EARLY AMERICAN STUDIES
Daniel K. Richter and Kathleen M. Brown, Series Editors

Exploring neglected aspects of our colonial, revolutionary, and early national history and culture, Early American Studies reinterprets familiar themes and events in fresh ways. Interdisciplinary in character, and with a special emphasis on the period from about 1600 to 1850, the series is published in partnership with the McNeil Center for Early American Studies.

A complete list of books in the series is available from the publisher.

Rebellion and Savagery

The Jacobite Rising of 1745 and the British Empire

GEOFFREY PLANK

PENN

University of Pennsylvania Press

Philadelphia

10   9   8   7   6   5   4   3   2   1

Published by
University of Pennsylvania Press
Philadelphia, Pennsylvania 19104-4112

Library of Congress Cataloging-in-Publication Data

Plank, Geoffrey Gilbert, 1960–
    Rebellion and savagery : the Jacobite rising of 1745 and the British Empire /
Geoffrey Plank.
        p.   cm. — (Early American studies)
    Includes bibliographical references and index.
    ISBN-10: 0-8122-3898-2 (alk. paper)
    ISBN-13: 978-0-8122-3898-3
    1. Jacobite Rebellion, 1745–1746.   2. Great Britain—Colonies—History—18th
century.   3. Scotland—History—18th century.   4. Jacobites.   I. Title.   II. Series.
DA814.5.P57   2006
941.07'2—dc22   2005042328

For Eleanor and John Plank

Contents

Introduction   1

Part I. The Response to the Crisis

1. Rebellion: Criminal Prosecution and the Jacobite Soldiers   29

2. Savagery: Military Execution and the Inhabitants of the Highlands   53

3. The 1745 Crisis in the Empire   77

Part II. Cumberland's Army and the World

4. Cumberland's Army in Scotland   103

5. Cumberland's Army in the Mediterranean   130

6. Cumberland's Army in North America   155

Epilogue: Cumberland's Death and the End of the Officers' Careers   181

Notes   193

Index   251

Acknowledgments   257

Introduction

On July 23, 1745, Charles Edward Stuart, the twenty-four-year-old grandson of England's long-dead, ousted King James II, landed in Moidart, on the western coast of Scotland, in the company of seven men. He intended to seize power in Britain, reverse the dynastic consequences of the Revolution of 1688, and on behalf of his father, who lived in Italy, restore the deposed Stuart family to the British throne. Before sailing for Scotland Charles Edward had been in correspondence with several British Jacobites, supporters of the Stuart dynasty, including prominent clan leaders and landlords in the Scottish Highlands. Some of these men greeted him near the coast, and with their help he raised a small army composed largely of Gaelic-speaking Highlanders. By mid-August he and his men were marching south. In September they took the town of Edinburgh, leaving the government's garrison beleaguered in Edinburgh Castle. Gaining new recruits along their route, and winning nearly all of their engagements with the government's forces, eventually the Jacobite army proceeded as far south as Derby, in the Midlands of England, before Charles Edward reassessed his circumstances and decided to turn back toward Scotland.[1]

While the Jacobites retreated, the government reassembled its available military forces and placed them under the command of the Duke of Cumberland, the second son of King George II.[2] Cumberland pursued Charles Edward northward, finally trapping the main body of his forces at Culloden Moor, near Inverness, on April 16, 1746. The battle that day was a violent rout. Hundreds of Jacobite soldiers were killed in the field, and the rest were captured or scattered. Charles Edward escaped. It took him several weeks, but he managed to leave Britain and sail to France.[3] Cumberland, in the meantime, led the government's forces on a punitive mission through Highland Scotland, disarming much of the population, burning crops, seizing livestock, and on occasion attacking entire communities, including old people and children, women and men.

While Cumberland was pursuing his military campaigns in the Highlands, he was struggling to restore order on the government's terms. Thousands of veterans of the Jacobite rising were brought into custody,

Map 1. The route of Charles Edward Stuart's principal forces, from Moidart to Culloden.

and evidence was gathered against hundreds of them in anticipation of formal criminal trials. Trying all of Charles Edward's soldiers proved logistically impossible, however. More than three hundred trials were held, and over one hundred defendants were found guilty and executed for rebellion. A larger number of prisoners, perhaps as many as eight hundred, were induced to plead for mercy and accept transportation to the colonies, where they were sold as bound laborers.

In order to understand the violence of 1746 it is necessary to comprehend the character and scale of Charles Edward's aims. He believed that his father was the rightful monarch of all Britain and Ireland, and he came to Scotland with the ultimate purpose of asserting his family's claim to those kingdoms and the entire British Empire.[4] As a result, the conflict had a powerful, almost intrinsically violent, moral component. Both sides accused the men in the opposing army of treason. As one writer with Jacobite sympathies put it, whenever a fighting man chooses the wrong side in a "civil or domestic" war, he puts "his soul in a most desperate issue," because "for every slaughter he makes of those on the right side, he is downright guilty of so many murders."[5] Another, less ardently partisan pamphleteer described the result when soldiers conflate military conflict with treason and murder: "rancor, ill-nature, and malice usurp the place of a noble resentment, and the unnatural contest is carried on without either decency or charity."[6] It is possible to go far toward explaining the violence of 1746 without mentioning that the fighting involved Scottish Highlanders.

Nonetheless, it is also clear that the army's operations were encouraged by a widespread antagonism toward the people and traditions of the Highlands. After the fighting had ended, one Lowland Scottish writer asked his readers to sympathize with the government's soldiers at Culloden by emphasizing the alien character of the Highlanders. The killing had been excessive, he acknowledged, "Yet one thing I own, that the rebels had enrag'd the troops; their habit was strange, their language still stranger, and their way of fighting was shocking to the utmost degree."[7] Kilts, the Gaelic language, and the wielding of broadswords distinguished the Highland soldiers in Charles Edward's lines. These attributes also, especially in the minds of the government's supporters, helped mark the Highlanders as primitive, contemptible, and dangerous.

In 1745 and for years thereafter, an array of commentators suggested that the Gaelic-speaking people of the Highlands were isolated, impoverished, and slavishly devoted to their clan leaders. The Highlanders were also, almost incessantly, described as gullible and violent. They seemed quick to take up arms in insurrection, and from the perspective of the government, their home region appeared almost impossible to police. For many, the Jacobite rising served as an object lesson demonstrating the link between civilization and political stability. Charles Edward had succeeded, to the extent that he did, by exploiting the savagery of the Highlands.[8]

Though Jacobites took up arms only in Britain, the rising was perceived as a crisis throughout the British Empire. Charles Edward's opponents emphasized the peculiar Highland character of the original Jacobite army, but they could not dismiss the insurrection simply as a local disturbance in northern Scotland. On the contrary, especially after the Jacobite forces reached England, the supporters of the government linked the Jacobite rising to global politics and trumpeted risks that they claimed the entire empire faced.

At the time of Charles Edward's landing, Britain was engaged in a long-running contest with the empires of France and Spain. In 1739 the imperial rivalry had turned violent, with the outbreak of war against the Spanish in the Caribbean. Over the next few years the fighting spread to engage most of the major powers of Europe, with combat on the European continent as well as in the Caribbean and in North America. By 1744 France had unambiguously aligned itself with Spain against George II. After Charles Edward landed in Britain one year later, his opponents suspected that the French were using him as a tool to advance their own imperial interests. Though France gave the Jacobites less support than they expected, a French ship had carried Charles Edward to Moidart, and later in the year a regiment of regular French troops landed in Scotland to fight for him.

Even before Charles Edward's arrival, many in Britain and the colonies had rallied to the ongoing war effort, believing that the British Empire was confronting the combined might of the world's major Catholic imperial powers. In actuality the war in Europe—known today as the War of the Austrian Succession—did not simply pit Catholics against Protestants, because Britain was allied with the Catholic Hapsburg dynasty in Austria. Nonetheless, for most Britons—at home and in the colonies—the Austrian dimension of the conflict was not the critical one. It mattered more that Britain's Spanish and French adversaries were Catholic. The religious element in the war increased in importance after Charles Edward arrived. Like his father and grandfather before him, Charles Edward was Catholic, and in Scotland, at least, he drew considerable support from fellow Catholics. In 1745 and 1746, nearly everywhere in the British Empire, Catholics were suspected of supporting the Stuart cause.

After Cumberland defeated Charles Edward at Culloden, many British colonists in North America rejoiced because they believed that the Jacobites, had they won, would have ceded large swaths of colonial territory to the Catholic French. The rising had served as a reminder of the colonists' dependence on the political stability, diplomatic leverage and military strength of the British government, and their vulnerability to the consequences of events across the ocean. Therefore, in America as well as in Britain, Cumberland acquired the status of a hero. He was celebrated as a champion of Protestantism, a guardian of British liberty, and a defender of Britain's imperial ambitions.

One of the most enduring effects of the Jacobite rising was to increase the public stature and political power of the army. Despite the long-standing controversy surrounding the maintenance of large armies in peacetime, after peace was restored in Europe in 1748, Cumberland remained captain general of Britain's land forces, with command over hundreds of officers and thousands of troops, and his soldiers continued to patrol the Scottish Highlands. He took advantage of the political capital he had gained from his victory in Scotland and concentrated his energies on strengthening the army, reforming it, and giving it a prominent role in the governance and defense of the empire. Cumberland faced vocal, at times strident, opposition to his efforts, and political imperatives required him to station the bulk of his forces outside England. In 1749 he introduced a system of rotation that cycled regiments between Scotland, Ireland, and the Mediterranean. Though North America was not formally part of the cycle, men were rotated between Scotland and the American colonies as well.

In the colonies and Scotland, the soldiers guarded vulnerable territories, but Cumberland and his supporters in the ministry believed that the army's mission involved more than defense, that garrisons should serve as agents of civilization. There was no detailed consensus, however, either within the army or in the counsels of government, over exactly what that project entailed. The officers in Cumberland's army participated in debates over the promotion of immigration, trade, and industry, the construction of infrastructure, the definition and enforcement of property rights, the spread of the English language, the advancement of Protestantism, and the education of children, in the Scottish Highlands and in colonies overseas. Their thoughts on these issues evolved as they gathered experience in various postings.

The narrative in *Rebellion and Savagery* returns repeatedly to a group of officers who served under Cumberland in Scotland and were later deployed in colonial posts: William Blakeney, Humphrey Bland, Edward Cornwallis, John Campbell, the Earl of Loudon, and James Wolfe. After serving with Cumberland in Scotland, Blakeney became lieutenant governor of Minorca; Bland assumed the governorship of Gibraltar; Cornwallis took commands in Nova Scotia, Minorca, and Gibraltar successively; Loudon became commander in chief of the British army in

North America; and Wolfe led the contingent of the British army that conquered Quebec. Under the direction of these men, and others like them, the army emerged from the crisis of 1745 with a sense of mission that both encompassed and transcended the northern hills and islands of Scotland.

In the immediate aftermath of Culloden, the army made policy in the Scottish Highlands, punishing some men and women as rebels or bandits and working with others cooperatively. As the weeks progressed Cumberland and his officers began to offer advice to the government drawing on their experience in the region, and over the next several years they contributed to an extended policy debate. Between 1746 and 1753, Parliament enacted statutes for the disarmament of Highlanders, the reform of the region's court system, the regulation of religious life, and the forfeiture of estates belonging to Jacobites. The ministry also established policies for the management of the forfeited estates, guidelines that were designed to promote commerce and Presbyterianism, the use of the English language, and loyalty to George II.[9] Military officers played a part in drafting these proposals, and once they were enacted, soldiers helped enforce them.

Though the army was never exclusively in control of the development of policy, in the late 1740s and early 1750s Cumberland's officers were engaged in similar, parallel reform efforts in their colonial posts. In the Mediterranean and in the forests and farms of North America, they faced similar challenges, patrolling populations that included many who did not speak English, in places where British legal institutions were weak or altogether absent. The officers traded advice across the waters and brought to their tasks a shared enthusiasm for the maintenance of security and the advancement of reform. As an institution, the British army of the early 1750s exhibited a new confidence in its power and influence. Cumberland's high officers, in particular, left Scotland with reinvigorated ambition. In their overseas assignments they sought to promote cultural transformation, encourage commercial development, and facilitate religious and political change.

Thus, the Jacobite rising influenced the administration of the empire in two distinct phases. First came the military confrontation itself, which affected all of Britain's domains. Then, after the immediate crisis was over, the British army assumed a new prominence in the governance of the Highlands and in the empire as a whole. As a reflection of this chronology, this book is divided into two parts. Part I is a discussion of the immediate crisis, emphasizing the army's 1746 campaign and its implications for the future direction of the empire. Part II examines the army in the years following 1746, relating its ongoing participation in the administration of Highland Scotland to its imperial mission, specifically in the Mediterranean and North America. The Scottish and colonial stories are interconnected. The debates surrounding the transportation of former Jacobites and reform in the Scottish Highlands had direct ramifications for the colonies. Events in North America, in turn, profoundly influenced the dynamic of politics in Scotland, most dramatically after Britain's renewal of hostilities with France in 1754. More generally, the political fortunes of Cumberland and the army affected the entire empire and carried particular significance for the countries in which soldiers were stationed.

Along with Cumberland, Blakeney, Bland, Cornwallis, Loudon, and Wolfe assumed their responsibilities with a distinctive view of political power and reform. In their words and actions they manifested an intense sense of indignation against certain kinds of cultural difference, characteristics which they variously described and condemned as savagery, infidelity, ignorance, superstition, sloth, or violent cruelty. Several of them also mixed their moral outrage with a self-consciously enlightened interest in ethnography. They tried to be systematic in their efforts to classify peoples, explain the beliefs and behaviors of the groups under their authority, and prescribe policies designed to advance the process of social development. The officers were generally fascinated with the peculiarities of their various assignments and drew sharp distinctions, for example, between the peoples of the Mediterranean, North America, and Britain. At the same time, however, they believed that they could learn much by making analogies, and all of them sought to contribute to ongoing policy debates in Scotland, the Mediterranean, and across the Atlantic, by citing the army's ever-widening pool of experience. The officers shared a belief that the army could operate as an agent for reform in uncivilized, rebellious, or contested lands. They insisted that the first step in that process was to establish Britain's undivided sovereignty over its territories, regardless of whether the inhabitants were ready or willing to be ruled.

Though Cumberland's officers were deployed in several places as military governors, for the most part they believed that military rule should be temporary. Nearly everywhere they went, in the early moments of their imperial projects, Blakeney, Bland, Cornwallis, Loudon, and Wolfe harbored hopes for a better future. They invested military manpower and resources in the construction of roads, bridges, docks, and public buildings, promoted manufacturing and commerce, and encouraged immigration. In regions populated by Catholics they sought to reform education, promote intermarriage, and facilitate Protestant conversions. In the long run they hoped to establish English-style governmental institutions, including civilian law courts. As far as was possible, consistent with the interests of the home country, the officers intended to place all the free inhabitants of Britain's possessions on a similar footing and make all of them loyal to the British regime.

* * *

In many respects, the operations of Cumberland's army after 1745 represented the continuation of a long historical process. At least since the Middle Ages, Anglo-Saxons, Anglo-Normans, English, and Lowland Scots, under the leadership of the kings and queens of England and Scotland, had been alternately battling and attempting to reform the Celtic peoples of Cornwall, Wales, Ireland, and the Scottish Highlands. Beginning in the sixteenth century, English imperialists had expanded these efforts, in effect, by turning their attention to North America. Considered in broad, schematic terms, this was a very old story.[10] Nonetheless, the official response to the crisis of 1745, and the subsequent operations of Cumberland's army, reflected British preoccupations that were distinctive to the era.

As Linda Colley has argued, the eighteenth century witnessed an official effort to create a new understanding of "British" nationality, one that accommodated various English, Scottish, and Welsh traditions and united the peoples of Britain by emphasizing a few antagonisms that they all allegedly shared, particularly against France and the Catholic Church.[11] These were also years in which many in Britain, and in Scotland in particular, were engaged in a fluid debate over the categorization of peoples, the attributes of "savagery," and the meaning of "civilization."[12] In large part because of the distinctive language and traditions of the Gaelic-speakers, and the complex relationship between Highlanders and the rest of the peoples of Britain, Ireland, and the colonies, these issues—the meaning of British nationality, and the steps between savagery and civilization—carried special significance in Scotland.

It is impossible to comprehend the actions of Cumberland's army in Scotland without considering the peculiar history of the Highlands, and the double-stigma that outsiders had long attached to the Gaelic-speaking inhabitants of the region as rebels and as savages. A deep-seated and widely shared suspicion of the Highlanders informed the violence of the government's military campaign in 1746. The reform efforts introduced after the fighting ended were similarly informed by regional history, and built on previous efforts to solve the "Highland problem" by introducing the Highlanders to civilization. In the eyes of many reformers, the region resembled North America in important ways. They viewed it as a place on the edge of the empire, where metropolitan standards of behavior, the rule of law, and the authority of the central government, were weak.

The Highlanders were one of the first peoples the English and Lowland Scots ever called "savages."[13] The Gaelic language and the Highlanders' clan-based social structure were common throughout Scotland until the high Middle Ages, when Germanic and Scandinavian invaders displaced the old Celtic traditions of the Lowlands.[14] For centuries thereafter the Highlanders' culture was assumed to be older than that of the Lowland Scots, and in Anglo-Saxon eyes, more primitive. As early as the fourteenth century, outside observers began identifying the Gaelic-speaking people of the Highlands as "savage and untamed."[15] By the eighteenth century, after the British encounter with North America and sub-Saharan Africa, the Gaelic-speakers had become, in the minds of many outsiders, representatives of an increasingly complex category of uncivilized groups. Some writers, stressing the importance of domesticated grazing animals in the Highland economy, suggested that the Highlanders had progressed further than the native tribes of North America. Others were less certain. In the aftermath of the Jacobite rising of 1745 one writer asserted that the Highlanders organized their lives according to principles of "patriarchal government" that were "suited only to those early ages before mankind had begun to form themselves into large societies."[16]

The phrase "patriarchal government" in this context referred to clanship, the hierarchical network of family ties and obligations that helped organize Highland society.[17] Under the customary terms of the clan system, men could demand protection and hospitality from their chiefs, who in return could summon them for military service. The military function of the clans involved more than protection against foreign invasion. Clans were active in settling local disputes and sought reparations against outsiders when the interests of their members were infringed. In the process they maintained order and regulated exchange in much of the Highlands and therefore performed an essential economic function, particularly among keepers of cattle. In parts of the Highlands, men, women, and children spent weeks every year following herds of livestock. The clans helped support these families and guarded their animals during their travels.

The men who guarded the cattle on the mountains were real. So too were the clans that protected them, but these were also powerful stereotypes. By the middle years of the eighteenth century many Highlanders lived quite comfortably without crossing hills on foot or calling on the services of clans. Not everyone was a herder, and there were financial and legal institutions that offered an alternative to the clan system for the negotiation of contracts or the settlement of disputes. Some prominent aristocrats in the Highlands were not clan leaders, and their powers as landlords had historical and legal foundations separate from clanship. Nonetheless, as social institutions that appeared to set the Highlanders apart, clanship and herding dominated most political discussions of them.

The term "Highlander" did not have a simple, consistent definition. In some contexts the word was used to designate the residents of a region encompassing the hills and mountains of northern Scotland, all of the British mainland north of Inverness, Scotland's northwestern coast, and the islands to the west. By an extension of that definition, former residents of the area were still considered Highlanders even after they had moved, particularly if they spoke Gaelic. Furthermore, the children and grandchildren of such Highlanders could inherit the status even if they had never seen the Highlands. Thus there were Highlanders born in Glasgow in the eighteenth century, and in several colonies abroad.[18]

Nonetheless, Highlander status was not always or universally understood to be hereditary. In some cases contemporary observers disagreed among themselves whether the offspring of Highland families retained the identity of Highlanders. One important example involved the Earl of Loudon, who led the government's Highland regiment against the Jacobites in 1745 and 1746. Like his father and grandfather before him, Loudon resided on a prosperous estate near the Irish Sea south of Glasgow, apart from the Scottish Highlands. His distant ancestors may have spoken Gaelic, but English was the language of Loudon's household. Loudon did not call himself a Highlander, and none of his associates in the army or the Scottish aristocracy applied that label to him.[19] After two years of service in the Highland regiment, he let it be known that he was weary of dressing in Highland kilts and "longed to have on britches" (see Figure 1).[20] Nonetheless, throughout Loudon's career, residents of the Highlands identified him as a member of Clan Campbell, one of the most powerful of the Highland clans. Opponents of the Campbells excoriated Loudon as a partisan for that clan's interest.[21] The Campbells, for their part, generally welcomed him as one of their own.[22]

Many purported descendants of prominent Highland families did not consider themselves Highlanders. The region contained an unusually prosperous English-speaking elite, and thanks to several generations of intermarriage, many well-born families in the area had cousins within the gentry and aristocracy of England.[23] The Highlands' English-speaking gentry impressed Daniel Defoe, who in his semifictional work *A Tour Thro' the Whole Island of Great Britain* declared that by the early 1720s the gentlemen of the Highlands had attained "the politest and brightest education and genius of any people so far north, perhaps, in

Figure 1. This engraving depicting the Earl of Loudon appeared in the *London Magazine* in 1755 after Loudon was named commander of the British army in North America. It is based on a portrait that had been painted in 1747 when Loudon held command of a regiment of Highland soldiers. Loudon did not consider himself a Highlander, and even in 1747 he let it be known that he "longed to have on britches." He did not wear a kilt in the 1750s. (Johannes Faber Junior, after Allan Ramsay. National Galleries of Scotland.)

the world."[24] The reputed sophistication of the Highland elite did not, however, necessarily undercut the frequently repeated assertion that the Highlanders as a group were uncivilized. On the contrary, some aristocrats and landholders in the region were among the most vocal and prominent commentators insisting that the local people needed civilization. Some members of the elite had plans for educating the rest of the inhabitants of the region.[25] They established model villages on their estates in a self-conscious effort to introduce civility and economic efficiency into areas they perceived to be primitive.[26]

In the years leading up to 1745, the landlords' efforts to reform and improve the lives of their Gaelic-speaking tenants became steadily more comprehensive and ambitious. The Campbells, under the leadership of the Earls and Dukes of Argyll, over several generations, were trendsetters. Beginning in the late seventeenth century the heirs of the Argyll estates altered their approach to estate management in order to establish stable, stationary year-round homes for their leaseholders, diversify the local economy, and direct more of the Highlanders' energies toward the accumulation of wealth. The Argylls established coal mines, slate quarries, orchards, and fish factories on their lands. In a break from prior practice, they used written leases and rented fields in small lots for relatively short terms of years. By the 1730s they had abolished most of the service requirements in their leases in order to place the market for land on a simpler cash basis. In all these efforts they believed that they were making their estates operate more like modern farms in the Lowlands of Scotland and England. These projects resembled colonial ventures, since the landlords accepted it as their mission to transform a society governed by irrational and unproductive tradition.[27]

Writers describing the Highlanders often modeled their analysis on discussions of allegedly primitive peoples overseas. In the early 1720s Defoe prefaced his description of the Highlands by declaring that England's "geographers" knew as little about the Scottish Highlands as they did about "the inner parts of Africa."[28] A decade later the English writer Edward Burt asserted that less had been published about the Highlands than about "either of the Indies."[29] Both Defoe and Burt responded to this perceived deficiency by providing descriptions of Highland life that they thought could stand beside ethnographic accounts of life in Africa and in the forests of North America. Missionaries launched similar projects. In 1714, after the Scottish Society for Propagating Christian Knowledge (SSPCK) sent its first Presbyterian ministers into the Highlands, its directors asked one of its emissaries to send back an "account of the superstitious customs of the people of the north."[30] The SSPCK was modeled on English and Dutch missionary organizations.[31] The society's charter directed it to serve the inhabitants of regions "where error idolatry superstition and ignorance do most abound," including "the Highlands, islands, and remote corners" of Scotland and "Popish and infidel parts of the world" abroad.[32]

By the early 1740s the SSPCK had established a network of itinerant teachers and small schools scattered throughout the Highlands.[33] It also funded much smaller projects to convert and educate the native peoples of North America, and in an effort to advance the purposes of its charter, it briefly considered undertaking missionary efforts in Asia as well.[34] The varied activities of the SSPCK strongly suggest that the Presbyterian directors of the organization placed Highlanders in a single broad category, that "great part" of the world's inhabitants "who live in barbarity and ignorance."[35] They believed that the Highlanders were uncivilized, but an examination of the actual activities of their organization makes it clear that the directors did not simply treat North America's peoples and the Scottish Highlanders equally. An intense hostility to Highland culture led the directors of the SSPCK, over the objections of several of their missionaries, to ban the use of the Gaelic language in missionary schools. The missionaries complained that this had the effect of alienating the students from their parents and prevented graduates of the schools from introducing their families and other members of their communities to the gospel.[36] The board of directors dismissed the missionaries' complaints, preferring to concentrate the society's resources exclusively on the children, cut them off from their family traditions, and ultimately (they hoped) consign Gaelic to an older, dying generation.

The SSPCK took a different approach toward the native peoples of North America. Initially, the chosen missionaries (New Englanders who had been recruited in the colonies) lived in forts and trading posts and made contact only with the adults who came to them.[37] Two pastors in Maine, for example, made "small compliments of pipes and tobacco" to the men who visited their fort and tried to speak to the men in their native Algonkian languages.[38] They met with little success. They taught none of their visitors English and boasted no conquests for Protestant Christianity.[39] Subsequently, the SSPCK insisted that its missionaries in North America learn native languages and "live and inhabit with the Indians in the wilderness."[40] Rather than taking children away from their parents or initiating a campaign against the Algonkian or Iroquoian tongues, they sought to convert influential tribal leaders and imagined they could introduce Presbyterianism to whole communities en masse.[41] This contrast in missionary strategies for Scotland and North America serves as a reminder that when British reformers in the eighteenth century labeled a community savage or barbarous, that was only the beginning of their analysis. An array of political considerations affected the proposals they advanced for the civilization of the ostensibly primitive group.

Before 1745 the Highlanders were most often compared not with North American groups or other societies across the ocean but rather with the Gaelic-speaking, Catholic Irish. One of the principal reasons the SSPCK was so determined to combat use of the Gaelic language in the Highlands was the close relationship between Irish and Scottish Gaelic.[42] The Scottish Highlands and Ireland had been linked, culturally and politically, for centuries. Prior to the sixteenth century the water separating the Highlands from Ireland had been far more important as a route for travel than as a barrier between peoples. In those years, extended families had branches on both sides of the Irish Sea, and no sectarian divisions impeded trade, cultural exchange, or the formation of political alliances. These circumstances changed dramatically in the second half of the sixteenth century, thanks in large part to a shift in English policy toward Ireland. The historian Nicholas Canny has suggested that English military officers and government officials in the Elizabethan era viewed themselves as colonizers and *conquistadores*, associating their subjugation of the Irish with the Spanish conquest of native tribes and empires in North and South America.[43] Other historians have placed more emphasis on the long history of English colonization in Ireland and on local precedents for the government's actions, but Canny has demonstrated that the English came to a new understanding of the process of conquest and colonization in the sixteenth and early seventeenth centuries, and that a new mode of imperialism arose simultaneously in Ireland and North America.[44]

During the wars in Ireland during Queen Elizabeth's reign, Scottish Highlanders went to fight with the Irish against the English regime. In response, the English government adopted a series of policies that established long-lasting, influential precedents that would eventually affect policy debates not only in Scotland but in various parts of the empire. In an effort to divide the Irish from the Highlanders, control both groups, and hasten the process of Anglicization, Elizabeth's successor as king of England, the Scottish king James VI (known in England as James I), planted a colony in Ulster, in northern Ireland, to insert a wedge between Ireland and Scotland. This policy had a far more devastating impact on Ireland than on Scotland, but similar colonies were planned for the western coasts of Scotland, and the project of controlling the Highlands through the planting of colonies would remain a major feature of public policy debate in the region for more than 150 years.[45]

Reform-minded writers in the eighteenth century frequently linked colonization with the formation of culturally mixed communities, which in turn they associated with global commerce, cosmopolitanism, the rejection of tradition, and wealth. They also associated mixed communities for historical reasons with England. As Defoe famously asserted in his satire "The True-Born English-Man," England was a product of successive invasions, a country where Celtic, Roman, Anglo-Saxon, and Norman traditions, among others, collided.[46] By contrast, the Scottish Highlanders, at least in the hinterlands, were generally considered pure Celtic.[47] The purity of the Highlanders' stock allegedly contributed to their backwardness. Edward Burt made the point this way: "The Highlanders are exceedingly proud to be thought an unmixed people, and are apt to upbraid the English with being a composite of all nations, but, for my own part, I think a little mixture in that sense would do themselves no manner of harm."[48]

In the Scottish context, one of the figures most commonly associated with colonization schemes was Oliver Cromwell. In the 1650s Cromwell's soldiers fought royalist opponents in the Scottish Highlands, and after securing victory he had hundreds of them transported as bound servants to Virginia and the West Indies.[49] Cromwell and his officers established garrisons in the Highlands.[50] Defoe praised the lasting influence of Cromwell's army in the vicinity of its forts, particularly around Inverness. After a unit had been stationed there, an "abundance of the English soldiers settled in this fruitful and cheap part of the country." The men, with their wives and children, introduced the English language and English farming methods into the region. By the 1720s, according to Defoe, the aftereffects of Cromwell's occupation were obvious. The inhabitants had acquired English "usages and customs" from the soldiers who had stayed with their families after demobilization. As a result, the people of Inverness dressed better, and their food was "much more agreeable to the English stomachs than in other parts of Scotland."[51]

Like Defoe, most commentators on Highland life in the early eighteenth century recognized that the region was divided. Many facets of life separated Highland communities from one another—differences in social class, language, and education, clan rivalries, differing levels of commercial development, and religious controversy. At least since the early seventeenth century, the divisions within Highland society had carried important implications for Britain as a whole, as England, Wales and Scotland struggled over the powers of the monarchy and the consolidation of state power. Political alignments in the Highlands were always fluid, and the apparent distinctiveness of various Highland communities invariably complicated any effort to stereotype the inhabitants as a group. On the other hand, when the region's politics turned violent, reports of combat served to reinforce the Highlanders' reputation for disorder. An ominous turning point came in 1688, when the old Stuart monarchy—or at least the old line of succession—was overthrown.

The Revolution of 1688, known as the "Glorious Revolution" in England, led to the removal of Charles Edward's grandfather, England's James II and Scotland's James VII, from the throne. The revolution introduced a new divisive issue into the politics of the Highlands, because the region was home to a significant number of defenders of the old constitution and dynasty. The events of 1688 transformed the supporters of James II and VII—henceforward known as "Jacobites"— from conservative backers of the ruling monarch into alleged subversives. A deep irony operated in public discussions of Jacobitism from that time onward. The Jacobites, in Ireland, Scotland, England, and elsewhere, exhibited a love of tradition. No other characteristic in religion, in political leaning, or in culture united them as firmly as their belief in a divinely sanctioned social and political hierarchy, with only one possible royal house in power.[52] Nonetheless, despite their professed devotion to law and ancestral rights, they were depicted by their opponents as outlaws. Even though Britain's Jacobites insisted that they were "for the greatest part, of the most ancient families of this island," all of them, and the Highlanders in particular, were singled out as exhibiting little respect for social order.[53] Over the long term, the Highlands came to be seen as a hiding place for rebels.

Concentrating on events in England, some historians have presented the Revolution of 1688 as a quick and easy affair. Viewed as an event in the empire as a whole, it was neither quick nor easy. Scotland's political leaders were divided and uncertain over the meaning of the revolution, and armed conflict erupted briefly in 1689, when a body of Highlanders, along with others from the Scottish Lowlands, fought against the new regime on the exiled king's behalf.[54] The revolution also unsettled colonial American politics, but the most intense theater of combat was Ireland.[55] James went to Ireland in 1689, and the fighting in that kingdom lasted for more than a year. The old Stuart king had never been a proponent of Gaelic culture, but the support he received among Gaelic-speaking Irish Catholics convinced many observers on both sides of the dynastic controversy that Gaelic traditions, Catholicism, and Jacobitism were linked.[56] The fighting was brutal, and it involved militia on both sides as well as the principal competing armies. One of the militiamen fighting for the revolution was the young William Blakeney, who carried emotional scars from the conflict for the next sixty-five years.[57] Though the fighting in Ireland engaged many men outside the regular armies, the negotiations leading to the decisive capitulation, the Treaty of Limerick of 1691, were conducted according to conventional rules of war. The government chose not to treat the Jacobite soldiers as criminals but rather as members of a legitimate military force. Instead of facing prosecution for treason, the men were allowed to depart with their leader for France.[58]

After 1691 the deposed King James never saw England, Scotland, or Ireland again, but in exile he continued to agitate for a return to the throne. He died in France in 1701, and eventually his son James Francis Edward Stuart tried to assert his own hereditary right to rule. In 1708 a French fleet took James Edward to the mouth of the Firth of Forth, but the French commanders turned back without allowing him to land.[59] In 1715 the British supporters of the Stuarts took up arms without the presence of their would-be king. Recruiting locally, Jacobite armies operated in Scotland and the north of England for more than two months before suffering decisive defeats. James Edward arrived only after the fighting was effectively over. He spent six weeks touring northeast Scotland before returning to exile in France.

The Jacobites' military efforts in 1708 and 1715 were timed to take advantage of two events that had promised to redefine their cause and expand their base of support. In 1707 a Treaty of Union had been concluded between the English and Scottish parliaments resulting in the dissolution of the parliament in Edinburgh and the arrival of Scottish representatives in the Houses of Parliament in Westminster. James Edward had come to the coasts of Scotland in 1708 carrying a proclamation calling for the repeal of the Treaty of Union.[60] By promising to restore Scottish independence, he hoped to gain the support of Lowland Scots and Highlanders who felt threatened by the parliamentary union with England. Six years later, in 1714, the Jacobites gained an opportunity to appeal to English pride when a German prince, the elector of Hanover, assumed the British throne as George I. During the rising of 1715, James Edward and his supporters derided the Hanoverians as foreigners with no hereditary claim to the crown and no understanding of the needs, values, or desires of the British people.[61]

The rising of 1715 was designed to bring the English and the Scots together in a common cause, and similarly to unite the inhabitants of the Lowlands with the Highlanders in Scotland. Though many Highlanders rallied to the Jacobite banner, they were hardly the only Britons to do so, and the rising in 1715 did not depend exclusively on their support.[62] Nonetheless, Highlanders were visible in the lines in Scotland, and they were conspicuous in the collective memory of the event. Years later the Jacobite army in Scotland was remembered as a body of Highlanders.[63] Partly because of this simplified recollection, many commentators viewed the 1745 rising as a replay of 1715. Consequently, they analyzed the government's response to the 1715 rising, concentrating on its policy in the Highlands, to find legal and practical precedents for punitive and ameliorative action and to discover why, after the 1715 episode, the government's efforts had failed. Every supporter of the Hanoverian dynasty agreed that the events of 1745 demonstrated the inadequacy of the government's response to the earlier rising.[64]

In the years following 1715, the government pursued an array of initiatives designed to punish the participants in the rising and alter the social conditions that had allegedly facilitated the mobilization of Jacobites. After the Battle of Preston in 1715, hundreds of captured Jacobite soldiers were persuaded to accept conditional pardons from George I requiring them to work in the colonies as bound laborers.[65] As a result, at least 639 men, mostly Highlanders, were sent in bondage to North America and the Caribbean. The prisoners were sold in Maryland, Virginia, South Carolina, Jamaica, Barbados, St. Kitts, and Antigua. In general, the places that took them had labor shortages and depended primarily on slave labor.[66] After the captured soldiers had been sent to America, other punitive measures were adopted by the authorities in the Scottish Highlands. The estates of several prominent Jacobite landlords were forfeited to the crown, and some justices of the peace were dismissed from their offices. Nonetheless, a powerful contingent of the Highland elite opposed these measures, and, partly as a result, the government failed to silence or impoverish all the Jacobites. Through a series of commercial transactions and legal maneuvers, many of the forfeited estates were transferred to relatives or friends of the original owners, and many Jacobite justices of the peace managed to keep their commissions.[67] In 1716 Parliament passed a Disarming Act for the Highlands, but its provisions were weak and the statute was not effectively enforced.

A second wave of government initiatives came in the 1720s, after Robert Walpole consolidated his power within Parliament. In recognition of the weakness of the previous enactment, a new Disarming Act was adopted, and General George Wade was appointed commander in chief in Scotland with a mandate to enforce it.[68] Among the military units serving under him were six new companies of Highlanders.[69] The Highland soldiers were seen as effective agents of law enforcement, and the creation of the new companies was intended to serve economic and political purposes as well. The units employed men who might otherwise have been idle or dangerous, and their initial assignment was to enforce the Disarming Act and guard the Scottish Highlands against French or Jacobite threats from abroad. Four additional companies were formed in 1739 and all ten were combined into a new unit which soon would be known as the Forty-second Regiment, or the "Black Watch." The Black Watch would eventually serve as a conduit for deploying thousands of young men from the Highlands into the British colonies, but in their first eighteen years of operation, the Highland companies never left Scotland.[70]

When Wade was sent to the Highlands to administer the Disarming Acts, some local leaders protested that using a standing army to police the region violated the laws of God, humanity, and Britain. They declared that the policy was "not fit even to be executed upon barbarians" and was certainly unsuitable for the "free Christian people" of the Scottish Highlands.[71] Particularly since much of the policing duty fell to Highland companies, Wade's "standing army" turned out to be less oppressive, in the short run, than the protesters feared. Nonetheless, the deployment of these troops set a precedent that affected government policy in 1745 and 1746. The domestic assignment of the soldiers reinforced the idea that military units could be used to police the inhabitants of the Scottish Highlands. It was also widely believed in official circles that Highland soldiers were the most appropriate men for the job.

The formation of the Highland companies was one component of a general program to establish a new legal order in the Highlands, tie the Highlanders to centralized governmental institutions, and connect them, politically and economically, to the wider British world. As part of this effort, Wade oversaw a road-building campaign (see Figure 2).[72] Soldiers formed work gangs of approximately twenty each and descended on communities along the projected routes.[73] In this manner they made their presence felt through large swaths of the Highlands, and they left a physical mark on the landscape. While primarily a military project, road building also served economic and cultural purposes. The roads facilitated internal commerce and brought outsiders into the region, though initially most of the newcomers were military men.[74] The soldiers themselves saw the roads as a way to improve the Highlanders' lives in accordance with the standards of the eighteenth century. One man compared Wade's roads with similar ones constructed by the British garrison on the Mediterranean island of Minorca. In both places, he asserted, the local people refused to use the new transportation links and instead preferred to travel on well-worn paths across the hills. He thought that both the Highlanders and the Minorcans were stubborn and obstinate "in refusing to make use of so great a conveniency because it is a novelty introduced by the English."[75] The Highlanders, like the people of that distant island, were narrow-minded and unable to appreciate the benefits that accrued from military construction.

Long before 1745, commentators from outside the region had identified a "Highland problem." The Highlanders in general, it was asserted, were ignorant, poor, and frequently violent. They were excessively loyal to their clans and also susceptible to the seditious persuasions of Catho-

Figure 2. General George Wade served as commander of the British army in
Scotland in the 1720s and 1730s. In that capacity he oversaw the construction of
roads and bridges across the north. In the background of this portrait a work
crew of soldiers can be seen building a road in the Highlands. (Attributed to
Johan van Diest. National Galleries of Scotland.)

lics and Jacobites. Ultimately, in the minds of those who thought this way, the Highland problem stemmed from the geographical isolation of the region and the backward condition of the people who lived there.

When Cumberland arrived in 1746, he came to a country that had already been the target of ambitious reform efforts. Missionaries, land-lords, and government officials had pursued efforts for decades to accel-erate the pace of cultural development. Among those interested in changing the lives of the Highlanders, it was already commonly assumed that the army would play a role in the process, by building infrastruc-ture, enforcing laws, employing Highlanders, and in general by expos-ing the people to civilization. The policies that the British authorities pursued in the Scottish Highlands after 1746, therefore, did not reflect a radical shift in aims. Instead, the events of 1745 had simply given urgency to a project that was already, if haltingly, underway. The crisis also had the effect of bringing more British subjects into the debates over the fate of the Highlanders. North American colonists, in particu-lar, paid more attention to them than ever before.

In the first half of the eighteenth century the Scottish Highlanders fit awkwardly into the British Empire. Their home region had long been the target of colonization schemes, and they had been subjected to mis-sionary work that in some ways resembled projects undertaken among the native peoples of North America. At the same time, however, some Highlanders were themselves colonists in the wider overseas empire. Prior to 1745, many colonists in America had actively encouraged them to come across the ocean to settle. Even after the 1715 rising, the govern-ment of South Carolina had petitioned for the importation of Jacobite Highlander prisoners, in order to bolster their colony's population of "white men."[76] In comparison to 1715, the 1745 rising generated a much stronger fear of Highlanders in America. In the late 1740s and early 1750s, the American colonists, like the English, commonly associ-ated the Highlanders with savagery, sedition, Catholicism, and the impe-rial ambitions of France.

The Highlanders' position in the British Empire was unusually com-plex, but similar uncertainties surrounded many of the empire's inhabi-tants. In Britain, Ireland, and the colonies, military officers, local civilian authorities, lawyers, and missionaries recommended divergent pro-grams for various populations according to their nationality, sectarian affiliation, and the progress the groups had allegedly made toward civili-zation. In their writings on political affairs, eighteenth-century policy-makers and commentators manifested an almost obsessive concern for the categorization of peoples. Nonetheless, uncertainty about the boundaries of categories, disagreements between observers, overlapping and often contradictory classification schemes, the peculiarities of local traditions, and complicating geopolitical relationships between different groups, made it impossible for anyone in the empire to prescribe or pursue a single, practical, coherent policy toward all Catholics everywhere, all purported savages, or all British peoples. These labels helped shape policy, but it would be futile to attempt to construct a simple explanatory framework based on these classifications, to suggest, for example, that one group within the empire was treated as it was simply because it was stigmatized or privileged on the basis of its purported status as "savage," "civilized," "Protestant," "Catholic," "British" or "foreign."

* * *

"Rebellion" and "savagery" were two concepts that simultaneously organized and confused British imperial policy. In times of armed conflict, identifying the crown's opponents as "rebels" or "savages" provided two potential, alternative justifications for suspending the operation of conventional rules of war.[77] In moral and practical terms, however, these categories of analysis had contradictory ramifications. Rebellion implied personal responsibility—an accusation could be pursued through formal proceedings, and if any of the accused were tried and convicted they were liable to severe punishment. Savagery, by contrast, was not a crime but a characteristic ascribed to entire communities and cultures. Though the imputation of savagery did not necessarily imply personal guilt, communities identified as savage could be subjected to correction collectively, through policies of expulsion, local punitive actions—sometimes directed against entire populations—and coercive projects aimed at advancing the process of civilization. Cumberland's officers believed they encountered both rebellion and savagery in Scotland, and, later, in the Mediterranean and in North America. They consistently asserted that everyone who resided on lands claimed by the British crown owed undivided allegiance to George II. In the Scottish Highlands and in North America they insisted that savages could be rebels. Repeatedly, however, this conviction left them uncertain whether to negotiate with their adversaries, punish them collectively, or arrest them in anticipation of prosecution. In Scotland and North America, Cumberland and his officers were often at their most violent when their classification schemes failed them and overlapping or contradictory ways of seeing the people around them left them confused over the direction of policy, without coherent guidelines to govern what they should do.

Many of the quandaries that Cumberland's officers faced may seem familiar in the early years of the twenty-first century.[78] In Scotland and on occasion in North America, the denigration of their enemies prevented the officers from observing diplomatic protocols or treating their opponents according to the normal codes of conduct governing European warfare. At the same time, an array of pragmatic considerations made it often seem impractical, if not impossible, to apprehend their adversaries as criminals and transfer them to the custody of civilian courts. There was always an element of opportunistic, tactical calculation in the choices the officers made. They understood that in times of crisis, military action and criminal prosecution served a common function, and that the coercive imposition of governmental authority, in a criminal trial setting as well as on a battlefield, rested ultimately on the threat or application of physical violence.[79] Nonetheless, for reasons peculiar to the circumstances of their times, they were anxious to justify their decisions by reference to specific constitutional and legal principles, accepted military traditions, and the dictates of enlightened social policy. They feared appearing arbitrary.

In March 1746, as his forces were preparing to execute punitive raids against rural communities in the Scottish Highlands, Cumberland pleaded with the ministry to define the parameters of acceptable action. He emphatically told the Duke of Newcastle, "there must be some rule and that must be closely stuck to."[80] But Newcastle did not know with any certainty what the rules should be, and he refused to respond positively to Cumberland's request, for fear of implicating the ministry in the soldiers' decisions after they had entered wild terrain.[81] This response frustrated Cumberland. He wanted to contrast himself to Charles Edward, whom he castigated as an outlaw, by operating only with authorization. He was also concerned to protect himself, and the army, politically and legally, within the halls of Parliament. At least since the Revolution of 1688, a powerful segment of the political nation had insisted that the survival of British liberty depended on limiting the powers of the army.[82] Even in the spring of 1746, many political leaders in Britain supported King George II but were wary of granting power to Cumberland or his soldiers. Cumberland also wanted guidance because he was worried about indiscipline among his men. Unregulated violence undermined his effort to transform the British army into an orderly, effective military force.[83] Furthermore, chaotic or arbitrary operations contradicted his understanding of the army's larger mission. In the Scottish Highlands and subsequently in the colonies, Cumberland and his officers sought to demonstrate that the army could impose order, establish the rule of law, and assert the authority of centralized governmental institutions. In the Scottish and the imperial contexts, they believed that the establishment of legal order was a necessary first step toward the achievement of pervasive social reform.

On none of these issues did Cumberland, or the officers around him, speak for all of Britain. They were extremely partisan and contentious men. Cumberland's position in the factious politics of Westminster shifted dramatically over his career. On occasion he alienated groups of his supporters, and considerations of political expediency forced him into temporary, pragmatic alliances with his political opponents.[84] Nonetheless, he always believed that he was constant in his support of the old Whig cause, as he understood it, the institutional interests of the army, and the needs of his father, George II.

Recently, historians studying the politics of imperialism have devoted considerable attention to popular agitation and the emotional importance of the empire to the British people at large.[85] Several scholars have identified the late 1730s as a turning point, when protests against the operations of Spain's *Guarda-Costas* in the Caribbean forced the Walpole ministry, despite its better judgment, into a colonial war.[86] Thereafter, through the middle years of the eighteenth century, an ever-larger segment of the politically active public in England, Wales, and Scotland took pride in the empire and defined the distinctiveness of the British nation by stressing the reach of its commercial and political power overseas. The anthem "Rule Britannia" was written in the heady early months of the war with Spain. Nonetheless, concentrating on the public rallies of the 1730s, and more generally on the emotive and symbolic resonance of imperialism, obscures profound, lingering divisions among the promoters of the cause of empire. Cumberland was too young to be engaged in the debates leading up to the war in the Caribbean, but by the time he reached maturity and turned his attention to colonial projects, he counted the imperial "Patriots" who had advocated warfare in the 1730s among his political rivals.[87] The problem was not merely that he identified them as Tories. Cumberland's vision of the empire's future—his belief that the army could conquer, regulate, and reform colonies on the edge of civilization—ran counter to the commercially oriented "blue water" vision that had been promoted by the early supporters of the Anglo-Spanish war.

In order to appreciate fully the significance of the divisions among the imperialists, it is necessary to study events on two sides of the water, in Britain and the colonies.[88] It was overseas, for example, in the Mediterranean, where the officers of Cumberland's army most dramatically confronted their adversaries among Britain's imperialists. Disputes between the army and the navy over the fate of Minorca began years before the French seized the island from the British in 1756. Jurisdictional struggles over the government of Minorca pitted Cumberland and his officers against their long-standing opponents in Parliament and in the view of some contemporaries, resurrected issues that had arisen earlier in the context of Cumberland's campaigns in Scotland. There is much to be learned by drawing connections between events in geographically separate and distant places. Tracing the progress of Cumberland's officers from the Scottish Highlands to the colonies can teach us much about British imperial history. It can also provide insight into the ideological significance, and the practical impact, of actions taken in Scotland in 1745 and 1746.

At no time during his political career or his command of the army was Cumberland in complete control of events. Every country his army entered had its own history, and in many places the officers could barely comprehend the local political dynamics, to say nothing of overriding or redirecting long-standing trends.[89] The level of Cumberland's political influence also fluctuated in Britain. Under these circumstances, all of his accomplishments were mixed with compromises, unintended consequences, and failures. To be sure, Charles Edward was defeated and Jacobitism faded after 1746. In the aftermath of Cumberland's campaigns in the Scottish Highlands, clanship gradually receded as a military threat. Over the ensuing decades the English language spread across the whole of Scotland, commerce increased, and the Highlands were integrated more fully into the cosmopolitan, British-imperial world. By the time Cumberland resigned his commission as captain general, the future of the British army seemed secure even in peacetime, and it had become a more coherently organized, professional force. Operating more effectively, the army had completed the conquest of French Canada by 1760, and in 1763 France formally ceded all of North America east of the Mississippi to the British Empire. Though Cumberland was no longer in command by that time, he had a hand in laying the groundwork for these events. Nonetheless it is important not to exaggerate his influence. Each of his accomplishments can be seen as an episode in a longer story, the continuation of a drama that had begun before he took the stage.

In the 1770s the British Empire would fracture again, with a rebellion in the American colonies that has often been interpreted, at least in part, as a reaction against the centralization and militarization of Britain's imperial government. These were trends that accelerated during Cumberland's command of the army in the Seven Years' War, but he should not be blamed for the breakup of the empire.[90] Though he briefly participated in the debates over the Stamp Act in 1765, he was dead well before the imperial crisis reached its climax and the American Revolution began. This book concentrates on issues that concerned Cumberland and his contemporaries in the 1740s and 1750s, questions involving the expansion and consolidation of the imperial domain, the deployment of the army as an agency for social progress, and the rules governing the use of force against different categories of inhabitants and strangers, savages and subjects. The debates over these issues would continue for decades and eventually affect all of the English-speaking world, including the nascent and expanding United States, those parts of the empire that the British retained after the Revolution, and the colonies they continued to acquire.

Cumberland participated in a particularly significant decision in 1756, when he argued in favor of sending Highland troops to North America and, after complex political maneuvering, secured support from the ministry. It is not clear whether he anticipated the consequences of this deployment. The mobilization of manpower from the region helped transform the politics of Highland Scotland. Landlords and military recruiters, including former Jacobites and officers from Cumberland's army, cooperated in recruiting soldiers, provisioning them, and embarking them for America. The war effort established and strengthened partnerships between members of the Highland elite, the army, and the government in Westminster and eased tensions that had lingered since 1745. After the fall of Quebec in 1759, Highlanders from various social conditions took pride in their participation in the North American campaign, and once the fighting was over, emigration from the Highlands increased.[91] The newcomers were generally welcomed in America. Only a few years earlier, in the late 1740s and early 1750s, many powerful leaders in the colonies had resisted proposals to settle Highlanders on their frontiers, but after the Highland soldiers fought for Britain in Canada, the colonists were persuaded to change their minds. Old stereotypes died hard, and wariness lingered. Charles Edward and his army were still remembered, but increasingly it seemed that he and the Highlanders who had fought for him belonged to a distant age. In North America and eventually throughout the empire, the Highlanders earned a new reputation, as useful settlers and champions of the imperial cause.[92]

Part I
The Response to the Crisis

Rebellion: Criminal Prosecution and the Jacobite Soldiers

In the summer of 1745, after the government in Westminster learned of Charles Edward's intention to come to Scotland, one of its first responses was to order him arrested. The Privy Council offered a reward of £30,000 to anyone who could take him into custody.[1] Upon learning of this, Charles Edward retaliated by declaring George II an outlaw and offering a reward for the apprehension of the king.[2] For the duration of the conflict, both the Jacobites and the government's forces employed the mechanisms of criminal law in their campaigns against their opponents. Before the scale of the rising was clear, some of George II's supporters hoped that ordinary law enforcement would bring the disturbance to an end. County sheriffs in Scotland prepared indictments against suspected Jacobites and sent deputies to effect arrests and prepare for trials.[3] The Jacobites, for their part, could not hope to indict all the loyal subjects of George II, but they dreamed of trying the most active and powerful among them. In Scotland Charles Edward ordered the arrest of several high government officials, including Duncan Forbes, the president of the Scottish Court of Session.[4]

For the Jacobites, these appeals to criminal procedure were largely symbolic, but for George II and his ministers, defeating the rising through criminal proceedings seemed viable. The government's decision to send regular army units against the Jacobites did not constitute an abandonment of the project of subjecting Charles Edward and his supporters to prosecution. Cumberland's army marched against them with orders to conduct investigations, make arrests, and hold suspects in custody.[5] Though no one ever managed to arrest Charles Edward, after defeating the rising the government jailed thousands of Jacobite soldiers and conducted hundreds of criminal trials. Dozens of those convicted were executed, and hundreds of others were transported to America after guilty pleas or convictions.[6]

It proved difficult, however, for Cumberland's soldiers to comply with the requirements of criminal procedure. Part of the problem lay in the scale of their undertaking. The Jacobite army fluctuated in size. Estimates of the number of men under arms varied considerably at every moment of the conflict, but everyone knew, from early September 1745 on, that Charles Edward had recruited thousands of soldiers. They proved a surprisingly effective military force. More than eight months passed before they were defeated decisively, and in the meantime the forces of George II lost several important engagements with them on the battlefield.[7] After the fighting ended the army held so many prisoners that simply identifying them proved difficult. Finding jail space, feeding them, and preparing evidence against them individually strained the government's resources at every step of the criminal proceedings.

By temperament, training, and experience, the soldiers and officers of the British army were poorly prepared for the task of readying criminal trials. To the extent that they thought of their campaign as a punitive operation, they preferred to impose punishment on the scene of battle without detaining suspects, gathering evidence, or deferring to the judgments of courts. Eighteenth-century military culture was more likely to excuse massive killing on a battlefield than to sanction the systematic execution of prisoners. The killing of war captives was seen, not only by soldiers but by most other observers of military action in Europe, as a violation of the rules of war if not an indication of savagery.[8] Nonetheless, in 1745 and 1746, Cumberland and his supporters insisted that rebellion was a capital offense and that the death penalty was what the Jacobite soldiers deserved. Therefore, government officials were at pains to declare that the rules of war did not apply in the context of the suppression of the rising. They asserted that the fighters Cumberland and his soldiers took into custody were criminal suspects rather than prisoners of war.

Though they referred to the Jacobites as criminals when they sought to justify suspending the conventional rules of war, the military men deployed against Charles Edward's army often used force to achieve tactical advantages rather than targeting violence in order to serve the ends of justice. Conditional threats served their immediate purposes, and efficient military operations frequently required commanders to allow their opponents to slip away or to bargain with them for surrender. Cumberland engaged in these practices even as he expressed disapproval of all negotiations. In the end, only one group of war captives was granted prisoner-of-war status, and made the subject of formal diplomatic negotiations: French troops, including those of British and Irish ancestry who had been born overseas and fought under the French flag. Anxious to avoid provoking France into suspending the rules of war on the Continent, the ministry ordered a careful examination of all the prisoners taken from French units to determine where the men were born.

Even Gaelic-speaking members of prominent Highland families were exempt from criminal prosecution if they could demonstrate that they had been born in France.[9]

The dilemmas that the government faced in the context of the suppression of the rising were common wherever an overt resort to military force was necessary to establish governmental authority. On the margins of the British Empire, where soldiers encountered diverse populations of uncertain loyalty, the application of justice in disputed regions often fell into the hands of military men who were ill educated or ignorant of the normal requirements of criminal procedure. British officers and soldiers in the Mediterranean, in North America, and elsewhere frequently had to distinguish between suspect groups and apply different codes of conduct in their actions against distinct segments of the local populations. Like the troops in Scotland, the men deployed to Britain's overseas domains often operated in places where they did not trust the local judicial authorities or where civilian courts were altogether lacking. The army's response to these problems in Scotland in the aftermath of the rising—arresting thousands of alleged rebels and arranging for individual trials in England—would have been impractical had it been attempted in the colonies. The trials of the Jacobite prisoners did not, therefore, set a specific precedent for the administration of marginal lands. Nonetheless, the army's response to the rising, and specifically its treatment of the Jacobite soldiers, reveals much about the instincts of the officers and the ideas they took with them when they moved from the Scottish Highlands to patrol other parts of the world.

*   *   *

Charles Edward arrived on the western coast of Scotland in late July 1745 with only seven companions, but with a rapidity that surprised nearly all concerned, by September he had gathered a formidable fighting force. The Jacobites intended to establish their credentials as the legitimate governing authority in Britain. Their ability to enlist troops in an orderly and lawful fashion, they believed, was an attribute of their sovereignty. In the early weeks of the rising Jacobite commanders in various parts of northern Scotland instituted a system of conscription, in some regions ordering all men between the ages of sixteen and sixty to enlist.[10] The recruiters drew heavily on the lowest ranks of the social order. Parishes were given quotas, and wealthy tenants paid cottars and servants to take their places in the ranks.[11] The Jacobites took advantage of the local social order as best as they understood it and ordered clan leaders to summon all the fighting-age men of their clans.[12] Throughout the Highlands, Jacobite recruiters emphasized traditional loyalties. They employed dramatic, ostensibly ancient rituals, such as carrying burning crosses as a call to arms.[13]

The hierarchical social structure of the Highlands often gave high-status women influence, and a few figured prominently in the mobilization effort. Charles Edward's opponents derided the Jacobites for relying on female recruiters, for example by lampooning the efforts of a woman named Jenny Cameron, who enlisted 250 men "and marched at the head of them" to Charles Edward's camp.[14] Anti-Jacobite pamphleteers retold Cameron's story elaborately, and with considerable creative license.[15] The work of Anne MacKintosh, the wife of the laird of Clan Chattan near Inverness, is documented more reliably. Her husband supported George II, but she disagreed with him and rallied the clan to the Jacobites.[16] Foot soldiers in Charles Edward's army referred to MacKintosh, who was only twenty-three years old in the spring of 1746, as if she were a formal military commander, and they took it for granted that she controlled the disposition of troops.[17]

Some Jacobite officials, particularly on the eastern and southern fringes of the Highlands, threatened "military execution" against those who failed to comply with their conscription orders.[18] That phrase was a familiar term of art, referring to a prerogative long claimed by the armies of Europe, to conduct punitive raids, usually involving the confiscation or destruction of property, against villages and regions where the inhabitants refused to provision troops or comply with military orders. Some who refused to cooperate with Jacobite recruitment efforts had their houses burned, while others had soldiers quartered in their homes.[19] The Duke of Perth declared that any of his tenants who failed to enlist would be treated as "rebels to the [Stuart] King." According to documents gathered after the rising ended, the punishments he inflicted on recalcitrants overstepped the traditional bounds of "military execution." Perth was alleged to have authorized his recruiting agents to seize young men and carry them off if they refused to join the Jacobite army voluntarily.[20]

While there is every reason to believe that many soldiers in the Jacobite army had been coerced into joining, there are also grounds for suspecting that the stories of intimidation and violence were exaggerated. Among supporters of George II, retelling violent accounts of the recruitment process was a way of demeaning Charles Edward's army. Captured Jacobite soldiers also had reason to embellish such tales in order to excuse themselves from punishment for participating in the fight.[21] Furthermore there were other reasons for young men to enlist. Many in the Highlands, particularly Catholics and Episcopalians, chose to join the army out of deep personal conviction in the justice of the Jacobite cause.[22] They opposed the ruling regime and welcomed Charles Edward both as the son of their legitimate monarch and as the champion of their interests. A few prominent leaders in the Highlands viewed the rising as an opportunity to increase their fortunes through preferment if the operation succeeded. Similar calculations were made by the desperately poor, who saw enlistment as a chance to start a new life and erase past mistakes.[23] Others joined with the Jacobites to escape prosecution for larceny or murder.[24] More commonly, men enlisted simply for money. Times were hard in many parts of the country, and the economy deteriorated after the rising began.[25] These conditions affected communities outside the Highlands. As soon as Charles Edward marched south he was able to recruit men in the Lowlands of Scotland and in England as well.[26]

Charles Edward believed that he could succeed in battle and win the loyalty of the people of Britain only if he led a restrained, conventional military force.[27] He ordered his recruits to procure uniforms, and as soon as he had gathered enough men to fill a parade ground, he began drilling them. Over the next several months he issued a variety of directives designed to maintain discipline, decorum, and morality within his ranks.[28] Despite these efforts, in the early weeks of the conflict most of George II's supporters spoke of the Jacobites with contempt. On first learning of Charles Edward's efforts, Cumberland, who was still in Flanders at the time, dismissively declared, "I hope that Great Britain is not to be conquered by three thousand rabble, gathered together in the mountains."[29] Cumberland's supporters continued to ridicule the Jacobite army for the duration of the conflict and long thereafter. Referring to their kilts, they called the Jacobite Highlanders the "bare asses," and even after the fighting ended, pamphleteers asserted that despite months of practice, Charles Edward's men had never learned to march in a straight line.[30]

While continuing to mock the Jacobite army as oafs, a large part of the British population began to fear them after they entered Edinburgh, and particularly in the aftermath of the government's first, failed effort to retake the Scottish capital in late September 1745. That attempt ended in a violent skirmish that came to be known as the Battle of Prestonpans. Loudon, who was present at the engagement, declared afterward that the government's troops had been "perfectly formed" to defend against an orderly assault but unprepared for the kind of attack they received.[31] Screaming and brandishing broadswords, Jacobite Highlanders took the government's soldiers by surprise, killing hundreds and leaving hundreds of others mortally hurt.[32] The wounds the swords inflicted were horrific, and they were remembered, redescribed, and embellished for years thereafter. In February 1746 the *London Evening Post* described the arrival in London of two hundred survivors from the battle. "The poor men were in a most miserable condition, some without arms and legs, others their noses cut off and eyes put out, besides hacked and mauled in many parts of their body, after a most terrible and cruel manner."[33] In 1748 a pro-government historian declared that the men who died at Prestonpans "were not killed, as in a battle, but slaughtered as by an apprentice butcher."[34]

Within minutes of their victory at Prestonpans the Jacobites knew that the carnage they had inflicted could damage them politically. They let it be known that when he learned that his soldiers had won the field, Charles Edward "mounted his horse, and put a stop to the slaughter."[35] He reportedly searched among the prisoners for surgeons and, discovering none, sent an express to Edinburgh to find competent men to dress the enemy soldiers' wounds. Far from providing evidence of their cruelty, the Jacobites claimed that their behavior at Prestonpans had demonstrated their "humanity" and "clemency."[36]

The Battle of Prestonpans came at a time when the leaders of the British government were beginning to reassess their strategy against the Jacobites. Initially after they learned of Charles Edward's landing, the leaders of the ministry and the army had expected to defeat him easily with the regular forces available in Scotland, including Loudon's new, half-completed regiment of Highland soldiers, and other local recruits informally deputized and armed to meet the occasion. Despite uncertainty within the Edinburgh legal establishment over the propriety of arming volunteers outside the army, militiamen were raised in several communities outside the Highlands.[37] In his capacity as the newly appointed lieutenant governor of Stirling Castle, William Blakeney had a role in the early efforts to distribute swords and muskets to volunteers. He authorized the dispersal of weaponry to the sheriff of Stirlingshire to allow him to arm men.[38] The hundred members of the Stirlingshire militia, so equipped, patrolled the roads of the area and seized several groups suspected of traveling to join Charles Edward and his army. Nonetheless, despite the availability of regular troops and local patrols, as early as mid-August 1745 the ministry had decided over Cumberland's objections to send reinforcements from Europe.[39]

In mid-July 1745 rumors had reached the ministry that the French were preparing for a possible "attempt" directly against Britain. The stories were vague and did not yet involve any specific information about Charles Edward and his intentions.[40] Cumberland was in Flanders at the time, helping defend the Austrian Netherlands from the French. There had been fighting in the European Low Countries since 1740, and though Britain did not officially declare war on France until 1744, Hanover, the homeland of George II and the rest of the royal family, had entered the fray early, and British troops had long been engaged. Many in Britain complained that the deployment of British troops in Flanders served the interests of Hanover to the detriment of Britain. Cumberland and his supporters defended their involvement by insisting that they were "saving the liberties of Europe," and Britain as well, by maintaining the balance of power and preventing the Bourbon French monarchy from dominating the Continent.[41] When he first learned that Charles Edward might be sailing for Britain, Cumberland was reluctant to shift any troops. Nonetheless he understood the need to convince the ministers (and the British public at large) that he was ready "to bring the whole British corps home in case it should be wanted."[42] When the call came, Cumberland moved slowly, and he fretted that, given the precarious position of his army in Flanders, any transfer of troops might "overthrow all the hope we have of saving these remains of the Austrian dominions."[43] He continued to resist redeployments until nearly the time of the engagement at Prestonpans.[44] By that time, however, with Charles Edward in Edinburgh, he had decided not only that more soldiers would have to be sent to Britain but that he would lead them.[45] Cumberland accordingly requested permission from the ministry to return to Britain, and he received it on October 8, 1745.[46]

Weeks passed, however, before Cumberland actually took command of the forces deployed against the Jacobites, and a great deal happened in the meantime. Loudon's Highlanders were redeployed to Inverness with orders to disrupt Jacobite military recruitment. The Duke of Argyll received permission to raise troops on the basis of a unique hereditary lieutenancy, and Highlanders loyal to the government, at least in the regions associated with Clan Campbell, belatedly gained the opportunity to take up arms without formally enlisting in the regular army. Militia companies were raised in counties and towns across England and Wales. The French sent a brigade of approximately a thousand troops, mostly men of Irish descent, to aid Charles Edward in the rising. At about the same time, thousands of Dutch soldiers landed in the northeast of England in the expectation that they would be ordered north to engage the Jacobites. The Jacobite army, however, skirted the Dutch to the west, marched through the north of England, entered Manchester, and proceeded into the English Midlands before retreating back toward Scotland. In all this time, the government's divided forces failed to engage them in any large-scale battles. When Cumberland assumed command on November 27, the Jacobites were in retreat, but Cumberland's army was in a poor condition to pursue them.

The units Cumberland brought from Flanders had been chosen with Flemish affairs in mind. They were the ones the commanders on the Continent could spare, and they did not arrive as a coherent fighting force.[47] In Britain, the various regiments, battalions, and independent companies that Cumberland led competed against each other, often antagonistically, for money and recruits.[48] They had their own financial accounts, their own enlistment practices, and very distinctive group loyalties.[49] The foreign forces that were sent to aid in the fight against the Jacobites—the Dutch and subsequently a unit of Hessians—had their own priorities, and Cumberland preferred not to use them in combat.[50] Throughout the army, communications between companies was frequently difficult. Especially in the early weeks after his arrival in Britain, Cumberland struggled to coordinate his scattered forces. One important episode from that period involved Georgia governor James Oglethorpe, who took command of a corps of volunteer cavalrymen from Yorkshire and nearly caught up with the Jacobites in the north of England.[51] Oglethorpe failed and met with disgrace.[52]

Cumberland believed he had to assert his overall authority in order to give a sense of unified purpose to the land forces in Britain. As part of that project, like Charles Edward, he issued orders almost incessantly related to the proper maintenance of uniforms, the deference owed to superior officers, parade etiquette, and drill.[53] Cumberland was assisted in these efforts by Humphrey Bland, a sixty-year-old Irish Protestant officer who had served as his quartermaster general in Flanders.[54] Bland had fought for Britain during the War of the Spanish Succession, and he had participated in the suppression of the Jacobite rising of 1715. Nonetheless, he was famous primarily as the author of the most widely cited drill book in the English language.[55]

Cumberland's obsession with drill exposed him to satire when his military operations were going badly. Following the Battle of Falkirk, one pamphleteer, referring to him as a "Bonny-plump lad," recommended that his forces be augmented by a "regiment of ladies."[56] The author suggested arming the female troops with a device that a future generation would call a nunchuck—two batons connected with a chain (see Figure 3). Calling this weapon a flail, the writer claimed that "half a dozen good strokes will mash to a paste the stoutest man in his Majesty's dominions."[57] Mocking the exercises favored by the eighteenth-century British army, the pamphlet included "Terms of Military Exercise for the Army of Ladies," as follows:

Pocket your flails,
Poise your flails,
Handle your flails,
Extend your flails,
Swing your flails,
Apply your flails,
Recover your flails,
Pocket your flails.[58]

Figure 3. A pamphlet entitled "The French Flail" was published in the early spring of 1746 when the government's campaign against the Jacobites seemed to be going badly. The author ridiculed Cumberland and his army and suggested that the British would be better defended if they deployed a "regiment of ladies" armed with nunchucks. (Courtesy of the University of Aberdeen.)

Some of this ridicule may have been deserved, but drilling served a serious purpose in training newly recruited soldiers and in integrating them, despite their scattered origins, into a coherent force.

In the process of bringing discipline to his army Cumberland was also consolidating and expanding his political power on three levels. First, within the army, he was establishing himself as leader. Cumberland was only twenty-four years old when he arrived to take command in Britain. Only the previous March he had received his commission from his father, George II, as "captain general" with authority over Britain's land forces.[59] Cumberland worked to build a body of supporters within the officer corps. He earned a reputation for socializing with well-born men of his own age and advancing their careers.[60] One young officer who would benefit professionally from Cumberland's friendship was Edward Cornwallis, the thirty-two-year-old son of a baron who had known the royal family since he was twelve.[61] Another, even younger recipient of the duke's attentions was James Wolfe, the eighteen-year-old son of a major general in the army.[62] Cornwallis and Wolfe both came to Britain from Europe in the redeployment of 1745, as did Bland.

Cumberland's leadership in the army gave him powerful leverage in Parliament. A significant number of officers serving under him had seats, including Cornwallis in the Commons and Loudon in the Lords.[63] A large number of others stood for election after serving in Scotland in 1746.[64] In the summer of 1747 Henry Pelham directed Cumberland to grant leave to all officers "whose presence is required at the ensuing elections."[65] This directive triggered a flurry of activity to support the Whig interest, and specifically Cumberland's influence in Westminster.[66] Some officers asked leave to stand for election. Loudon was temporarily excused from his combat duties to secure votes for preferred candidates for the House of Commons.[67] Employing a military metaphor, Cumberland's associates described these efforts as their "home campaign."[68] As captain general he had enormous patronage power. Cumberland had ultimate authority over the selection and promotion of officers, military provisioning, transportation, and the payment of troops.[69] In short, he organized the army as an institution, and those who sought profit, professional advancement, or political influence through the distribution of commissions were well advised to maintain his favor.

Leading the army against the Jacobites served Cumberland's political interest on a more popular level as well. Many common soldiers were thrilled at the sight of him. According to Wolfe they were "ready to undertake anything, having so brave a man at the head of them."[70] Some private men may have been more cautious than Wolfe suggested, but a large part of the army was impressed by Cumberland's royal status. In Scotland he was obliged to issue orders for his soldiers not to stare at him while they were on parade.[71] Additionally, Cumberland led many who were not soldiers. Some officers and enlisted men brought their wives with them on the campaign, and other women provided various services to the troops. Among other tasks, these women were assigned the job of cleaning and repairing clothes and milking cattle and goats.[72] Some were paid directly by the army, while others, women and men alike, followed the troops in hope of more informal employment. In the closing weeks of Cumberland's service in Britain, dozens of shopkeepers, barbers, butchers, laborers, carpenters, and others lived in huts surrounding the army's main camp.[73] These civilians formed part of a procession, and for Cumberland they were also an audience. Not only during parades and drills but also at concerts, hangings, and evening walks with his officers, he made sure that he was visible to all.[74]

The army's march north was a necessary military operation, but it functioned as a pageant as well. Cumberland self-consciously displayed his authority, and one effect of his service was to enhance his personal position in future contests with political rivals, including opposition members of Parliament. Cumberland had an unusually partisan way of interpreting British politics. He credited "the old Whig cause" with placing his grandfather on the throne in 1714, and throughout his career he believed that only the Whigs could be trusted as defenders of the Protestant succession and the royal family.[75] Party politics remained on his mind in 1745 and 1746, but Cumberland also knew that Charles Edward's challenge transcended ordinary partisan divisions. Sovereignty was directly and explicitly at issue, and as the most active and visible member of the reigning household, Cumberland sought to dramatize and demonstrate its majesty, power, and right to rule. He was determined to be regal as well as popular, and a central element in that project was denying his military opponents any legitimacy or respect.

Though he never admitted it publicly, Cumberland knew, as a practical matter, that as long as the Jacobites retained a coherent fighting force they held leverage over him, and their ability to retaliate limited the range of his policy options. Soon after his arrival in England he complained that he could not pursue summary justice against Jacobite prisoners and put them to death, because "they have so many of our prisoners in their hands."[76] By altering his actions to avoid a violent Jacobite response, Cumberland engaged in a kind of silent negotiation. Other political and military leaders in England and Scotland would have preferred to speak more openly with the Jacobites and explicitly offer them minimal concessions.[77]

In the month prior to Cumberland's arrival, General George Wade, with the approval of the ministry, offered official clemency to any Jacobite soldiers who surrendered to him within a two-week grace period.

Wade directed his offer to individual private men and justified it by observing that many of them had been forced to enlist in Charles Edward's army by the "threatenings" of their "chiefs and superiors."[78] Blakeney, less formally, pursued a similar policy from his post in Stirling-shire. Jacobite soldiers who deserted their units and passed by Bla-keney's garrison at Stirling Castle were disarmed and then allowed to "go quietly home."[79] While Wade and Blakeney were offering leniency to individual soldiers, Loudon, for his part, was interested in negotiating with officers. Fearful of entering into an unauthorized "correspon-dence," he wrote the ministry to ask whether such negotiations would be legal. He never received a firm response, at least not from White-hall.[80]

Loudon's question was quickly and simply settled after Cumberland arrived. The answer came when the government's army retook the town and castle of Carlisle, which had been seized by the Jacobites a few weeks earlier. When the Jacobites had taken the town, Charles Edward and his officers had entered into elaborate formal negotiations with Carlisle's original defenders, and they had celebrated their victory with ceremon-ies of submission.[81] Cumberland's entry into Carlisle was equally dra-matic but in a different way. Initially he had refused to submit to any negotiations, but he begrudgingly agreed to a short exchange of let-ters.[82] In his first communication he ruled out any possibility of a pris-oner exchange but offered no details on the terms he would accept. The Jacobite defenders of the castle responded by asking him to be more specific. Cumberland replied, "All the Terms his Royal Highness will or can grant to the Rebel Garrison of Carlisle are, that they shall not be put to the Sword, but be reserv'd for the King's Pleasure."[83] Once the garri-son had surrendered Cumberland expressed regret that he had con-ceded so much.[84]

After the government's forces retook Carlisle, Cumberland ordered the mayor and town clerk arrested on charges of high treason because they had negotiated for the surrender of the town to the Jacobites.[85] He and his supporters in the ministry exerted pressure to have the two men tried and punished, but the mayor and town clerk evaded prosecution.[86] As the campaign continued, and long after it was over, other men, including both civilians and military officers, faced prosecution on simi-lar charges. One of the most prominent was Archibald Stewart, the pro-vost of Edinburgh, who had failed to offer much resistance when Charles Edward entered his city.[87] In October 1747 the provost was tried, but acquitted.[88] Bland, for one, considered the trial judgment "shame-ful" and attributed it to a pro-Scottish bias in the judges.[89]

The army had its own system of discipline, and while civilian courts handled the cases against mayors, clerks, and provosts, military tribunals considered the cases against officers who surrendered forts in the Highlands.[90] Blakeney served as presiding judge in one of these trials.[91] Bland presided in another, with Cornwallis sitting as a judge by his side.[92] Military officers were scrutinized and punished with increasing frequency after 1745, not only for conducting allegedly treasonous negotiations but also for lapses of judgment, incompetence, and cowardice. Among those facing trials after the suppression of the rising were Georgia's governor James Oglethorpe, who had failed to catch the Jacobite army with his volunteer cavalry, and General John Cope, who had held overall command of the government's army at the Battle of Prestonpans.[93] Those two men were acquitted at their trials, and most of the high officers who were convicted received lighter sentences than the statutes allowed. Nonetheless, appearing as a defendant in a court martial, in and of itself, represented a disgrace. As far as negotiating with the Jacobites was concerned, the official policy was clear after the capture of Carlisle: no one was to do it, and those who did might find themselves on trial.

Cumberland gloried in this stubborn stance and cooperated in a publicity campaign presenting him as an uncompromising hero (see Figure 4). Blakeney, who successfully defended Stirling Castle against a Jacobite siege in January 1746, similarly acquired heroic status. Eleven days after Charles Edward's army took possession of the town of Stirling and surrounded his castle, Blakeney sent word to Edinburgh that the Jacobites had "summoned him twice" for negotiation. Each time, according to Blakeney, "his answer was, that he had always been looked upon as a man of honour, and that they should find he would die so."[94] On the same day this report reached Edinburgh, excited government officials relayed it to London, and eventually Blakeney's words were incorporated verbatim into several published histories of the rising.[95] Blakeney would not enter talks on any matter. Indeed, according to one biographer, when Jacobite commanders requested permission to carry away the corpses of those who had died at the walls of Stirling Castle, Blakeney refused to hold fire and allow it. He declared that "the weather was very cold" and therefore "their bodies were not like to be offensive."[96] According to contemporary understandings of the rules of war, all civilized peoples allowed their military enemies to bury their dead.[97] In this conflict, however, those rules seemed not to apply.

Cumberland occasionally issued conditional threats to the Jacobites, but once the army was under his direct command he maintained a consistent policy against cordial negotiations between the commanders of the two armies.[98] Cumberland's highest officers generally understood these guidelines and struggled to comply with them. But the ban on negotiation affected all the ranks, and among lower officers and com-

Figure 4. This print was made to celebrate Cumberland's refusal to negotiate with the Jacobites, specifically during his siege of Carlisle. The heading reads "The Duke of Cumberland refusing to treat with the Rebels." (Courtesy of the Carlisle Library.)

mon soldiers it was much more difficult to define and enforce. Every soldier who dropped his weapons and asked for quarter entered into a bargain with the enemy, and for most of those who asked for quarter, that was only the beginning of the deal making. Cumberland believed that even in cases involving individual soldiers, entering into an agreement with Charles Edward's army constituted treason, and his position contributed to a deepening alienation between the men of the opposing armed camps.

In September 1745 the government soldiers captured at Prestonpans were brought to the city of Edinburgh, which was then under the control of the Jacobites. Eventually the effort to house the prisoners forced the removal of all the civilian criminals and debtors from the city's cells.[99] Military recruiters visited the men in prison and offered to release any of them who agreed to enlist in the Jacobite army. Those who agreed were given uniforms; those who refused were transferred to darker, damper quarters in the jails.[100] On September 28, 1745, twenty former prisoners who had joined Charles Edward's army fled from their new commanders to the government's garrison in Edinburgh Castle. In response the Jacobites ordered all their prisoners out of the city. They took the men north to Atholl, but found inadequate prison facilities there.[101] It soon became obvious that the only practical option was to negotiate with the prisoners and offer them conditional release. In October 110 Highlanders who had fought in Loudon's regiment at Prestonpans were set free on parole and given travel money to allow them to return to their homes.[102] In exchange for their liberty the men promised not to return to combat.[103] For the duration of the rising, prisoners held by the Jacobites could gain their freedom by offering similar pledges.[104]

These arrangements caused consternation among the Jacobites. One officer declared that it was foolish ever to trust the prisoners' promises, because many of them broke their word and returned to the field of battle. It would have been smarter, he declared years later, simply "to put all the enemy to the sword."[105] From their own perspective, many in the government's army expressed similar sentiments. Cumberland, disgusted with the way the men honored the promises they made to the Jacobites, hinted that he would have liked to see all the officers among them hanged.[106] The findings of an inquest held in January 1746 foreclosed that possibility, so Cumberland contented himself with ordering the men to violate the promises they had made in exchange for release from the Jacobites' custody. He wanted them back in his camps.

Cumberland was aided in this effort by several members of the Presbyterian clergy, who argued that the men had never been bound by the pledges they gave when they were held prisoner by the Jacobites.[107] The clergymen asserted that the soldiers' promise not to fight had been "illegal" and that it carried no weight "in comparison with the legal one" they had made when they first enlisted in the government's army.[108] Some of the men who had vowed not to return to combat were initially unconvinced by this argument and sought to avoid service by pleading sickness or otherwise evading the military authorities.[109] As late as February 1746, some soldiers who had accepted parole in the aftermath of the Battle of Presonpans resisted returning to the government's service, but in general, when they were threatened with prosecution for desertion, they relented and rejoined their original corps.[110] The Jacobites, for their part, observed these proceedings closely, and in February they published a broadside in Aberdeen warning that the failure of these men to honor their parole agreements might make it difficult for any individual soldiers in the future to negotiate terms for surrender.[111]

All of the men who surrendered to the Jacobites faced scrutiny in the spring of 1746, and many risked prosecution for desertion or treason.

Those who had enlisted with the Jacobite army suffered the worst legal jeopardy. It became almost a routine ceremony each time the government took a Jacobite stronghold: former government soldiers found in arms with the Jacobites were summarily tried before courts martial and hanged.[112] But even those who fled from their captors and tried to rejoin their old military units were investigated to make sure they had not aided the Jacobites in any way or entered into any subversive agreements as a way of securing their release. Wolfe was one of the officers responsible for conducting these investigations.[113] The official policy against negotiating with the Jacobites created a dynamic that heightened animosity and distrust. Anxious to forestall any suggestion that they had maintained friendly relations with their captors, prisoners held by the Jacobites spread self-serving reports that they had been mistreated. Their testimony lent credence to stories that had circulated since the rising started that the Jacobites were cruel jailkeepers. Furthermore, as the rising continued, and the material circumstances of the Jacobite army deteriorated, the allegations of mistreatment had a stronger basis in fact.[114]

One Jacobite leader, Donald Cameron of Lochiel, advocated hanging prisoners one at a time, systematically, to avenge specific outrages. Lochiel published his views and they were distributed widely, both in manuscript and printed form.[115] In February a rumor circulated among the government's soldiers that the Jacobites had hanged at least one prisoner.[116] That spring rumors spread through Inverness that Charles Edward's men intended to kill all the prisoners they held in country churches. Years later, the men who eventually gained release from those churches continued to believe that they had barely escaped with their lives.[117] By March 1746 nearly all the conventions governing the treatment of war captives seemed to be breaking down, and some of Cumberland's soldiers and officers believed that the Jacobites were on the verge of dispensing with the taking of prisoners altogether.

In December 1745 a small group of soldiers from Bland's regiment had skirmished with a body of Jacobite Highlanders. Fewer than a dozen men had been involved, and among the government's troops only one man was wounded, with "four cuts upon his unlucky noddle."[118] Nonetheless, the fight was significant because the soldiers returned to camp with a report that the Highlanders had approached the field of battle "howling as they do" and then yelling (in English?) "murder 'em, no quarter." Those yells were remembered for weeks and eventually formed part of an extensive, though largely debatable, body of evidence supporting the claim that the Jacobites refused to allow fighting men to surrender.[119] In the meantime, the Jacobites spread rumors of their own, and unlike the government they could produce a document to support their claims. It was an order, purportedly issued by Cumberland himself, outlining how at least some of his men were to behave if they encountered "such of the rebels as may be found in arms." First, according to the directions, the soldiers were to demand an immediate surrender, and if any of the "rebels" offered resistance, the government's soldiers were to engage and kill them, offering "no quarter."[120]

The Battle of Culloden was brief and brutal. Cumberland complained after the fighting was over that the Jacobites were "dastardly cowards" for giving him the victory "so cheap."[121] One soldier reported that hours after the battle it was difficult to cross from one end of Culloden Moor to the other because the ground was covered with the dead.[122] Several reports indicated that in the aftermath of the fighting, Jacobite soldiers had been systematically executed. The survivors among the Jacobites reported this; their stories were confirmed, more or less explicitly, in the way the government's soldiers defended themselves, not by denying the allegations but rather by offering self-justification.[123]

Shortly after his moment of victory Cumberland began to anticipate controversy, and on the next day he issued a general order directing his officers and soldiers "to take notice that the public orders of the rebels yesterday was to give us no quarters."[124] The Jacobites consistently denied the existence of any written orders to that effect, and when pressed, no one in Cumberland's army could produce the documentation.[125] Nonetheless, Wolfe was one of many soldiers who repeated Cumberland's version of events eagerly. On the day Cumberland told the soldiers to "take notice" of the existence of the Jacobites' written orders, Wolfe wrote at least two letters repeating the allegation. In one he declared, "The rebels, besides their natural inclinations, had orders not to give quarters to our men. We had an opportunity of avenging ourselves for that and many other things, and indeed we did not neglect it, as few Highlanders were made prisoners as possible."[126]

Some defenders of the government attributed the killings to the soldiers' "passion," suggesting that months of mounting anger found release when the men found the Jacobites vulnerable before them.[127] Anger may indeed explain these events, but the men who killed at Culloden did so deliberately, and not in a blind rage. This is best illustrated by the example of Bland, who, according to Cumberland, "gave quarter to none but about fifty French officers and soldiers he picked up."[128] Bland made a careful distinction. Officers and soldiers with French commissions were protected by the protocols of diplomacy and the ability of the French to make reprisals if the British failed to proceed in their cases according to conventional rules of war. The British Jacobites, by contrast, were helpless, and if Cumberland is to be believed, Bland's men physically attacked them all. More than a month after the battle, Bland continued to believe that it was better to kill Jacobite soldiers than to maintain them as prisoners. On May 22 he gave orders to Loudon to pursue one of the lingering remnants of Charles Edward's forces. His directions specified that Loudon was to "destroy" as many of the Jacobites as he could, "since prisoners would only embarrass him."[129]

The word "embarrass" did not necessarily carry the same meaning in the eighteenth century that it does today. Bland could have meant any of several things by suggesting that the taking of prisoners would "embarrass" Loudon: possibly that it would constitute an encumbrance and impede his freedom of action, or that it might cost him money, or that it might perplex him.[130] In truth, Bland knew from experience that holding Jacobite prisoners did all these things. The officers of the army had been struggling with the ordeal for months.

After the Jacobites left Edinburgh in November 1745 the officers in the government's garrison asked permission to transfer some or all of the 172 prisoners they held in the castle to naval ships in the harbor. The soldiers complained that they could not maintain and guard so many prisoners, but the navy, for its part, refused to receive them, pleading that it did not have enough fresh water on board its vessels to support so many.[131] Some of the government's prisoners were eventually transferred from the castle to the city's jails, but in January, after the surrender of Carlisle, hundreds of new captives were brought to Edinburgh.[132] The prisoners were paraded before the townspeople, and according to one account, their "miserable state" created a false impression that the fighting was nearly over.[133] Combat would continue, however, for months, and more prisoners would arrive, overcrowding Edinburgh's jails. Jailkeepers and garrison commanders faced similar problems across Scotland and northern England. Prisoners were shifted from one strongpoint to another, eventually accumulating by the dozens on ships despite the earlier protests from the navy and a subsequent order from the privy council that all prisoners should be housed on land.[134] Conditions on the prison ships were so poor that by August the Admiralty was concerned that they would spread disease through the ports of England.[135] Through the summer of 1746 the leaders of the army, the navy, and the ministry shared a growing sense of urgency. It was necessary to dispose of these captives quickly and permanently.

Though Cumberland's instructions had directed him to gather evidence against the Jacobite prisoners his army captured, his forces were distracted by other concerns and in a poor position to begin preparing for trials. Scotland's juridical authorities were hardly equal to the challenge either, but even if they had been ready to prosecute Jacobites by the thousands, several jurisdictional conflicts had to be resolved.

Within the army, no one understood the jurisdictional issues better

than Bland. In the summer and fall of 1746 Bland took over command
at Stirling Castle.[136] During that time he oversaw the activities of Gabriel
Napier, the sheriff of Sterlingshire, and others who gathered evidence
against the Jacobite prisoners.[137] Bland and Napier had an uneasy relationship. In July they received a directive issued by the Duke of Newcastle and Lord Milton, the lord justice clerk of Scotland, ordering them
to release prisoners on bail if the government lacked specific evidence
indicating that they had committed "some hostile act on the part of the
rebels" or had marched with the Jacobite army.[138] This order was in
keeping with the standard practice of criminal procedure, and Napier
immediately put it into effect, offering bail to several prisoners. Bland,
however, would have none of it, and issued orders that those prisoners
Napier had released should be rearrested despite the ministry's directive. Bland insisted that he would follow instructions only from his military commander.[139] Within a week of notifying Cumberland of this
stance, Bland received orders to respect the "civil power." Bland
expressed relief upon receiving this order, because, he wrote, "we military men make very bad judges."[140]

Bland was fascinated by the constitutional relationship between what
he called the "civil" and the "military" powers in Britain, but his principal concern, in this episode and throughout his career, was neither the
preservation of civil liberties nor the protection of the prerogatives of
the soldiers. Bland's overriding worry was the internal regulation of the
army and the maintenance of its discipline. In this case his greatest fear
was that disputes between civilian and military authorities would confuse
or disrupt the chain of command. According to Bland, Cumberland's
powers were, in effect, unlimited, and had he wished to do so Cumberland could have placed the "whole country" under military rule. But
Cumberland had not made that decision, and it was not in the power of
subordinate officers, even after consulting judges and ministers, to make
the decision for themselves. Even the thought that they could do so was
pernicious, Bland suggested, since it might tempt "officers of a lower
station" and private men to take the law into their own hands. This
would result in "licentiousness." In fact, Bland thought that in some
units it already had.[141]

The government faced the prospect of trying thousands of prisoners.
Given the enormity of the task, it was virtually impossible to regulate the
relationship between the civil and military authorities neatly. Some officers never received coherent orders, while others, including Cumberland himself, remained reluctant to comply with the requirements of
criminal procedure. These problems were compounded by the difficulty
of keeping track of the men in custody. As a result, despite Milton's
directives, military commanders held dozens of prisoners for months

without formally charging them or gathering evidence against them. Some were virtually abandoned in small jail cells in the mountains of Scotland, while others were lost in the crowds of prisoners on ships in the Thames or in Edinburgh Castle and the castle in Carlisle.[142]

The Jacobite defendants fell into three categories. The most famous were four Jacobite peers, who were tried before the House of Lords and beheaded. Next came a group of forty-two individuals named in a Parliamentary Act of Attainder on June 4, 1746. By statute they were given until July 12 to surrender and face justice. Otherwise they would be declared guilty of high treason without facing trial.[143] But by far the largest category of defendants was the third—those who were liable to prosecution more or less in the same way ordinary criminal suspects were. There were thousands of these, and credible, usable evidence against them as individuals was often difficult to find.

By mid-February 1746 preparations were underway to try the Jacobite defendants with rigorous procedural formality.[144] Witness lists were prepared for each trial, and procedural issues meticulously debated. In the summer, when the trials began in the vicinity of London, "all the judges that were in town" attended the early proceedings, either as members of the bench or as vocal observers.[145] The defendants were allowed to examine potential jury members; one defendant challenged the qualifications of so many jurors that his trial had to be delayed.[146] The court heard challenges to the prisoners' indictments, and with the assistance of counsel, the defendants raised an array of defenses, including, in at least two cases, the insanity defense.[147] Translators or Gaelic-speaking attorneys were provided for those who needed them, and all defendants retained the right to confront the prosecution's witnesses.[148] The government, therefore, had to offer live testimony in every trial. Moreover, the prosecutors had to be careful about the way they presented their evidence. In one case in Carlisle, the court directed an acquittal because the prosecuting attorney had failed to produce a written document that had been the subject of live testimony, in violation of the best-evidence rule.[149]

The insistence on live testimony created enormous logistical difficulties, compounded by the choice of venue for the proceedings. One of the first pieces of legislation passed by Parliament after the Battle of Culloden was one authorizing the prosecution of Jacobites in any county of Britain.[150] As early as May 12, Newcastle informed Cumberland that the Jacobite prisoners would be tried outside Scotland.[151] Remembering this decision years later, Bland asserted that it was predicated on a distrust of the Scots. "Few or none" of the prisoners would have been convicted if the trials had been conducted in Scotland, according to Bland. These circumstances "laid the ministry under the necessity of trying the rebels in England."[152] This decision made it much more difficult to assemble witnesses for trials, and the government was forced to rely on the testimony of the prisoners themselves. Jenny Cameron was one of those who were briefly considered potential witnesses. After her capture Cumberland identified her as one who knew a large part of the Jacobite army. "I fancy she may be a useful evidence against them if a little threatened," he declared.[153] Before the trials began in Carlisle, investigators prepared a list of those "who may be willing to become witnesses from the hopes of mercy."[154] Jenny Cameron was not mentioned. It was a short list, because the Jacobites, as a group, generally remained loyal to each other and to their cause. Therefore the prosecutions depended on only a few informants and the cases became repetitive as the same witnesses offered testimony against their fellow-prisoners, trial after trial, one at a time.[155]

One hundred sixty-nine trials were scheduled in Carlisle in September 1746. According to one account, the first trial was over "in a minute," while the second lasted from ten in the morning "to near five at night."[156] With so many cases to hear, the court had to learn to proceed expeditiously, and efficiency increased as the weeks proceeded. Five trials were held on September 13, and fourteen on September 19.[157] By the end of the month, fifty prisoners had been convicted and thirty-six acquitted. Forty-one prisoners had pled guilty, and thirty-four had been released without trial.[158] The courts in London were more efficient still, trying as many as seventeen cases in a single session.[159]

As these numbers suggest, many of the prisoners facing trial received acquittals because the government's evidence was often weak. Those who advanced affirmative defenses fared worse, in general, than those who stayed silent and relied on deficiencies in the prosecution's case. One affirmative defense that failed spectacularly was the assertion raised by members of the Jacobite garrison at Carlisle that capital punishment violated their rights under prevailing codes of conduct for the treatment of prisoners of war.[160] Early in the proceedings the judges had declared that the defendants before them could not claim the protections usually granted conventional war captives.[161] Furthermore, in the specific case of Carlisle, Cumberland had never offered prisoners mercy, but only promised that they would be "reserved for his Majesty's pleasure." The king had chosen "that they shall have a fair trial."[162] Eight months after surrendering, several members of the Jacobite garrison of Carlisle were hanged.

A second, common defense that failed repeatedly was that of coercion, a claim raised primarily by footsoldiers in the Jacobite army who argued that they had never wanted to support Charles Edward but rather had been forced by their landlords or neighbors to join the fight.

In an early, precedent-setting trial south of London, the judge instructed the jury "that there is not nor ever was, any tenure which obligeth tenants to follow their lords in rebellion. And as to the matter of force . . . the fear of having houses burnt or goods spoiled . . . is not excuse for joining and marching with the rebels." Only "a present fear of death" could excuse participation in the Jacobite rising, and then only if the accused fled the army as soon as he had a chance.[163]

The coercion defense implicated questions that had preoccupied the political world of Britain since Charles Edward landed.[164] Had the judges accepted the defense without tight restrictions, they might have prevented the government from pursuing criminal prosecutions against any but the most prominent leaders of the rising.[165] To sustain the prosecution, the government had to reject any assertion that the great landlords or the clan leaders held irresistible authority over those who answered to them. Nonetheless, once the trials were concluded, the debate over the powers of clan leaders and Highland aristocrats resumed almost as if there had never been a judicial ruling suggesting that the Jacobite soldiers were personally responsible for their actions. After 1746, policy makers generally accepted the premise that landlords and clan leaders in the Highlands wielded enormous coercive power, and a central aim of government policy was to weaken the authority of the region's aristocrats and clans. Supporters of this effort suggested that it was necessary for political stability.

The prosecution of Jacobite soldiers and officers resulted in a short burst of dramatic violence. There were four beheadings in the Tower of London and dozens of hangings elsewhere, often with the defendants drawn and quartered.[166] George II took a personal interest in seeing these sentences carried out. He worried that any temporary reprieves might become permanent, because "whenever criminals are reprieved, it always looks like a hardship when they are executed afterwards." Therefore he advised the ministry to avoid procedural delays.[167]

Through the summer, courts and prosecutors struggled to follow the king's advice, but in the early autumn of 1746, increasing numbers of former Jacobites received reprieves.[168] Many of those who escaped prosecution were "induced to petition to be transported," under the terms of informal agreements.[169] Plea bargaining was not a common practice of the English courts, though similar arrangements had been made earlier, for example in the case of Jacobite prisoners seized in 1715.[170] The government's resort to the tactic in 1746 is one indication among many that Britain's criminal justice system was overwhelmed. The authorities in some jurisdictions chose another, more impartial mechanism to handle their unmanageable caseloads. They held lotteries. In Carlisle, Chester, Lancaster, Lincoln, and York, once the lottery process began, nineteen out of every twenty defendants, randomly chosen, were offered the chance to plead guilty and travel as bound servants to America.[171] One newspaper reported that the prisoners still held in London in mid-December were all to be "transported beyond seas" after Christmas.[172] This policy was encouraged by reports that the Highlanders would be welcomed in the colonies. As early as July 1746 the *Caledonian Mercury* had published a story indicating that "petitions from the merchants in Jamaica and South Carolina have been presented to his Majesty, praying that the common men amongst the rebel prisoners may be sent over as servants."[173]

In the spring of 1747 the *Scots Magazine* reported that 430 prisoners had recently been boarded onto ships in Liverpool to be carried to "the plantations." Overall, according to the correspondent, nearly a thousand prisoners had been sent overseas by the beginning of May. Among the most recent were men who had been held in jails in Carlisle, Chester, Lancaster, Lincoln, and York.[174] Historians have been unusually meticulous in trying to count the number of Jacobite prisoners who were executed, banished, or transported across the ocean. It is impossible, however, to be simultaneously comprehensive and precise. The number executed exceeded one hundred, and a comparable number died in prison or on shipboard. At least six hundred went to America as bound servants, and approximately two hundred more were sent simply into exile. Hundreds of others are unaccounted for in the historical record.[175]

*   *   *

Historians analyzing the government's response to the Jacobite rising have broken official policy into stages.[176] While there are various ways to describe and delineate the steps the army took, if one concentrates on official policy toward Jacobite officers and soldiers, at least three successive policies appear: a period of almost unrestrained battlefield violence, followed by a concerted effort to prosecute the soldiers according to formal legal norms, concluding with what might be called a period of conditional reprieve, during which former Jacobite combatants were given the opportunity to bind themselves over for service in North America and the West Indies. While these were distinct stages, underlying them all was a single, coherent, and consistent ideological purpose. Cumberland and his supporters made an uncompromising assertion of George II's sovereignty, and everything they did served to demonstrate the government's insistence on maintaining its monopoly on the use of force. They would not formally recognize the Jacobites' bargaining power or do anything that seemed to confer legitimacy upon them.

Some historians have suggested that the Jacobite soldiers were treated as they were because so many of them were Highlanders and therefore demeaned as a savage "out group" unentitled to the benefits of the rules of war.[177] A stronger case can be made, however, at least with respect to the official policy toward the soldiers, that they were punished severely not because they were an "out group" but rather because they were subjects of the British crown. Thanks in part to evolving understandings of the "rights of Englishmen," we have grown accustomed to thinking that only advantages accrue to those who can claim the status of "British subject." The fates of the soldiers captured in the rising make it clear that there were disadvantages in receiving the designation. Being British exposed the prisoners to trial for rebellion and execution. A similar logic affected the administration of Britain's colonies, where, in the absence of reliable courts, some groups identified as treasonous subjects faced draconian punishment without the purported benefit of formal trials. Many of those communities—various native peoples in North America, for example—suffered also from being labeled "savage." According to contemporary understandings of the terms, savages could be British subjects in the middle years of the eighteenth century.[178] Even while the Highlanders were understood to be subjects, they were also stigmatized as a distinctly savage people. The effect of that stigma can be seen most dramatically not in the army's treatment of enemy soldiers but rather in its relations with noncombatants in the Highlands.

Chapter 2

Savagery: Military Execution and the Inhabitants of the Highlands

Charles Edward Stuart hoped to gain support throughout the British Empire, but nonetheless, from the early days of the rising forward, his enterprise was widely associated with the Scottish Highlands. This was so for the simple reason that he landed in northwest Scotland and raised his first recruits among Gaelic speakers. When they first heard the news, some advisors to George II feared spontaneous, parallel risings in Ireland, Wales, or among Catholics in northern England, but nothing like that occurred, and within weeks it was generally agreed that the Jacobites could never have raised an army anywhere outside the Highlands.[1] This belief did not reflect any widespread complacency about other regions and peoples. Supporters of the ruling regime continued to harbor suspicions about the Lowland Scots, the Welsh, and Catholics of all nationalities. Nonetheless, the accusations they lodged against other groups were quite different from those they brought against the Highlanders. Jacobites outside Highland Scotland were generally thought to be either silent and passive supporters of the rising—as the Earl of Chesterfield described the Lowland Scots—or subversive minorities, cleverly manipulating implements of power in the law courts, the councils of government, and the church to achieve their ends.[2]

The Highlanders were Charles Edward's most visible, and most talked-about, fighters. This circumstance shaped the way the British in general responded to the events of 1745. Much of the initial commentary, particularly from opposition members of Parliament, concentrated on the weakness of centralized governmental institutions in Highland Scotland and suggested that the ministry could have foreseen and prevented the rising if the region's coasts had been effectively patrolled and the Highlands and islands better policed.[3] Some commentators, within the Scottish elite and in England as well, assumed that ordinary Gaelic-speakers had little contact with national institutions and virtually no interest in British politics, and that those who joined with their clan leaders in support of Charles Edward did so only in response to local pressures and concerns. In the long run this analysis would inspire reform efforts for the Highlands, but in the early weeks of combat its greatest impact was on the government's military tactics.

Many influential leaders assumed that the Highlanders cared more about their home communities than they did about Britain. Taking that for granted, less than a month after the rising began, the Earl of Stair, a prominent officer in the British army, argued that Charles Edward could be easily defeated because the Highlanders would quit the field when they discovered that they had left "their wives and children to the mercy of their enemies."[4] Stair recommended sending troops to "the countries which the rebels have left," to "live at discretion."[5] This idea quickly spread through the army's ranks and by early October 1745 it animated the actions of commanders in the Highlands. By the spring of 1746 it had become a central piece of the government's strategy.[6]

Long-standing stereotypes of the Highlanders as savages made the adoption of such tactics acceptable to government ministers, military leaders, and the English public; and especially after the Battle of Prestonpans and the Jacobite Highlanders' entry into England, denigration of Highland culture became more common and vehement. For many, the Highlands' traditions seemed flawed and sinister in their entirety, and everyone who belonged to the region's ancient cultural world, or participated in it, was complicit in maintaining an evil presence in Britain. This point of view was expressed in a poem published in *London Evening Post* and subsequently reprinted in the American colonies, identifying the Highlanders as "Sons of Murder" and suggesting that they were linear descendants of the Bible's first outlaw, Cain.[7]

On the face of it, the phrase "Sons of Murder" referred only to the men and boys of the Highlands. Nonetheless, women and girls were targeted in Cumberland's campaign to punish and subdue the inhabitants of the region. With the tacit approval of the ministry, in the spring and summer of 1746 Cumberland ordered his soldiers to destroy houses, burn crops, and kill livestock, leaving some families to starve. As the men attacked women and girls in the hills, on occasion they raped them, receiving neither commendation nor censure for their actions. The officers who directed these operations justified themselves by invoking military necessity. Both Loudon and Wolfe, for example, claimed that "molesting" the wives of Jacobite soldiers was the most effective way to convince the men to abandon Charles Edward's cause.[8] The officers' readiness to sanction such violence increased as they approached Gaelic-speaking communities. The events of 1745 and 1746 confirmed deep-seated cultural animosities that contributed to an impulse among many in the army to punish Highlanders regardless of their sex or age.

At the same time, however, particularly among high officers and members of the elite, a variety of social and political dynamics contradicted and undercut that impulse. The 1745 rising divided the Highlands more dramatically than it did any other part of Britain.[9] From the start, but especially after Charles Edward retreated back into Scotland in 1746, the authorities relied on help from supporters within the Highlands, including the Gaelic-speaking soldiers in Loudon's regiment, the Argyllshire militia, Presbyterian ministers, and prominent members of the aristocracy. Furthermore, even before the dissolution of the Jacobite army at Culloden, Cumberland and his supporters in the ministry recognized the need to establish a new legal order, one that they knew they could not impose simply through the exercise of indiscriminate violence. By the summer of 1746, well before Parliament enacted any detailed legislation, the army, with the help of cooperative Highlanders, assumed the task of law enforcement and undertook a few initial steps toward instituting long-term reforms. Loudon played a central role in this redirection of policy, and in doing so he forged alliances with several prominent Highland families, including some who had supported Charles Edward during the rising. The friendships Loudon established lasted years, and contributed to his ability to mobilize the Highlanders after 1756 to engage the French in North America during the Seven Years' War.

*   *   *

During wars and in peacetime, armies in eighteenth-century Europe routinely issued orders to noncombatant populations. Landlords were required to lease houses to soldiers and make fields available for the grazing of regimental livestock. Farmers and merchants were required to sell soldiers produce and equipment. On occasion officers seized property and destroyed it on a claim of military necessity. The details of the requirements varied from country to country, but such obligations were imposed nearly everywhere, by all European armies, whether or not the soldiers were pursuing a policy of punishing, intrusively regulating, or reforming the local population. In general, the troops were expected to behave respectfully, and the noncombatants were supposed to comply with the armies' orders without resistance. The 1743 edition of Bland's *Treatise on Military Discipline* took these traditions for granted and contained detailed recommendations on the quartering of soldiers, the patrolling of streets, and the maintenance of order in militarily occupied towns.[10] In his capacity as quartermaster general in Flanders, Bland had worked closely with shopkeepers, magistrates, physicians, and others in various Flemish communities to arrange housing, supplies, and medical care for the soldiers.[11] Especially in the early weeks after his arrival in Britain, Bland monitored and assessed the army's relations with the inhabitants of the regions it traversed. In England, during the long march north in November and December 1745, he was pleased with what he saw.[12]

Like the commanders of the government's forces, Charles Edward assumed that he had authority to quarter soldiers in private houses and to requisition horses, carriages, and porters from the towns his soldiers passed through.[13] In many towns the Scots accepted their obligation to house the soldiers, but they expected Charles Edward's men to comply with local custom and not exceed the traditional limits governing how many men could be lodged in each home.[14] The Jacobites, in general, were anxious to operate within such rules. One pamphleteer asserted that prior to the Battle of Prestopans, a unit of Jacobite Highlanders had marched "close by the Earl of Stair's house without hurting a chicken."[15] This refrain recurred frequently in Jacobite literature: Charles Edward's men fought according to established rules and would not harm anyone off the field of battle.[16]

To be sure, Charles Edward confiscated property. From July 1745 onward he needed financial resources to maintain his army, and this required him to exert authority over all the British people within his reach, regardless of their opinion of the rising. Had he relied only on monetary support from his willing followers, he would have, in effect, fined them for rallying to his cause.[17] A more even-handed approach, taking funds from friends and opponents alike, made choosing the Jacobites seem less onerous, and it also made the exaction appear more like a legitimate governmental tax. Seeking to distinguish coerced financial contributions from plunder, Charles Edward took care to label them "excises," land taxes, and customs duties, and he claimed to collect them according to established, published rates.[18] At the end of September 1745, for example, he sent an order to the customs collector in Ayrshire, the site of the Loudon estates, demanding his books and "all the money due" according to the custom house accounts.[19] There is no reason to think the Jacobites received any taxes from Ayr, but in some regions they were able to convince the local excise men to collect the taxes owed to the government and deliver them over for the use of the insurgency.[20]

Though he based his family's claim to the throne on heredity, Charles Edward understood that the success of his efforts would depend to a great extent on the support he received from the British public. Mindful of local politics, he repeatedly issued orders barring his soldiers from arbitrarily seizing produce from the countryside.[21] During his siege of Carlisle, he told the mayor, "we shall take care to preserve you from any insult" and assured him that the good treatment the people of Carlisle received would "set an example to all England."[22] While at Carlisle the

Jacobites asked the inhabitants to bring them "wheat, rye, oats, barley, beans, butter, cheese, poultry, eggs, black cattle, sheep, hogs, and such other provisions and merchandise as they have." Speaking for the Jacobite army, the Duke of Perth assured the townspeople that the soldiers would pay for everything, and that "all people with their horse, carts, and other effects" would be safe.[23]

The truth, however, could never be so simple. As they passed through southern Scotland on their way to Carlisle, Jacobite soldiers killed deer in the forests of several aristocratic estates. These actions infuriated the steward of one property to such an extent that he confronted Charles Edward personally and threatened to make the Jacobites' names "stink in England, and have their barbarity published in all the English prints." Worried about his reputation south of the border, Charles Edward ordered his men to desist.[24] Almost from the moment Charles Edward entered Edinburgh, reports circulated that "outparties and stragglers" from the Jacobite army, beyond the control of their leaders, "pillaged the country and robbed passengers of their money."[25] Charles Edward responded by denying that the robbers were soldiers, asserting instead that criminals posing as Jacobites were roaming the countryside demanding bribes for protection and committing thefts. One man accused of leading such a band faced a court martial conducted by Charles Edward's officers. He was sentenced to death and shot by a firing squad.[26] Shortly thereafter Charles Edward issued a proclamation against impersonating a Jacobite soldier and ordered all enlisted men to assign themselves to units so that their movements could be regulated more closely.[27]

Cumberland's army inflicted far more damage to property in Scotland than the Jacobites did. The government's soldiers occupied houses, released horses and cattle into fields, seized and slaughtered livestock, confiscated boats, pulled down bridges, and rendered fords impassable. In the fall of 1745, Blakeney, from his post in Stirling Castle, impounded all the boats on the River Forth.[28] After a few days the owners of the boats took their property back, which led Blakeney to organize periodic patrols to retrieve any vessels that could be easily discovered and destroy "such of them as were found concealed."[29] Blakeney also oversaw the destruction of the local bridge over the Forth and of the fords.[30] Other government units, operating from Edinburgh Castle and elsewhere, similarly disrupted transportation, in effect cutting off the Highlands from the rest of the world. As a result, the regional economy collapsed. Trade in the north of Scotland nearly ended, money stopped circulating, and in several areas the Highlanders were barely able to feed themselves.[31] Especially after January 1746, the damage the soldiers inflicted had an increasingly punitive purpose, but it is important to remember that many of their actions were sanctioned by tradition, consistent with common practice, and justified, according to widely accepted norms, by military necessity. The destruction of private property was not always punitive. Cumberland's army began destroying bridges, for example, while it was still in England.[32]

As Cumberland's army moved into Scotland, even in the south of the country, its actions became at once more overtly punitive and at the same time, paradoxically, more indiscriminate. Often trouble began with a simple request for provisions, but whole regions were subjected to punishment for failure to respond promptly to an officer's commands. At the beginning of February, for example, Cumberland ordered his men to acquire coal from the people of Falkirk, adding "if coal is not immediately furnished," the soldiers could "burn anything but houses."[33] Cumberland assumed that any failure to supply the army's needs was evidence of widespread treason. Bland employed a similar logic in March, when he subsisted his troops on cattle, sheep, and hogs taken from estates in the Scottish countryside. He argued that this was necessary because the "country butchers" had not "brought in any meat to sell."[34] Throughout Scotland Cumberland's army had greater difficulty securing cooperation than it had in England, in part because the Jacobites were better organized in the northern country. Some Scots refused to aid the government out of loyalty to the house of Stuart, while others feared retaliation from the Jacobites if they complied with the soldiers' demands.

From the autumn of 1745 on, Blakeney, in Stirling, performed a great deal of police work, interviewing informants and cross-checking the reports they made on their neighbors, in an effort to obtain intelligence on the activities of the Jacobites.[35] Over time he established a network of informants, some of whom were paid for information.[36] Unlike many other commanders in Scotland, Blakeney secured the cooperation of the local civilian authorities, but even with their assistance he could not control the county. Gabriel Napier, the local sheriff, moved into Stirling Castle in August 1745, shortly after learning of Charles Edward's landing. He stayed there for eighteen months, afraid to return to his home.[37] An alternative, Jacobite government eventually asserted its authority in Stirlingshire, and in December 1745 the Jacobites issued a summons to the sheriff demanding £650 in overdue taxes and allegedly unpaid rent.[38] After Napier failed to appear and pay the money, Jacobite soldiers took furniture from his house, cattle from his fields, and hay and oats "to a considerable value."[39] Other officials who cooperated with Blakeney similarly lost valuables from their homes.[40]

In the fall of 1745 Charles Edward tried to install new local governments not just in Stirlingshire but in all the parts of Scotland under his control. In Aberdeen, for example, he named Lewis Gordon lord lieutenant of the county.[41] Gordon had difficulty recruiting effective administrators, and a large part of the local community refused to comply with his orders. Under these circumstances he could gain obedience only by crudely exerting force, for example quartering solders in households that failed to pay the Jacobites tax.[42] According to one of those who resisted him, Gordon's orders were "enforced by fire and sword to men, houses, planting and corn yards."[43] While these circumstances might, under some theories of justice, have excused the townspeople of Aberdeen for acquiescing in Gordon's demands, when Cumberland arrived in February 1746 he wanted to punish them. He declared that housing the Jacobite soldiers had been a crime, and he and Milton, the lord justice clerk, also thought that charges might be brought against the local magistrates and the sheriff for failing to arrest Gordon and his men.[44]

Of all the government's commanders in Scotland, Loudon faced the longest ordeal, and the greatest difficulty, confronting rival Jacobite assertions of authority. With the survivors in his regiment he went by sea to Inverness soon after the Battle of Prestonpans. He came with orders to restore the government's authority and impede Jacobite efforts to raise money and men.[45] Many of Loudon's troops, as Highlanders, had the advantage of local knowledge, facility with Gaelic, and the ability to comprehend and negotiate the ways of Highland politics far more effectively than other troops. They lacked military experience, but their task near Inverness initially had more to do with law enforcement and political persuasion than with conventional tactical operations. These considerations contributed to the decision to send Loudon to Inverness.

Nonetheless, the deployment isolated Loudon in what was to him an alien environment, and he found his task nearly impossible. The opposition he faced seemed grounded in a set of political and social institutions more mysterious and deeply rooted than the ad hoc Jacobite governmental authorities faced by Blakeney in Stirling or Cumberland (later) in Aberdeen. Loudon attributed the Jacobites' success around Inverness to their ability to summon "kindred" assemblies.[46] In several instances he claimed that young men had been "forced out and dragged to rise in rebellion" from such gatherings.[47] He was particularly concerned about the Fraser clan, whose purported leader, Simon Fraser, Lord Lovat, had once been a friend of the government in the region. Lovat fought for George I in 1715, and he had cooperated closely with General Wade after that reform-minded officer arrived in Scotland in 1724.[48] Nonetheless, in the late autumn of 1745 large numbers of "Frasers" had joined with the Jacobites. When Loudon arrived in Inverness, Lord Lovat, who was then seventy-eight years old, denied that he had rallied his clan for Charles Edward. He claimed that his son, Simon Fraser, the nineteen-year-old "Master of Lovat," was the leader of the Jacobite Frasers. Loudon spent weeks trying to discern the truth of the matter; in the meantime he struggled to gain Lord Lovat's cooperation, by force if necessary. Loudon had Lovat arrested in December 1745, but the old man escaped, and with the help of his son proceeded to raise more soldiers for the Jacobite army.[49]

More than once, Loudon was confused and defeated by his opponents in the vicinity of Inverness, who seemed able to operate against him with impunity and in secrecy, thanks in large part to the protection they gave to fellow members of their families and clans. Perhaps his most embarrassing defeat came in February 1746, when Anne MacKintosh hosted Charles Edward in her home and helped spirit him away when Loudon learned that he was there.[50] The episode was a great humiliation for Loudon, who had far more soldiers at his disposal than Anne MacKintosh did.[51]

Blakeney, Loudon, and all the other military commanders in Scotland faced the problem of assessing culpability in regions where the Jacobites held power over the local noncombatant populations. Cumberland's instructions directed him to inform himself of "all suspected persons" and upon finding grounds for suspicion, to apprehend them and place them "in safe custody."[52] In England, where the Jacobites had failed to establish lasting local governments, the operation had seemed relatively easy. Physicians, apothecaries, storekeepers, postmasters, informal letter carriers who had served Charles Edward, along with others who had merely cheered the Jacobites on, were seized by Cumberland's army and held on suspicion of treason.[53] Cumberland gathered evidence against all of them, and not only those who had formally enlisted in Charles Edward's army. Cumberland also ordered the arrest of women who had followed the Jacobite soldiers, and if the women had small children with them, the young ones were brought into custody too.[54] The parade of prisoners leaving Carlisle in January 1746 included thirty-seven women and seven children.[55]

Cumberland might have at one time hoped to arrest everyone in Scotland who had obeyed commands from Jacobite soldiers, but that was never a practical option, and indeed after Culloden the ministry issued orders restricting formal criminal prosecution to those who had committed "some hostile act on the part of the rebels" or had marched with Charles Edward in his army.[56] Nonetheless there was a widespread belief among many prominent supporters of George II in Scotland that individuals who gave material aid to the Jacobites deserved punishment, and not just the young men who had joined the rank and file. One Presbyterian commentator argued that all those who furthered the Jacobite cause were sinners, including "some paying contributions, cess, and excise, others contracting for so much to keep their cities or towns from being plundered; some taking oaths to them, others, receiving protections from them." The writer acknowledged that "a great many of the poorer kind" had never had any choice but to cooperate with the Jacobites, yet he considered all voluntary compliance with Charles Edward's demands sinful.[57]

Cumberland, for his part, was most concerned about those who consented to quarter Jacobite soldiers in their houses. In early February 1746 he anticipated that this problem would get worse once Charles Edward's men had completed their retreat into the Highlands. He predicted that the Jacobite Highlanders would scatter "into their holes and hiding places" and that it would be impossible, from that time forward, to distinguish the fighting men from ordinary householders with arms.[58] Loudon had already expressed a similar fear as an argument for attacking communities near Inverness. Loudon declared that he could not tell the difference between a Jacobite soldier and a Highlander armed to defend his home. "The distinction between these classes of men in point of guilt or innocence," he wrote, "is too fine for me to observe."[59] Echoing Loudon, Cumberland told Newcastle that "orders should be given to kill all that have arms in their houses."[60] But even as he expressed this sentiment, Cumberland intimated that he did not have the authority to give such orders on his own. In hopes of securing the necessary legal authority, his aide de camp sent a letter to Milton, asking him to issue a proclamation placing an affirmative obligation on everyone in the Highlands to deliver up any Jacobite soldiers who fled into their communities. Milton refused, insisting that none of the judges in Scotland had the power to give such an order. Instead, Milton suggested, Cumberland could make the proclamation himself, relying on his military authority.[61]

Reluctantly, and "cautiously," as he put it, Cumberland took Milton's advice.[62] On February 24, 1746, he issued a proclamation requiring "all common ordinary people, who have born arms or otherwise been concerned in this rebellion," to deliver all the weapons in their possession to the local magistrates or ministers of the Presbyterian Kirk, to register their names and places of residence, and "to submit themselves entirely to the King's Mercy." Anyone else, "all manner of persons," who had knowledge of weapons belonging to the Jacobites, was ordered to seize the weapons and bring them to the magistrates or Presbyterian ministers.[63] The proclamation ended with a warning. In an early draft Cumberland had planned to declare that that all those who failed to comply would be "pursued with the utmost severity as rebels and traitors by military execution." Milton had suggested a different enforcement mechanism, and on further reflection Cumberland amended his statement.[64]

The final proclamation suggested that those who failed to cooperate would face punishment in one of two ways: through "due process at law or military execution."[65]

That final warning was thoroughly ambiguous, and neither due process nor military execution fully satisfied the army's needs or perfectly justified the actions Cumberland wanted to take. "Military execution" involved the destruction of property in regions that failed to comply with the army's orders. It was a sanction familiar to the men of the army, but it was difficult to justify legally on British soil. When Milton saw a draft of the proclamation he warned Cumberland that the exaction of "military execution" would violate constitutional norms.[66] Due process was a mechanism that would allow Cumberland to inflict targeted, personal punishments, but employing formal legal procedures seemed impractical under the circumstances. Cumberland remained uneasy about the whole issue. He wanted expanded powers, but he also wanted explicit legal authority and guidelines defining what his soldiers could do. Cumberland sought guidance from the ministry, but despite his requests, the ministers refused to give him directions or explicitly endorse the terms of his proclamation.[67] Writing formally on behalf of the government, Newcastle told Cumberland that "no general rule can be given for your Royal Highness's conduct."[68] In a separate, private letter, he admitted that political considerations had impeded the ministry's ability to discuss the question. "Your Royal Highness knows how delicate the point is, and consequently how difficult it is, to give any general order upon it." Even conceding that much in writing was a risk, and Newcastle asked Cumberland to burn the letter.[69]

Cumberland's proclamation was published and distributed to dozens of Presbyterian churches in the Highlands, where it was read to the assembled congregations.[70] Immediately thereafter Presbyterian ministers began collecting weapons from Highlanders who wished to comply. Cumberland's supporters cited his proclamation as an indication of his good intentions toward the Highlanders. A letter in the *London Evening Post*, published several weeks later, overstated what Cumberland had promised and insisted that he had approached "the rebels in a gentle, paternal way, with soft admonitions, and a gracious promise of pardon and protection to all the common people, who would bring in their arms and submit to mercy." Nonetheless, everyone knew that the proclamation had the effect of sanctioning reprisals on a large scale. That same letter in the newspaper, purportedly written by an officer under Cumberland's command, indicated that the Highlanders' recalcitrance "obliged his Royal Highness to lay the rod more heavy on them, by carrying fire and sword through their country, and driving their cattle . . . In short, our army hath detachments at present in all parts of the Highlands, and the people are deservedly in a most deplorable way, and must perish either by sword or famine—a just reward for traitors."[71]

Even before Cumberland issued his proclamation, his soldiers had adopted the policy of destroying homes as a way to punish, demoralize, and incapacitate the Jacobites. In February 1746, after one officer was killed in an ambush, government soldiers burned the houses of Inverlochy, confident that "there was not an inhabitant belonging to it but was in the rebellion."[72] By March Cumberland was detaching units of a few hundred each into allegedly "disaffected" parts of the Highlands, with orders to "destroy" everyone found "in arms" and to "burn the habitations of all those who have left them, and are with the rebels."[73] Looking back on the campaign nine years later, James Wolfe proudly recalled the efficacy of the government's tactics. "A body of troops," he wrote, "may make a diversion by laying waste a country that the male inhabitants have left to prosecute rebellious schemes. How soon must they return to the defense of their property (such as it is), their wives, their children, their houses, and their cattle!"[74]

There is evidence that on occasion these campaigns worked exactly as Wolfe remembered, and that some Jacobite soldiers deserted to return home and protect their families.[75] Nonetheless, in the upper reaches of government, confusion reigned over the legality and propriety of the army's actions. By citing military codes to justify his reprisals against noncombatants, Cumberland undercut the repeated assertions that he had already made when justifying his treatment of Jacobite soldiers, that military codes of conduct did not apply to this conflict. Cumberland's supporters, inside and outside the military, made similarly contradictory assertions in the effort to legitimize what the army was doing. Chesterfield, for example, was adamant that Jacobite soldiers should be executed, either on the field of battle or after they had been taken prisoner.[76] In support of this policy, a contravention of the rules of war, he insisted that the Jacobites were "not enemies, but criminals. We cannot be at war with 'em."[77] On the other hand, when Chesterfield advocated cutting off food supplies to all Scotland, he maintained that the Scots deserved none of the advantages of criminal or civil procedure. "If Scotland is not now to be considered and treated as an enemy's country," he wrote, "I don't know what country ever can."[78]

Rather than responding to Cumberland's inquiries by clarifying this conundrum, the ministry's only official response was to indemnify the soldiers. After men serving under General Henry Hawley ransacked the estate of a pro-government landlord in central Scotland, "a great clamor" arose in Edinburgh, where "even friends of the government" thought it would be right to the prosecute the general.[79] Fearful of the consequences if such a legal case went forward, George II's ministers shepherded through Parliament a bill relieving the government's soldiers in Scotland of criminal liability.[80]

Though Parliament freed the soldiers in Cumberland's army from the threat of criminal prosecution, military discipline, as Cumberland understood it, required that all of them proceed by rules. As he traveled north he remained concerned to maintain good relations with the farmers and merchants who sold provisions to his men.[81] He also knew that if his units attacked the countryside without restraint, it would be difficult to direct them effectively as a military force. In his *Treatise on Military Discipline* Bland had warned that armies could dissolve into chaos if soldiers were given unbridled liberty to plunder. In order to keep control, it was necessary to prevent, or at least regulate, the collection of loot.[82] These considerations led Cumberland to establish military courts, which imposed dramatic, painful punishments on those who seized property or attacked noncombatants without proper authorization. In one extreme instance six men were sentenced to receive 1,500 lashes each, for "plundering under the pretended orders of H.R.H. the Duke."[83]

In a further effort to regulate the actions of his soldiers, Cumberland established a precise distribution system to make sure that every soldier who participated in orderly punitive raids received his stipulated share of plunder.[84] One of those charged with enforcing these regulations was Wolfe, who sent directions to commanders in the field, specifying the share allotted to each man according to his rank.[85] When Wolfe himself participated, he did so with self-possession and a small measure of restraint. One woman remembered him approaching her in her home "and desiring a gentleman who was with me to go out of the room." Wolfe then "said that he was come to tell me, that by the Duke of Cumberland's and General Hawley's orders, I was deprived of everything I had, except the clothes on my back."[86]

After Cumberland's proclamation in February, "military execution" proceeded with increasing comprehensiveness and regularity. Though the proclamation had only mentioned arms belonging to Jacobite soldiers, the program expanded until it involved disarming all the inhabitants in areas that were alleged to have given the rising support.[87] The residents of each targeted community first received a summons requiring them to deliver up their weapons, with a warning attached that those who failed to respond would face severe punishment. Men who complied with these orders and delivered up their arms were asked to appear before a Presbyterian minister or an officer in the army, register their names and places of residence, and sign a statement signifying that they would remain in their homes until "the King's pleasure be known." The process involved elaborate paperwork. Orders were issued to maintain lists of every person giving up arms, with an enumeration of the weapons delivered, along with a written attestation of the oath.[88] Other lists were required for those who failed to cooperate with the disarming process. In effect, in several regions, soldiers were sent to take a detailed and comprehensive census of all the adult male inhabitants, listing their place of residence, their political leanings, and all their arms.[89] Though no one was promised a pardon for cooperating with this process, men whose names appeared on the right lists were eventually exempted from criminal prosecution.[90] There was no guarantee, however, that their households would be preserved. On the contrary, Cumberland's officers asserted that in each community "the whole of the clan" was "answerable for each particular, and on the non-appearance of any one, the rest [would] forfeit everything."[91]

In the aftermath of the Battle of Culloden, Charles Edward's army disintegrated. Those Jacobite soldiers who survived and escaped capture scattered into the country, to the homes of their friends, relations, and sympathetic neighbors. This was what Cumberland had feared, and his response had consequences for everyone in the Highlands. Immediately after the battle, Cumberland ordered his soldiers to "visit all the cottages in the neighborhood" to search for "rebels."[92] The men were directed to destroy the farms and seize the livestock wherever Jacobites were found.[93] Further afield, Cumberland sent orders to Loudon to "distress whatever country of rebels you may pass through."[94] Loudon's campaign brought devastation to several areas. He reported that in some places "the whole people fled with most of their goods to the hills" on hearing he was coming.[95] The punitive campaign lasted weeks. At the end of May, to pursue it more efficiently, Cumberland moved his headquarters to Fort Augustus, on the western end of Loch Ness.[96] This was, as the *Caledonian Mercury* reported, "the most centrical place for sending out detachments."[97] Among those who served under Cumberland at the fort were Bland, Cornwallis, Loudon, and Wolfe.

By the time Loudon arrived at Fort Augustus he had already spent six months commanding troops in the Highlands. Many there identified him as a partisan of the "Campbells," and they blamed him, and his purported clan, for the violence of official policy. One Jacobite leader, Donald Cameron of Lochiel, insisted that Loudon was personally responsible for the government's practice of burning buildings, seizing livestock, and harassing women and children in regions that provided Charles Edward support. According to Lochiel, it was only in response to Loudon's repeated requests that Cumberland had issued orders authorizing the scorched-earth policy.[98]

On May 22 Bland ordered Loudon into the country of the Camerons, advising him, "If any of the country people did not come in immediately, deliver all their arms, and submit to the King's mercy, he was to burn and destroy their habitations, seize all their cattle, and put the men he found to death, being pretty well assured it will be difficult for him to shed innocent blood in that country."[99] One of the officers involved in the operation reported afterward that the event did not "answer our expectations." Loudon's soldiers seized one man who had pointed a pistol at them. Later they met a larger group of Highlanders carrying weapons who "went off into the hills" on seeing the patrol. The soldiers took six prisoners but killed no one despite the encouragement they had received from Bland.[100] The next day Loudon received a message from the men who had fled from him, indicating that they were ready to surrender their arms and "throw themselves on his Majesty's mercy." Loudon agreed to receive them and scheduled two meetings where he accepted their formal submissions en masse.[101] At one signing ceremony four of the Camerons signed their names, and eighty-five others marked their names with "x."[102] When he learned of these events Cumberland doubted that the signatories had given up all their weapons. "Almost every Highlander is possessed of two or three sets of arms," he claimed.[103] In response, Newcastle told Cumberland that among the ministers in London the submission of the Camerons was deemed a success.[104]

Though some of the Camerons had blamed Loudon for violent acts committed by the army in the Highlands, after the Battle of Culloden he may well have been the most moderate of British officers. On several occasions Loudon avoided confrontation with former Jacobite soldiers, and he intervened in cases in which his men attacked Highlanders who had taken oaths in accordance with Cumberland's proclamation.[105] Loudon's behavior contrasted sharply with that of other men serving at Fort Augustus. A more typical officer was Cornwallis, who in May received orders from Cumberland to lead a detachment of three hundred men and march "through the country of the Camerons, and then to turn up to the head of Loch-Arkaig." Vaguely, he was instructed to "clear everything down to the River Lochy."[106] From there he was "to drive through the countries of the MacDonalds of Moidart, and Knoidart, and the Camerons north of Lochy."[107] Cornwallis's operation was remembered years later as one of unrestrained violence. Men were killed if they looked away when they saw his soldiers coming. Others were summarily executed because weapons were found in their houses, and at least one elderly woman, a beggar "blind of an eye," was raped and then shot, allegedly because she failed to give the soldiers useful information.[108]

Women were frequently targeted for violence by the government's soldiers in 1746. In regions that had supplied Charles Edward with troops, they had often been left by themselves or with only children and elderly men, vulnerable to raids. Sometimes, with the help of small children, they tried to barricade their doors when the troops arrived to plunder or destroy their homes.[109] On occasion they fought the men with firelocks, knives, or fists.[110] Sometimes the very futility of these struggles enraged the soldiers and officers. One colonel conjectured that the Jacobites were trying to use their families as shields, "thinking by that to escape the first violence and rage of the pursuers out of tenderness for the ladies." He declared that the gambit would not work. Professing himself "stark raving mad," he felt certain that the women deserved punishment as well as the men.[111]

In the late spring of 1746, as increasing numbers of troops from Charles Edward's army gave up the battle and fled home, many women in Highlands assumed responsibility for sheltering the deserters.[112] On more than one occasion they did so by concealing the fleeing men within female society, offering them women's clothing and traveling with them as if the former soldiers were women themselves. The *London Evening Post* reported in March that "upwards of 100" Jacobite soldiers had been seized in Aberdeen in women's clothes.[113] That particular report may have been fabricated for rhetorical purposes. Accounts of Jacobite men disguising themselves as women predated 1745 and conveyed the message that the Jacobites were subversive, deceptive, and deficient in the masculine character that undergirded the prevailing social order.[114] But in 1746 the reports carried more than symbolic significance. They had immediate, practical implications for the women of the Highlands. The danger was not that women would be mistaken for Jacobite men in female costume (the disguises, in general, were unconvincing at close range) but rather that women would be held culpable for helping the men escape justice.

The most prominent cross-dresser was Charles Edward himself, who in June 1746 reached the Isle of Skye disguised as a female servant attending to the needs of a young woman named Flora MacDonald (see Figure 5). Immediately upon arriving on Skye, Flora went to visit Margaret MacDonald, the wife of a prominent local ally of Cumberland, Alexander MacDonald of Sleat.[115] Margaret kept her silence—she later claimed she knew nothing—and Charles Edward moved on, eventually managing to escape Britain altogether and sail for France. Once this story became known, Charles Edward's clandestine visit to Skye subjected both Flora MacDonald and Margaret to close scrutiny. Many supporters of George II wanted the two women punished severely.

No articulated philosophy in Europe, no code of conduct in warfare or legal doctrine, gave approval to physical attacks against unarmed, civilized women. Writing in the middle years of the eighteenth century, the French philosopher Emmerich de Vattel expressed the common view in general terms: "Women, children, the sick and the aged, are in the num-

Figure 5. Charles Edward Stuart dressed as a woman to facilitate his escape from Britain in the summer of 1746. This print, recalling the moment, was made in the late 1740s. (J. Williams. National Galleries of Scotland.)

ber of enemies . . . but these are enemies who make no resistance, and consequently give us no right to treat their persons ill, or use any violence against them, which is so plain a maxim of justice and humanity that at present every nation, in the least civilized, acquiesces in it."[116] Invoking similar principles, Charles Edward and his supporters railed against the government for attacking the women of the Highlands. Lochiel, for example, declared, "When courage fails against men, it betrays cowardice to the highest degree to vent spleen against brutes, houses, women, and children, who cannot resist."[117]

Cumberland's supporters responded to the Jacobites' protests without denying that the government's soldiers had attacked women. Instead, in justification they cited the behavior of the Jacobites. The discovery of female soldiers would, at least according to the thinking of some theorists on the rules of war, relieve the government's forces from ordinary strictures prohibiting physical violence. As Vattel put it in the 1750s, "if women are desirous of being spared, they are to employ themselves in the occupations of their sex, and not play the men in taking arms."[118] From personal experience, Cumberland knew that women could be useful militarily. He employed them in his own army, not only doing laundry and performing other normal "occupations of their sex" but also gathering intelligence and keeping watch over plundered livestock.[119] Nonetheless, virtually all observers agreed that Charles Edward relied on the support of women more heavily than the government did. Writers claimed that women in the Highlands gave themselves over to his service entirely, without restraint or reason.[120] This pattern of behavior, it was suggested, raised doubts about the Highlanders' civility, which in turn, implicitly at least, raised the question of whether they deserved to be treated according to civilized norms.

Perhaps the most elaborate propagandistic effort surrounding these issues involved Jenny Cameron, a middle-aged woman who helped raise troops for the Jacobite army and who allegedly conducted a brief and torrid love affair with Charles Edward, a man barely half her age.[121] According to one pamphleteer, Cameron's depravity stemmed not from any bad choices she made but rather from flaws deep in her character. She had been born with a "hot and violent" temper, and her parents, rather than bringing her "to herd," had failed to restrain her natural self-indulgence.[122] In her youth Cameron degenerated quickly and began dressing and behaving as a boy. At the age of fifteen, after she had been sent away to relatives in Edinburgh, she started going into the city dressed as man, "picking up women of the town, with whom they sometimes went to the bawdy-house, and carried the frolick as far as their sex would permit them."[123] Her support for the Jacobite cause, the writer suggested, was only the last expression of her lifelong perversity.[124]

Pamphlets such as these contributed to a deepening and increasingly widespread belief that the Highlanders lived beyond the reach of ordinary civilized norms, and that rape could be a legitimate component of a campaign designed to treat them as they deserved. One writer went so far as to propose a policy of nearly universal violence against women, to kill or incapacitate them and prevent the Highlanders from producing offspring.[125] Proponents of such views sought strength for their position in often-repeated though less-well-documented accounts of rapes committed by Highlanders and Jacobites.[126] Within weeks of Charles Edward's landing in 1745, violence against women became a central theme of propaganda for both sides.[127] By the time the Jacobite army reached Manchester in the autumn of 1745, its soldiers had gained such a reputation for violence against women and children that mothers fled the city, pulling their infants along with them.[128] They ran even though many in Manchester expected their homes to be plundered.[129]

Flora MacDonald and Margaret MacDonald were too prominent and well connected to face a significant risk of sexual assault, but in more obscure parts of the Highlands, for example in the territories crossed by Cornwallis's companies, soldiers assaulted women with impunity.[130] It was official policy to confront them in their homes, though none of the commanders ever explicitly declared that rape was an appropriate punitive measure. Nonetheless, even as men were subjected to courts martial for collecting plunder without authorization, none of the government's soldiers in 1746 faced any kind of tribunal or sanction for the commission of rape.

By the spring of 1746 some distant observers of events in the Scottish Highlands began to fantasize about concocting a famine devastating enough to eradicate the region's population.[131] As lord lieutenant of Ireland, Chesterfield promoted the idea of starving the Highlands and did what he could to cut off Highland Scotland's food supplies.[132] He proudly declared that as long as he was lord lieutenant, he would make sure that not even "the loyalest Highlander" would "have an oatcake" from Ireland.[133] In London the Privy Council responded to Chesterfield's bluster as if it were a joke, but his words are a measure of the depth of the animosity engendered by the rising.[134] Anonymous pamphleteers in 1746 similarly recommended starving the Highlanders or otherwise comprehensively destroying them.[135]

Nonetheless, even when the denigration of Highland culture was at its height, political realities forced Cumberland to distinguish between loyal and disloyal communities in the Highlands. Charles Edward's retreat into the region had increased the military significance of Loudon's regiment. Similarly, as the rest of Cumberland's army followed the main Jacobite forces north, the Argyllshire militia served alongside many of his regular units, and the government's commanders were increasingly reliant on them. Several prominent officers in the army had ambivalent feelings about employing Highland troops. Loudon himself, fearing for his reputation after his misfortunes near Inverness, let it be known that his soldiers were unreliable and prone to desert.[136] Bland, for his part, blamed the Argyllshiremen under his command after some of his soldiers ransacked the home of a supporter of George II. Bland explained the incident by declaring that "all the Highlanders are naturally thieves."[137] Cumberland had his own misgivings, though his views were diametrically different from Bland's. He insisted that the Argyllshiremen exhibited excessive "favor" and "partiality" toward other Gaelic-speakers and "absolutely refused to plunder any of the rebels' houses."[138] Outside the army, Chesterfield was critical of the government's reliance on Highland soldiers. He quoted the proverb "set a thief to catch a thief" but then declared, "I beg leave to except Scotch thieves."[139] In the end, however, military action salvaged the Argyllshiremen's reputation. In March Bland commended a company serving with him north of Aberdeen, and two weeks later his comments were repeated verbatim in a newspaper in Edinburgh.[140] Far more significant honors came after Culloden, where several companies of Argyllshiremen distinguished themselves in action. Cumberland singled them out for praise.[141]

The irregular soldiers' "Campbell" identity, and Loudon's personal association with that clan, affected the way many observers interpreted the fighting, with a direct impact on the stereotypes surrounding the Highlanders. According to some supporters of the government, the Campbells were the only good people in the region. One writer eventually went so far as to suggest that the various clans in the Highlands were racially and physically distinct.[142] Eager to avoid punitive measures after the defeat of the rising, some communities in the Highlands struggled to assert that they were really "Campbell" even though they went by different names.[143]

The Battle of Culloden represented a turning point in relations between Cumberland's army and the inhabitants of the Highlands. While violence spread over a wider area, soldiers and officers found themselves increasingly enmeshed in the existing social structures of the region as they sought to police the Highlands and initiate efforts at reform. Uncertain how to proceed after Charles Edward's army dispersed, Cumberland sought advice from prominent English-speaking Highland landlords, including Duncan Forbes, the Earl of Findlater, and Alexander MacDonald of Sleat. Especially in less well traveled areas, Cumberland relied on Highland companies much as earlier British commanders had done since the 1720s and 1730s. The complexity of the tasks facing his forces convinced him to keep the Argyllshire militia in the field beyond their original terms of enlistment.[144] Cumberland was also forced to acknowledge the utility of Loudon's regiment, despite lingering doubts. These arrangements strengthened the hand of several political factions in the Highlands. They served the interests of the Duke of Argyll, a man Cumberland never liked, and they aligned the government more powerfully than ever behind local supporters of the Presbyterian Kirk.

In the summer of 1746 Cumberland and his officers deployed the army violently on the side of the Kirk in the Highlands.[145] Bland was particularly active in this part of the campaign. He oversaw the arrest of Catholic priests and Episcopalian pastors who had allegedly failed in their legal obligation to swear allegiance to George II.[146] Presbyterian Highlanders fought alongside Bland and took an active role in punishing the Catholics and burning their places of worship. The leader of one company of Highlanders, Sir Harry Munro, pursued the project with so much enthusiasm that he earned the nickname "flagellum eclaesie Romanae."[147] Supporters of the SSPCK celebrated these efforts and began making plans to bring missionaries and Presbyterian schoolmasters into the communities the Episcopalians and Catholics had apparently been forced to abandon.[148] In general, Presbyterians welcomed Cumberland's army into the Highlands.[149] At least one pastor invited the soldiers to engage in a campaign of thoroughgoing destruction. With reference to the Atholl estates he declared, "if you were to hang throughout all that country indiscriminately, you would not hang three people wrongfully."[150]

Many other ministers of the Kirk sought to moderate or regulate the application of force. Presbyterian clergymen offered their services as clerks and administrators for much of the disarmament program. They publicized Cumberland's proclamations and maintained records as the army collected arms and information.[151] They also assumed a role in the dispensation of mercy, and men arrested for participation in the rising routinely sought out testimonials from Presbyterian pastors. If the prisoners gained support from the ministers, their petitions for mercy were much more likely to succeed.[152] The army needed the Kirk's clerical help, because in much of Highland Scotland courts of law were scarce and seldom open.

Even as he recruited Presbyterians to help him, Bland expressed misgivings about undertaking tasks that would ordinarily be performed by civilian judicial authorities. He justified his actions by referring to historical precedent—similar operations had been conducted in "Oliver's time" in the 1650s—and also by invoking practical necessity, because, he insisted, in the areas where his units were operating "we have no justice of the peace or magistrate."[153] Bland exaggerated slightly, but in many parts of the Highlands, particularly in those designated as "disaffected" or where landlords had sided with the Jacobites, civilian judicial authorities were difficult to find. Some magistrates went into hiding just as the problem of law enforcement was at its worst.

Not all the violence that summer was politically motivated. Many men were hungry and desperate, and on occasion they resorted to cattle raiding, burglary, and theft simply in an effort to survive. In much of the Highlands, landlords and tenants resisted giving up their weapons on the grounds that they needed them to defend their homes from raiders.[154] Loudon was sympathetic to their concerns and struggled to interpret his orders in a way that would allow him to avoid taking weapons away from the government's "friends."[155] He also recognized that, for pragmatic reasons, the disarming process brought with it an obligation to restore order. By early June 1746 Loudon's soldiers were serving as a rural police force in some areas, pursuing alleged cattle thieves and highwaymen.[156] Loudon and other officers met with inhabitants from various districts to consult on the best methods for deterring crime and pursuing thieves. In some instances these informal discussions led to the development of plans that, had they been effectively carried out, would have entailed significant changes in the economic and social life of the region. On their own initiative, some officers declared it their policy, for example, that the hills in their districts be cleared of shelters for cattle herders and shepherds, since those structures served as cover for robbers. In issuing the order, one officer declared that it would serve the interest of "civilized subjects," meaning those who lived year-round in permanent houses.[157]

As the soldiers negotiated with local leaders in Highland communities, many women assumed important roles as mediators. Some who had formerly cooperated with the Jacobites took tentative steps toward reestablishing peace. They were aided in these efforts by a complex set of social and emotional dynamics. Several of the women had family ties to officers in Cumberland's army, but even when they had no intimate connections with the leaders of the government's forces, the men surrounding Cumberland found it difficult to punish women outside the violent context of raids and battles.

Within hours of the Battle of Culloden, the army took several leading Jacobite women into custody (see Figure 6).[158] Anne MacKintosh was one of them, and according to legend she was so distraught at what she had seen on the moor that day that she asked the men who seized her to shoot her.[159] The soldiers did not do so, but Cumberland hoped to punish at least some of the women severely. "The ladies must be taught to know they may be punished for rebellion," he is reported to have

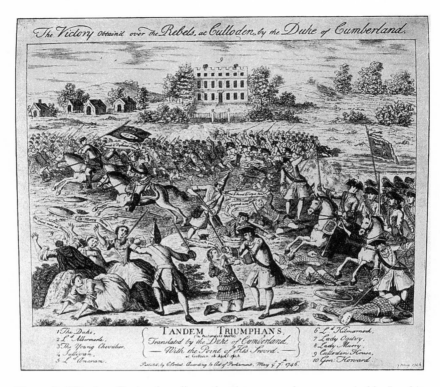

Figure 6. "Tandem Truimphans" was the slogan on a banner carried by Jacobite soldiers at the Battle of Culloden. This print, made with the purpose of mocking the Jacobites, illustrates how the words were "translated by the Duke of Cumberland with the point of his sword." Several women captured by the government's forces near the scene of action are depicted in the lower left-hand corner.

said. Those around him interpreted his comment as indicating that he believed that "one female rebel must suffer," presumably by execution. An officer who heard the remark later told Loudon, "I am hopeful our wrath against the fair may soon pass."[160] Not only at Culloden but for months thereafter, soldiers and officers in Cumberland's army often came to the defense of women held in custody. Flora MacDonald, for example, admitted to helping Charles Edward escape, for which she might have been considered among the guiltiest of them all, but her "modest behavior" as a prisoner reportedly "gained her many friends." Indeed, high naval officers and at least one general pleaded on her behalf and insisted that she be spared incarceration.[161]

Loudon intervened in the case of Anne MacKintosh, whose husband

Aeneas had done what he could to help him since the time of the formation of Loudon's regiment.[162] Loudon had skirmished with Anne Mac-
Kintosh in the spring of 1746, but after she was taken prisoner he took up
her defense.[163] Perhaps Loudon recognized the long-term political value
of maintaining good relations with her. Perhaps he defended her out of
deference to her husband, or perhaps instead, as it was widely suggested,
he had been seduced. When Loudon fled Inverness in the spring of
1746, Aeneas MacKintosh went with him.[164] Anne, alone in a town filled
with Jacobite soldiers, acquired a reputation as a woman with time to
spare for unattached men.[165] Her reputation may have been undeserved,
but for years thereafter she was widely considered a temptress.

In the summer of 1746 Loudon reprimanded a subordinate officer
for destroying part of the MacKintosh country.[166] The following autumn,
after reports spread that Loudon was keeping company with Anne
MacKintosh, that officer declared that "considerations of love or lust"
had clouded Loudon's judgment. Loudon was in love, and when Anne
MacKintosh suffered, according to a rumor, he was "hurt."[167] In the
autumn and winter of 1746 Loudon frequently visited Inverness, and he
certainly grew close to Anne MacKintosh. Some observers considered
the evolving relationship scandalous, while others accepted it with
aplomb, closing their letters to Loudon by writing, "My respectful compliments to Lady MacKintosh."[168] Loudon was not the only prominent
person to enjoy the company of the young lady. Others, including Duncan Forbes, also visited her frequently and protected her.[169] Nonetheless,
jokes circulated at Loudon's expense, including one alluding to "Mark
Antony and Cleopatra."[170]

Loudon nonetheless persisted in his friendship with Anne Mac-
Kintosh and her husband, and indeed, despite increasingly elaborate and
damaging accusations leveled against him, he cultivated alliances with
other former Jacobites as well.[171] In the summer of 1746, the most immediately valuable contact he made was with Simon Fraser, the "Master of
Lovat," the son of the Jacobite lord. Young Simon Fraser crossed swollen
rivers in August 1746 to reach Fort Augustus and surrender to Loudon.
After drying himself out he spoke extensively, recounting his varied
experiences over the previous months, identifying prominent Jacobites,
and expressing "great remorse and repentance" for his own participation in the rising.[172] Loudon was grateful for the information, expressed
compassion for the young man, and helped save him from a formal
criminal trial. Several Presbyterian ministers also petitioned on Fraser's
behalf, arguing that he had been "seduced" by the Jacobites even
though his "principles" were fundamentally sound.[173] The young "Master of Lovat" was held in Edinburgh Castle until August 1747, when, as
part of a settlement reached to avoid prosecution, he agreed to move to

Glasgow and "not to stir out of the limits thereof without His Majesty's express permission."[174] In the 1750s he gained full freedom and stood at Loudon's side in North America. Though they remained in Scotland, Aeneas and Anne MacKintosh would similarly work closely with Loudon after he turned his attention to colonial affairs.

* * *

One way to interpret the friendships that Loudon made with former Jacobite leaders would be to see them as part of a general healing within the Scottish aristocracy and gentry, as family ties and social connections reestablished themselves despite the disruptions of 1745. Something similar, arguably, happened after the rising of 1715.[175] The links Anne MacKintosh established and maintained with members of Scotland's ruling elite contributed, in the long run, to a widespread reassessment of the Highlanders' character, their political loyalties, and the role they could play in Britain's imperial project. Nonetheless, it is important to remember that years would pass before these effects were felt. In the meantime Highlanders were still vilified, and Britain's leaders remained uncertain that political stability had been achieved.

In the summer of 1746 Loudon convinced Simon Fraser to provide evidence against his seventy-eight-year-old father, who was facing a capital trial. Fraser cooperated, and after Lovat was convicted, thousands of spectators came to the Tower of London to watch the execution. Lovat was a Catholic, and some of the publicity surrounding his case emphasized that he had converted as an adult.[176] Supporters of the government eyed the crowd at the Tower carefully, worried that Catholics and Jacobites would transform the event into a rally, and that the pathetic spectacle of the old man's beheading would turn the assembled multitude violently against George II.[177] No one was certain yet that the crisis was over.

Many supporters of George II continued to fear for the future. They did not believe that the defeat of the Jacobites in Scotland necessarily meant the end of political subversion. Suspicions and apprehensions lingered in England and throughout the British Empire. The rising had been a crisis for all of Britain's domains, even in places that did not see armed conflict. In America, particularly on the colonial frontier, Jacobitism was perceived to be part of a wider, persistent threat, and despite Cumberland's victory at Culloden, George II's authority did not seem secure.

Chapter 3

The 1745 Crisis in the Empire

In early May 1746 a ship left Dublin with a small crew and a crowd of passengers below the decks. The vessel sailed for Virginia, where the people on board, eighty men and twenty-six women, were to be sold as bound servants. Unexpectedly, approximately ten days into the voyage, in the Atlantic three hundred miles from Ireland, the men and women seized control and ordered the captain to steer for the Isle of Skye. The leaders of the mutiny declared that they wanted to go to Scotland to "join the Pretender."[1] According to testimony gathered after the event, none of the passengers had done anything to support Charles Edward prior to leaving Dublin. Their aim now was primarily to regain their freedom and avoid transportation to America. Initially the mutineers had planned to sail straight back to Ireland and find refuge somewhere in their home country, but someone had warned them that "if they went to Ireland they'd be hanged," and so they made the remarkable decision to seek the protection of the Jacobite army.[2] Others facing a risk of prosecution, closer to the scene of combat, made similar gambles in 1745 and 1746.[3]

En route to Skye the leaders of the mutiny spoke bravely of capturing English ships, and they made their captain drink a toast to Charles Edward. Some on board were skeptical of this performance and suspected that the captain had been colluding all along in the enterprise with the hope of claiming a share of prize money from the Jacobites and collecting insurance for his ship and its cargo.[4] As the vessel approached the Western Islands, a small detachment of the mutineers left in a small boat and rowed to Stornoway, on the Isle of Lewis, seeking information on Charles Edward, his whereabouts, and his fortunes. It was then that they learned that the rising had been defeated. They gave up on the project of going to Skye and ordered the ship back to the north of Ireland.[5] On May 29, before they reached the Irish shore, their vessel was stopped by a British warship, and sixty-five of them were taken into government custody.[6]

This servants' mutiny brought the armed conflict of 1745 and 1746 as close to North America as it would come. There were no similar actions taken in the colonies, and indeed this was an unusual event for Ireland. Viewing Britain's domains generally, the rising came and went without provoking pitched battles anywhere beyond the reach of Charles Edward's army. Outside Scotland there were no large-scale spontaneous insurrections, and nowhere beyond the Highlands were the Jacobites able to recruit large numbers of soldiers without the coercive assistance of an occupying force. Historians have amply documented the presence of Jacobites in England and Wales in 1745. Their failure to rise in favor of Charles Edward was largely the result of poor communications, factional infighting, and disorganization. The English and Welsh Jacobites proved unable to lend each other support or orchestrate any significant show of strength, hence many who might have fought for Charles Edward calculated that taking action would not be worth the risk.[7] Jacobites are more difficult to find in the historical records of Ireland and the colonies. Though a few Irish men crossed over to Britain during the rising to offer their services to Charles Edward, and others participated in a clandestine trade to feed and otherwise support his soldiers, such activities were generally conducted in secret and involved only individuals or small groups. In America the Jacobites were probably even fewer in number, but since Charles Edward never made any overtures toward them, they had little opportunity to reveal their political aspirations to each other, their neighbors, or posterity.

As an armed conflict, the Jacobite rising of 1745 was an event restricted almost exclusively to the island of Great Britain. Considered more broadly as a crisis, however, it affected British subjects in Ireland and farther across the sea. In Ireland and the colonies, politically aware men and women read newspapers eagerly and interrogated ship captains and travelers for news from Scotland and England. They also watched their neighbors closely, testing each other's loyalty and anxiously assessing the prospects for political stability and domestic peace. In various parts of the empire Scots came under suspicion, regardless of whether they spoke Gaelic or traced their lineage to the Highlands. Catholics were also carefully watched. The Jacobite rising provoked an anti-Catholic response nearly everywhere in the British Empire. In Britain, in Ireland, and especially in the colonies, it was widely asserted that the Catholic Church was operating in league with the Jacobites and the king of France.

Though the story of the Irish servants' mutiny did not reach America, had it done so, it would have confirmed many of the colonists' most deeply held fears. Stories were circulating in Maryland, Virginia, and elsewhere that native warriors, French provocateurs, and local Catholics were forming an alliance (perhaps also hoping to gain support from slaves) in order to overthrow the social order and deliver the colonies to a Catholic king.

Outside the Scottish Highlands and away from Cumberland's army, 1745 marked a crisis of different kind. Those who lived along the path of the Jacobite forces in Lowland Scotland and northern England faced immediate danger, and they were forced, whether they liked it or not, to make decisions that affected not only their own safety but the course of grand political events. Elsewhere in the empire no one's life was in jeopardy, but living at a distance from the scene of combat often contributed to a sense of helplessness, because it seemed that everyone's future depended on events far from home. The length of the conflict, continuing for months after it was expected to end, gave the people of England, Wales, Ireland, and the American colonies time to think about the consequences of a Jacobite victory in ways the Scottish Highlanders never could. Weeks of worrying generated conspiracy theories and sightings of Jacobites even where there were none.

When the news from Culloden finally arrived in North America, colonists celebrated fervently. Though the battle had taken place thousands of miles away, Cumberland's American supporters had never thought that the enemy was distant. They had interpreted the rising in the context of imperial rivalry and believed that Charles Edward had been coordinating his actions with Catholic France. This way of thinking helped make Cumberland a hero in the British colonies. It also helped sustain a sense of lingering danger in North America, even after the Jacobite army in Scotland had dispersed.

In 1747 hundreds of war captives began to arrive as bound servants in Maryland and the British West Indies, and proposals were circulating to send entire communities of Highlanders into exile in the Caribbean and North America. Though the war captives had military experience and had demonstrated their willingness to engage in rebellion, their arrival in the British West Indies and Maryland generated less local controversy than might have been expected. Slave owners and other masters were accustomed to accepting strangers as servants, and they believed that they could control and exploit bound workers, even those who came from reputedly dangerous groups. While the colonists were willing to accept Highlanders as bound laborers, the idea of receiving entire communities of Gaelic-speakers generated fear. Influential colonial leaders objected to the suggestion of bringing Highland clans to North America, particularly if the exiles were to be relocated near the native peoples of the continent, or the French, on the colonial frontier.

*   *   *

In order to understand the impact of the 1745 rising on the lives of the people of southern England, Wales, Ireland, or the colonies, it is necessary to acknowledge that most of the inhabitants of those regions knew little about Scotland, and when they first learned of Charles Edward's landing they took it as Scottish news. Those who wished to inform themselves further searched for information on the northern country, much as many of them had demanded materials on the Caribbean in 1739 at the start of the colonial war with Spain. Even when the fighting reached the English borderlands, it still seemed distant from London. In early October 1745 the *London Evening Post* reported "great demand" for maps of northern England.[8] As Charles Edward and his army moved south, the war came closer to home for most of the English and increased in importance for nearly everyone else, but for many of those who saw the soldiers, the experience paradoxically increased their sense of distance from the wellsprings of the rising. The most noticeable Jacobite soldiers were Gaelic-speaking Highlanders in distinctive clothing, and the majority of Charles Edward's English-speaking fighting men were Lowland Scots who spoke with an accent. In the view of most of the government's supporters in England, the Jacobite army was a foreign invasion force, and not the armed wing of an indigenous insurrection.[9] Weeks later, after Cumberland's army entered Scotland, the English soldiers' letters home only reinforced the sense that the Jacobites represented Scotland, a place that they saw as foreign (and disagreeable). One published journal, purportedly by a soldier in Cumberland's army, contained complaints that Scotland's women were "ugly" and "nasty" and that "the nastiness of their food, together with their dirty beds, makes me always fear of either a surfeit, or itch."[10]

As the historian Murray Pittock has suggested, one effect of the 1745 rising was to blur the distinction between Highlanders and Lowland Scots in the stereotypes that informed most published accounts of Scottish life and culture.[11] Mindful of this trend in public commentary in 1745 and 1746, many Lowland writers exaggerated the difference. One writer maintained that Highlanders were "confined to a particular corner of the kingdom, speak a different language, and differ as much in their manners and customs from the rest of Scotland as the Chinese does from the Turks. They are so much a different people, that they agree in nothing, but in being inhabitants of one island, and subjects to the same government."[12] Despite such protests, anti-Scots feeling escalated and encouraged some powerful commentators—Chesterfield most famously—to impugn the loyalty of everyone in Scotland.[13] In one letter to the ministry, Chesterfield suggested that the government's troops in Edinburgh Castle ought to have "battered" the town. Had Edinburgh

been destroyed, he asserted, "not five of the king's real friends would
have suffered by it."[14]

In the early weeks of the rising, many supporters of George II feared
that Charles Edward would exploit Scottish resentment against the 1707
Treaty of Union to transform his movement into a campaign for Scotland's independence.[15] Such a gambit, pursued effectively, might have
broadened the Jacobites' base of support in Scotland. After he entered
Edinburgh in September 1745, Charles Edward declared the Treaty of
Union void, but he never convened a Scottish parliament, and his subsequent actions, particularly his march into England in the autumn of
1745, made it clear that he did not have Scottish national interests prin-
cipally in mind.[16] To be sure, Charles Edward received some support
from the Lowlands of Scotland. He laid claim to dynastic loyalties that
dated back centuries in the old northern kingdom. Scottish Episcopalians and Catholics were generally conservative and had their own sectarian reasons for supporting a change in regimes. Pittock has argued
strenuously against any facile assumption that Scotland's Jacobites were
all Highlanders, and he has proved his case by extensively documenting
the mobilization of Lowland Scots on behalf of the rising.[17] Soldiers
from the Lowlands enlisted in the Jacobite army, and the recruits were
fed, housed, and supplied wherever they went. Nonetheless, historians
face nearly insurmountable difficulty in assessing the depth of Jacobite
support in Lowland Scotland, particularly in the south. In that region,
those who offered their services did so in the face of intimidating, coercive pressures, only after the original body of Charles Edward's forces—
the Highlanders—had arrived.

Nearly everywhere in the Lowlands there was a sectarian pattern in
the response to the rising. Religious conservatives were more likely than
others to enlist with the Jacobites, but the most dramatic religious element in the politics of the time was the unambiguous, vigorous support
the government in Westminster received from the Presbyterian establishment.[18] Through their synods and the actions of individual clergymen, Scotland's Presbyterians discouraged Jacobite recruitment, gave
assistance to the government's forces, and prayed only for George II.[19]
Edinburgh's established clergy fell silent after Charles Edward entered
their town. Church bells rang for services, but no ministers appeared in
the pulpits, and the clerical strike continued until the Jacobites had
left.[20] The sectarian pattern in responses to the rising was even more
dramatic in Aberdeen and along the northeastern coasts of Scotland,
where Cumberland declared that the "only people to be trusted" were
the members of the Kirk.[21]

Some Presbyterian clergymen had a theologically informed, providen-
tial understanding of the events of 1745. According to their sermons and

tracts, God had sent Charles Edward to test the British and punish them for violating holy commands. The pastors confidently declared that the Jacobite army would remain in Britain until it had accomplished the task that Providence had assigned it, but in the long run the forces of order and righteousness, the Protestant cause, would prevail.[22] Similar pronouncements echoed from pulpits in England, Ireland, and the North American colonies, but outside the churches it was common to discuss the religious dimension of the dynastic controversy in less metaphysical terms.[23] Throughout the empire, supporters of George II had long claimed that the Jacobites were part of an international conspiracy, a "three-headed monster" advancing the interests of the pope, the Stuart family, and the rulers of France.[24] For those who subscribed to this vision of world politics, the events of 1745 seemed only to confirm their worst fears. Charles Edward, after all, was Catholic. He had been raised as a child in Italy, and prior to his arrival in Scotland he had mustered his forces, small as they were, in France. A French ship had carried him north.

The Jacobites knew how widespread, and how powerful, this way of interpreting their movement was, and so they repeatedly and insistently declared their devotion to religious liberty, British sovereignty, and the integrity of the English and Scottish constitutions.[25] Nonetheless, Jacobitism was so commonly associated with Catholicism, tyranny, and foreign influence that even some of Charles Edward's supporters had misgivings about his cause. A carefully ambiguous poem published in an Edinburgh newspaper at the time of the Jacobite occupation hinted at uneasiness even as the poet ostensibly cheered the rising on.

Go on, victorious Prince, with heaven's applause,
Fight for thy own, and for thy country's cause;
Leave us our laws, and our religion free,
And let no bigot find approach to thee . . .[26]

Despite such pleas, and the protestations of the leaders of the Jacobites, the rising inspired fear and anger in many parts of the British Empire, directed not only at Highlanders and Scots but toward all representatives of the Catholic Church. In the words of one writer, the Jacobites were agents of the Roman "Antichrist," "Join'd with a Hellish Band of Highland Thieves."[27]

In England one of the first official responses to news of the rising was an effort to enforce a variety of long-dormant statutes regulating the behavior of Catholics. Some of these laws had been first enacted in the sixteenth century, and taken together they barred Catholics from owning weapons, keeping horses valued at more than £5, living in London, or gathering in large numbers for public worship.[28] As early as 1744, when the ministry first heard rumors that the French might support an insurrection on behalf of the Stuarts, preemptive orders were issued from Westminster, requiring all the country's Catholics to give up their arms.[29] Similar directives were issued by various national and local authorities through the time of the rising.[30] Three regions of the country were particular areas of concern: London, where subversive elements could attack the institutions of government; the north of England; and the West Midlands. In the autumn of 1745 Newcastle anticipated that Charles Edward would march south from Scotland down the western side of England, because there were "a great number of Roman Catholics in Lancashire," and furthermore because the Jacobites might expect "to be joined by numbers from Wales."[31] A few weeks later, while he was still in Flanders, Cumberland received a detailed report suggesting that as many as two thousand men, mostly "Papists," were ready to enlist and fight for Charles Edward in Shropshire.[32] After the Jacobite army marched into England along the route Newcastle had predicted, many observers expected it to attract Catholic recruits.[33]

The government's military response included deploying regular troops to face the Jacobite army and encouraging the formation of local militia companies and other irregular units to maintain control of the English countryside and assist at the margins of the field of battle. Initially Cumberland had high expectations for the irregular forces. He recommended to the authorities in Lancashire that they raise a "posse comitatus" to "harass" the Jacobite army until the government's regular forces could reach them.[34] Cumberland also thought that the militiamen could exact a kind of violence that would be unseemly for his troops. In particular he believed that the "country people" could put Jacobite prisoners to death, something neither the magistrates nor the army dared to do regularly without extended formal proceedings.[35] On rare occasions some irregular units met Cumberland's expectations. At the northern borders of England they seized horses and supplies from the Jacobite army, and after Cumberland arrived, during the government's siege of Carlisle, they watched the town's fortifications.[36] On at least one occasion when a man tried to escape by jumping from the wall, the militiamen killed him before he could get to his feet.[37]

Most English militiamen never came near to the scene of combat, however.[38] In the majority of the communities where militia mustered, the men stayed near their homes, honored their officers, and paraded only to dramatize their loyalty to George II.[39] The officers who enjoyed the honor of leading these men were subsequently rewarded financially with lucrative pensions. After the rising was defeated, the militia units therefore became an object of bitter controversy, and they were widely denounced as a militarily useless conduit for the distribution of political patronage. The militiamen took more aggressive action in the north of England than elsewhere in the country, however. This was so, in large part, because many of the companies in the north, including those near Carlisle, were violently Protestant. Furthermore, in many northern communities, it was difficult to distinguish between the actions of the militia and those of local anti-Catholic crowds. On one occasion a militia company in Stokesley, North Yorkshire, protested the arrest of a boy who had vandalized a Catholic chapel.[40] The militiamen marched through the town and the surrounding villages, "with drums beating and colors flying," and in the course of their parade enlisted thirty or forty new recruits. They ended their march at the chapel, gutted it, and carried their loot to a bonfire. Before throwing the clerical vestments into the flames, one man put them on and mockingly performed the role of a priest.[41] Similar actions took place across the north of England.[42] When Cumberland traveled through Newcastle in January 1746, he passed a private chapel burning. According to a report in the *London Evening Post*, "the house and appurtenances being vastly large, it was a terrible sight, and was very near the height of the blaze when the duke passed by."[43]

On April 30 and again on May 20, 1746, crowds destroyed houses in Liverpool that some believed served as chapels for Catholic worship.[44] Nonetheless, by then at least in some English circles, the climate of opinion had begun to change. England's Catholics, in general, had kept quiet during the rising, and some moderate political leaders had been arguing all along that it was wrong to provoke them.[45] Rather than congratulating the militia for intimidating the government's enemies, many supporters of George II belatedly concluded, to their own surprise, that the "Papists" had never been Jacobites at all. One of Cumberland's most ardent publicists, the historian Andrew Henderson, acknowledged after the fact that when Charles Edward arrived in England, "Yea the Roman Catholicks themselves abhorred the thought of a change [in kings]."[46]

If the supporters of George II were gratified and surprised by the response of England's Catholics to the rising, they were all the more pleased by the behavior of the Irish. Prior to the summer of 1745, Ireland was assumed to be, along with the Scottish Highlands, the most vulnerable part of Britain's domains. Like the Highlanders, the Gaelic Irish were widely denigrated as primitives and Catholics. Furthermore, communal memories of 1690, when much of Ireland rallied to the deposed king James II, led many to assume that the Irish people still honored the Stuart family's claim to the throne. Indeed, when he first heard reports that Charles Edward was sailing in the Irish Sea, Cumberland speculated that he might be headed for Ireland. Like many others within the counsels of government, he assumed that the Jacobites would be greeted warmly there, because "the common people" were "almost all Roman Catholics."[47]

The Protestant minority in Ireland, which over the preceding decades had consolidated its hold on the country's political institutions and taken possession of most of the land, was terrified.[48] At the end of August 1745 Chesterfield assumed authority as Lord Lieutenant, and within hours of his arrival in Dublin he heard rumors that a large number of Irish Jacobites, between two thousand and three thousand, had openly declared their support for the rising.[49] The rumor was unfounded, but fearing the worst, the Protestants prepared for a crisis. Pamphlets circulated containing dire warnings of the consequences of a Jacobite victory. One writer predicted that the Protestants would lose title to their lands.[50] Another described the stakes in apocalyptic terms. "The consequence to us would be the same as if this whole frame of heaven and earth was to be broken, and thrown into its first darkness and confusion."[51] The writer reminded his readers of how their grandparents had purportedly suffered under James II, when an army of Catholics "was let loose" upon them whose "only pay was the pillage and plunder of Protestants." During those harrowing months "No place was a refuge." The old king's soldiers "perpetuated all kinds of villainy; they invaded the marriage bed, they compelled the parents to behold the rape of their daughters . . . and if we resisted, we were dragged to execution for rebellion."[52]

After quickly assessing the state of affairs in Ireland, Chesterfield concluded that his first priority was to calm down the Protestants. He surrounded himself with "ceremony and noise," deployed "drums and trumpets with a vengeance," and organized public displays of support for George II.[53] In a bombastic and ineffectual gesture, he offered a reward of £50,000 for the "head of the Pretender's son," in the event that Charles Edward set foot in Ireland.[54] But Chesterfield resisted calls to treat Ireland's Catholics as enemies. He had the authority to restrict the Church's activities, even without the enactment of new statutes, but he did not want to provoke the Catholic majority unnecessarily or upset the island's tenuous peace.[55]

By Chesterfield's reckoning, Ireland's Catholics outnumbered the Protestants four to one.[56] The most vulnerable parts of the country, he believed, were the places where the greatest concentration of Catholics lived, in the south and west.[57] He doubted that they would take action without assistance from the main Jacobite army. By early October he had concluded on the basis of bulletins from England that Charles Edward was concentrating his attention on London and planned to turn to Ireland only after seizing the British throne.[58] Though Chesterfield was not complacent, he reported that there was "nothing stirring among the

Papists here."[59] As for the Protestants, he succinctly and accurately described them as "unanimously zealous, but unanimously frightened too."[60]

Chesterfield believed that events in Britain and on the continent of Europe would determine Ireland's future, and that "this country must necessarily follow the fate of England."[61] In September 1745 he declared, "I never expected mails from any place with half the impatience with which I now expect every mail from England. Every event both at home and abroad is now important."[62] By the following spring it had become clear to nearly everyone that the Irish could affect the outcome of the fighting only if they traveled to Britain or offered the opposing armies in Scotland information and supplies.

In the spring of 1746 the Irish Sea assumed great strategic importance. The Royal Navy used Irish ports as bases for operations against the Jacobites on Scotland's western coasts.[63] The Jacobites, for their part, traveled across the water in smaller craft. In March 1746 Chesterfield reported an increase in the circulation of Spanish and Scottish currency in Ulster, interpreting this as indicating that agents from the Jacobite army had purchased grain in the province. His response was a vigorous effort to cut off Scotland's trade in food.[64] He wanted the government to maintain control of the Irish Sea and block all passage to Scotland, but he did not want to militarize the mainland of Ireland.

As it was in Ireland, so it was in the colonies in North America. The events of 1745 served as a reminder of the primacy of Britain's politics within the empire. The news from Scotland heightened tensions in America and set many colonists on guard to ward off local insurrections. Nonetheless, most of the inhabitants simply followed the British news with apprehension, believing that their future was at stake and that nothing they could do could affect the outcome of the crisis. In January 1746 the governor of Pennsylvania appeared before the colonial assembly to report that several ship captains had confirmed the story that had been circulating since mid-October, that Charles Edward had landed in Scotland. "At this distance," he declared, "we can only pray."[65]

Daniel Wadsworth, a pastor in Hartford, Connecticut, followed news of the Jacobite rising from its early days until its end.[66] On February 22, 1746, he prematurely recorded in his diary "the news of the defeat of the Pretender's army."[67] Though weeks passed before it was refuted, that story was false, and reports of the Battle of Culloden would not reach America for several months.[68] On July 4, Wadsworth wrote that stories were circulating "from abroad" that the Jacobites had been "totally defeated." It was not until July 17, however, eight and a half months after his first diary entry related to the rising, that Wadsworth was confident enough to record that the rumor had been verified.[69]

The slow dissemination of information had a profound effect on the colonists' response to the crisis.[70] The long duration of the conflict, and delays in the transmission of news, made events in Britain seem more ominous. Only fragments of information were available in America, and the colonists had difficulty assessing the strength and extent of the insurrection. Those who wanted fresh, reliable news were repeatedly frustrated, and the published reports that came from Britain, with their concentration on military events and high politics, amplified the sense of crisis. In Boston, the Reverend Charles Chauncy found material for a sermon in the October issue of London's *Gentleman's Magazine*.[71] As late as March 1746, when Charles Edward was retreating into northern Scotland, South Carolina's newspapers carried a report that Jacobite Highlanders were ransacking the Midlands of England.[72] The time it took for such stories to cross the Atlantic reinforced the colonists' sense of powerlessness. Even if they had a reliable source of information, they could respond to events only several weeks after their occurrence.

The inhabitants of North America had reason to take an interest in British events. Members of the oldest generation had memories of the reign of James II, when Charles Edward's grandfather revoked colonial charters, suspended assemblies, and altered the terms of religious establishment in several colonies. After James was deposed in 1688, unrest continued for several years, and in some places, New England particularly, the old political system was never fully restored.[73] In his sermon in February, Chauncy reminded those too young to remember that "our fathers here in New England" had "groaned under the oppressive burden" of "Popish and tyrannical power."[74] He warned everyone that if the Stuarts took the throne again they would be a "plague" to Britain's "dependencies."[75] Unfortunately there was not much the New Englanders could do, except "bow the knee before the throne of mercy." Chauncy declared that prayer was "the only way wherein we, who live at such a distance, can help our king and nation."[76]

The colonists were worried about their own rights in 1745 and 1746. After the crisis was over, Benjamin Franklin expressed the worst fears of many of them when he asserted that if Charles Edward had won, "we were all to be converted to the Catholic faith."[77] Many in America were also concerned about the international ramifications of a Jacobite victory, particularly the impact it would have on their relations with the Spanish and the French.

Over the previous six years the colonists had engaged themselves in Britain's imperial war efforts in a variety of contexts on an unprecedented scale. In the early months of Britain's war with Spain in 1739, colonials had enlisted by the thousands to fight the Spanish in the Caribbean. When France declared war against Britain in 1744, the French, operating from Cape Breton Island, attacked Nova Scotia, and the government of Massachusetts responded by sending hundreds of men to augment the regular British army's garrison in the colony. Nova Scotia had been officially British only since the Treaty of Utrecht in 1713, and most of its colonial inhabitants were French-speaking Catholics, descended from the French founders of the colony, which had originally been known as Acadia.[78] For several years, successive waves of New England soldiers patrolled the Acadian community and engaged in intermittent combat with the French army and its Algonkian and Iroquoian allies. New England's most dramatic contribution to Britain's broad imperial project came in 1745 when, with support from the Royal Navy, an army of colonists seized Louisbourg, France's principal settlement near Nova Scotia, on Cape Breton Island.[79] As part of the capitulation agreement, all the French settlers on the island, numbering over a thousand, were transported, via Boston, to France.[80]

The seizure of Cape Breton Island inspired a wave of imperial patriotism throughout the British colonies. When the news arrived a few months later that Charles Edward was leading an insurrection in Britain, many in America began to worry that if the rising succeeded, the Stuart royal family, restored to the throne, might reverse the colonists' recent gains. The Jacobites had long relied on French and Spanish assistance, and the pamphlets they published during the rising denounced George II's imperial adventures as a profligate waste of money and men.[81] One Scottish Jacobite pamphleteer rhetorically asked "the People of England," "Would you be an island again?"[82] The writer assumed that the English were tired of fighting for the empire, and he took it for granted that the answer would be yes. It is very unlikely that the New Englanders had access to this literature, but they could guess at what a Stuart king might do. After the news arrived in Boston of the Battle of Culloden, one preacher declared that the Jacobites might have restored Gibraltar, Minorca, and Jamaica to Spain and returned Cape Breton Island, Nova Scotia, the fishing grounds of the north Atlantic, and the eastern shores of Newfoundland to France.[83]

The imperial implications of the 1745 rising convinced some colonists that the conflict was closer to home than Charles Chauncy and the governor of Pennsylvania suggested, and that there was more that they could do for George II than pray. Throughout Britain's colonies in North America and the West Indies, from Montserrat to Massachusetts, there were supporters of the ruling regime who believed that the rising had been instigated by a large transatlantic conspiracy with a secret membership. Some predicted that the kings of France and Spain would exploit a Jacobite victory by consolidating their hold on the Appalachian Mountains, the American south, and the west and would seize several additional Caribbean islands. In their bleakest moods they expected Charles Edward to deliver all of British North America to France. Many groups were suspected of complicity in this project, including American native tribes, Scottish colonists, Catholics of all nationalities, and at the head of it all, the French.[84]

There was very little evidence of subversive activity in America, but the smallest hint that someone might have divided political loyalties was enough to bring that person under suspicion. In the winter of 1745–46 a Protestant missionary named David Brainerd came to Elizabeth, New Jersey. Within hours of his arrival the townspeople accused him of being "engaged in the Pretender's interest." Brainerd wrote in his diary that he was "generally taken to be a Roman Catholic, sent by the Papists to draw the Indians into an insurrection against the English." Some of his accusers were too afraid of him to talk, while others sought to have him jailed.[85] Brainerd was surprised and distressed, and he struggled to reconstruct everything he had said since his arrival in Elizabeth. As far as he could remember, he had never mentioned British politics, Catholicism, or the imperial conflict with France. He was worried, however, that he might have inadvertently dropped a word leading some of the townspeople to suspect that he was "stirring up the Indians against the English." After searching his memory he concluded that he was guiltless, since all he had done was to argue in defense of the "rights of the Indians" and object to "the horrid practice of making the Indians drunk" and "cheating them out of their lands."[86]

Brainerd had difficulty conceiving how anyone could suspect him of Jacobitism, and in retrospect the accusation does seem farfetched. The Susquehanna people he worked with were not allied with the French. He was not a Catholic. Indeed, though he was a Connecticut man, he worked under the auspices of the SSPCK, an organization that constituted, along with Cumberland's army, the most aggressive proponent of the Whig interest in the Scottish Highlands. But the colonists of New Jersey were not well informed, and had anyone in Elizabeth known that Brainerd was receiving Scottish pay, that probably would have served as evidence against him.

In several colonies Scots were subjected to scrutiny in 1745 and 1746, even if they traced their ancestry to the Lowlands and strongly supported George II. The Scottish governor of North Carolina, Gabriel Johnston, was one of those who were watched.[87] Rumors spread that he secretly favored Charles Edward. When Johnston smiled after hearing news of Charles Edward's success, it was noted. After he failed to celebrate adequately when the news was good for the government, that too was noticed.[88] Years earlier, in the late 1730s, Johnston had invited Gaelic-speaking colonists from Argyllshire into North Carolina.[89] The colonial assembly had supported him in the effort, and officials from other colonies were engaged at the time in similar schemes, to place Highlanders in southern Georgia, for example, and in western New York.[90] Nonetheless, in 1745 North Carolina was the only colony in North America with a self-sustaining Scottish Gaelic-speaking community.[91] Though North Carolina's Highlanders were quiet in 1745 and 1746, the governor's association with them hardly won him much political support. As late as 1749 some German settlers in western North Carolina believed that Johnston intended to establish a new colony of Jacobite Highlanders on the eastern slopes of the Appalachians.[92]

Perhaps the most violent display of controversy in British North America in 1746 occurred in Boston when a body of sailors from merchant ships struggled against navy press gangs and took to the streets to object to the Royal Navy's practice of recruiting seamen against their wills.[93] As the protesters marched, the crowd swelled, because the sailors won support from other angry inhabitants of Boston. Together with their allies they took several naval officers hostage and drove Massachusetts governor William Shirley out of his house and out of town. The sailors who initiated the action included Scots who had recently arrived from Glasgow, and Shirley insisted that the "greatest part" of the crowd was "Scotch."[94] The governor did not accuse anyone of Jacobitism. With carefully chosen words, in negotiations with the sailors' leaders, he demonstrated that he knew the difference between Lowland Scots and Highlanders.[95] Others, however, were less discriminating. The admiral whose recruitment policies had inspired the protests reportedly responded to the crowd by declaring that "all Scotchmen were rebels."[96] After William Douglass, a prominent Scottish-born journalist, complained about that admiral's actions, Douglass was sued for libel, and in the subsequent proceedings, according to observers sympathetic to him, the prosecution suggested that "not only the defendant, but the whole Scots nation were disaffected to the government."[97]

There were many in Massachusetts who disliked Douglass for reasons unconnected to his national origins.[98] In his years in America he had expressed strong opinions on issues as diverse as smallpox inoculation, currency reform, religious revivalism, and the New Englanders' recent expedition against the French on Cape Breton Island. Douglass had opposed the New Englanders' seizure of the island. All of his positions were controversial, and his opponents remembered what he had said. While the 1745 rising affected the way his enemies described him, the crisis in Britain was not the principal reason Douglass was maligned. Brainerd, Johnston, and the anti-impressment rioters were similar in this respect. All of them were involved in controversies that predated 1745, and the opposition they faced was based on array of factors, many of them unrelated to the Jacobite rising. The events of 1745 affected colonial American politics by widening and hardening divisions that already existed in local politics, and Scots were among the groups who suffered as a result. In the aftermath of the crisis, in moments of tension, colonists redefined the sectarian, factional, and racial fissures within their societies, and on occasion accused their rivals of Jacobitism.

Of all the colonies, Maryland was the one most unsettled by the news of the Jacobite rising. Maryland had a substantial Catholic minority which, generations earlier, had ruled the province. Though the colony's political leaders were now Protestants, many of them were closely linked to the old Catholic elite through marriage and other social ties. The governor of the colony, Thomas Bladen, was Protestant, but his mother was Catholic.[99] Because of his family connections and other links to members of the Catholic Church, Bladen had to be careful in the way he responded to the crisis. He had to be cautious, but at the same time his attachments gave him incentives to protect Catholics from large-scale reprisals. A greater number of prominent figures were accused of Jacobitism in Maryland than anywhere else in America, and it is possible that some of the accusations were true.[100]

On March 13, 1746, Bladen heard a report that Catholics were stockpiling weapons in a large house on the banks of the Monacy River.[101] In response he summoned Richard Molyneux, the ecclesiastical leader of the Catholics of Maryland, before the provincial council. The allegations concerning weapons proved unfounded, but other damaging stories were circulating. In particular, there were vague indications that Molyneux had responded to the news from Britain "in a seditious manner contrary to his due allegiance," and this had led some observers to conclude that he was "a person very ill affected to his Majesty's person and government."[102] Bladen did not order Molyneux arrested. Instead he warned him that the Catholics' "unguarded" behavior had "exceeded all bounds of prudence and decency." Bladen told Molyneux to be discrete; then, with a telling reference to the greatest underlying fears affecting the Protestant elite in Maryland, he told him to stay away from the colony's "Negroes." Any "concourse" between white Catholics and blacks, the governor predicted, would "give suspicion of something else being designed than a bare exercise of religion."[103] A few months later Bladen repeated the warning and made it more general, by issuing a proclamation barring Catholics from initiating any efforts to win converts.[104]

Throughout the British Empire, the opposition to Charles Edward was almost intrinsically anti-Catholic. Chesterfield's Ireland was an exception to the general pattern, but in Scotland, England, and elsewhere throughout the empire, defenders of the government commonly sought to restrict the activities of Catholics during the rising. On the Mediterranean island of Minorca, the governor required a group of Catholic friars to post bond because he suspected that they were trying to convert his soldiers and convince them to desert to Spain.[105] More significantly, in November 1745 the Privy Council modified the terms of religious establishment on Minorca, requiring the Catholics to tolerate other Christian groups.[106] In the Caribbean, on Antigua and Montserrat, Protestants attempted to impose permanent changes in the law, to restrict the Catholics' political rights and limit Catholic immigration.[107] Everywhere these policies reflected long-standing local concerns. In the Mediterranean and the Caribbean the fear of French and Spanish subversion was grounded in regional politics and not at all dependent on conspiracy theories associated with the Jacobite rising. The fear of Catholicism was not new, nor was it something that set Maryland, or the colonies as a group, apart. The distinctive feature of the American response to the rising was the way in which the colonists associated the 1745 crisis with imperial expansion.

Even among those who believed that the zone of colonial settlement should expand, the process of taking territory invited controversy in British North America. Colonists argued over the status of indigenous peoples, the allocation of land, and the conduct of trade and diplomacy with the colonies of Spain and France. Those who supported peaceful commerce and restrictions on the expansion of British power did not advocate the destruction of the British colonies, but their opponents often accused them, especially in 1745 and 1746, of advancing subversive and destructive plans developed by the French. David Brainerd's defense of the rights of native peoples, Johnston's support for Scottish Gaelic settlement in North Carolina, the Bostonians' protests against naval impressment, and Douglass's more general opposition to New England's militarism all implicated questions related to imperial expansion. Accurately or not, each of these figures was accused of advancing (in their own small way) a grand design, to deliver Britain to the Stuarts, and most of North America to the French.

While they spoke out generally against wasteful colonial wars, the Jacobites were never in a strong enough position in Britain to formulate a detailed, long-term foreign policy, certainly not one that directly addressed the concerns of colonial Americans. Nonetheless, inadvertently, their actions affected the interests of the colonists, primarily by helping keep the navy on the European side of the Atlantic Ocean. In July 1746 the *Virginia Gazette* carried a report indicating that privateering activity off America's shores had increased "since the unnatural rebellion," because "the King's ships, which should have been employed in the protection of trade, were obliged to be stationed almost round Scotland."[108] Later that summer the colonists had more to complain of, after the ministry canceled its plan to send naval ships to the St. Lawrence River to assist in a projected campaign against French Canada. Thousands of colonial troops had volunteered for the operation, but without the British navy they could not proceed.[109]

The cancellation of the 1746 expedition against Canada was a major disappointment for the colonies' militant expansionists, but it did not turn them against George II, Cumberland, or the ministry. The news from Culloden had arrived by that time, and most colonists believed that Cumberland's victory over the Jacobites had saved them from a terrible fate. Indeed, in the mid- to late 1740s, repeatedly and extravagantly, the colonists praised Cumberland as their champion and celebrated the defeat of Charles Edward as a victory for the empire. After the news of Culloden was confirmed, preachers delivered laudatory sermons.[110] Colonial assemblies passed resolutions of thanks.[111] Bonfires were lit on plantations, on farms, and in cities, and the colonists danced.[112]

These celebrations elevated Cumberland to a nearly godlike status. Preaching in Philadelphia, the evangelist George Whitefield declared that Cumberland should be "blessed above men" because "thro' his instrumentality, the great and glorious Jehovah hath brought mighty things to pass."[113] Several months later, in *Poor Richard's Almanac*, Franklin compared Cumberland to Hercules.[114] These were the most extravagant tributes, but the most enduring ones were place names. In the years following Culloden, forts were named for Cumberland in Nova Scotia and Maryland, in places where his name was ultimately given to the local county and the local town.[115] Other counties were named for him in present-day Maine and Vermont and in New Jersey, North Carolina, Virginia, and Pennsylvania.[116] Rhode Island, Massachusetts, and Maryland named townships or parishes for Cumberland, and in 1750, in perhaps the most symbolically resonant honor, a traveler named Thomas Walker came to a river west of the Appalachians that had been formerly called the Shawnee.[117] He named it the Cumberland River and subsequently identified the nearby mountains as the Cumberland range (see Figure 7). Eventually Cumberland's name would be attached to the Cumberland Gap, a landmark celebrated for generations as the pioneer's gateway into the American west.[118]

The settlers' encomiums to Cumberland reflected anxiety as well as gratitude. Most of the worries that had plagued them in 1746 continued for years thereafter. The French remained in the west and north, the Spanish in the south, and Britain's relations with North America's native tribes remained as fraught as they ever had been. No one knew for certain that the Jacobite movement had been finally defeated, and it was more difficult in America than in Britain to assess the Stuart claimant's

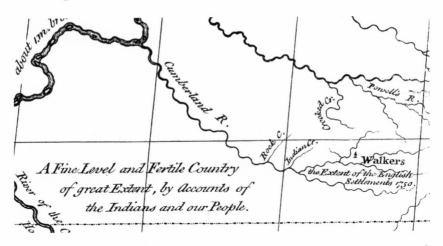

Figure 7. The Cumberland River, formerly known as the Shawnee, was renamed for the Duke of Cumberland in 1750. This is a detail from a map of North America published in 1755. (Courtesy of the Special Collections and Archives, University of Kentucky Libraries.)

strength. The 1745 rising had served to emphasize the colonists' dependence on British authority, which made them eager to honor, or flatter, the kingdom's great men. When the inhabitants of Cumberland, Rhode Island, named their town, they did so in part to win support from their sovereign and secure themselves politically against the territorial claims of Massachusetts. When military officers in Maryland and Nova Scotia named their forts for him, they were motivated, at least in part, by considerations of patronage. Cumberland led the British army, and the army, even if it was stationed at a distance, seemed increasingly influential in American life.

North America was uneasy in 1746, but from the perspective of Britain, the colonists had made a convincing show of loyalty to the ruling regime, and not only by naming counties or publishing congratulatory declarations. Despite the efforts of the conspiracy-minded, virtually no Jacobites had been discovered in America, and if any of the colonists had favored Charles Edward, they had been isolated and generally mute. The apparent ease with which the colonies weathered the crisis fit an overall pattern. Outside the Scottish Highlands and away from the rival armies, throughout the British Empire, the rising had passed without violence. The government's supporters, therefore, came to an almost inevitable conclusion: there was something uniquely wrong with the Scottish Highlands. In their debates over future policy, ministers and military officers looked to England, Ireland, and America for models of effective governance, and they thought the colonies, in particular, were places where Highlanders in need of reform could be sent.

In 1747, after most of the criminal trials were concluded, hundreds of war captives from Charles Edward's army were boarded on ships and sent across the Atlantic. The merchants and ship captains who took custody of the prisoners were selective in where they brought them. In general, they carried the former Jacobite soldiers to places with a high demand for labor and an established infrastructure for disposing of bound servants in large numbers. Hundreds of men were taken to the British West Indies, where, in ceremonies that might have seemed legally superfluous, they were induced to sign contracts of indenture. None of the prisoners had signed such contacts before their arrival in the Caribbean, and the government officials who had arranged their passage assumed that the men could be sold for lifelong service whether or not they agreed to any terms.[119] Nonetheless, plantation owners on the islands refused to buy any of the prisoners as servants unless they signed a contract, because they wanted to dispel any ambiguity about the men's status. Captives brought across the ocean after the 1715 rising had maintained legal challenges to their bondage for years.[120] In 1747 the terms offered the prisoners were attractive. In Barbados, after 125 prisoners arrived in July, 120 of the men agreed to sign contracts immediately, and all but 3 of them were quickly sold.[121] A similar sale took place later that year in Jamaica.[122] The contract for the servants sold in Jamaica survives. Though the men were bound over for lifelong service when they left Britain, those who signed the indenture in Jamaica had their term reduced to seven years.[123]

Several factors facilitated the negotiation of these contracts. The prisoners had limited bargaining power; those who refused to enter into contracts were left in jail with an uncertain future. On the other hand, as a result of the insistence of the masters, no sales could take place without the prisoners' consent, and by refusing to sign contracts the men could delay the proceedings indefinitely. The ship captains and merchants involved in these transactions were in a hurry to complete the sales. The ships had other places to go and other cargo to carry. The merchants had other deals to transact, and no one wanted to clutter the docks. For the plantation owners, labor was scarce, and the short life expectancy of servants in the Caribbean made the reduction in the term of service less of a concession. Men bound for life often died anyway before working for seven years. Furthermore, there were advantages in making an accommodation with the prisoners. In the tense world of the sugar plantations, masters were always conscious of the possibility of violence. They believed that they would be safer if they could prevent the former soldiers from associating their own status with that of the slaves. From the perspective of the masters it appears that the accommodation worked. Demand for the servants was high, and ships continued to arrive in the Caribbean with prisoners from Charles Edward's army at least until 1749.[124]

The only colony on the American mainland to receive Jacobite prisoners was Maryland.[125] Maryland had a well-established market for the sale of bound servants, and anecdotal evidence suggests that in the years leading up to 1745 the Chesapeake region, and Maryland in particular, had taken on more Highlanders as bound servants than any other part of British North America.[126] Like their compatriots in the Caribbean, the prisoners brought to Maryland were invited into negotiations prior to their entry into the servant market.[127] The talks took place while the men were still on shipboard, in irons below decks awaiting disembarkation. On one of the ships, according to one account, most of the prisoners refused to sign contracts of indenture even after they were offered a reduction in the term of service from life to seven years. The men relented and agreed to the contracts only after their ship captain promised to find purchasers from among the colony's Catholics.[128]

The arrival of the prisoners in Maryland sparked controversy. Within six weeks of their arrival two were put on trial and convicted for "drinking the Pretender's health."[129] Reports spread that most of the two hundred men who had been brought to the colony had been purchased by Catholics, and some in the colony feared that the Highlanders' new masters intended to deploy them in a subversive plot to overthrow the Protestant regime.[130] Maryland's political structure was less vulnerable, however, than the alarmists suggested. The colony had been shared by Catholics and Protestants for more than one hundred years, and tacit, workable compromises had been reached. Throughout the eighteenth century there was far more talk of sectarian violence in Maryland than actual conflict. Bound service was the basis of the colonial economy, and, as individual workers, the Jacobite newcomers could be absorbed and controlled easily. Isolated on farms and in homes, they were too few in number to upset Maryland's domestic peace.

In the American colonies overall, there were very few protests against the importation of former Jacobite soldiers. Such complaints as there were concentrated on other, broader and more ambitious proposals emanating from Britain. Within weeks of Charles Edward's arrival in Scotland, British pamphleteers and officials had begun discussing large-scale emigration schemes involving the involuntary removal of entire populations from the Highlands to America—not just Charles Edward's soldiers and other convicted Jacobites but communities including women and children. One pamphlet published in Britain presented the argument that the Highlanders, as "lineal descendants of the ancient Scots," were endowed with a character well suited to the rigors of colonial life. They were "brave and prolific," the writer insisted, and their "warlike disposition" could make them useful for the defense of the colonies, particularly in the "northern parts of America" where their settlements might serve as a "fence" against enemy native groups and the French.[131]

In the spring of 1746 Cumberland endorsed the idea of transporting whole communities of Highlanders across the ocean, though he did so for his own reasons and the details of his proposals make it clear that his project was different from the one previously advanced by pamphleteers. Cumberland developed his scheme after consulting with several of his supporters in the Highlands, including Duncan Forbes and Alexander MacDonald of Sleat.[132] Alexander MacDonald of Sleat had been one of the government's most courageous supporters in 1745 and 1746. After a large part of his clan had enlisted with Charles Edward, he himself had recruited soldiers for the government and provided the Argyllshire militia intelligence and logistical support.[133] In the spring of 1746 Alexander MacDonald had helped rescue Loudon and his regiment after their retreat from Inverness.[134] In light of this service Cumberland had praised MacDonald directly to his father the king.[135] At the time, Cumberland had not learned that MacDonald's wife Margaret was suspected of helping Charles Edward escape Britain.

There had long been divisions within the MacDonald clan. In 1739 MacDonald had allegedly arranged the kidnapping of dozens of his own tenants, with the intention of sending them away for sale as bound servants in America.[136] Cumberland's proposal in 1746 can be seen, at least in part, as a modified version of that earlier, illicit proposal. Cumberland recommended that "whole clans be transported," including "the entire clan of the Camerons," and part of the "MacDonalds," particularly those on the mainland of Scotland, who in 1745 had challenged Alexander MacDonald's leadership within his clan by contributing troops to Charles Edward's army.[137] Cumberland wanted to send the exiled Highlanders to the West Indies, where he thought that they might enrich themselves, generate profit for merchants, and increase British trade. Though he believed that the targeted clans were dangerous, and therefore wanted them out of Britain, he did not want them sent as bound servants, or "slaves."[138] Living in exile, but otherwise in freedom, the Highlanders would be "much happier," he insisted.[139]

Cumberland was at the height of his influence when he made this proposal, but nonetheless he failed to gain official support. Objections were raised that transportation was too expensive, that the plan was too harsh, that it was legally suspect, and that it would jeopardize the security of the colonists already in America.[140] The debate lasted years, however, and it had an influence on events in Scotland and America.[141] In 1748 the Duke of Bedford, with Cumberland's approval, was making preparations to send Highlanders to the colonies.[142] By that time the sense of immediate crisis had passed, and Bedford knew that he could not send any families against their will. He proposed instead to send disbanded soldiers from Loudon's regiment to Nova Scotia to strengthen Britain's hold over the colony. The men would be required to reenlist as soldiers for a short term before receiving grants of land.[143] The project faltered because Loudon's Highlanders had suffered so many casualties in three years of combat and intermittent disease that few if any of his veterans were healthy enough to go.[144] Still, the idea lingered. From his post in Scotland in 1751 Wolfe fantasized about transporting Gaelic-speakers to Nova Scotia. They were "hardy, intrepid," and "accustomed to a rough country," Wolfe asserted. Furthermore, it would be "no great mischief" if they died.[145]

In the late 1740s and early 1750s, most of the inhabitants of Britain's American colonies had never seen a Highlander. If they knew anything about the people at all, their knowledge was derived from material they had read. In 1745 and 1746, the news arriving from Britain had been troubling, and the colonists' wariness was intensified by a wide variety of imported literature, some of which was reprinted in America, including political poems and satirical writings.[146] After the defeat of the rising, official histories, soldiers' memoirs, and fictive biographies were added to the mix.[147] By 1750 there was even an American edition of *The Life and Surprising Adventures of Miss Jenny Cameron*, including details of Cameron's alleged sexual escapades and the services she had performed for Charles Edward's army.[148] Some colonists may have been amused by the Jenny Cameron story, but as a whole the literature imported from Britain was enough to convince anyone that the Highlanders would make bad settlers.

At one time it had been different. Between 1715 and 1745, colonial officials in North Carolina, Georgia, and elsewhere had classified Highlanders as "foreign Protestants," a broad category of potential immigrants whom they actively recruited, especially in the 1730s, as part of a concerted effort to settle and defend the colonial frontiers.[149] Those who had sought to bring Highlanders in groups to North America had been familiar with their reputation for savagery and rebelliousness. Nonetheless, they had expressed confidence that life in the backcountry would change the people forever. As one agent for Georgia had asserted in 1735, life in the colonies would "effectually civilize our Highlanders and divert that boisterous humour, which used, upon the least commotion, to fly out in the face of their sovereign."[150] No one in America made any similar declarations in the decade after 1745, and in general the colonists were much less sanguine about placing Gaelic-speakers near their borders.

In Massachusetts, Governor Shirley, for one, was adamant that Highlanders were inappropriate colonists for border regions. They were "a set of poor, ignorant, deluded wretches just come out of a most unnatural rebellion," he declared, and if they were planted in Nova Scotia, or anywhere near, they would immediately offer their services to the French.[151] The German settlers in North Carolina advanced a slightly different argument, but they were equally insistent that Highlanders should not be sent to live in separate communities near them. They believed that any plan to place Highlanders in the west was part of a Jacobite plot, and they did not want Gaelic speakers occupying the available land.[152] In the American colonies generally, Highlanders who arrived as bound servants did not provoke protests. This was so even after the former Jacobite soldiers had completed their terms of service and began to travel alone. The colonies were willing to have Gaelic-speaking servants, but in the late 1740s they did not want such people living in groups, especially not at the edge of the zone of settlement.

*   *   *

Before the start of the Seven Years' War in 1754, none of the proposals that were circulating to transport intact communities of Highlanders to North America reached far enough along in the planning stages to raise widespread alarm. Furthermore, outside of North Carolina there were too few Highlanders living in concentrated settlements to make their presence a matter of concern. Nonetheless, for those who thought about the matter, the controversy surrounding Highland settlements in America was part of an ongoing debate over the future of the colonial frontier. The preoccupations that had distinguished the colonists' discussion of the 1745 rising continued to affect their thoughts about Highlanders after Charles Edward's defeat. From the perspective of many colonists, the greatest danger associated with bringing Highlanders to America was that it might interfere with the colonies' territorial expansion.

In 1746 the colonists commonly assumed that Cumberland had advanced the cause of empire by defeating an army of Highlanders. Ten years later, in 1756, North America would witness a surprisingly different drama, when, still in command of the army, Cumberland sent Highland troops to the colonies to combat the French. From that time forward the Highlanders assumed a different role in the politics of imperial expansion. It was a change in status that reflected developments both in Scotland and North America, as well as shifts in the fortunes, aspirations, and political program of the leaders of the British army.

Cumberland and his officers had turned their attention to reform in the Scottish Highlands almost immediately after the Battle of Culloden, and their participation in the project of reshaping the region continued over the next decade. The restoration of peace in Europe in 1749 served to broaden the scope of the officers' ambitions, with new deployments overseas. Veterans of Cumberland's Scottish campaigns were given authority in Gibraltar, Minorca, and Nova Scotia, and in each colony, as in Scotland, they sought to promote civilization as they understood it by encouraging immigration, building infrastructure, promoting trade and industry, and limiting the power of Catholics and the Catholic Church. In the short run they made little progress, in part because they were politically weak; the return of peace had diminished Cumberland's influence within the counsels of government. Cumberland's full power returned to him only with the renewal of warfare against the French in North America, in 1754. Nonetheless from 1746 onward the army's operations in the Highlands had been tied to its projects overseas. In 1754 the outbreak of combat near the fork of the Ohio River was a turning point for the British army, and consequently for the Scottish Highlands and the empire as a whole.

Part II
Cumberland's Army and the World

Chapter 4

Cumberland's Army in Scotland

Cumberland's victory over the Jacobites in 1746 bolstered the stature of the British army, strengthened Cumberland's leadership within the ranks, and gave him, and the military as a whole, new influence on the direction of political life. Controversy continued to follow him and the army in general, but for years after Culloden Cumberland was able to influence policy not only in Scotland but also in the colonies and anywhere else Britain projected its power overseas. Even after he resigned as captain general in 1757, the army was able to pursue a new, more deliberate and vigorous imperial agenda, thanks in part to his efforts. Northern Scotland, however, was the first place where Cumberland and the men under his command visibly and self-consciously assumed the role of reformers.

In 1745 and 1746 the "Highland problem" received the concentrated attention of the British public, and within the counsels of government it acquired an urgency it had not had before.[1] This led to years of effort to reform the character of the Gaelic-speakers and integrate their region more fully into Britain's political structure and the world of commercial exchange.[2] Parliament initiated much of this program, by amending the laws of Scotland, confiscating the property of Jacobites, and managing the newly acquired lands in ways designed to improve the Highlanders' condition. The army also played a significant role. Cumberland and his officers became advisors to the ministry as it designed its reform program, and after the new legislation was enacted, they helped determine how it would operate in practice.

In the immediate aftermath of Culloden, much of the Scottish Highlands was militarily occupied territory, and the troops pulled back from their combat and policing functions only slowly. The number of soldiers stationed in the region gradually declined, as did their power to seize property or arrest and detain the people of the country. A turning point came in the autumn of 1747, when the crown pardoned all those who had given assistance to the rising without taking up arms.[3] After that, the army's position in the Highlands resembled what it had been in the 1720s and 1730s. Units patrolled the coasts, and in the interior soldiers lent assistance to civilian law enforcement, conducting investigations, for example, of alleged subversive activity. The troops also built bridges and roadways, pursuing the program General George Wade had instituted a quarter-century before. Nonetheless, the relationship between the Highlanders and the army had changed.

In large parts of the Highlands, communities were devastated, impoverished, and angry. Some Highlanders sought redress for their grievances, on occasion by going to court to demand compensation for damaged crops and slaughtered herds or the return of confiscated property. The army as a whole resented these complaints, and several officers asked to be stationed outside the region. Some soldiers, unhappy in general with the conditions of life in Scotland, vented their frustration in criminal activity, including thefts, vandalism, sexual assaults, and fights that occasionally escalated into large-scale brawls. These circumstances resulted in constant jurisdictional conflict, as magistrates and military officers argued over the prosecution of soldiers and the power of the army to investigate crime. The arguments proved nearly intractable, in part because the rules governing Highland life were changing. The government had undertaken the task of restructuring the legal institutions of the region and the customs of the inhabitants. Many of the rules governing community life, therefore, were assumed to be temporary, provisional, or obsolete.

As advisors to the government, the leaders of the garrisons in the Highlands generally thought that it was their responsibility to become experts on the laws, social customs, and economy of the region. They consulted with local aristocrats, sent subordinate officers into the field, and prepared reports that they sent to Westminster to assist in the formulation of reform plans. The longer the soldiers stayed in Scotland the more they came to believe that they were knowledgeable about it, and they found themselves increasingly enmeshed, often uncomfortably, in the society they were trying to reform. Few of the army's English or Irish officers lived easily in Scotland. As a group they were given to disparage their neighbors in the north. Enlisted men in the lower ranks of the army often hired themselves out to do manual labor or craft work in local communities, sometimes all but abandoning their soldierly authority in the process.[4] The higher officers refused to integrate themselves so thoroughly into Scottish society. Indeed, their letters and order books indicate that they were anxious to keep a distance between themselves and those they governed, in order to maintain an aura of discipline and strength. Nonetheless, the necessity of governing the Highlands forced several officers into local partnerships, particularly with the country's Presbyterian, English-speaking elite.

The officers' experience in the Highlands helped change their understanding of the army's role in the empire. A few of the men involved in making reform proposals began reading theoretical literature on education and cultural development. Partly as a result of such reading, they came to believe that their expertise extended beyond the Highlands, and that they were specially qualified to direct the administration of exotic lands. The Scottish Highlands, for these men, remained a zone on the edge of civilization. Though they boasted of success in deterring crime and suppressing political subversion, in the early 1750s few if any of them believed that the old, ostensibly regressive and dangerous tendencies within Highland culture had disappeared. That was why they believed that others should value their experience and expertise. In the view of the most enthusiastic officers, the army was engaged in a project of enormous magnitude—the transformation of a region and a people. It was a task, they assumed, that would take decades to achieve.

*   *   *

On a winter day in 1745, a unit of the government's Highland soldiers encamped near London received instruction in Gaelic from a man who would become a leading figure of the Scottish Enlightenment. The speaker, Adam Fergusson, was a Presbyterian minister, and soon he would be appointed a professor of moral philosophy at the University of Edinburgh. In 1745 Fergusson was a military chaplain and, officially at least, he continued to serve Highland soldiers in that capacity until they were deployed in North America in 1756.[5] On this occasion he expounded on the origins of social responsibility. He declared that infants, as soon as they entered into the world, "stand in need of the assistance of others." Life would be "forlorn and comfortless," he told the soldiers, if mutual assistance were not "afterwards reciprocally given and received through the whole of our lives." He declared, "If society is a thing so indispensably necessary to the human nature, and if every individual member reaps such inestimable advantages from their joint confederacy, we can no longer hesitate in drawing our conclusion, that each member is bound, both on account of his own and the public welfare, to maintain that league from which he derives so many blessings."[6] Fergusson's immediate purpose in delivering this sermon was to remind the men of their obligation to fight to defend the community that raised them, including its leader George II. Nonetheless, he spoke in general terms and introduced the soldiers to the theory that children derive their political values from their social environment, and that this process begins at the moment of birth. These assumptions underlay much of Fergusson's subsequent philosophy, and in the middle years of the eighteenth century, similar ideas about childhood and culture informed many scholarly discussions of historical change.[7]

Britain's soldiers in 1745 were fighting in the presence of philosophers.[8] The crisis inspired scholarly inquiries into the source of political order and the loyalty Britons owed to George II.[9] After Culloden the commentary continued and drew in a greater number of less well known writers with a different agenda—analyzing the distinctiveness of the Scottish Highlands and prescribing programs to accelerate cultural change.[10] The ministry received lengthy essays on Highland life, with recommendations for reform, from Highland landlords, Presbyterian missionaries, members of the Edinburgh legal establishment, and constitutional experts closely associated with the House of Lords. In general the writers of these pieces are not remembered as careful scholars, but many of them were eager to display erudition and abstract thinking. Some sought to locate the Gaelic-speakers on the spectrum of human development between savagery and civilization. Many employed the logic of political economy. Some offered theoretical discussions on the socialization and education of children.

Cumberland entered the official debate over the long-term future of the Highlands in February 1746, on the invitation of the Duke of Newcastle.[11] That following June Newcastle sent Cumberland a list of four bills, with several provisions each, which the ministers planned to introduce in Parliament. Two weeks later Cumberland returned the document, adding extensive marginal notes.[12] Cumberland's comments reveal the extent of his interests and the volume of information available to him about life in the region. His recommendations reflected his firsthand experience in the Highlands, but much of his detailed knowledge came from conversations with the Earl of Findlater and Seaforth, a reform-minded aristocrat with close ties to the Lord Chancellor, the Earl of Hardwicke.[13] Cumberland also consulted with other prominent landlords, including Alexander MacDonald of Sleat and Duncan Forbes, though he worried that Forbes was "Highland mad" and overly inclined toward "lenity."[14] With the help of these advisors, he instructed Newcastle on fine points of Scottish property law, the operation of civilian courts in the Highlands, the significance of tartans, naming practices among Gaelic-speakers, and the methods of consecrating Scottish Episcopalian priests.

Nearly all of these features of life were investigated by members of Parliament in the years following Culloden, and the rising inspired considerable legislative activity.[15] The first new enactments focused on the political structure of the Highlands, with the aim of reducing the region's autonomy and reinforcing the British government's monopoly on the use of force.[16] Disarmament was part of that initial effort, as was

the prohibition of tartans, which were widely viewed as military uniforms.[17] Under new legislation, only Highland soldiers in the regular
British army were allowed to wear plaid kilts. Other initiatives sought to
weaken the political power of landlords and clan leaders. In 1747 Parliament outlawed wardholding, the customary practice which had traditionally placed tenants under an obligation to perform military service
for their superiors.[18] "Heritable jurisdictions" were also abolished, so
that after 1747 the Highland aristocracy could no longer convene their
own law courts.[19]

All of these proposals generated controversy. The abolition of heritable jurisdictions, in particular, upset many in Scotland.[20] Nonetheless, it
was the future of the lands belonging to convicted Jacobites that caused
the longest-lasting and most complex debate. This was so because a large
swath of territory was at stake, and powerful, conflicting interests were
involved. Landlords in the Highlands were very interested, as were many
of the most ambitious reformers, who hoped to transform the Jacobite
estates into model communities and direct their management with the
aim of transforming the local inhabitants' character. Some reformers
predicted that the policies the government introduced for the administration of the Jacobites' lands would be emulated by neighboring landlords and that Parliament, through strategic purchases, would acquire
new properties and establish a vast "royal district" spanning the Highlands.[21] Controlling this territory, they thought, would give the authorities the leverage they needed to effect lasting, fundamental social
change.

The proponents of this program sought, in the long run, to make the
Highlanders loyal subjects of the British king. They assumed that this
could be achieved only by undermining the independent authority of
the region's aristocrats and the power of the clans. To combat clanship
they intended to strengthen the law courts of the region, so that the
clans would cease to punish outsiders on account of their distinct
national identities or names. The reformers also sought to place the
region's economy on a cash basis, to place all commercial actors on an
equal footing, and to put an end to the traditional practices of barter
and the reciprocal exchange of services, practices that seemed, histori-
cally, to strengthen the clans. Policy makers were particularly concerned
to eliminate service requirements from leases, because demanding service from one's tenants was seen as a demeaning expression of hierarchy
and an inefficient allocation of energy. Furthermore, in times of crisis,
calling one's tenants physically to one's home was often the first step
toward mobilizing men for military action. The justifications offered for
these reform proposals often mixed economic and political interests.
Nearly all the reformers assumed that economic growth would promote

political stability, because young men with good economic prospects were unlikely to take the risk of going to war.[22]

Nearly all of the reformers focused their attention on the young. Like Adam Fergusson they assumed that education began early, and that children and young adults acquired their political values from the full array of influences acting on them, including their families, churches, schools, and the wider economic community. One anonymous advisor to the ministry was particularly concerned about the children of aristocrats, who, the writer asserted, learned laziness and arrogance from watching their fathers demand services from their tenants.[23] Another argued that everyone in the Highlands was corrupted by the whole tenor of Gaelic culture. "The songs recited at their festivals, the fables transmitted from their ancestors, the continual strain of their conversation, all this nourishes their martial spirit, and renders them, from their cradle, compleat soldiers in every thing but the knowledge of discipline."[24] To combat the allegedly pernicious effects of Highland culture, conditions could be placed on leases to require that all those who lived on the forfeited estates speak English, accept Presbyterianism, and send their children to authorized schools.

Nearly all of the reform proposals involved bringing in new settlers to live with the Highlanders, including English army veterans, Scots from the Lowlands, and perhaps even a few "foreign Protestants" from the continent of Europe.[25] The most ambitious schemes entailed shifting populations out of the countryside in order to establish planned villages, where the Gaelic-speakers could live with newcomers from outside the region (see Figure 8).[26] Explaining one such proposal in Parliament, Hardwicke declared, "It is not to be supposed, I hope, that we are to banish, transport, or exterminate all the natives . . . we are only to get a few intelligent and industrious farmers and masters of manufactures, with some servants and journeymen, and a few who understand fishing and curing of fish, to go and settle there, in order to serve as examples to the people of the country, and to instruct and employ such of them as may incline to be industrious."[27]

While most reformers concentrated on the future of the forfeited estates, there was an alternative model of change, one that emphasized the influence of the army. Several military officers and others advocated the permanent stationing of soldiers in a network of five or six outposts, not only as a guarantee against attack and insurrection but also because the presence of the troops was expected to trigger a complex sequence of changes in Highland life. Forbes, one of the most articulate advocates of this plan, suggested that each of the garrisons would attract bakers, laundresses, retailers, barbers, surgeons, and workmen, until eventually the core of a new municipality would be formed. New roads and inns

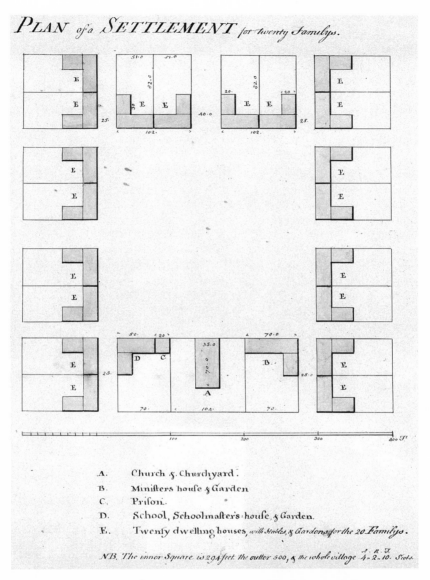

PLAN of a SETTLEMENT for twenty familys.

A.   Church & Churchyard.
B.   Ministers house & Garden
C.   Prison.
D.   School, Schoolmaster's house, & Garden.
E.   Twenty dwelling houses, with Stables, & Gardens, for the 20 Familys.

NB. The inner Square is 294 feet, the outter 500, & the whole village 4.2.10. Scots.

Figure 8. In the late 1740s and early 1750s, schoolteachers, missionaries, estate factors, aristocrats, lawyers, military men, and government ministers exchanged dozens of proposals for establishing model communities in the Scottish Highlands. This plan, from the early 1750s, envisioned housing twenty families alongside a church, parish house, school, schoolteacher's house, prison, and burial ground, in a space measuring 500 feet squared. (Courtesy of the Royal Archives © Her Majesty Queen Elizabeth II.)

would be established to link the communities and facilitate travel. Forbes recommended that the government establish schools near its military outposts, including "spinning schools to draw the idle females of these countries into the manufacture." Once those schools were in place, he predicted, weavers would come. Once the communities had grown, the government could formally grant them municipal powers. This would aid law enforcement, promote commerce, and gradually undermine the traditions of Highland life.[28]

None of those involved in the reform effort believed that their aim was to reverse historical trends. On the contrary, virtually all of the proposals considered by the ministry after 1745 were presented as efforts to accelerate developments that were already, at least in some places, underway. Forbes, for example, cited changes that he believed had occurred on the eastern and southern fringes of the Highlands. In those places, he maintained, "within memory, the inhabitants spoke the Irish language, wore the Highland dress, and were accustomed to make use of arms." Now, he suggested, "after the accidental introduction of industry," the people spoke "a sort of English," wore "Lowland clothing," and "took up the plough in place of weapons."[29] Bland and Milton, the lord justice clerk of Scotland, in their influential proposal for reform in the Highlands, cited similar developments further afield. They claimed that "none succeed better" than the Highlanders when they "reside or are employed" elsewhere in Britain or in the colonies, "remote from their barbarous Highlands."[30] This proved that the Gaelic-speakers were responsive to changes in their environment. Rather than moving the Highlanders out of Scotland, they proposed altering the conditions of life at home. It was generally assumed that the government could change the region only gradually and slowly. Cumberland wrote Newcastle in April 1746 that the "Jacobite rebellious spirit" was "so rooted in this nation's mind that this generation must be pretty wore out before this country will be quiet."[31] His words were echoed in many of the reform proposals. Writers indicated that none of the government's efforts would come to fruition until "the present generation dies out."[32]

Both the land-based model for change and the idea of using garrisons drew upon precedents from before 1745, and in broad terms the strategies were compatible with each other. Bland, for one, believed that the army had a role to play in the administration of the Jacobites' lands. In 1747, shortly after his appointment as commander in chief in Scotland, he sought out Milton, and together they developed a detailed plan for the forfeited estates. They proposed stationing large numbers of troops at strategic outposts and settling veterans on the confiscated lands.[33] Nonetheless, despite Bland's efforts at compromise, the debate over the direction of policy in the Highlands became increasingly contentious among the reformers, and by the early 1750s many had come to believe that the land-based and garrison-centered approaches represented the interests of different constituencies. Cumberland's most ardent supporters emphasized military encampments and worried that concentrating resources on the forfeited estates would enrich the inhabitants of precisely those parts of the country that had risen in favor of Charles Edward, in effect rewarding them for the trouble they had caused.[34] Many in Scotland, on the other hand, resented Cumberland's troops and feared making their presence permanent.

One consequence of this disagreement was to slow the enactment of effective policy. In 1747 Parliament passed a Vesting Act, which authorized a survey of land titles throughout the Highlands and directed the Scottish Barons of Exchequer to assume temporary administration over the Jacobites' estates. By 1749 surveyors were crossing the hills. They examined titles to land, and in their reports they detailed the family histories of the title-holders, concentrating on the political leanings of family members and any possible links to Jacobitism.[35] They also examined the situation of the tenants, and when they identified circumstances that seemed to promote sedition or lawlessness, they recommended remedial measures for the future consideration of those who would administer the property.[36] In all, fifty-three estates were surveyed and forty-one acquired by the barons of Exchequer. Most of the estates were sold off, however, to pay creditors, so that after the passage of the Annexing Act in 1752 only thirteen properties were seized.[37] Even after that, controversies impeded reform efforts. The commission for overseeing the annexed estates was not appointed until 1755.[38]

One of the challenges the reformers faced was finding precedents for official action. This was necessary both to support the constitutional legitimacy of their proposals and to demonstrate, by reference to past experience, the likelihood of success. For those seeking local historical precedents, Cromwell's policies seemed relevant, and he was cited by several policy makers including Hardwicke, Milton, and Bland.[39] Cromwell had deployed troops across the Highlands in the 1650s and placed local government in English hands. Milton and Bland suggested that these actions had been wise but had not accomplished enough, because as soon as Cromwell's army left, the Highlanders had "returned to their natural barbarity."[40] At least one writer, in a widely disseminated essay, cited the Georgia colony in America as a precedent that established the legitimacy of using public funds to subsidize long-term social reform.[41] But it was Ireland that most frequently captured the reformers' attention.

Much of the commentary focused on Ireland's "charter schools," a network of approximately twenty boarding schools which had been established, beginning in 1734, to spread English, the work ethic, and Protestant Christianity among Catholic Irish children.[42] None of these schools had been open for more than eleven years, and no more than 250 students had graduated from them before the time of the rising.[43] Nonetheless, in part because the schools were self-consciously modern and designed to effect radical change in the population, they were studied intensely by eighteenth-century reformers and were widely praised.[44] After the Irish failed to rally to Charles Edward, the charter schools were given some of the credit for transforming and pacifying the people and keeping Ireland loyal.[45] It was far more credit than the educators deserved.

The founders of the Ireland's charter schools had sought to erect an educational system based loosely on the ideas of John Locke.[46] Proceeding on the premise that children acquire their fundamental character from their environment, the designers of the curriculum wanted the schools to operate year-round, twenty-four hours a day, to keep the students permanently away from their parents and home communities. Children who returned to their parents at night, or took employment too close to home after graduation, were considered vulnerable because their families and priests would have "too frequent access to them" and "draw them back to Popery."[47] The founders of the schools therefore sought to direct children away from their parents at the end of their school years "by transplanting the children either to other schools, or to services remote from the influences of their Popish relations."[48]

In 1749 Findlater urged Hardwicke to do more to establish educational institutions in the Highlands "in the manner of the charter schools in Ireland."[49] To investigate the practicality of the plan, he eventually sent the philosopher Fergusson to investigate the operation of the Irish schools.[50] Fergusson went and reported back that the teachers in the schools taught their students to read English, "with some arguments against Popery, but most of their time is employed in work. The oldest of the boys are employed in what they can do without doors. The younger boys knit stockings and the girls spin. When their time is out they are put apprentice to Protestant tradesmen, or to service under indentures." Fergusson indicated that he had heard "pretty good accounts" of the success of this program, even though the schoolmasters complained that it was difficult to recruit children, "because the Papists are averse to the design."[51]

The widespread praise for Ireland's charter schools after 1745 was coupled with condemnation of the ongoing educational and missionary efforts of the SSPCK. The Scottish society had concentrated on children since the time of its founding, and indeed, as early as 1729, before they knew of any similar efforts in Ireland, some members of the society proposed establishing working schools for young pupils.[52] Nonetheless, no money had been allocated to that effort, and after 1745 it was widely asserted that the missionaries operating in Scotland were employing antiquated methods. One writer argued that the trouble with the SSPCK schools was that the children "only go to them in the morning from the houses of their parents, and return home at night."[53] The Irish approach, it was commonly claimed, would work better. One of the most ambitious proposals for the Scottish Highlands involved a parliamentary outlay of £10,000 per year to subsidize "5,000 boys and girls with the masters necessary to teach them." The children would be kept in boarding schools from age eight to age fifteen, "without ever seeing their parents." During that time, "they could be taught to speak and read English, the principles of Christianity with a strong bias to the Whig and Protestant side, and the easy parts of manufacture and agriculture."[54] The SSPCK began raising funds to establish working schools in 1747 and opened several, beginning in 1750.[55] Some, following the Irish model, taught spinning, knitting, weaving, gardening, and fishing.[56]

Nonetheless, few of the schools prospered, and they failed, in part, because of resistance from parents. One school opened on the forfeited lands of the Earl of Lovat, for example, but closed within weeks after a rumor spread "that every mortal who came to that school were to be transported to his Majesty's plantations."[57] The historical significance of the reformers' educational program should not be measured solely by the number of boarding schools built or the effectiveness of those institutions in introducing children to Presbyterianism, industriousness, and the English language. Like the charter schools in Ireland, the projects launched to reshape the habits of children in the Highlands had an impact beyond the classroom, because they were widely discussed, and the commentary surrounding them engaged the minds of powerful men.

Of all of Cumberland's officers, none was more prepared to participate in the debate over policy in the Highlands than Bland. He was an Irish Protestant with an intense sympathy for the Presbyterian cause. When Bland was in Scotland he spent most of his time in Edinburgh, where he socialized with members of the country's Presbyterian political elite. Almost from the moment he arrived he began to visit Milton and the judge advocate for Scotland. They spent days in conversations that extended beyond simple questions of law. They consulted with each other on local politics, followed the news from the continent of Europe and Westminster, and speculated about the direction of policy in Highland Scotland.[58] Bland often approached these discussions with outward reticence. He was self-consciously diplomatic, and when talking with Scots he was careful to hide his low opinion of their country.[59] Furthermore, almost as a reflex, he denigrated his own education and expertise, though throughout his career he drew freely upon wide-ranging reading.[60]

Bland made it a habit, as he put it, to "call philosophy to my aid."[61] In the 1743 edition of his *Treatise of Military Discipline*, for example, he discussed the innate qualities that distinguished the English from the Dutch, differences he attributed to varying quantities of phlegm. The *Treatise* continued, however, with comments that foreshadowed Bland's later concerns, indicating that while "nature" might play a role in determining how easily a nation's soldiers could be trained, "art has the greatest share." Bland noted that the Dutch army contained soldiers "of different nations," and this suggested to him that natural inclinations could be altered, and native characteristics changed.[62] Bland employed similar reasoning in his contributions to the ministerial debate over the forfeited estates. His views were respected and his writings, particularly the essay he wrote with Milton, were credited with helping to steer the direction of policy.[63] In his position as commander in chief in Scotland, from 1747 to the summer of 1749, and again from 1753 to 1756, Bland helped determine how the government's new programs would be put into effect.[64] In his last years as commander in chief he also served on the commission overseeing the annexed estates, and he was its most active member until he departed from Scotland in 1756.[65]

Cumberland's other officers had less influence but they also, in general, took their role as reformers seriously and worked to become experts on the life of the Highlands. After Blakeney took command of the garrison at Inverness, he entered into consultations with the community's "sensible men," and within weeks he thought he had learned enough about the operation of the criminal courts to recommend significant changes in procedure.[66] By the summer of 1747, after approximately one year in his post, Blakeney believed that he was in a position to give advice to the cattle herders in the hills around Inverness on the precautions they should take to protect their herds.[67] Loudon, after nearly two years in the region, similarly claimed to have gained expertise on the life of Gaelic-speakers. He professed that initially he had been skeptical about the stories he had heard concerning clanship, and he claimed that he was surprised to learn from experience that some of them were true.[68] His friends came to believe that Loudon was uniquely qualified to analyze the conditions of life in the Highlands and to negotiate with local leaders to effectuate reforms. As the Earl of Stair put it, "your apprenticeage has been a little rude, but now that it is over, the knowledge that you must have acquired in the north, and the different people that inhabit that country, and of their different interests, may be of great use to the public."[69] Loudon's career in the Highlands was cut short, however, in part because some critics thought that he had frater-nized too closely with clan leaders, and particularly that he was consort-ing with Jacobites. Bland weathered similar criticism. According to Wolfe, Bland was reputed to be "a good deal under" Scottish influence in the late 1740s.[70]

Wolfe, who returned to Scotland after more than a year's absence in 1748, had perhaps the darkest view of the country of any of Cumber-land's officers. He considered Presbyterians tedious, and even in the Lowlands of southern Scotland he described the inhabitants as primi-tives who did not know how to run farms efficiently, restrain their appe-tite for liquor, or behave themselves in polite society.[71] The Highlanders, from his perspective, were only worse.[72] When Wolfe left Scotland for the last time in 1753, he wrote to his father, "A mile on this side the river that divides England from Scotland one begins to perceive the differ-ence that labor and industry can make upon the face of a country. The soil is much the same for some space either north or south, but the fences, enclosures, and agriculture are not at all alike. The English are clean and laborious, and the Scotch excessively dirty and lazy."[73]

Unfortunately, perhaps, from Wolfe's point of view, the soldiers' mis-sion in the aftermath of 1745 was not to make all Scotland function like England. Their task was somewhat less ambitious than that. The army had orders to maintain security, aid in law enforcement, rebuild roads and military infrastructure, and enforce the parliamentary program for social reform. Some aspects of that reform program, particularly those related to religious life, affected all of Scotland. Nonetheless, the most ambitious new projects centered only on the Highlands and Western Islands, where the ministry hoped to introduce fundamental changes in the landscape and economy and, in the process, transform the character of the people.

From Bland's perspective, when he thought about his responsibilities in detail, one of the most urgent tasks facing the army was strengthening the transportation system. This was necessary to integrate the Highlands into British society and to facilitate troop movements in the event of a crisis. Working with the magistrates of Stirling, he helped finance the reconstruction of the bridge over the River Forth that had been destroyed on Blakeney's orders in 1746.[74] He also revived and expanded General Wade's plans to build roads and bridges across the extent of the Highlands.[75] Bland deployed work-gangs to survey, clear and build the roads, beginning in the summer of 1748.[76] After his arrival in the High-lands, Wolfe oversaw some of these crews.[77] In May 1749 Wolfe dis-patched three hundred soldiers, including men trained as pavers, carpenters, smiths, miners, and bricklayers, for construction work.[78]

One reason the army was engaged in this task was to make it easier to respond to emergencies and send men to the Western Islands. In 1747, around the time that Bland took command of the troops in Scotland, there were rumors that the French were sending Catholic priests and other emissaries into the islands and the adjacent coasts with promises that France would aid the Highlanders in a new insurrection.[79] Cumberland doubted that the Jacobites would trust the French to lead them to victory after what had happened in 1746, but nonetheless the reports continued to circulate, and in response to them, Bland developed an elaborate system of patrols. Initially he sent companies of the government's Highland troops to the region, and later he employed crews in small vessels to ply the coastal waters of western Scotland.[80] In addition to searching for smugglers and French agents, these units had orders to "seize all the Popish priests they can meet with."[81]

The leaders of the military, with the support of the ministry and much of the Scottish legal establishment, insisted that the regulation of Scotland's religious life was a security issue. Six weeks after his arrival in Edinburgh, Bland sent a circular letter to his subordinate officers declaring that nonjuring Episcopalian and Catholic congregations were "the source and nursery of all the evils that fall on this land."[82] The illegal churches, he argued, instilled "into the minds of the people Popish principles, contempt of the law, and disobedience to his Majesty's mild and merciful government."[83] One year later, further down the chain of command, Wolfe made a similar speech to his men.[84] A new statute enacted in 1746 had stipulated that the only Episcopalian clergymen allowed to officiate in Scotland would be those ordained by English or Irish bishops, and that the pastors had to pray for George II at every service.[85] Bland ordered soldiers to investigate and help prosecute clergymen who violated the law. He sent troops to religious observances, but even on the rare occasions when the men gained entry, they often found it difficult to gather evidence. The members of the congregation were seldom willing to assist in any prosecutions, and the soldiers had little way of telling whether the pastors had the right kind of ordination or whether they had spoken the requisite prayers for the well-being of the king.[86]

The military men had an equally frustrating time trying to enforce those provisions in the Disarming Act that banned the wearing of tartan kilts. Wolfe had just arrived in Scotland when the law first went into effect.[87] He ordered his troops to seize any man wearing prohibited plaid and carry the offender directly to the civil magistrates for prosecution. Anticipating difficulties in the presentation of evidence and the interpretation of the law, Wolfe told his soldiers not to allow any violators to change their clothes before they appeared before the court.[88] Wolfe's men seized a large number of men, so many in fact that the civilian authorities complained that they could not afford to feed the prisoners the soldiers brought to them.[89] Soon difficulties arose concerning definitions. One Highlander arrested for wearing a kilt protested that the loose-fitting plaid garment he was wearing was a tunic and therefore not covered by the statute. Exhibiting an impressive familiarity with criminal procedure, he insisted that penal statutes had to be strictly construed.[90] Another adopted a similar but even more daring stance, protesting that the garment he was wearing was a "woman's petticoat."[91] One man said that he had been arrested wearing a blanket.[92] A report from 1749 described "the variety and oddity of the dresses they [the Highlanders] have chosen, some having made their plaids into something resembling nightgowns, others like cloaks or great coat."[93] Plaid trousers became a particular concern of the British authorities in 1749.[94]

While they sought to regulate Scotland's religious life and struggled over the definition of the word "plaid," the soldiers in the Highlands were engaged in a variety of other law enforcement activities. Considerable time and resources were invested in the prosecution of thieves.[95] The protection of livestock, in particular, was made an urgent priority. Bland asserted that Highlanders felt free to seize cattle because they believed "that all creatures that live on grass ought to be in common, and therefore think it no crime."[96] In a typically grand pronouncement, he declared that "suppressing theft" was "the foundation of the whole reformation" the government hoped to achieve in the Highlands, "for when people can't steal, they will be under a necessity of supporting themselves and families by their own labour."[97]

Participating in law enforcement required the soldiers to locate and recruit cooperative witnesses and work effectively with the officers of the local courts. Often the task was too difficult for them. Blakeney, for example, offered rewards for information and promised confidentiality to informants, but he declared that he had been "thwarted in everything" by the local magistrates.[98] Bland, by contrast, had good relations with prominent Scottish lawyers in Edinburgh, but even he suspected that no one in the Highlands wanted to prosecute illicit Episcopalians. On the advice of Milton and others, in December 1747 Bland issued a general threat that if the magistrates failed to enforce the new statutes, he might order his troops to take the law into their own hands and bypass the civilian authorities.[99] On a small scale, that is what Wolfe did. In cases where the civil magistrates refused to cooperate with him, he authorized his men to hold prisoners until other, more compliant judges could be found.[100]

Several factors contributed to tension between the military and Scotland's judicial authorities. The officers and the magistrates had contrasting training and inclinations, and the military men were often frustrated by the formalities of the criminal law. The magistrates complained that they were short of resources. Highland Scotland was impoverished, still recovering from insurrection, and the new statutory regulations were expensive to enforce. There was no money to bring witnesses to court, and holding prisoners in jail cost more than some jurisdictions could afford.[101] There were also disagreements over substantive issues. At least one sheriff refused to prosecute a man for wearing a plaid blanket because he did not believe that it had been Parliament's intent to "oppress the poor."[102]

Though there were ways to interpret these controversies without reference to general tension between the soldiers and the people of the country they patrolled, cultural animosity and chauvinism made it difficult for the army to cooperate effectively with civilian officials. Even Bland, with all his Scottish friends, in unguarded moments denigrated the Scots, and he was particularly harsh in his comments about Gaelic-speakers. In reference to the Highlanders, he complained in the autumn of 1748 that it was "ridiculous to talk of law to a parcel of savages, who never observed any but lived at large, preying on everything that came their way like many lions and tigers."[103] Similar sentiments were expressed by men at all ranks of the British army.

On April 16, 1750, soldiers observed the anniversary of the Battle of Culloden by building a bonfire in the center of Inverness. Some went to the river with fireworks and set off rockets from the bridge. For at least some of the men, the celebration was mixed with anger. A group of three walked up a street from the river, and one of them hurled a rock through a window. A neighbor seized the stone-thrower, expecting the man to be punished, but an alarm reached the rest of the soldiers and a group of approximately twenty, armed with muskets and bayonets, came to the rescue. They marched to the house with the broken window and, using the butts of their weapons and throwing more stones, systematically broke the rest of the windows. In the midst of the excitement the original stone-thrower escaped. At least one of the company suggested that they should all go to supper and then return to break every window in town. In the end the troops were not nearly so comprehensive, but at least three houses were damaged that night.[104]

Compared to the violence the men were commemorating, this was a minor incident. Nonetheless, it reflected ongoing animosity and the power of memory to disturb the lives of soldiers and civilians alike. There were similar altercations in scattered sections of Scotland in the decade following Charles Edward's defeat. On occasion fights erupted after the troops seized property by asserting their military authority.[105] Often, resentful soldiers simply committed theft.[106] More than once, patrols committed daylight attacks on women, sometimes culminating in gang rape.[107] Those accused of assaulting members of the local community were usually tried before courts martial, but at least two of the rapists were tried and convicted in local criminal courts.[108] In other instances, including an attack committed by soldiers in Wolfe's regiment in which several women were assaulted by both soldiers and civilian men, no prosecutions occurred.[109] From the perspective of the Scots, the men of the army repeatedly exhibited what the council of Inverness called "manifest contempt of the law of the land."[110]

In the late 1740s and early 1750s, Highlanders and other Scots with grievances against the army appealed repeatedly to the law. In some parts of the Highlands they began making preparations for litigation as early as June 1746, when Cumberland's army was still at its most aggressive in the field. An agent to one landlord whose estate was attacked by the government's troops advised the tenants to stay in their houses when the soldiers approached them. He told them to "make no opposition, but let them do as they would, only to take notice who were the officers, and what their behavior." The tenants were also advised to keep a record of the actions of the enlisted men. The agent wanted the tenants to bring this information to him, so that he could have "an exact account of all" after the army left the country.[111]

Parliament that spring had passed a bill indemnifying the soldiers for their actions suppressing the rising, but that law did not effectively preclude all suits.[112] From 1746 on, several soldiers and officers faced legal actions demanding the restoration of improperly seized property.[113] In the winter of 1747 a close advisor to Cumberland declared that if the lawsuits persisted, "very few officers" who had served under him in 1746 would "dare to appear" in the Highlands.[114] One captain was summoned to court repeatedly from February 1747 through January 1751 over a demand that he return a misappropriated horse.[115] That horse had been seized, allegedly, in 1745. Other cases arose from actions the soldiers had taken after the rising had been defeated. In 1748 several officers from the garrison in Stirling were sued for battery after a fight in a public house. According to the officers, they had been drinking by themselves when they overheard a group of men in the next room making some "most indecent expressions toward his Majesty." The officers rose from their seats and, by their own confession, beat the men in the adjoining room. One of those beaten brought suit against them. The officers countersued, but before the case came to trial the matter was settled, though not very amicably.[116] Most of these cases were defeated by procedural means. By filing motions and interlocutory appeals, the defendants could delay trials for years.[117]

Though they generally ended inconclusively, these lawsuits had political significance. Cumberland and his associates interpreted them as evidence that Scotland's judicial authorities leaned "too much," in Bland's words, "to the country side against the military."[118] In 1752 Cumberland and his supporters took this grievance to the ministry and incorporated it into a wide-ranging protest against the direction of government policy in the Highlands.[119] They argued that military officers in Scotland should be given commissions as justices of the peace and that greater efforts should be made to prevent former Jacobites from purchasing, leasing, or otherwise profiting from the forfeited estates. They claimed generally that Jacobites were favored by the civilian administrators of Scotland.[120]

By the time these allegations reached Whitehall, Cumberland's popularity in England had declined. In the immediate aftermath of Culloden he had been a hero.[121] For at least two years, public acclaim had reinforced Cumberland's political power, and the most influential members of the ministry, Newcastle particularly, sought out his support and advice. Nonetheless, beginning in 1748 Cumberland's position began to deteriorate. First he fell out with Newcastle.[122] Then the conclusion of a peace treaty with France lessened public support for military expenditure and revived a long-running debate in British politics over the maintenance of professional land forces in times of peace. After the wars of the preceding decade, there was a consensus in favor of maintaining a "standing army." Rather than calling for full demobilization, those who worried about the power of the military focused much of their anxiety on Cumberland and his personal authority over the officers and troops. In 1748 Cumberland entered into a divisive political debate with his older brother, Prince Frederick, over the power of military courts to discipline demobilized officers. He won the argument, but at considerable political cost.[123]

During the process of demobilization Cumberland asked to retain command of a regiment of dragoons. Henry Pelham, who along with his brother Newcastle dominated the ministry, opposed him, warning "in the strongest light, the ill consequences" of the proposal. Pelham hinted that Cumberland's regiment would be seen as an independent force unaccountable to Parliament. He suggested that if Cumberland insisted on keeping the unit he might jeopardize the public standing of the royal family.[124] The two men eventually secured a compromise on this issue. Cumberland gave up his regiment in exchange for other provisions strengthening the peacetime army. Specifically, Pelham agreed to the stationing of 12,000 soldiers in Ireland.[125] Cumberland also gained Pelham's approval for stationing approximately 2,500 troops each in Gibraltar and Minorca.[126] Nonetheless, even after these agreements were reached, Pelham continued to worry about Cumberland's militaristic public image and the damage it might do to the dynasty. In a letter to his brother in the summer of 1750 he indicated that Britain had to avoid another war with France because, thanks in part to Cumberland, a Jacobite rising in 1750 might do better than the one in 1745. "I fear this country is not so well disposed to some branches of our royal family as they were upon the late rebellion," he declared. Cumberland, according to Pelham, had not conducted himself "prudently, with regard to the temper of this country, and constitution."[127]

Pelham's innuendo would be repeated, in stronger language, in the coming months. In 1751 Parliament debated charges of libel stemming from a broadside entitled "Constitutional Queries, earnestly recommended to the serious consideration of every Briton," which had been circulated among members of the House of Commons and the Lords, and outside Parliament through the cities of London and Westminster. Implicitly it compared Cumberland to Cromwell and Richard III and warned that his experience in Scotland had inured him to exercising dictatorial power. Cumberland might seize the throne by military force, the writer claimed, despite his brother's superior claim to succession. The Lords condemned the broadside and ordered it burned by the common hangman.[128] Later that year Prince Frederick died, and Pelham and Newcastle reacted in a way that almost suggested that they believed the allegations contained in the scandalous broadside. They ushered through Parliament a bill that barred Cumberland from becoming regent, should Frederick's son George (the future George III) ascend to the throne underage.[129]

Cumberland was still recovering from these setbacks when he raised his objections to government policy in the Highlands. His immediate concerns involved Scottish politics. He wanted to limit the power of the Highlands' aristocrats, and he was particularly worried about the leader of the Campbells, the Duke of Argyll, whom he saw as a rival power in the north and a representative of the traditions of clanship.[130] But Cumberland was also concerned to protect his reputation and defend the army as an institution. Cumberland's supporters, in their submissions to the ministry, emphasized the military's effectiveness as a force for order in a chaotic world. They asserted that the military presence in the Highlands had made private property secure. The construction of roads and bridges had promoted commerce. The soldiers had also spent thousands of pounds of their own money in the region, encouraging growth in the local economy. In more general terms, the men had had a good influence on their neighbors. "Mixing with the soldiery in the service civilizes the rude inhabitants." Indeed, at least one writer claimed that the presence of army had done more to change the Highlanders than all the legislation passed by Parliament since 1745.[131]

These submissions reflected views long expressed by Cumberland's high officers, nearly all of whom believed in the value of their mission in Scotland. Furthermore, with the possible exception of Blakeney, all of them, almost in spite of themselves, found ways to find pleasure in the northern country. When he was in Edinburgh Bland attended the meetings of the "Revolution Club," where he met with fellow Whigs and Presbyterians, drank, traded gossip, and joked about the state of affairs in the Highlands.[132] Even Wolfe, whose correspondence is littered with sneering commentary about the people of Scotland, obtained invitations to dances in the Highlands where he enjoyed the company, so he claimed, of the daughter of a Jacobite chief.[133] Nonetheless, Bland, Wolfe, and many of the others believed that their talents could be usefully employed elsewhere and would have preferred to be posted outside Scotland. Bland, who was aging, sought an assignment that would require less travel. Wolfe, by contrast, aspired to a more exotic posting overseas.[134] Though it could not answer all their expectations, Gibraltar seemed to offer what both men wanted. Wolfe at one time dreamed of going there, or to Minorca.[135] Bland, in 1749, actually went.[136] Other officers serving in Scotland were transferred to America, specifically to Nova Scotia. While in Scotland, Wolfe maintained correspondence with fellow officers in Gibraltar and Nova Scotia; his letters to the North American colony, in particular, reveal much about his understanding of the imperial project and its relationship to the army's task in the Scottish Highlands.

Nova Scotia and neighboring Cape Breton Island held the attention of much of Britain in the late 1740s. In 1745, just before Charles Edward landed in Scotland, a body of New England troops had seized the French fort of Louisbourg on Cape Breton Island. Thereafter, for the duration of Britain's war with France, a great deal of diplomatic and military maneuvering had centered on France's desire to get Louisbourg back. In Scotland, both the government's soldiers and the Jacobites followed these events closely, because they believed that their own fortunes might be at stake. In the counsels of the French ministry in the winter of 1745–46, the project of retaking Louisbourg competed against proposals to assist the Jacobites in Britain.[137] A disastrous, failed effort to retake the American fortress in the summer of 1746 employed resources that France might have otherwise sent to aid Charles Edward. When Scotland's Jacobites learned that a convoy had sailed from France, they believed that it was headed straight north to help them. According to one account, they waited "several weeks" with "extreme impatience" before learning, to their disappointment, that the ships were headed across the Atlantic.[138] The French failed to retake Louisbourg militarily but they ultimately regained it through diplomacy. Under the terms of the peace treaty of 1748 the American fortress was returned to France.

Soon thereafter the British ministry announced a plan to establish a new, fortified town on the Atlantic coast of Nova Scotia, to rival Louis-bourg. Halifax, the new stronghold, would give the British army a large permanent garrison in the region, and an administrative role in a settlement scheme that was similar to, and had been influenced by, the government's efforts to bring order and civility to the Scottish Highlands. Nova Scotia, at the time, was inhabited primarily by the native Mi'kmaq bands, and by the French-speaking Catholic Acadians. In 1748 some policy makers had recommended sending Highlanders to live in Nova Scotia, and not just as a way to export the "Highland problem" to America. They had also intended to send the government's reform program as well. Emphasizing the allegedly salutary effects of intermingling distinct populations, the Duke of Bedford and others argued that both the Highlanders and the Acadians could be transformed into useful and loyal British subjects, if they were "intermixed" and made part of a cosmopolitan society.[139] Even after the idea of transporting Highlanders was abandoned, Cumberland and his allies in the ministry remained committed to bringing immigrants into Nova Scotia to surround and assimilate the local French-speaking population. They faced opposition. Henry Pelham in particular opposed the project, thinking it precipitous and unnecessarily provocative toward the French.[140] Nonetheless, in 1749 Parliament allocated £40,000 for the fortification and settlement of Nova Scotia, an unprecedented sum.[141]

Wolfe had just returned to Scotland when this project was announced. His immediate commanding officer, Edward Cornwallis, was chosen to serve as governor of Nova Scotia.[142] Cumberland visited Scotland in the spring of 1749 to meet with Cornwallis, discuss Nova Scotia, and oversee the division of Cornwallis's troops.[143] Cumberland gave Wolfe command of Cornwallis's regiment in Scotland, but ordered several of the regiment's officers to travel with their old commander to America. In a letter to a friend who had been sent away to Nova Scotia, Wolfe confidently declared that the British army's presence would benefit the Acadians. "Within the influence of our happy government," he insisted, "all nations are in security." The British, he asserted, could harm no one because "A free people cannot oppress." He did not discuss the details of the government's project across the ocean, but he told his friend that he should read the recently published work of Montesquieu, *L'esprit des lois*. Wolfe wrote, "It is a piece of writing that would be of great use where you are."[144]

In *L'esprit des lois* Montesquieu presented a complex analysis of cultural development, with recommendations for governing foreign lands. His premise was that each society's system of governance reflects the totality of its historical and environmental circumstances. Because each nation experiences distinctive challenges and responds to them in accordance with its own traditions, legal systems must vary around the world in order to be viable. Montesquieu reveled in the complexity of human affairs, and as a result he did not provide universal, programmatic solutions to the problem of conquest or the governance of culturally distinct peoples. Nonetheless, his work contained a general model for successful conquest, one suggesting that vanquished peoples should be subservient only temporarily and gradually brought to a position of full equality with their conquerors through cultural assimilation. "When, after a certain length of time, all the parts of the conquering state are bound to those of the conquered state by customs, marriage, laws, associations, and a certain conformity of spirit, servitude should cease."[145] Montesquieu emphasized the role of marriage in this process: "Nothing strengthens a conquest more than unions by marriage between two peoples."[146] Almost since the moment of its publication, Montesquieu's work had captured the imagination of reformers in the Scottish Highlands.[147] Wolfe's decision to recommend the book to his friend in Nova Scotia reflects a more general spread of ideas from Scotland to the colonies following the 1745 rising.

Wolfe initially viewed the settlement and fortification of Nova Scotia as part of a larger campaign, which he described as "the propagation of freedom and truth."[148] But as the years passed and the inhabitants of the colony resisted assimilation, he became increasingly disillusioned with the effort. His friend, in the end, was miserable in Nova Scotia, and scared. By 1751 Wolfe was commiserating with him. "Yours is now the dirtiest as well as the most insignificant and unpleasant branch of military operations; no room for courage or skill to exert itself, no hope of ending it by a decisive blow, and a perpetual danger of assassination."[149] When, after many petitions, his friend was reassigned to a post back in Scotland, Wolfe described it as an escape, and he later wrote that in comparison with Nova Scotia, the Scottish Highlands were a paradise.[150] Wolfe had not seen Nova Scotia when he wrote those words. He would be sent there, however, at a pivotal moment in the Seven Years' War, in 1758.

The actions of Cumberland's soldiers in North America will be discussed in more detail in Chapter 6. Especially in Nova Scotia, but also during Wolfe's drive to Quebec in 1759, the army's challenges, and its response to them, resembled its previous mission in Scotland, though the sequence of policy shifts was reversed. Initially, at least in Nova Scotia, Cumberland's officers believed that they could civilize the French-speaking Catholics and make them loyal to the British crown. When that project faltered they faced an administrative quandary over the use of military force and the applicability of the criminal law. They called various groups rebels and savages, and the level of violence escalated in part as result of their confusion over the applicability of rules. Scottish Highlanders played a new role in North America during those campaigns, one that helped alter the way the rest of Britain thought about them.[151] By the time Wolfe arrived in North America, the contrast he had drawn between Nova Scotia and the Highlands, suggesting that the Highlands were a paradise by comparison, had been repeatedly and forcefully delineated in the press. The Highlanders were also widely contrasted with North America's native peoples. In the context of America, it seemed, the Gaelic-speakers were not savage at all, at least not when compared to the New World's natives.[152] By 1758, many of Cumberland's officers had become skeptical of the civilizing mission as it applied to the Catholic French colonists and native peoples of North America. Yet they still believed in the efficacy of their mission in Scotland.

Several factors contributed to the sense that Scotland's Gaelic-speakers, as a group, no longer constituted a threat. The process was a gradual one extending over many years, and it cannot be dated precisely. The Highlanders seemed less dangerous in part because Jacobitism as a political movement was on the decline. In the immediate aftermath of defeat, the exiled Stuart family splintered, and Charles Edward managed to antagonize most of his French supporters.[153] Over the next several years he traveled Europe seeking new allies, but with little success. In the 1750s he received new overtures from France. Proposals circulated within the French ministry to place him in command of the expedition to Minorca in 1756, and in the winter of 1758–59 the ministers discussed bringing him to Britain again with a large invasion force. As an alternative it was also briefly suggested that he might lead a French expedition against the British colonies in North America.[154] Nonetheless, in 1756 and again in 1759, the deliberations foundered when Charles Edward himself began to participate in the debate. He could not bring himself to trust the French, and without them or any other powerful allies to work with, he was in no position to take action alone. The Jacobites in general lost their sense of direction. They became a lost cause.

In the meantime, stories emanating from the Highlands suggested that elements of the government's program were working. The SSPCK claimed conversions to Presbyterianism.[155] Soldiers boasted that the Highlands were secure.[156] Travelers started coming to the region in greater numbers, in part to seek out reminders of the legendary, bygone heyday of the clans. Eventually their writings would engulf the Highlands in a cloud of romantic myth.[157] On a more human level, the leaders of Highland society were accommodating themselves to a new political reality. For many this meant developing a working relationship with the officers of Cumberland's army. It was a difficult process, and no one struggled harder, or faced the intrinsic challenges more directly, than Margaret MacDonald, the widow of Alexander MacDonald of Sleat.

Alexander MacDonald, the friend of the government, died in November 1746, leaving his estate to his wife Margaret, who in the previous summer had helped conceal Charles Edward (inadvertently or not) during his flight from Cumberland's army.[158] Margaret always professed innocence, but she could never dispel the suspicion of Jacobitism. She escaped prosecution, thanks in large part to the support she received from Loudon and several other of her husband's friends.[159] Nonetheless, her position became more perilous after the death of her husband. She was then left alone with two small boys, the eldest of whom, James, was four years old.[160] By the spring of 1747 Cumberland had decided that James, as Alexander MacDonald's heir and the possible future leader of a powerful clan, should be educated in England.[161] Margaret MacDonald disagreed, and she resisted the authorities' efforts to take her son south for the next nine years.

In 1754 Bland made it a special project to render the Isle of Skye "so disagreeable" to Margaret MacDonald that "she would be glad to quit it." He suspected that she was still a Jacobite, and his suspicions seemed confirmed after his soldiers arrested the manager of her estate for multiple violations of the Disarming Act. Shortly after that arrest Bland sent fifty men to patrol the island in the vicinity of the MacDonald home. Terrified of the troops, Margaret MacDonald wrote to Bland asking "for God's sake that some assistance might be sent to her to convey her and her son out of the Isle of Skye." Bland was delighted by the request, because, as he put it, "This was the very point I aimed at."[162] Soon thereafter Bland launched an effort to get Margaret MacDonald's son, the twelve-year-old James, transported out of Scotland altogether. Life in Skye, Bland insisted, had instilled "Jacobite principles" in the boy and had given him a "high, but weak, notion of clanship and his own importance." Bland thought that if James were educated in England he might become a good influence on Skye. "Brought up in right Protestant principles," James might "strengthen his Majesty's interest in those remote parts of the Highlands, and boot out Jacobitism from amongst his numerous clan."[163] Margaret MacDonald had legal custody of the boy, but with soldiers on her land and her overseer in jail, she was in a poor position to bargain. After weeks of pleading she agreed that her son could be educated in England.[164] James MacDonald traveled south with his mother, attended Eton, grew up, proceeded to Oxford, and then toured Europe. He spent part of his continental tour in the company of Adam Smith, and with Smith in Paris he met the philosopher David Hume. In short, though he retained his Scottish identity, he gained a better education than either Cumberland or Bland had ever imagined for him, and he integrated himself quite effectively into Britain's social and intellectual elite.[165]

Bland's confrontation with Margaret MacDonald reflected his preoccupations, and those of most of the reformers in the Highlands, in the early 1750s. Bland was worried about the region's ancient social hierarchy, which, he believed, made clan leaders arrogant, powerful, and potentially disloyal to the crown. He thought that the ultimate solution to the problem lay in education, and he took it for granted that children absorbed their political values from their social environment and the company they kept. The strategy Bland adopted in James's case was a scaled-down version of his program for the Highlands as a whole. He used all the coercive power at his disposal to encourage migration, travel, and social mixing, with the ultimate aim of bringing James, and the whole of his community, closer to the English.

Though James died young, in Italy at the age of twenty-six, his education serves as a reminder of the mixed results of the reformers' schemes. Certainly Bland does not deserve all the credit for the young man's career, but in James's case, and in Scotland as a whole, the army had a role to play in bringing the Highlanders more fully into the cosmopolitan world. This was achieved in part through compromise. In the end the reformers did not undermine aristocracy in the Highlands or make anyone forget their names. Rather than eliminating the cultural distinctiveness of the region, flattening its social hierarchy, or making the local economy run on a simple cash basis, the government's program served to guarantee the loyalty of the social elite that was already there. Eventually that elite, in cooperation with the government, would help send thousands of less privileged Scottish Highlanders to North America.

*   *   *

Even before large numbers of Highland soldiers were deployed in America, the influence of the government's policies in the Highlands extended well beyond the region. Reports on the reform efforts spread. In various parts of the British Empire, many commentators were eager for news from Scotland. One man who was particularly interested in developments in the Highlands was William Douglass, the controversial Scottish-born doctor who had lived in Massachusetts for twenty years.

Douglass developed his own idiosyncratic theories, based on his reading, his personal experience, and the vague reports he received from Scotland. He classified Highlanders as "sylvestres, wild people like our American Indians" and suggested that the British government, in its response to the 1745 rising, might have learned from the example of

Massachusetts in its policies in the aftermath of the seventeenth-century "Pequot war."[166] After killing a large part of the population, and selling others, including children, into slavery in Bermuda, the New England colonists had agreed to a cessation of hostilities with the remaining Pequot only "upon condition of their abandoning their name and country." Douglass suggested, "Perhaps some expedient of this nature might be used with regard to some of the incorrigible clans of Highlanders in the northern and western parts of Scotland."[167]

While Douglass believed that the British government might learn from the New Englanders' example, he also suggested that the American colonists might learn from the SSPCK. He was a strong supporter of the society and paid attention to its activities.[168] Douglass was not entirely well informed, but he asserted that the missionary organization ran 136 schools in Scotland in 1750 and maintained approximately 7,000 pupils.[169] Believing that the society had adopted the Irish "charter school" system of education, he commended its "reading and working" schools as models for a pedagogical program that might be applied for the education of North American colonists and native people alike. He thought that the schools in America should be overseen by Church of England schoolmasters, but otherwise his proposed educational program was identical to that allegedly pursued in Scotland. "In the incorporated charitable schools of Scotland and Ireland," he wrote, "they only regard the rising generation, where without any strained allegory it may be called the sowing the seeds of Christianity, loyalty, and industry. The . . . working schools have lately been attended with great success and benefit to the countries: that is reading and writing being required, the boys are sent to sea, to husbandry, and other laborious trades, the girls to spinning and other services with peculiar restrictions."[170]

Douglass presented these ideas in a mammoth, rambling two-volume history of the British Empire. In the same work, in his speculations about the empire's future, he theorized further about the role of education in imperial expansion. Douglass was worried that the colonies might be acquiring territory too rapidly and attempting to absorb too many distinct cultures into a single polity.[171] These concerns led him to advance a detailed plan for assimilating foreigners by reeducating children through a program that drew upon ideas similar to those he believed animated the work of the Irish charter schools and their SSPCK counterparts.[172] Douglass argued that any immigrants in the colonies who did not speak English, along with the members of any conquered populations, should be dispersed and prevented from recongregating in "separate districts." They "ought to be intermixed with the British settlers," he declared, and "English schools only allowed for the education of their children." Borrowing a phrase from Defoe, he asserted that such a policy would make all of the pupils "true born Englishmen."[173] Douglass cited two cases showing what he called "the bad effects of not observing this regulation." In Nova Scotia the Acadians had stayed French and Catholic, and in New York (the old Dutch colony of New Netherland), the Dutch were still Dutch. At least Douglass thought so.[174]

Douglass participated in the debate over the fate of the Acadians in Nova Scotia, and his works were cited by Benjamin Franklin during the controversy over the future of French Canada.[175] His writings reflected a wider trend. The ongoing effort to reform the lives of the Scottish Highlanders affected the thoughts of a diverse set of colonists, commentators, and officials who hoped to transform the lives of other groups, both in North America and in the Mediterranean. The project of assimilating foreigners, Catholics, and alleged barbarians was embraced by many imperialists and did not belong exclusively to the men of Cumberland's army. Nonetheless, in the 1750s the political fortunes of Cumberland, and the future of such efforts, were closely linked.

Chapter 5

Cumberland's Army in the Mediterranean

In the autumn of 1748, as he was completing his first full year as commander in chief of the land forces in Scotland, Bland began suffering "a frequent stoppage of urine" that made riding horses, or even traveling in carriages, painful to him. His duties required him to traverse great distances, sometimes on rough roads, and by November his disorder had become so severe that performing his responsibilities became an ordeal. Seeking a command "that would not be attended with much bodily labor," he asked to be appointed governor of Gibraltar.[1] In the 1740s and early 1750s it was rare for British soldiers to believe that a posting in the Mediterranean would improve the material circumstances of their lives in the short run, and Bland was almost unique in thinking that the small size of Gibraltar was a positive advantage. When Bland arrived, the only way in or out of the post was by water, and when the winds blew west, months could pass between the arrival of ships from Britain.[2] Gibraltar, along with Britain's other outpost in the Mediterranean, the island of Minorca, was an isolated place. Thousands of soldiers lived in each post, and for decades they had suffered from disease, boredom, and drink in almost perfect obscurity.[3] At the end of the War of the Austrian Succession, the two outposts acquired new political significance, however. Bland, despite his age and ill health, was proud of the appointment.[4] Blakeney, who in 1748 was appointed lieutenant governor of Minorca, believed so strongly in the importance of the assignment that at one critical moment he told a group of assembled islanders that he had been chosen for his office by God.

Along with the Scottish Highlands and Nova Scotia, Gibraltar and Minorca were testing grounds for the proposition that the British army could serve as a civilizing influence and, with the help of civilian settlers, transform the character of culturally distinctive, marginal places. The inhabitants of Gibraltar included Genoese Italians, Greeks, and Sephardic Jews. Most of the people of Minorca were Catalan-speaking Catholics, but the island was home to a small, politically significant immigrant community of Orthodox Greeks. During the 1740s there had been controversy over Britain's failure to encourage more Protestant immigration into its Mediterranean possessions, or to convert the inhabitants to Protestantism.[5] Bland declared in 1751 that if Gibraltar had been properly governed since its conquest, every house in the enclave "would have come into the possession of Protestants by this time."[6]

After Bland and Blakeney arrived, the army's administration of Gibraltar and Minorca became a test of Cumberland's political influence and the viability of his approach to governance and reform. The task of governing the outposts posed many of the same challenges that had confronted the army in the Scottish Highlands. Both Bland and Blakeney thought that they were leading transitional, military governments, and they hoped to implement reforms that would eventually alter the religious inclinations and legal status of the inhabitants of their territories. Gibraltar, according to Bland, had no constitutional structure of government and no institutions that he could have deferred to if he had wanted to share power. Blakeney, for his part, thought the islanders of Minorca were arrogant, gullible, and parochially minded, and that as lieutenant governor he was struggling against irrational traditions and the international reach of the Catholic Church.[7] Both governors promoted commerce, immigration, and legal reform as ways to bring their outposts more fully into the cosmopolitan, British-imperial world. On Minorca, Blakeney also concentrated much of his energy on battling the islanders' way of educating their children. To the greatest extent possible, he wanted to draw Minoroca's next generation away from the influence of Catholic friars and priests.

Neither Bland nor Blakeney drew direct comparisons between the Mediterranean and Scotland, however, in part because of the ominous position of Africa in their thoughts. Both governors associated Africa with an array of evils, including ignorance, political instability, violence, greed, and disease. Service in the Mediterranean gave the two men a sharpened sense that Europe as a whole was a distinct, coherent place, fundamentally different from North Africa. Bland, in particular, began to praise the common heritage and disposition of all Europeans. He was unable to reconcile this way of thinking with his contempt for Scottish Highlanders; as a result, when he wrote about Europe as a continent, he simply failed to mention the Scottish Highlands.[8] Forgetting the Highlanders was made easier for him by the general absence of Highland soldiers in the Mediterranean garrisons.

While Bland and Blakeney seldom related their activities in the Mediterranean to the army's administrative role in Scotland, others did. At least one commentator cited precedents from Scottish history as a guide for the formulation of policy on Minorca, and another went so far as to suggest that the islanders themselves were descended from ancient Celts.[9] This theory was repeated, with greater poignancy, after a French expeditionary force landed on Minorca in 1756.[10] The Minorcans, in general, exhibited little zeal for George II on that occasion. It seemed that they had not been raised to value their allegiance to the British crown.

From the time of Blakeney's arrival on Minorca, some ministers and military men in Britain questioned the utility, or even the propriety, of trying to alter the islanders' institutions or character. The Admiralty, in general, was among the skeptics and represented a rival military service capable of performing many of the duties that the army had assumed in the Mediterranean. Almost from the moment Bland and Blakeney arrived at their posts, the Admiralty objected to several elements of their reformist schemes.[11]

The Mediterranean garrisons figured prominently in debates over the powers of the British army. For decades, Gibraltar and Minorca had functioned as places where the government could warehouse troops outside the view of opposition politicians. They continued in that capacity after 1748, but as part of his effort to centralize authority and make the army more adaptable and efficient, Cumberland introduced a new system of rotation. Soldiers were sent south much more frequently, if only on a temporary basis. Cumberland hoped to use Gibraltar, in particular, as a place to discipline and train fighting men. Cumberland's opponents described Gibraltar as a place of authoritarian rule, dissipation, and corruption, while Cumberland and Bland struggled to make it operate as a model of efficiency.

The political conflict that erupted in Britain after France attacked and seized Minorca in 1756 became, in part, an argument over the officers' pretensions. While the land forces suffered less than the navy did as a direct result of that controversy, the disturbing outcome of the dispute—the execution of Admiral John Byng—revealed the violent underpinnings of military discipline, and its potentially corrosive influence on Britain's political process and the rule of law. The loss of Minorca made North America all the more important for Cumberland, and for the future of the army's imperialist ambitions.

*   *   *

Gibraltar was captured by the English army in 1704, during the War of the Spanish Succession. The English took the enclave on behalf of the Hapsburg claimant to the Spanish crown, but in the peace agreement that ended the war in 1713, the Hapsburgs lost Spain and Britain retained Gibraltar. The town, with an estimated population of "1200 families" had suffered enormous damage in the 1704 siege, and many of its original inhabitants had fled.[12] Treating the place as abandoned,

Britain's military authorities claimed possession, demolishing some damaged buildings, confiscating others, and charging rent from the townspeople who wanted to stay in their homes.[13] Gradually a new community developed, largely dependent on the army, composed of Greeks, Italians, Jews from North Africa and Europe, and others. Some immigrants, from Italy and elsewhere, worked as laborers and fishermen.[14] Many others, including a few Muslim North Africans, found employment in trade. A contingent of "old Spanish settlers," supporters of the Hapsburg cause, remained in the town, though their numbers declined as the years progressed, especially after Spain laid siege to the enclave in 1727.[15] By 1752, a descendant of the "old Spanish" claimed that only two such families remained in Gibraltar.[16]

British Minorca had a different history. The British took the island by force in 1708, but initially they held it in the name of the Hapsburgs.[17] A large part of the island's population supported the Hapsburg dynasty, which made the initial occupation much easier than it might have been.[18] In 1712, anticipating the defeat of its allies in Spain, Britain claimed sovereignty over the island, and the victorious Bourbon regime formally ceded Minorca to the British at the end of the war.[19] There were approximately 16,000 islanders in 1713. The population grew over the next several decades, though not as spectacularly as the British sometimes claimed. A census in 1750 counted 21,619.[20] Immigration accounted for some of the increase. A number of "foreign" sailors had arrived on British ships, left their vessels, and taken Minorcan wives.[21] Greek merchants began arriving on the island as early as 1719, and by the early 1740s they had established a small community.[22] Taking advantage of the Privy Council's order of 1745, they supported a priest who conducted services in their language, according to Orthodox rites.[23] For the most part, however, the population of Minorca remained what it had been before the British arrived: Catholic, Catalan-speaking families maintaining their old traditions and living in their ancestral homes. After Britain took sovereignty, the first governor announced that the islanders would retain their property rights, that the local "magistrates and other officers" would stay in their positions, and that the people of Minorca could remain in the Catholic Church.[24] These promises would pose a challenge to subsequent governors, and especially to Blakeney.

Bland arrived at Gibraltar on June 18, 1749. He came with a fleet of twenty ships and thousands of men to replace the garrison. As Bland's soldiers disembarked, the old contingent stumbled onto the transport ships in their place, heading for redeployment in Ireland.[25] Some of the departing soldiers had to be shaken awake. Bland reported that from the dock he saw "dozens dead drunk in the streets."[26] Bland's appointment represented a new start for Gibraltar. Not only the soldiers but nearly the entire British administration of the town was replaced. The former governor, William Hargrove, had been charged with embezzlement on a large scale.[27] Bland came with orders to investigate Hargrove's misdeeds and to establish new regulations for the collection of revenue, the payment of officers, the distribution of property, and the administration of the town.[28]

Before leaving Britain, Bland had submitted a plan for the governance of Gibraltar. His proposals reflected detailed research and a reform agenda even more intricate than the plans he had recently developed for the forfeited estates in Scotland. Bland developed guidelines for the licensing of Jewish and Genoese dockworkers, the grazing of cattle on the hill surrounding Gibraltar's famous rock, and the distribution of milk. He proposed a survey of all titles to land, the collection of moderate and consistent rents, and taxes on wine and liquor. He also endorsed what he called a "free market" in provisions, which meant allowing Jewish and Genoese merchants to sell produce "without paying any duty for the same to the governor or those employed by him."[29] Bland relayed his ideas to Cumberland, who endorsed them and sent them on to the Privy Council.[30] The Privy Council approved the outline of regulations, so that the instructions Bland brought with him to Gibraltar had been written by himself.

Bland looked on the enclave as a complex, integrated community. To keep it safe, and assure its effectiveness in protecting British trade and otherwise strategically defending the interests of the empire, he regulated a wide variety of aspects of life. He worried about letting hogs run on the hills below the rock, for example, because it was necessary to save the pasture for cattle.[31] He was also concerned about street cleaning, because the outpost was small, densely populated, and vulnerable to disease.[32] His position as governor gave Bland an opportunity to experiment, and he became Gibraltar's most enthusiastic reformer, adopting a set of initiatives that by his own account transformed the settlement in a matter of months. Mindful of the effects his policies would have not only on the town but also on the character of the soldiers, Bland altered the sentencing policies of his courts martial, so that men convicted of minor offenses were put to labor rather than whipped. He used petty convicts in public works projects. Sweaty, remorseful men, many recovering from nights of illicit drunkenness, carried stones and wielded axes to build roads over the enclave's hilly terrain.[33] Similarly, Bland used his power to regulate the local markets to convince the retailers of wine and liquor to agree to the payment of duties, which he used to finance the construction of a new wharf and to purchase a town clock.[34] The wharf, in particular, became a source of pride for him. He claimed to have contributed his own money to the project, in part because he knew he had no formal authority to impose taxes.[35]

Bland believed that ultimately none of the elements of his reform program would be viable in isolation from the others. Specifically, it would be impossible to reform the lives of the soldiers, or raise revenue from liquor taxes, without regulating the drinking habits of the sailors as well and keeping watch over all of the enclave's inhabitants. In his first months in office he was intensely worried about Gibraltar's civilians, whom he described as "Jews, Genoese, Spaniards, Portuguese, Irish Papists, Scotch pedlars and English bankrupts who fled from justice or could not get bread at home."[36] Bland argued that special care would be needed in dealing with the townspeople, particularly when it came to the imposition of taxes and imposts, because they were "ready to commit any fraud in their power, and consequently not at all scrupulous of cheating the king of his duties."[37] His suspicion of the Jews and Catholics lay behind his decision to restrict the liquor monopoly to "British merchants only."[38] A few of those who initially gained licenses to trade were Irish Catholics, but he turned against them. Within weeks of the introduction of the new regulations, Bland accused two of them of smuggling and suspended their right to trade.[39] In general Bland assumed that "rank Irish Papists" were "inveterate enemies to our present happy establishment." Therefore he questioned whether they should be allowed to live or work on Gibraltar, even though, he conceded, they were "his Majesty's born subjects."[40]

Prior to his arrival Bland had requested, and received, orders from the Privy Council authorizing him to inspect the title to every plot of ground, house, or building in Gibraltar, and upon finding title valid, to impose a "moderate ground rent to the king" on each property.[41] The Privy Council warned him (borrowing his own words) that Gibraltar was now inhabited primarily by "Jews, Moors and Papists of different nations," and that this "may prove of dangerous consequence to the town." In pursuance of his instructions Bland surveyed the land titles. When he discovered that Catholics or Jews held title, he added a restriction. While they could leave their property to their children, they could not sell their real estate to anyone other than "his Majesty's natural born Protestant subjects."[42] Bland also charged differential ground rents, with Protestants paying only one half of the rent due from Catholic tenants.[43] The purpose of these regulations, as Bland described them later, was to "get by degrees the property out of the hands of foreigners and Papists," in part for security reasons but also in order to assure that the wealth generated at the outpost flowed through British hands into the British-imperial economy.[44]

In the long run, Bland hoped to replace Gibraltar's population with

English-speaking Protestants. In the meantime he believed he could maintain order by exercising his military authority. The townspeople, after all, were virtually unarmed, and "not numerous enough" to challenge the soldiers. Their economic interests also kept them subservient, because the army controlled the distribution of economic licenses and real property.[45] Nonetheless, Bland did not think that concentrating power in a military governor would serve the empire's interests, or those of the army, over the long term. "How strange it will appear," he wrote, "to anyone who should take a view of the English constitution, which is so wisely founded for the ease, safety, and happiness of the subject, to find that a place of such importance to the power and commerce of Great Britain should be left for so many years under the arbitrary will of the governor, without the least check to control him!"[46]

Bland was aware of the political and legal risks he took by governing the enclave in the way he did.[47] He worried about lawsuits and also fretted about criticism he might receive from "the anti-courtiers and the city merchants," political opponents who would dissect his actions with an eye toward embarrassing Cumberland.[48] By 1750, the Admiralty had objected to some of his plans, particularly those that restricted the sailors' access to liquor.[49] Bland was certain that the sailors and his other critics would find a receptive audience in Britain. Speaking for the army as a whole, he declared, "the unthinking multitudes are but too apt to look upon us as invaders of their liberty and property."[50] As a partial solution to this problem, he asked the ministry to establish civilian criminal courts for Gibraltar, but none were established during his time in office.[51]

Gibraltar, with its small population and territory and its formidable garrison, seemed open to wholesale reform. Though it was difficult to recruit new settlers for the enclave, Bland could easily imagine evicting its Catholic and Jewish population gradually to make room for newcomers and redesigning the government without consulting the townspeople. Minorca, however, was larger. Though some British administrators in 1717 were rumored to have considered transporting all the islanders, after Blakeney became lieutenant governor he never believed that he had that option.[52] Everyone involved in the policy debate over Minorca agreed that any fundamental change in the island's governmental structure would require a new accommodation with Minorca's present inhabitants.

Around the time of Blakeney's appointment, a few ambitious promoters of colonization schemes circulated elaborate plans designed to alter the character of the people of Minorca. One writer suggested bringing "British and Irish" families to the island and encouraging the soldiers to marry local women.[53] The heads of these new households—soldiers and immigrants alike—would be provided incentives to purchase homes, giving them a stake in the community and helping to "reconcile" them with the islanders.[54] In support of this proposal the writer specifically cited the experience of Scotland, where marriages between Lowland and Highland families had inspired conversions to Presbyterianism.[55] That same writer also praised the Irish charter schools and suggested that they might serve as a model for educating and converting the children of Minorca to Protestantism.[56]

Blakeney shared this writer's reform agenda, though he did not have the resources to carry out the scheme in detail. It had been a struggle for Cumberland simply to retain 2,860 soldiers on Minorca, and there was no parliamentary money available to subsidize immigration. Blakeney therefore could only use the power of his office, and the influence of his soldiers, to affect change in Minorcan society. On the day after he disembarked he declared his intention to oversee the operation of the island's convents and monasteries, which served as schools for the islanders' youth. He did not trust the resident friars, and he was determined, he declared, to make sure that the children would not attend "schools of rebellion."[57] A few months later, Blakeney was involved in a dispute with the leaders of Minorca's Catholic Church over three young women whom his troops had lured out of a convent. All three women professed a conversion to Protestantism, and two of them wanted to marry British soldiers.[58] For Blakeney the controversy implicated fundamental questions of human liberty. "As I was born free and bred up in a free country," he wrote, "how can I find fault with any one for having fled bondage [in a convent] and asserted their liberty, which I have always looked on as the birthright of all mankind?" He also responded to the women's departure from the convent in religious terms. "As a member of the English Church, how shall I answer it to God, if I hinder any one from the exercise of that religion which I myself look upon as the most surest guide to heaven?"[59]

Blakeney's correspondence from Minorca reads very differently from the letters that Bland, at this time, was sending from Gibraltar. Bland presented himself as an abstract thinker and a designer of grand, constitutionally significant governmental schemes. He expected his writings and policies to guide the decisions of his successors in office for years to come.[60] Blakeney, by contrast, presented himself continuously as a man under siege, struggling just to assert his authority in a chaotic and disrespectful society. Part of the difference can be attributed to the contrasting personalities of the governors. Blakeney shared many of Bland's interests, but he was not nearly as creative or systematic a thinker. Minorca depressed him, and furthermore he was showing his age. During his eight years on the island, according to some accounts, he gradually withdrew from human company. According to one witness, by 1756 his face was frozen in a vacant and unreadable smile.[61] Senility may have eventually set in, but even before it did, Blakeney had always lacked what Bland called "philosophy." He made up for it by being adamant. When he tried to take over the Franciscan schools, for example, he declared, "God and the King has set me over one and all in this island, and I should be unworthy of the honor if I suffered anyone to laugh at my orders, or if I should share the authority with anyone whatever, much less a mendicant friar, sprung out of a dunghill."[62] Although adopting this stance failed to make Minorca governable, similar tactics had worked for him in the past. At Stirling Castle, for example, Blakeney's refusal to negotiate had made him famous.

The failure of the Blakeney's administration of Minorca was, in part, a personal one, but there were many features of community life on the island that made the place resistant to change. The civilian inhabitants of Minorca outnumbered the soldiers considerably, and in contrast with their counterparts in Gibraltar they shared a common language, church institutions, legal traditions, and mechanisms of law enforcement. They had ways of speaking coherently as a community and making their views heard. The islanders, in general, wanted to protect their churches, schools, and law courts, institutions that predated the British conquest. Many of them were also concerned to defend the accommodations they had reached with previous British administrations, and with the officers of the Royal Navy. Most of the islanders who struggled against Blakeney's reform proposals believed that Minorca could retain its cultural integrity, its language, religion, and legal institutions and still remain a part of the British Empire. The friars who objected to Blakeney's proposal to take control of the island's convents and monasteries, for example, made their case in petitions to the Privy Council.[63]

In the forty years that had passed since 1708, many islanders had prospered. The British fort and the warships in the harbor gave Minorca a kind of influence in the Mediterranean world it would never have enjoyed, divorced from a strong imperial power. Within the range of British guns it was easy for Minorca's port officials to board French, Spanish, Genoese, Maltese, and African ships and demand the payment of anchorage duties. One British official asked, rhetorically, what would have happened if the Minorcans had tried to board foreign ships without Britain's protection. If a visiting captain chose to be obstinate, the port officials would have been thrown overboard.[64] A similar dynamic operated on the high seas. Minorca's merchants sailed with "Mediterranean passes," letters which in effect guaranteed that the ships enjoyed the protection of the Royal Navy. Merchants with these passes were able to travel, usually unmolested, along the coasts of North Africa. The British made it possible for Minorcan merchants to sell foodstuffs and other commodities in Algiers.

Commerce on Minorca generally flowed along established lines, among friends, in family groups, or at least within well-defined local communities. Many of the most prosperous traders saw themselves as a coherent block, and they objected to the presence of Dutch ship captains, Greeks, and other competitors who came to Minorca from across the water. Blakeney, for his part, wanted a greater variety of merchants to come to the island, in order to increase the volume of trade and weaken the power of Minorca's Catalan-speaking, Catholic elite. He took a particular interest in supporting two French Protestant merchants on the island and a small number of Orthodox Greeks.[65] The island's Catholic clergy objected to this, as did many local merchants from the town of Port Mahon. In 1750 Blakeney received a petition from several of the merchants complaining that they could not stand the competition, and that their livelihoods were getting "sacrificed to the advantage of foreigners."[66]

The struggle that ensued played itself out in several forums. The clergy sent petitions to London, insisting that Minorca should remain a preserve of the Catholic Church. Landlords refused to rent or sell to foreigners, and at least one French Protestant family received a judicial order for eviction. Blakeney suspected that the Church, the landlords, and the judges were operating in league together, using their control of real property to "drive the Greeks, and all the Protestants out of the island."[67] There were also threats of violence.[68] Blakeney responded by ordering a curfew barring islanders from walking in the streets of Port Mahon "without a light in the night time." The order angered many of the townspeople. One man accosted the lieutenant governor himself, declaring "a fig to the English—we are twenty Spaniards for one Englishman." Blakeney escalated the confrontation by mounting new guns over the town.[69] He wanted to use military force to intimidate his opponents on Minorca, but more than once they reminded him that they had him outnumbered. Indeed, "a fig to the English—we are twenty Spaniards for one Englishman" (or "one soldier") seems to have become a popular slogan, or chant, among them.[70] One of Blakeney's first initiatives had been to order the disarmament of the island's population, but on occasion angry islanders were ready to confront his soldiers with rocks.[71]

In the long run, however, the most politically resonant struggle centered on the local Vice Admiralty court, which held jurisdiction over commercial disputes. The judges of the court were Catlan-speaking islanders, though they held commissions from the Royal Navy. Dutch and Greek merchants accused the chief judge of the court, Gabriel Olivar y Pardo, of favoring an inner circle of established merchants, engaging in trade himself, and adjudicating cases in ways that promoted his own commercial interests and those of his friends.[72] Olivar insisted that his court was independent of the governor's authority, that his commission came from the navy, and that it had been a consistent policy of the British since the time of the conquest to respect the autonomy of the island's courts. Blakeney, for his part, insisted that he had plenary authority over Minorca, including the power to oversee the operations of the courts in every civilian jurisdiction on the island.[73] By 1755 the struggle between Olivar and Blakeney had effectively shut the court. Blakeney confiscated the case files in several controversial cases, preventing Olivar from reviewing the records in order to issue rulings.[74] Olivar responded by traveling to London to present the dispute directly to the Admiralty.[75] Blakeney disapproved of the appeal and tried to dismiss Olivar from the bench. The appeal went forward nonetheless, and the Admiralty ruled in Olivar's favor, sending a strong complaint of its own to the Privy Council protesting that Blakeney had encroached on its jurisdiction by trying to replace the judge. The Privy Council, for its part, responded by restoring Olivar to office.[76]

Blakeney was furious with this order. Not only did he see it as a personal affront; he worried that those who had relied on his help in the factional politics of the island—the Greek merchants, for example, and others who had complained against Olivar—would despair of receiving any help from the governor's office. Blakeney was running short of friends on Minorca in 1755, and it seemed as if the navy had no interest in supporting him. Neither, it appeared, did Cumberland or his other old supporters in London.[77] As early as 1753, a number of men in Cumberland's circle, including Cumberland himself, Henry Fox, and Bland, had decided that Blakeney would have to leave his post.[78] They proposed sending Blakeney's nominal superior, the absentee governor of Minorca James O'Hara, Baron Tyrawley, to take over daily administration on the island. They hoped that Tyrawley would implement far-reaching reforms in Minorca's legal and ecclesiastical affairs, policy initiatives that seemed, from the perspective of Westminster, beyond Blakeney's abilities.[79] One of the proposals they considered would have placed all the island's Catholic chapels, convents, and monasteries under the supervision of the British and beyond the jurisdiction of Rome.[80] Tyrawley, however, never arrived to implement the plan, and Blakeney was left to struggle by himself.

At the heart of this controversy were differing understandings of the nature of British rule. Blakeney did not believe that the people of Minorca were ready to govern their own affairs, and in the meantime he sought to consolidate authority in the governor's office, in order to use that power to effect a general transformation of Minorcan society. He wanted to promote immigration and protect the interests of non-Catholics and speakers of languages other than Catalan. Even after they had lost faith in Blakeney personally, Cumberland and his advisors supported the aims of his program.[81] Olivar, on the other hand, held a more conservative vision of the future of the island. He favored the retention of an independent local court system, the protection of local trading interests, and, in general, no abrupt change from the social arrangements that had functioned in the past. Minorca's old elite, including several lawyers and established merchants, supported him in this view. So too, apparently, did the Royal Navy.

The Admiralty's intervention in this dispute fit a pattern. While it is important to recognize that the navy was changing in the eighteenth century, and that naval officers had conflicting views on Britain's imperial project, in general the Admiralty concentrated its attention and energy on the defense of sea lanes.[82] The "blue water" strategy most commonly associated with the navy and its political supporters suggested that Britain could expand the volume of its trade and maintain security by patrolling the water. In the "blue water" vision of the future, colonial dependencies could remain foreign so long as they gave British merchants their trade. Cumberland was always skeptical of this way of thinking, and he believed that the navy's manner of projecting power overseas was antithetical to his own.[83] In this particular controversy, the Royal Navy, in general, cared less than the army did about changing the character of the people of Minorca, or the island's system of internal governance. For Cumberland, and for Blakeney, these were matters of concern.

By 1748, Cumberland and his officers were accustomed to thinking of the army as a civilizing influence in distressed societies, as a temporary agency of law enforcement, and as a promoter of cultural and commercial exchange. This, they believed, was the army's mission in Scotland, and now soldiers had been assigned similar duties in the Mediterranean and in Nova Scotia as well. The soldiers' tasks in the overseas outposts differed significantly from their old assignment in Scotland, however, because on the margins of the British Empire there were people beyond the immediate reach of the army's reform efforts. For Bland and Blakeney, North Africa loomed nearby, and neither of them imagined any imperial project aimed at conquering, assimilating, or even improving the character of the Africans.

The economic vitality of both Gibraltar and Minorca depended on trade with North Africa. The residents of both Minorca and Gibraltar were eligible for passes to enter North African waters without exposing themselves to attack by privateers.[84] Bland considered the passport system a success, though it only worked in regions at peace with the British Empire, and controversies surrounded it almost continually in practice. One major issue complicating the "Mediterranean pass" system was defining which merchants and mariners were eligible for the protection of the British crown. German-speaking merchants from Hanover created unusual problems. Bland spent more than a year trying to convince the local authorities in Tetuan, on the coast of Morocco, that five Hanoverians in their custody were "his Majesty's subjects," something the North Africans had "no idea of."[85] Before he could convince them, one of the Hanoverian captives died.[86] Bland complained that the Moroccans were "unacquainted with geography."[87] The Moroccans had similar complaints about the British, for example when British ships entered disputed territories to trade.[88]

Just as traders in Gibraltar conducted commerce with their counterparts in Morocco, merchants based in Minorca carried on a lively trade in Algiers.[89] Some Algerian leaders suspected British merchants of supplying rebel groups within their jurisdictions. The alleged rebels, for their part, asserted long-standing independence.[90] As a result, almost from the moment of his arrival, Blakeney was involved in controversies surrounding trading privileges, captive taking, and the ransoming of prisoners. To negotiate such disputes, like Bland at Gibraltar, Blakeney had to insert himself into a complex and unfamiliar political landscape. He was not studious, however, and unlike Bland he did not develop any personal theories on North African politics. Instead he relied almost entirely on the advice of merchants and emissaries familiar with the Algerian coast.[91]

Shortly after Bland's arrival in Gibraltar, a pestilence struck Morocco. Bland discussed the matter with "several African Jews, and some Greeks who lived long in that country." They told him that the summers were healthier than the springs, which led Bland to conjecture that "the sun may purify, or exhale those malignant vapours, and by that means destroy their forces." He conceded, however, that it would be best to leave such theorizing to the members of the Royal Society.[92] He was less reticent in advancing a cultural explanation for the diseases that plagued North Africa. Muslims were fatalists, he asserted. "They say God has fixed the time which every man is to die, and set it down in the book of fate, so that none can shorten or prolong it." This was a stance that prepared them to accept death, but it also kept them from saving themselves by prudent measures such as avoiding contact with disease.[93]

Contagion preoccupied both governors and affected their thoughts about the relationship between Minorca, Gibraltar, and North Africa. When disease struck the North African ports, no ships from Africa were allowed to dock at Gibraltar unless they stayed in the harbor for an extensive period of quarantine. When the epidemics were most virulent, or perceived to be so, quarantine was considered an inadequate precaution, and trade with those ports entirely ceased.[94] Bland thought of illness as a continental phenomenon and believed that by guarding against African disease he was defending the European continent as a whole.[95] In the autumn of 1748 Blakeney struggled to refute reports that disease had struck Minorca. He oversaw a rigorous quarantine process in the harbors of the island, to make sure that no diseases arrived from North Africa or the eastern Mediterranean.[96] Despite Blakeney's efforts, the French in Marseilles never admitted that commerce with Minorca was safe. Ships arriving in France from the island were routinely required to spend weeks in quarantine before anyone could disembark.[97] Blakeney suspected that France and its allies had ordered these precautions to isolate Minorca, weaken its merchants and the British garrison there, and impede the growth of Britain's Mediterranean trade.[98] He accepted the idea that ships from certain regions—North Africa in particular—had to be treated as dangerous, but he considered it a French slander to suggest that Minorca lay on the south side of the line, in the zone of disease.

It was Bland, however, who concentrated his thoughts most intensely on the border separating Europe from Africa and the features that distinguished the two continents. This was so not only because of his scholarly inclinations but also because he arrived at Gibraltar at a time of diplomatic tension. Thirty-nine hostages claiming British protection—thirty British subjects, five Hanoverians, and four Catalan-speaking residents of Gibraltar—were being held in Morocco.[99] Prior to Bland's arrival as governor, one effort to buy the hostages' freedom had failed spectacularly, with the British negotiators themselves taken captive.[100] Bland was charged with resolving the dispute in a way that would free the captives and guarantee, to the greatest extent possible, the future security of British traders. He also had to safeguard the honor and reputation of the British government, not only internationally but also within Parliament and "out of doors" in the streets and lanes of Britain. Operating through emissaries he sent to North Africa, Bland engaged in sporadic, difficult negotiations with a variety of leaders, until in the early spring of 1751 the last hostages were released.[101]

Like his British army counterparts in North America, who arrived with strong and negative preconceptions about America's native warriors, Bland had come to the Mediterranean prepared to hate the Muslims of North Africa. For centuries, captive taking had figured prominently in Mediterranean warfare and diplomacy, and war captives had long been traded and sold as slaves on both sides of the sea. While the British occasionally participated in captive taking in the Mediterranean, they generally blamed the Africans for the practice. When large groups were taken at once, as had happened before Bland arrived in the region, the events were widely publicized and the captive takers were vilified as representatives of a depraved and violent culture.[102] Nonetheless, Bland was unwilling to rely solely on old public commentary in his assessment of North Africa's peoples. During his negotiations he studied Mediterranean politics. He interviewed "some of the British merchants and principal Jews" in Gibraltar and "some of the noted Jews in Barbary" in order to construct a detailed, dynastic history of Morocco, which he put in writing and preserved for his own edification and that of his successors in office.[103]

In his history and in his letters to the ministry, Bland employed several labels to identify the diverse inhabitants of the North African coast, whom he described variously as "Moors," "Arabs," "Barbary Jews," and "blacks."[104] On occasion Bland tried to be meticulous in distinguishing between these various communities, tracing their histories, their interests, and specific features of their purported character. Nonetheless, particularly in moments of diplomatic tension, he grouped them all into a single category, "Africans," or, alternatively, "Barbarians," and suggested that they were "a set of ignorant, obstinate people, entirely unacquainted with the rules of right and wrong."[105] When a fatal contagion struck North Africa in 1750, Bland declared that if there had been no Europeans endangered by the disease he would "rejoice if the whole race of that country were extirpated from the face of the Earth."[106] In Bland's view, Africans were distinguished by an "immoderate love of money," which encouraged them to "break through all laws human and divine."[107] They were "thieves from their cradles."[108] "None but fools," he wrote, would trust them.[109]

Of all the groups that Bland classified as "African" or "European," Sephardic Jews occupied the most ambiguous position, in part because they frequently crossed between the continents. Bland asserted that the largest volume of trade between Gibraltar and North Africa was "carried on by our Jews."[110] He employed Jews as informants and advisors as he formulated policy.[111] Nonetheless, when his negotiations for the release of the hostages turned sour in the fall of 1750, Bland blamed a "rascally Jew" who had (according to the British negotiators) insinuated himself so thoroughly into the counsels of a local Muslim leader as to take control and manipulate the negotiations to maximize his own profits. After a break in the negotiations, Bland's emissaries insisted that the North Africans "employ none of the Jews" during subsequent negotiations.[112] In the context of diplomacy, Bland did not trust the Jews, and he feared that their influence might complicate the Africans' negotiating stance.

Bland believed that he understood Africa, and his assessment of the

Africans' character had a direct effect on his approach to negotiations. He associated the African continent with despotism and suggested that British power in the region could be maintained only by appealing to the Africans' self-interest and simultaneously keeping them in fear. Bland insisted that Muslims "think it a meritorious action" to plunder Christians "when they can do it with impunity."[113] "Their notion of justice," he asserted, was "very different from what we have in Europe; their government being founded purely on force, to which alone they submit."[114] In consequence, he declared that it was "absolutely necessary to take the first opportunity to mortify those people in order to bring them to a true knowledge of their own weakness."[115]

Bland advocated a mixture of economic coercion and military force in dealings with the peoples of North Africa. He believed that some towns in Morocco were entirely dependent on their trade with Gibraltar, and if the leaders refused to cooperate with the British, they would jeopardize the flow of commerce and risk popular revolt. Bland's confidence would weaken later, but early in his negotiations with the governor of Tetuan he asserted that the North African leader had to work with him, because if he did not, Bland could easily starve his town. The townspeople would then rise up and kill their leader. Bland believed, accordingly, that as long as the negotiations continued, the governor lived in "continual dread."[116] He argued that it was necessary to maintain "an air of superiority" in his dealings with Africans.[117] In his negotiations, Bland grandly reminded the leaders of Morocco that "us Europeans" had a low opinion of "African faith."[118]

Bland took a starkly different approach in his negotiations with his European neighbors. When he arrived on Gibraltar, Spain and Britain had just concluded a peace agreement ending nine years of official war. During that time Spain had blocked all overland communication with the enclave, leaving Gibraltar dependent on North Africa for food. Bland, unhappy with this situation, worried that in the absence of trade with the Spanish, the appearance of an epidemic in Africa might force Gibraltar's garrison into a choice between plague and hunger. Therefore, one of his first initiatives was to open up trade with Spain.

Bland had served in Spain during the War of the Spanish Succession, and he believed that his experience in that war gave him a rare expertise that served him well during his negotiations with neighboring officials. He was confident in his assessment of the Spanish temperament and operated on the assumption, so he insisted, that the Spanish "esteemed themselves the first people in the world."[119] Bland claimed that the "Spaniards" and the "Barbary Moors . . . differ as much from one another in their customs and manners as they do in their religion, and hate one another with an ardent, pious zeal without a possibility of their ever being reconciled till the Messiah reigns on Earth."[120] The Spanish, from his perspective, were European, which made it easier to negotiate with them, even if he always had to be on his guard. Bland negotiated for Spanish merchants to visit Gibraltar, but only if they came by sea. Spain did not open the land border, and Bland was satisfied with the result. He had worried that had the gates on the border been opened, the Spanish "might send in clever people in disguise, and form cabals to seize this place by surprise." Furthermore, his soldiers, bridling under his government, might desert from Gibraltar and move permanently to Spain.[121]

From Bland's perspective in Gibraltar, the Mediterranean Sea divided two cultural zones. While he remained distrustful of many European groups, including Jews and Irish Catholics, he also believed that the people of Europe shared values that the North Africans lacked. There were very few Scottish Highlanders on or near Gibraltar in the early 1750s, and Bland had no occasion to discuss whether he thought that they belonged to the group he called "us Europeans." Nonetheless, at least one of his letters suggests that he still thought of the Scottish Highlands as a savage country, similar to North Africa's Atlas Mountains. In a letter to the Duke of Bedford, he wrote that the "mountain Arabs" of Morocco were "greater thieves and as wild as the Highlanders in Lochaber."[122] Bland had not changed his opinion of the Scottish Highlands. In general, Highlanders were more likely to be defined as "European" and relatively civilized in places where they constituted part of the colonial community or participated in Britain's imperial project. Highlanders would assert themselves and alter their reputation later in the decade, after large numbers of Gaelic-speakers began moving into distant, contested zones in North America during the Seven Years' War.

Bland left Gibraltar in the summer of 1751 and eventually returned to his position as commander in chief in Scotland. He had served in the Mediterranean in a time of relative peace, and he was satisfied with his accomplishments. Blakeney, on Minorca, remained for five more years, and it was his misfortune to face a military crisis.

In the early spring of 1756, when he first learned that the French were preparing to attack Minorca, Blakeney summoned a council of war which resolved to ready the defenses, appeal for help from the navy, and determine "what dependence and assistance" could be expected from the Minorcans.[123] Blakeney sent out recruiters with drums, asking the island's young men to enlist in the army. On the promise of pay, thirteen volunteered, though only three men appeared for service. One of the three reportedly fled from the fort after the French arrived.[124] By that time Blakeney had concluded that the islanders would be unhelpful, and he complained to the ministry that a "disaffected, ungrateful party of the inhabitants" had obstructed his efforts to prepare a defense.[125] Within two days of the French landing on Minorca in April, Blakeney wrote to Henry Fox that "the natives in general on this important occasion have shown the highest disaffection to his Majesty's service."[126] Three days later, the governor lost contact with the ministry; he remained isolated for nearly two months during the siege. After he surrendered, Blakeney continued to excoriate the islanders. "To the reverse of joining in the defense of the island, they have done everything in their power to obstruct the service, and have made fully appear (what I have often represented), that they are a disaffected people, no way attached to his Majesty's government."[127]

Since 1748, Blakeney had consistently assumed that the people of Minorca owed allegiance to the British crown. In moments of tension he had accused his political adversaries on the island of "sedition" and called them "rebels," using a language that could only be applied to British subjects.[128] While chasing rebels, Blakeney had also tried to find loyal allies among the islanders, nearly always failing in the face of opposition from the leaders of the Church and the courts. In a desperate effort to establish a local government that would cooperate with him, in 1753 he had tried to establish a new municipality called "St. Phillips," composed of those "dutiful and quiet" people who lived within gunshot of the British fort.[129] He was still negotiating the legal status of "St. Phillips" when the French arrived. After the fighting ended, Blakeney was criticized for failing to destroy "St. Phillips."[130] Like the rest of the island, the community had failed to support him; burning it might have served military purposes during the siege.

The French siege of Minorca inspired a great deal of public commentary in Britain. One of the most ambitious publications, published first in 1752 and reissued while Blakeney was under attack, was an ethnographic study of the islanders. The writer, John Armstrong, had lived on the island in the early 1740s, and he asserted in his book that the islanders, "though they make a part of our British dominions, are as utter strangers to the good people of England, as the hunters of Ethiopia, or the artificers of Japan."[131] Like the English traveler Burt in the Scottish Highlands, Armstrong hoped to fill a gap in the literature with his own careful study of an underexamined group. He declared, on the basis of his own historical research and archeological speculations, that the people of Minorca were the cousins of the Highlanders and lineal descendants of Europe's ancient Celts (see Figure 9).[132]

Other writers concentrated more on the recent past and lamented the failure of the British government to introduce Minorca to Protestantism and English culture. Emphasizing the purported economic benefits of such a policy, a short essay in the London Evening Post suggested that after

Figure 9. In his *History of the Island of Minorca*, first published in 1752 and reprinted in 1756, John Armstrong argued that the islanders were of Celtic origin. In support of this assertion, he described ancient ruins on Minorca, including the altar and cairn depicted here, which he claimed closely resembled pre-Christian monuments in Scotland, Wales, and Ireland. (Courtesy of the Annenberg Rare Book and Manuscript Library, University of Pennsylvania.)

acquiring sovereignty the British government should have purchased half the land on Minorca and distributed it to British settlers. If that had been done, the islanders would have gradually adopted the practices of the industrious Britons who surrounded them, and would thus have pursued economic "improvements."[133] One pamphleteer claimed that the failure to introduce settlers had been deliberate. Since 1708, the island's governors had "taken care that none of our industrious people should ever settle there." Military men, this writer asserted, were no substitute for settlers, because "the natives could not learn industry from our soldiers."[134] The pamphlet argued that the British government should have long ago exerted itself "to convert, without compulsion, the natives to the Protestant religion."[135] The authorities should have pursued gradual legal reform with the goal of making the island operate according to the doctrines and procedures of English law. English should have become the language of official business. "In short, their laws, their language, their religion, ought to have been made the same with those in England." The pamphleteer asserted that if such a policy had been adopted, "almost every native of Minorca would have been a zealous

Protestant, and as faithful a subject, and as ready to take arms for the defense of our government, as any soldier we have now in the garrison."[136]

These publications appeared in the tense two-month period before the news of Blakeney's surrender was confirmed. Once the British knew that the island was lost, public commentary shifted focus. Blakeney's capitulation agreement avoided declaring whether the islanders were British, Spanish, or French subjects. The document identified them simply as "*les naturels de l'isle*" but unambiguously stipulated that they would remain on the island and that France would assume responsibility for their government.[137] Whether or not the inhabitants had ever owed allegiance to Britain, the issue, for now, seemed moot. From the perspective of Britain they were beyond reach, unavailable for either punishment or reform, and the public's attention turned to the military commanders.

Admiral John Byng had been dispatched from England with a fleet of ships in April 1756 to help defend Minorca. He sailed first to Gibraltar with a body of troops and orders to embark more men detached from Gibraltar's garrison. The officers at Gibraltar objected to this plan, not only because it would weaken their defensive position against Spain but also because they believed that the French were too strong and that it was too late to save Minorca. To make a show of complying with Byng's orders, they gave him some troops, though fewer than he ordered. Eleven days after sailing from Gibraltar, Byng came within sight of Minorca. He saw a large number of French ships patrolling the coasts, a French army in Port Mahon, and the British flag flying over Blakeney's fort. After one inconclusive engagement with the French fleet, Byng convened a new council of war. He knew that Blakeney still held his position, but the garrison was obviously outnumbered. Indeed, the French may have landed as many as 15,000 men.[138] The admiral, who had earlier argued in favor of proceeding, reversed his position, and his advisors, many of whom had participated in the first council of war and argued then against any effort to relieve Minorca, agreed with him this time. The shipboard council resolved to turn back, judging that any effort to relieve the fort would be costly and futile and would permanently weaken the garrison at Gibraltar through the loss of valuable troops.[139]

Prior to the officers' decision to abandon Minorca, rumors had spread across the Atlantic world that Byng had gained a major victory against the French. A shipmaster in Philadelphia reported that Byng had "gained the advantage" against the French fleet.[140] Another in Newport, Rhode Island, spread the news that Byng had "beat the French and secured the garrison."[141] A newspaper in Antigua also reported Byng's victory, and that press account spread at least as far as Rhode Island, Connecticut, and Massachusetts. The Antigua newspaper cited the captain of a ship who had heard the story in Madeira from a man who had learned of the victory while in Gibraltar. That man, in turn, claimed to have been present when the governor of Gibraltar received the news. According to this account, Byng had faced the French fleet in two engagements, each lasting twenty-four hours. He had sunk three ships and taken three, while losing one. In the meantime on Minorca, Blakeney had taken the initiative. Though under siege, using fortress guns and sallies from their post, his men had killed ten thousand of the French.[142] Yet another report reached Virginia, and from there traveled to New York, indicating that Byng had won the day, losing three ships while sinking eleven. This report, like the others, indicated that Minorca was saved, and this one specified that the French army had lost 7,000 men.[143]

Similar rumors reached England, though the news traveled more quickly in European waters.[144] In the weeks that passed between Byng's departure from Portsmouth and the arrival of the disappointing report that he had turned back, a large part of the British public discovered that it cared about Minorca in a way it never had before. The loss of the island sparked widespread fury. Crowds burned Byng in effigy in coastal cities and towns across England.[145] The City of London, several towns, and the councils of nine English counties sent addresses to George II demanding an inquiry.[146] Coming less than a year after General Edward Braddock's humiliating defeat against the French in North America, the loss of Minorca seemed to confirm a pattern—either the ministry was incompetent in the conduct of military affairs, or something more sinister was at work.[147] Newcastle, worried for his political future, promised a delegation from London that the admiral would be hanged.[148]

Byng demanded a court martial, and for the next several months, until his execution in March 1757, he and his supporters prepared an elaborate defense intended to spread responsibility for the loss of the island. One man they implicated was Edward Cornwallis, who in 1756 had held command over a regiment on Minorca, though he had been away, at Gibraltar, when the French attacked (see Figure 10). Cornwallis had participated in the council of war on Gibraltar, and he had recommended against sending Blakeney reinforcements.[149] Cornwallis had subsequently sailed with Byng and had taken part in the second council of war, again siding with those who thought that Minorca was beyond saving.[150] If public attention had focused on Cornwallis's role in this affair, his career would have been ruined. Wolfe, among others, was worried for him.[151] As it turned out, however, Cornwallis had friends at the proceedings, including one witness who claimed to have overheard him exclaim, when he first learned that the French had attacked Minorca, "I wish to God I had been with my regiment."[152]

Figure 10. On a rare visit to Minorca in 1755, Cornwallis had his portrait painted by an itinerant artist named George Chalmers, who was briefly on the island and also painted a likeness of Blakeney. Blakeney was already considerably more famous than Cornwallis, and in 1756, during the public debates surrounding Britain's loss of Minorca, the Chalmers painting of Blakeney was reproduced as a print for sale in London. The Cornwallis portrait, by contrast, fell into obscurity. When the painting was offered for sale by Christie's auction house in the 1920s, Cornwallis was misidentified as Blakeney. (Charles Kingsley Adams to John Clarence Webster, August 16, 1929, Edward Cornwallis file, National Portrait Gallery, London.) (Cornwallis portrait courtesy of the Nova Scotia Archives; Blakeney portrait © National Portrait Gallery, London.)

Newcastle and the leaders of the army struggled to simplify the controversy by focusing on Byng. Byng was a coward, they said, and to dramatize their point they contrasted him with Blakeney, whom they depicted as a hero. Pamphleteers reminded the British public of Blakeney's service in Scotland during the 1745 rising.[153] One writer claimed that at Stirling in 1746 Blakeney had "cut down" the Highlanders "like grass under a scythe."[154] That writer asserted that Blakeney had been the first person in Britain to fight effectively against Charles Edward's forces.[155] Others expounded imaginatively on Blakeney's futile efforts to hold back the French at Port Mahon. According to one, Blakeney pronounced these words when the fate of Minorca became clear to him: "O England! O England! 'tis not for myself I mourn, but for Minorca's woes, and for thy loss—for such I fear 'twill be."[156]

Byng's defenders, and others who opposed the ministry and the army, turned on Blakeney in response, to discredit the government's version of events on the island. One writer suggested that Blakeney had been bribed to surrender Minorca and that he had held Stirling Castle in 1746 only because the Jacobites had been unable to offer enough money to tempt him.[157] Others suggested that Blakeney was senile and inattentive, and that he had been chosen for the command on Minorca in the expectation that he would fail.[158] The ministry, according to this theory, was willing to lose the island to France and was concerned only to avoid censure for its actions.

Some of the passion surrounding the public response to the loss of Minorca stemmed from antagonism between the army and the navy and between their different political constituencies in Britain. For years supporters of the navy had depicted the service as the mainstay of Britain's defense, and one that posed no threat to British liberty. Byng's detractors turned those claims against him, by suggesting that a display of weakness in one admiral might be symptomatic of problems throughout the naval ranks. Such behavior, they claimed, "may cost us more than Minorca—our navy and kingdom too."[159] The admiral's defenders, for their part, suggested that Byng was a scapegoat, punished to divert attention from the failings of the army and the ministry.[160] Some attributed the trial to a complex conspiracy organized in part by Cumberland himself, who avoided public scrutiny by posing as an unequaled champion of British liberty. Mockingly praising the men of Cumberland's army, one writer asked, "Can all the far-famed heroes of antiquity . . . compare all their accumulated victories to the single defeat of Culloden?"[161]

No one, however, was in charge of the events leading to Byng's execution. Nearly all of the principal players involved in military operations in the Mediterranean—in the ministry, and in the army and the navy—were targeted for scathing criticism in the autumn of 1756, and in general they responded defensively and reactively, anxiously hoping to salvage their careers. As the case proceeded toward its conclusion, high officers in both the navy and the army came to realize that they had a common interest in the outcome, and many came to regret that the prosecution had gone so far. The trial ended in a mixed verdict. Byng was acquitted of the most serious charges and convicted only of negligence. Nonetheless, the court martial condemned him to die.[162] The officers who issued this ruling believed that it was mandated by the wording of a recent statute. Recognizing the injustice of the result, they unanimously recommended that the king commute the sentence. The king was unwilling to intervene in the controversy, however, and Byng was shot by a firing squad.[163]

*   *   *

Bland and Blakeney had arrived in the Mediterranean with great enthusiasm. They were part of an effort to reform the British army and to demonstrate its effectiveness as a civilizing influence in the world. By 1756, both of their experiments had faltered. Minorca was lost, at least for the time being, and, less spectacularly, many of the reforms that Bland had implemented were abandoned by Gibraltar's subsequent governors.[164] After the loss of Minorca, Cumberland and his associates suspected that double agents in Gibraltar had sabotaged the effort to save the island. They therefore recommended that a new governor be appointed and that he be ordered, among other things, to "send out of the garrison the consuls of other nations residing there, and in general all such persons as he may think dangerous or disaffected."[165] It was almost as if Bland had never been there.

The failure of these experiments put pressure on the army's North American ventures. When news of the loss of Minorca reached Britain, correspondents immediately relayed it to Britain's military commanders across the Atlantic.[166] The burden was on them, many believed, to reverse the effect of Blakeney's defeat. Loudon had just arrived in North America as the new commander of British forces. Upon learning of the loss of Minorca, several of his friends in Scotland took it upon themselves to relay him the news. In contrast to the Mediterranean actions, Scots were deeply involved in the American war effort. One writer in Edinburgh told Loudon, "A lucky stroke in America under your Lordship's conduct will make some amends for our misfortune in the Mediterranean."[167] Milton, the former lord justice clerk of Scotland, similarly wrote him, "Port Mahon can only be recovered in America."[168]

Loudon, however, was wary of the attention. He longed for fame and glory, but the controversies surrounding the loss of Minorca had exposed the political and legal vulnerabilities of military officers, not only in the navy but in Cumberland's army as well. Furthermore, the army's record of accomplishment in North America had long been disappointing. Since the time of Edward Cornwallis's arrival in Nova Scotia, the army had been engaged in efforts in America similar to its projects in Scotland and the Mediterranean. In the regions they patrolled, the officers and soldiers hoped to exert pervasive influence, encourage the spread of a common Protestant culture, obtain the loyalty and obedience of all the inhabitants, and confront the British Empire's external enemies from a position of military strength. From 1749 onward, the army's influence had been greatest in Nova Scotia, but with the outbreak of armed conflict in 1754, Britain's regiments had assumed a more prominent role in the governance and defense of the colonies on a continental scale. The army's administrative and military efforts had generally gone badly, however, and though Loudon had not despaired, he knew that it would be difficult to turn failure into success.

After the execution of Admiral Byng, British generals in North America worried about acting cautiously, because, as one observer put it, they feared that if they held their fire against the French and their native allies they might be haunted by "Byng's ghost."[169] Loudon was one of those anxious men. After he postponed an operation against Louisbourg in 1757, he jailed an insubordinate officer for declaring that the leaders of Britain's American armies should "suffer" like "Mr. Byng."[170]

Chapter 6

Cumberland's Army in North America

On June 21, 1749, Edward Cornwallis sailed into Chebucto Harbor, on the Atlantic coast of Nova Scotia. Remaining on board his ship, the newly appointed governor awaited the arrival of dozens of other vessels, bringing settlers, soldiers, and supplies, from England, Cape Breton Island, and Boston. Approximately 2,500 settlers joined him in the harbor before any shelter was constructed on land.[1] Then, together, the settlers and soldiers began to build the town of Halifax, in a region that had been under the continuous control of Mi'kmaq hunting bands since before the arrival of Europeans in North America. Cornwallis sent men ashore to clamber across the hills; from the deck of his ship he could view the sweep of the wooded landscape. Virtually from the moment of his arrival he was modifying his town plan, making decisions on the location of house lots, roads, forts, fish-drying stations, and docks.[2] Within two months he had a map, and he reported that "everyone knows where to build his house."[3] By October, three hundred houses had been built, and though Cornwallis had difficulty mobilizing labor, he had overseen the construction of a stockade around Halifax, two forts, and several miles of road heading toward the interior of the continent.[4]

Like Bland in Gibraltar, Cornwallis supervised a range of interconnected aspects of community life. In addition to roads, docks, forts, and stockades, he oversaw the construction of a sawmill, a brewery, and a church.[5] He regulated markets for liquor, livestock, and fish.[6] With suppliers from Boston, he arranged for the importation of lamps so that the streets of Halifax could be illuminated at night.[7] As early as November 1749, he was issuing orders for the protection of shade trees, as an "ornament and shelter" for the town.[8] He was also struggling to establish English-style institutions of government. Cornwallis appointed a provincial council, and eventually he divided Halifax into wards and arranged for the election of ward officers.[9] Though the nearest trained lawyer lived hundreds of miles away, he established a civilian law court, which met in an ordnance storehouse in August 1749. Conforming "as near to the English customs as possible," the court convened its first capital trial.[10]

There was a considerable amount of crime to prosecute. Cornwallis complained that the first settlers to arrive were "poor idle worthless vagabonds" who had come to Nova Scotia only to receive free transportation across the ocean and the subsidy offered by Parliament.[11] To improve his situation he endorsed a proposal to recruit "foreign Protestant" settlers from the continent of Europe. Parliament accepted the project, and beginning in 1750, thousands of immigrants from Germany and Switzerland began disembarking in Halifax.[12] These European newcomers pleased the governor. Cornwalis described the Swiss, in particular, as "regular honest & industrious men," and he believed that he needed them to make Halifax work.[13]

Ultimately, however, Cornwallis was frustrated in Nova Scotia. Pursuant to his instructions, he insisted on consolidating the authority of the provincial government and requiring an equal share of obedience from all of Nova Scotia's inhabitants. He refused to allow the Acadians any formal exemption from military service, disavowing a concession they had won from a previous governor twenty years earlier. In the long run Cornwallis hoped to erase the distinction between the Acadians and other British subjects, not only on the question of military service but in nearly all respects. His instructions directed him to build a culturally integrated province, where Protestant immigrants could mingle freely with French-speaking Catholics, and introduce them gradually to new forms of worship and standards of piety, new ways of commerce and new political allegiances. By 1750, if all had proceeded according to his original plan, the zone of Protestant settlement would have extended from Halifax across the peninsula to the coasts of the Bay of Fundy, where the Acadians lived.

The Mi'kmaq, it turned out, were an obstacle to this plan. In the autumn of 1749 Mi'kmaq warriors took up arms against the newly arrived settlers, and as early as March 1750 Cornwallis had decided that it would be too dangerous, in the short term, to locate any new settlements far from the stockades of Halifax.[14] Over the course of the next year Mi'kmaq leaders, in cooperation with the French, made speeches and threatened force and convinced several hundred Acadians to move out of British-controlled territory. Writing in general terms to the ministry, Cornwallis complained that the Mi'kmaq and the French had "stirred up his Majesty's subjects [the Acadians] to rebellion."[15] This was, from the governor's perspective, an illegal insurrection. He would not officially acknowledge that his battles with the Mi'kmaq constituted a war. His predecessors in office, in similar circumstances, had done so, but Cornwallis maintained that if he declared war on the Mi'kmaq he would "own them a free people" and undermine Britain's claim to rule over the colony and all its peoples.[16]

Cornwallis had come to Nova Scotia as a representative of Cumberland's army. He believed that soldiers could take a leading role in reforming society and that one aim of imperial policy should be the promotion of cosmopolitan, industrious, and Protestant populations. Military occupation, government investment, and the encouragement of immigration were common tools to this end. After his efforts to carry this program to the Acadians foundered in the face of armed opposition, he confronted many of the same dilemmas that the army in Scotland had faced a few years earlier. Cornwallis believed that he faced a savage enemy, and he wanted to find a way, without the help of effective judicial machinery, to suppress and punish alleged rebellion.

Reports of the troubles in Nova Scotia spread through the army and affected the way many officers thought about North America. Loudon received letters indicating that the Mi'kmaq in Nova Scotia maintained "ascendency" over "all our French inhabitants."[17] Wolfe's friends in the colony sent him similar accounts.[18] The Nova Scotia project had initially represented, for Wolfe and others, an expression of the army's highest aspirations.[19] Wolfe lost much of his enthusiasm after the Halifax settlement faced armed resistance. Cornwalis himself became disillusioned, and he left Nova Scotia in the spring of 1752.

The Seven Years' War began in North America two years later, and it raised for the leaders of the army many of the same issues that had confronted Cornwallis at the time of the founding of Halifax. In 1756 Loudon came to North America to direct Britain's war effort against the French and their native allies. Loudon stayed less than two years. After he departed, Wolfe arrived in a slightly less exalted capacity. Like Cornwallis, Loudon and Wolfe were trying to assert British sovereignty in the face of violent opposition, in regions lacking English-style institutions. They struggled with the assignment of culpability, and in their policies toward French Catholics and native peoples, they had difficulty determining which groups should be liable for collective punishment, and what kind of sanctions could appropriately be imposed. They believed they were confronting rebels and savages, but just as in Scotland, "rebellion" and "savagery" were fluid concepts in North America. The officers thought that the status of their enemies should affect the British army's strategy and conduct, but they could not develop a coherent, consistent, and easily applicable guide for the soldiers' behavior in operations against French regular soldiers, militiamen and native warriors.

At least with respect to the issues facing the officers, the Seven Years' War in North America bore some resemblance to Cumberland's campaigns in the Scottish Highlands. The soldiers' quandaries proved that the theoretical issues that the army had struggled with in 1746 remained unresolved. In another important way, however, the American war seemed to bring the troubles of 1745 to a conclusion. After 1756, several battalions of Highland soldiers served in the army in North America. From the perspective of most British observers, their service in the war dispelled the association between Highland culture and rebellion. In the American context, on the contrary, the Highlanders were part of the legitimate, punishing authority. Furthermore, at least a few of the Highland soldiers came to see their work as a first step in a larger civilizing project. Like colonists in other places, they imagined that they could transform whole landscapes, spread commerce, generate wealth and power for Britain, bring comfort to themselves and their families, and perhaps even improve the fortunes of the native peoples of the continent.

*   *   *

George Washington's skirmish with the French near the Ohio River in the summer of 1754 abruptly and dramatically increased Cumberland's power in British politics. Almost as soon as the news arrived from America, Newcastle invited Cumberland into the inner counsels of government, and within a matter of weeks the captain general was taking a leading role in the direction of British North America's military affairs.[20] Loudon was among those eager to take advantage of this change in Cumberland's political fortunes, and when the decision was made to send two regiments from Ireland to the colonies, Loudon hoped that he might be given the command. Loudon, at the time, led a regiment of English troops in Ireland, but for several years he had wanted a post in the colonies. He was most interested in Jamaica, but rumors circulated before 1754 that he would have accepted the governorship of New York.[21] Now a commission was available to lead all of Britain's troops on the American continent. After the assignment went to Edward Braddock, an officer who slightly outranked him, Loudon received a personal note of apology from Cumberland's closest ally in the ministry, Henry Fox.[22]

The unfortunate General Braddock marched his regiments into an ambush in the forests of western Pennsylvania in the summer of 1755.[23] He was killed, and his soldiers retreated in disarray. In Britain, this outcome was wholly unexpected, and it did not take long before Braddock's defeat was publicly compared to the Battle of Prestonpans.[24] Braddock and his men had been attacked with unexpected quickness by an apparently savage enemy. Most of the attackers were native warriors, and the soldiers had panicked and run. According to some observers, the event proved that the army lacked discipline.[25] Others, opponents of the ministry, suggested that Braddock's defeat demonstrated that North American affairs had been neglected and that Cumberland and his allies were overly concerned with the defense of Hanover and other continental European affairs.[26] In the aftermath of the battle the ministry looked for a new commander for North America, one who would bring a new, stronger order to the ranks, prove the ministry's commitment to the colonies, and restore the army's reputation. Loudon volunteered.[27]

Loudon's commission as commander of British forces in North America was accompanied by an appointment as the titular governor of Virginia, a post that had been added in order to increase his authority over the colonists.[28] Loudon's supporters had argued that he should become a dominant figure in British American politics, because he was a man of "of quality" and a prominent military leader. With the governorship of Virginia and command of the army, he could demand respect and would wield the power necessary to impose his will. Some advisors to the ministry hoped that the governorship would serve as a platform for making Loudon a transformational leader of British North America, restructuring the governance of the empire, and, as one writer put it, would "rescue them [the colonies] from themselves." Proposals were already circulating for legislation defining the colonists' "privileges and subordinations." The alternative, some feared, would be to "leave them independent."[29]

In order to establish "harmony" and "union," the Earl of Halifax hoped that Loudon would convene "a council of governors, and deputies of the [colonial] assemblies" immediately after his arrival in America.[30] This would be necessary to coordinate the war effort, but Halifax also saw it as part of a broader effort to assert British sovereignty more forcefully. Halifax hoped that Parliament would authorize British taxation in America, and he speculated on the specific taxes that could most easily be imposed, including a poll tax, a land tax, and a stamp tax. Considering the alternatives, he concluded that stamp duties would be "most eligible."[31] Halifax was nine years ahead of his time, but as a group the members of the Privy Council resolved to grant Loudon "every power civil and military that can legally be given him."[32]

After crossing the ocean, Loudon was preoccupied almost exclusively with military affairs. Nonetheless, even though he never addressed issues such as peacetime taxation, his manner of asserting command over the colonies plunged him, almost immediately, into fractious disputes with colonists seeking to defend their autonomy and prerogatives.[33] The colonial assemblies and local authorities resisted Loudon's demands that they provide quarters for his soldiers without compensation from the army.[34] Colonists objected to the scope of Loudon's recruitment efforts, and among the fighting men, colonial officers and soldiers resented his efforts to subject them to the regular army's severe system of discipline.[35] Nonetheless, Loudon's first dispute with colonial officials involved the colonists' wartime policy toward native peoples, specifically the practice of scalping. This issue, as Loudon understood it, implicated fundamental questions about the structure of authority in the empire and the ability of the British to project their sovereign power coherently in an American context.

Massachusetts governor William Shirley had held command in North America on an interim basis between the time of Braddock's death and Loudon's arrival on the continent. During that year, Shirley had encouraged the colonial authorities to offer bounties for the scalps of men, women, and children belonging to enemy tribes.[36] Colonial governments had been offering such prizes, intermittently, for decades. There was a tit-for-tat logic behind the practice, a belief that since native warriors occasionally scalped colonists, it was appropriate to deploy the tactic against them. As a colonial policy, scalping had a punitive purpose. It also reflected a recognition on the part of the colonists that they could not regulate the lives of the native peoples or control them. The colonial militia could not police the woods, and in wartime they were rarely able to surround and capture significant numbers of native warriors. Under these circumstances, militiamen and volunteers inflicted violence on those individuals they could find; and in order to intimidate others, they mutilated the corpses to maximize the dramatic impact of the killing. This had been the function of scalping for centuries, since long before the colonists arrived.[37]

In 1755, Pennsylvania's governor was one of those colonial officials who took Shirley's advice and offered bounties for scalps. Using formulaic language borrowed from earlier Massachusetts proclamations, the governor declared that "the Delaware Tribe of Indians, and others in Confederacy with them" were "rebels and traitors," and he offered graduated prizes, according to the sex and age of the individuals killed. Specifically, he promised to pay 150 pieces of eight for the scalps of "Delaware" (Lenape) men over the age of twelve, 130 pieces of eight for women over twelve and younger boys, and 50 pieces of eight for the scalps of girls eleven years of age or younger.[38] The government of New Jersey adopted a similar, if slightly less elaborate, scheme.[39] Prior to Loudon's arrival on the scene, these efforts had received the endorsement of Benjamin Franklin, who belonged to a commission appointed to direct Pennsylvania's war effort against native groups.[40] In support of the program, the commissioners had resolved that "the best means of securing our inhabitants was to carry the war into the enemy's country, and hunt them in all their fishing, hunting, planting and dwelling places."[41]

Despite the support the policy received from many colonists, within days of their arrival in America Loudon and his second-in-command James Abercromby sought to void the New Jersey scalp-bounty program.

They expressed no qualms about the targeting of children, nor did they suggest that the prize system violated the rules of war. Instead they complained that the colony's initiative had undermined the diplomatic efforts of Britain's newly appointed superintendent of Indian affairs.[42] Each colony seemed to be making policy for itself. In fact the colonies had been doing so, with respect to their relations with native peoples, since the time of their founding, but Loudon was certain that this tradition had to change. He complained that in North America "not only the different colonies . . . but even private communities . . . and even single persons" negotiated with the native tribes, and he worried that this arrangement all but foreclosed the possibility of peace.[43] Loudon's objections to the practice of scalping were always logistical and pragmatic rather than moral, and despite his misgivings about the bounties, during his subsequent campaigns in North America he oversaw the payment of bounties for scalps.[44] In most of these operations Loudon worked with rangers, mixed irregular units composed of provincials and native warriors. He disliked doing so, but he believed he had to use the rangers because, as he explained to Cumberland, they were "able to deal with Indians in their own way."[45]

At least from the time of the founding of Halifax, British officers arriving for combat in North America had routinely paid bounties for scalps. Cornwallis, in the autumn of 1749, called the practice "the custom of America" and offered prizes for the deaths of Mi'kmaq men, women, and children.[46] Edward Braddock, similarly, began offering bounties for the scalps of Native Americans in the early days of his doomed campaign.[47] Cumberland's officers identified the native peoples of America as savages and assumed without qualms that they could fight native warriors unconstrained by the rules of war. It was only right, they believed, to fight them "in their own way."[48] Even Emmerich de Vattel, the leading European authority on the rules of war, acknowledged that the normal standards of conduct would not apply when "the war is with a savage nation, which observes no rules."[49]

While European conceptions of savagery helped inform the British army's response to Native Americans, a second dynamic was also at work. Cumberland's officers came with the intent of asserting Britain's sovereignty over eastern North America; they believed that the continent's purported savages, regardless of their character or customs, owed allegiance to George II. In his first proclamation offering bounties for the scalps of the Mi'kmaq, Cornwallis, with his council, used language that he could easily have used four years earlier with reference to Scotland's Jacobite Highlanders. The Mi'kmaq, he declared, "ought to be looked on as rebels to his Majesty's government, or as so many banditti, ruffians, and treated accordingly."[50] The range of available policy options dif-

fered, however, between Scotland and America. As Cornwallis knew too
well, North America was short of lawyers, especially in frontier regions.
There were virtually no translators in Nova Scotia who could work in the
Mi'kmaq language and English, and no apparatus of civilian law
enforcement equal to the task of trying the Mi'kmaq individually for
their purported crimes. On the other hand, the American continent was
huge, and the native bands seemed mobile, especially in the north and
the maritime region. These circumstances made it easier to contemplate
campaigns to eradicate local populations, whether through the "custom" of scalping or by other means. As he was unloading his ships in
Chebucto Harbor, Cornwallis declared that it would be "very practicable
with an addition of force by land & sea to root them [the Mi'kmaq] out
entirely."[51] He allowed an ambiguity to linger in this statement, whether
he imagined killing or driving the Mi'kmaq westward off the peninsula.
Cornwallis was not insistent on destroying all native peoples, and as
governor he negotiated with tribes living beyond the intended zone of
colonial settlement.[52] As long as the Mi'kmaq were "rooted out" of peninsular Nova Scotia, their ultimate fate was not his concern.

   No one in the British army or government in the 1740s or 1750s was
so cavalier about the future of the French settlers in North America. The
French had not traditionally been stigmatized as savages, and subjecting
them to indiscriminate violence had long been considered beneath
the standard of decency. As one writer in Maryland put it, "to extirpate
and destroy our enemies is not the custom of British conquerors, nor
agreeable to that lenity and generosity that Englishmen are famed
for."[53] These sensibilities restrained the colonists much more in their
combat against the French than against the native peoples of North
America. Prior to the Seven Years' War, those who imagined conquering
Canada and clearing it of its colonial population had assumed that the
French Catholic inhabitants of Quebec would be "treated with the
utmost humanity, and carefully conducted home to their own country
[France]." By 1754, however, the population of the French settlements
lining the St. Lawrence River had grown to such an extent that it no
longer seemed "practicable" to send the settlers across the ocean.[54] The
alternative of simply dispersing the Canadians, driving them west like an
aboriginal band, was never contemplated. With their numbers, wealth,
technology, and presumed diplomatic leverage, French colonists were
viewed as a security threat.[55] Furthermore, a central aim of British strategy was to keep them away from the native tribes.

   At least until 1758, the principal goal of British policy in North
America was to concentrate the zone of French settlement by expelling
settlers from contested regions outside the densely populated core of
Canada.[56] Cumberland advised Loudon to force the French to retreat

into the valley of the St. Lawrence River and to send colonial volunteers to "break up as much as they could" the "unguarded" French settlements elsewhere.[57] The destruction of those communities would dramatically assert British sovereignty over the disputed territories. Some supporters of the strategy also hoped that the influx of refugees into Quebec and Montreal would overtax local resources and impede the operations of the French army.[58] Beginning as early as 1754, British military commanders sought to "extirpate" French settlements on the isthmus of Chignecto, in the St. John River Valley, along the Ohio River, on Lake Champlain, at Niagara and at Detroit.[59] On occasion, when the French surrendered their outposts, the capitulation agreements required civilian French settlers to move to the St. Lawrence.[60] In the long run, the British hoped to bring their own colonists onto the vacated lands, for the benefit of the settlers themselves and also to contain the French geographically and disengage them from the affairs of the native tribes.

From the British perspective, one of the problems of imperial policy in North America was that the continent lacked any obvious landmark comparable to Humphrey Bland's Mediterranean Sea, delineating the boundary between the domains of the Europeans and those of the purported savages. To be sure, even in the Mediterranean context, Bland and Blakeney had worried about Dutch and French meddling in North African politics, and they believed that "Barbarians" could be manipulated by rival European powers.[61] France's apparent influence with the native people of North America was of a different character, however. For more than a century, in various places, the French had lived closely with the original inhabitants of the lands they colonized, often establishing families with them, worshipping with them, and sharing in a complex, sometimes violent, network of ritualized diplomacy, reprisal, and material exchange.[62] The French in North America, therefore, seemed peculiarly, and somewhat mysteriously, dangerous. It was never clear whether they were complicit in the actions of native warriors.

One expression of anxiety over contacts between French Catholic colonists and native people came from peninsular Nova Scotia in the summer of 1755. Before ordering the relocation of the Acadian population, Nova Scotia's provincial council asked the newly appointed chief justice of the province, Jonathan Belcher, Jr., to provide an advisory opinion justifying the action on legal grounds. Answering the council's request, Belcher cited the long history of British-ruled Nova Scotia, emphasizing the Acadians' relations with Nova Scotia's Mi'kmaq bands.[63] On several occasions over the previous decades the British had gone to war against the Mi'kmaq, while the Acadians had continued to fraternize and trade with them.[64] Though few Acadians had taken up arms against the British, Belcher argued that maintaining ties with the Mi'kmaq had been treasonous, and that this pattern of behavior revealed the Acadians' "inveterate enmity to the English." Belcher cited this history, along with the Acadians' refusal to acquiesce in the possibility of a military draft, to support his conclusion that the Acadians were "rebels to his Majesty." This was not a judgment issued against individuals, or a sanction based on a specific set of alleged infractions of British law. It was a ruling against the entire people, men, women, and children, and it was written to justify an effort to punish and reform them collectively.

In the autumn of 1755, nearly seven thousand Acadians were taken from their homes near the coasts of the Bay of Fundy and transported to English-speaking colonies to the south.[65] The decision to transport the Acadians stemmed from a recognition that the program undertaken by Cornwallis, to surround the Acadians with new settlers and absorb them into a new, cosmopolitan colonial society, had failed. On the other hand, transporting the Acadians constituted a last, slightly desperate attempt to achieve the same goal. The colonies receiving Acadian exiles dispersed them widely, in the hope that they would learn English from their new neighbors and gradually adopt English-colonial ways. If they could not be absorbed into the new Nova Scotia, perhaps they could be assimilated in other British colonies, where they would form a much smaller part of the population.

The decision to transport the Acadians was made in Nova Scotia, but it represented in many respects the culmination of a set of policy initiatives that Cumberland and his officers had supported for years. At the start of the Seven Years' War Cumberland had increased the number of troops in Nova Scotia over Newcastle's objections, and he had won the argument only after his ally in the ministry, Henry Fox, circumvented ordinary ministerial procedures and appealed directly to the king.[66] When the news arrived in Britain that those soldiers had been used to transport the Acadians, some within the ministry had expressed dismay.[67] Cumberland, by contrast, adjusted to the news easily, and in the spring of 1756 he convened a meeting in his apartment to discuss, among other issues, "the state of Nova Scotia when the French inhabitants are drove out."[68] Loudon, for his part, had followed events in Nova Scotia for years before his appointment as commander in chief, and in the winter of 1755, as the Acadians were boarded onto transport ships and soldiers burned their old farms and homes, he received reports in England from the scene.[69] After he came to North America, Loudon remained interested in the Acadians as exiles. He was particularly concerned with the future of their children.

In Philadelphia Loudon confronted a body of Acadian protesters who objected to recent provincial legislation requiring the destitute among them to bind their sons and daughters over as servants in Protestant homes.[70] The group included a number of men who threatened "to leave the women and children, and go over to the French in the back country" if their grievances were not addressed. They sent Loudon a memorial in French objecting to the Pennsylvania government's plans. Loudon told the men he would not consider their complaint, because he "could receive no memorial from the king's subjects but in English." After consulting as a group, the Acadians resolved that they would not communicate with him in any other language than French. At that point the negotiation ended. Loudon identified five "ringleaders" among the protesters, had them arrested, and sent them to England "to be disposed of as his Majesty's servants shall think proper."[71]

Loudon saw this dispute, in part, as a contest over the Acadians' willingness to obey the law, recognize their status as British subjects, and exhibit proper deference to sovereign authority, for example by petitioning Loudon in English. He had no interest in considering the merits of the underlying dispute because it struck at the core of imperial policy toward the Acadians. Since 1746, most proposals for reforming Acadian society had involved placing as many children as possible in families with Protestant fathers, either by promoting intermarriage or by removing Acadian boys and girls from the Catholic families of their birth.[72] During this controversy Loudon took advice from a man named Alexandre de Rodohan, a man who in many ways embodied the assimilationist program as it had been originally designed. De Rodohan was a French Protestant who had come to Nova Scotia during the Cornwallis administration. He had maintained friendly ties to Cornwallis, and, almost uniquely among the "foreign Protestants," he had married a Catholic Acadian woman. In the winter of 1755 he had left Nova Scotia with the exiles, eventually settling with his family in Pennsylvania.[73] De Rodohan had a unique perspective on the Acadians, and he agreed with Loudon's punitive response to those who refused to cooperate with the government's programs. He suggested that the protests had been the work of a small group of provocateurs. With the five "ringleaders" sent away, it might still be possible to get the others to submit "to any regulation made in the country, and to allow their children to be put to work."[74]

Loudon believed what de Rodohan told him, but as the weeks and months progressed, it became increasingly difficult to find others in the colonies who still thought that the Acadians as a group could be forced to adopt English, Protestantism, and industry and demonstrate their loyalty to George II. The Acadians, in general, were not cooperating with the program, and an increasing number of officials were coming to the conclusion that their presence in the colonies was a security risk. Military leaders were particularly concerned about groups of Acadian exiles who had stealthily made their way north toward French-controlled regions in the St. John River Valley, on Cape Breton Island, along the coasts of the Gulf of St. Lawrence, and around Quebec. It was generally assumed that these refugees were angry. Shirley declared that if the Acadians reached French-ruled territory they would be "worse than Indians," and he relayed his concerns to Loudon.[75] As Loudon was preparing for operations against the French on Cape Breton Island in 1757, he heard similar warnings.[76]

These admonitions came near the end of Loudon's American career. After extensive consultations with his subordinate officers, Loudon decided against attacking Cape Breton Island, in effect canceling his only ambitious strategic campaign. In 1756 he had arrived in North America too late in the summer to take any significant offensive actions, and in 1757 he had concentrated his resources on the Cape Breton campaign. While that effort came to nothing, British forces had been suffering losses farther west. Late in 1756 the French had established a new outpost at Ticonderoga, at the southern tip of Lake Champlain, and in 1757, at just about the time that Loudon's Cape Breton expedition was canceled, French forces had seized Fort William Henry, the British outpost on Lake George. Loudon's assertion of authority over the colonists had already won him political enemies, and these military setbacks exposed him to ridicule and angry denunciation. Before he left North America that winter, Loudon hurriedly collected his papers so that he would be able to defend himself and ward off criminal prosecution.[77] Cumberland predicted that he would be "pulled to pieces," and Loudon did not want to meet the fate of Admiral Byng.[78]

Loudon avoided a trial, but his loss of command had become a virtual certainty late in the autumn of 1757, after Cumberland resigned his commission as captain general of the army. Earlier in the year Cumberland had taken command of the defenses of Hanover, and by nearly all accounts he had performed badly. Cumberland's losses in Germany, combined with an array of setbacks in North America, capped the first phase of the Seven Years' War, a period that the historian Lawrence Henry Gipson has succinctly described as "the years of defeat."[79] The British public, by and large, was relieved to see the captain general give up his post. According to one observer, resigning was one of first things Cumberland had ever done that met with "universal applause."[80] Cumberland blamed his political opponents for his demise, but ultimately he resigned because his father had lost confidence in him.[81] His departure from the army jeopardized the careers of several officers who had depended on his patronage. When Cumberland wrote Loudon to tell him of his resignation, he closed his letter by declaring himself Loudon's "useless friend."[82] Thereafter, William Pitt became the principal director of Britain's war effort, and one of Pitt's first decisions was to dismiss Loudon from command in North America.

Observing these events, Cumberland worried that the policies he had adopted over the years, and specifically the approach he had taken toward the American war, would be abandoned. In a letter to Henry Fox, he wearily predicted that the "Tory doctrine of a sea war," which he had always opposed, would henceforth guide the foreign policy of "our children's children."[83] Some of his concerns were justified. Pitt adopted a more conciliatory approach to the British-colonial governments, and he refused to grant any of his general officers the kind of supervisory authority that had been held, at least in theory, by Loudon. He also abandoned the project of bringing the Acadians into the English-speaking colonies. The exiles who had already been transported were left where they were, but Pitt demonstrated no interest in pursuing coercive programs to assimilate them. After Pitt took command, the five men whom Loudon had sent to England were released. Loudon had wanted them punished for defending the Acadians' parental rights. Instead they were allowed to return to their families in America.[84]

The shift in policy was not, however, nearly as comprehensive as Cumberland feared. His resignation from the army had coincided with an ideological realignment in British politics, a change in the terms of public debate with ramifications for both the army and the empire. For a variety of reasons—some having to do with the reform of the English militia after 1757—England's long-standing popular hostility to the army lost much of its political force.[85] Simultaneously, several of Cumberland's most powerful opponents in the ministry embraced his strategy for the conduct of the war in North America. Pitt, in particular, accepted the premise that this was a struggle over territory, and like Cumberland he sought to clear most of North America of the Catholic French.[86]

Even before he wrote Loudon to inform him that he would be replaced, Pitt had chosen Wolfe to serve as part of a team of new commanders in North America.[87] Wolfe was selected in part because he was young, and Pitt assumed therefore that he would be tractable and do little to upset his superiors and elders.[88] Had Wolfe lived longer, this probably would have proven a miscalculation. Wolfe was ambitious and generally dismissive of the prerogatives of seniority.[89] He remained loyal to Cumberland throughout his career, and he came to North America with the simple resolution to do better than his older predecessors. He denigrated Loudon. "Our American affairs," he wrote, "were running into the utmost confusion under his pen and ink administration."[90] Though Wolfe had been appointed only as a second-in-command, he arrived determined to act vigorously and to succeed where, he believed,

Loudon had failed. His first assignment was to participate, under the direct command of General Jeffery Amherst, in a campaign to complete the operation that Loudon had abandoned in 1757, and take the fortified French port of Louisbourg, on Cape Breton Island.

Wolfe landed in North America in Halifax, Nova Scotia, in the early summer of 1758 and almost immediately began receiving warnings about the Mi'kmaq. For at least six months a story had circulated in Halifax that Mi'kmaq warriors, in disguise, frequented a particular tavern in town, where they gathered news, disseminated messages from the French governor of Louisbourg, and planned attacks. Rumors indicated that when groups of Mi'kmaq left Halifax, they frequently took prisoners with them, and that they scalped soldiers and settlers before returning to the woods.[91] Soon after Wolfe arrived, reports indicated that the army's transport ships, which numbered more than a hundred, had been inspected in detail at night by Mi'kmaq warriors who paddled silently around the vessels in canoes.[92] The warriors were presumably preparing to attack, and Wolfe was warned that it was their common practice to "scalp and mangle the poor sick soldiers and defenseless women." This was a reference to the women who traveled with the soldiers as wives and servants. Therefore, Wolfe was told, it was necessary to fight the Mi'kmaq "in their own way" in order to "preserve the women and children of the army from their unnatural barbarity."[93] Wolfe took these messages to heart, and on his first day of combat on Cape Breton Island, his soldiers began collecting scalps.[94] He boasted, with reference to the Mi'kmaq, "We cut them to pieces whenever we found them, in return for a thousand acts of cruelty and barbarity."[95] Nonetheless, Wolfe had to admit that the stories of the warriors' ferocity had been exaggerated. Like many British commanders in comparable circumstances, he was surprised to discover that his opponents would not stand and fight. Their tactics exasperated him. The Mi'kmaq, Wolfe declared, were "the most contemptible, cowardly scoundrels in the creation—we have destroyed some few, and the rest are trembling in the woods, flying before the meanest of our rangers."[96]

The siege of Louisbourg lasted six weeks. British naval vessels blocked the harbor, while the army patrolled the surrounding country and forced the French soldiers and civilians to seek refuge behind the fortress walls. The siege ended after an intense twelve-hour bombardment, which left more than four hundred dead.[97] The French surrendered. Under the terms of the capitulation agreement, the soldiers of the garrison were transported to England, while the civilian townspeople and all the colonists on Cape Breton and nearby Ile St.-Jean (known today as Prince Edward Island) were boarded onto ships for France.[98] Some of the civilians, particularly on Ile St.-Jean, resisted capture and managed to escape.[99] For the most part, however, the conquerors met with note-worthy cooperation. Approximately two thousand civilians were transported from Louisbourg alone.[100] Wolfe, by his own account, was disgusted with this course of events. Shortly after the garrison surrendered, he visited the town and met a group of French "ladies," who, he reported, were thin and pale, and "heartily frightened."[101] Wolfe was polite to the women, but later, after a group of townspeople told him that it had been "cruel to fire shot and shells into the town," he responded by declaring that "American war was different from all others, and must be carried on upon the principles which our enemies have thought fit to establish." Wolfe told these civilians that he was sorry the garrison had surrendered so quickly, because with one more day of bombardment the British might have done considerably more damage. This would have been appropriate, Wolfe suggested, to avenge "the unheard of and unprecedented barbarities exercised by the French, Canadians and Indians." He claimed that Britain's forces had killed or wounded "about a thousand of those scalpers," but he hoped that they would be able to "add something to that number."[102] Wolfe would get his wish, but not on Cape Breton Island.

His next assignment, in late August and early September 1758, was to take three battalions to Miramichi Bay, on the mainland coast of the Gulf of St. Lawrence, and destroy the French fishing settlements clustered there.[103] Wolfe thought it beneath his dignity "to rob the fishermen of their nets, and to burn their huts," but he performed the mission with a careful attention to detail.[104] The status of the settlers in the Miramichi region had not been raised in the negotiations at Louisbourg, because the British insisted that George II held sovereignty over the mainland coast of the Gulf of St. Lawrence under the terms of the 1713 Treaty of Utrecht. The French settlements there had to be destroyed because no one had the right to live on the mainland without swearing allegiance to Great Britain. The settlers were deemed to be intruders, and their crime was compounded because scores of Acadian refugees had fled to Miramichi after 1755 to escape the British army. Furthermore, the fishermen and refugees had received support and protection from members of two local native tribes, the Mi'kmaq and the Wuastukwiuk. Miramichi Bay, therefore, seemed to be a wellspring of resistance to British rule. In his orders for Wolfe, Amherst identified the settlements as a staging ground for "renegades."[105]

The settlers along the coasts of Miramichi Bay heard that Wolfe was coming days before he arrived. The Acadians among them warned the others that Wolfe's soldiers would give them "no quarter," and almost everyone fled.[106] According to Wolfe, his soldiers encountered "no enemy in a condition to oppose us."[107] Nonetheless, he directed his detachments to destroy every house. He ordered his men to seize furs, fish, livestock, and food and to burn every building, but he also admonished them that "he would not suffer the least barbarity to be committed upon any of the persons of the wretched inhabitants."[108] Wolfe insisted on orderly operations, and pursuant to his orders he wanted the French and Acadian colonists captured so that they could be transported to France. Summing up his operations at the end of the season, Wolfe declared that all the "houses, stages, magazines, shallops, nets, stores, and provisions" in the region had been burnt. One hundred forty colonists had been seized, "and the rest of these miserable people will in all probability be forced to abandon their settlements, and retire to Quebec."[109] One of Wolfe's admirers succinctly wrote, "Wherever he went with his troops, desolation followed."[110]

Wolfe returned to the region in the summer of 1759 in command of a much larger body of troops. His operations that year, culminating in his death and the capitulation of Quebec, in some ways mirrored his actions at Miramichi in 1758. Once again, he marched into abandoned communities, because the French inhabitants on the shores of the St. Lawrence, warned in advance of his approach, had fled.[111] Once again, Wolfe's soldiers burned the settlements, almost as comprehensively as they had done upstream. There were, however, important differences. Along the St. Lawrence Wolfe faced hostile fire, from regular French soldiers, French-Canadian militiamen, and native warriors allied with the French. Furthermore, at some vague geographical point along the river, Wolfe lost his ability to claim that the French settlements he entered were illegal encampments on British territory. Therefore he needed a different argument to justify the seizure and destruction of property, and he needed to invoke new rules if he wanted to set appropriate parameters around acceptable violence.

As he approached Quebec, Wolfe issued a proclamation which, from his perspective, laid the ethical and legal groundwork for proceeding against the French Canadians in accordance with the principles of military execution. He declared with self-conscious generosity that "the king of Great Britain wages no war with the industrious peasant, the sacred orders of religion, or the defenseless women and children." He promised the settlers that they could "remain unmolested on their lands, inhabit their houses, and enjoy their religion in security." But then he warned the inhabitants of Canada that if any of them took up arms against the British, "they must expect the most fatal consequences—their habitations destroyed, their sacred temples exposed to an exasperated soldiery, their harvest utterly ruined."[112] A few French Canadian villages were spared destruction on the basis of their ability to convince Wolfe's officers that they would abide by the terms of his proclamation.[113] More, however, were deemed to have failed to cooperate, because they had contributed men to the regular French army and the local militia. As he approached Quebec, Wolfe claimed that nearly all the men in the region were carrying arms against him. He reported to the ministry that "old people seventy years of age, and boys of fifteen fire on our detachments, and kill or wound our men from the edges of the woods" and that "old men, women, and children" hid in the forests alongside the fighting men.[114] Wolfe believed that most of the communities had violated the terms of his proclamation, and in response he set their villages on fire, often after taking the women and children hostage.

Though it proved difficult, Wolfe tried to maintain order within the violence. He threatened to prosecute and put to death anyone who seized plunder without authorization.[115] Similarly, he warned his troops, "No churches, houses or buildings of any kind are to be burned without orders. The persons that remain in their habitations, their women and children, are to be treated with humanity. If any violence is offered to a woman, the offender shall be punished with death."[116] There was no rush for loot, in part because the French Canadian settlements were generally a poor source of plunder.[117] Wolfe had greater difficulty controlling violence against "persons," because he had no clear conception what the rules should be, since he was fighting a mixed force of French soldiers, colonial militiamen, and native warriors.

Wolfe believed that he should fight France's native allies "in their own way," and as part of his campaign against them he offered prizes of five guineas each for scalps.[118] On at least two occasions his soldiers scalped French Canadians, but Wolfe insisted that he had never encouraged the practice and that as a policy he would not pay for the scalps of the French.[119] Indeed, Wolfe decried "the inhuman practice of scalping, except when the enemy are Indians."[120] On July 29, 1759, he issued a statement to the French at Quebec. He made a plea "that the inhuman practice of scalping, either by Indians or others, may be put a stop to," and he accompanied his request with a vague warning, that if scalping continued it would be "severely revenged."[121] Wolfe accompanied this statement with a gesture. He delivered up twenty-five French Canadian women who had been taken prisoner by his men a few days before. Neither the plea, nor the warning, nor the release of the female prisoners seemed to have much effect. The French denied that they were responsible for the warriors' actions. As one British observer put it, "notwithstanding this, and a great many other instances of our lenity shown to the enemy, we find little benefit accrue to us from them. They continue to scalp every person who is unhappy enough to fall into their hands."[122] This was an exaggeration, but on several occasions during the closing weeks of the campaign native warriors took the scalps of Briish men they had killed.[123]

Wolfe blamed the French, as a group, for the practice of scalping, and he was ready to deploy violence against them collectively in his effort to get the practice stopped. While he was not willing (at least openly) to countenance the scalping of French colonists, by all accounts he was ready to threaten violence against women. As they approached Quebec, Wolfe and his men took many women captive. Most were held for short periods and then returned in the context of negotiations on combat-related matters. In a private letter, General George Townshend indicated that he saw "captive women and children" brought into his camp near Quebec "every day."[124] On July 21 a British detachment landed at the village of Trembleau and took approximately three hundred prisoners, "mostly women," according to a British report on the action.[125] One soldier under Wolfe's command claimed that on September 2, 1759, "We have at least three, if not four transports, full freighted with French females: some of them women of the first rank in the country." He described the prisoners' diplomatic utility in crude terms. The soldier claimed that when the French had threatened to deliver their prisoners over to the "Indians," Wolfe had responded to the French commander, "He might do as he pleased; but, at the same time, he might be assured, that the very instant he attempted to carry his threat into execution, all the French ladies, without distinction, should be given up to the delicate embraces of the English tars."[126] Gradually, as it had in the Scottish Highlands, rape became an illicit instrument of policy, more often the subject of cruel jokes than proclamations, but nonetheless (at least as a threat in the case of the French Canadians) part of the British army's arsenal against an enemy society (see Figure 11).

British missiles set the city of Quebec on fire on July 16, 1759; it would burn again on at least three occasions.[127] In early September Wolfe reported that the town was "totally demolished, and the country in a great measure ruined."[128] After Wolfe was dead, and Quebec had surrendered, one soldier tried to calculate the destruction precisely. "During the whole siege from first to last, 535 houses were burnt down, among which is the whole eastern part of the lower town (save 6 or 8 houses) which make a very dismal appearance. We also destroyed upwards of fourteen hundred fine farm-houses in the country, &c."[129] General James Murray, who succeeded to command after the death of Wolfe, declared that "with skill and management, twenty years will hardly restore the province to the state it was in the beginning of the year (see Figure 12)."[130]

The British army had traveled a great distance between the construction of Halifax in 1749 and the burning of Quebec ten years later. By

NO MERCY TO CAPTIVES BEFORE QUEBECK

Figure 11. This caricature has been attributed to Brigadier George Townshend, who served under Wolfe during the siege of Quebec. Wolfe holds his proclamation in his hand and, waving his finger in the air, announces that "the pretty ones will be punished at headquarters." The man facing him declares, "I understand you completely, General—strike 'em in the weakest part, Egad." The man behind Wolfe thinks apprehensively, "I wonder if I shall have my share." (Courtesy of the McCord Museum of Canadian History, Montreal.)

the time the French surrendered the ruins of their city, Cornwallis and Loudon had returned to Europe, Cumberland had resigned as captain general of the army, and Wolfe was dead. Nonetheless, though the veterans of Cumberland's army in Scotland no longer had the power to direct imperial policy in Canada, their general ideas were espoused by others and survived them. In 1760, during the debate over whether Britain should retain sovereignty over the conquered province, Benjamin Franklin argued in favor of annexation. He emphasized Canada's potential (rather than its current) wealth and warned that leaving the French in control of the colony would be dangerous. Franklin compared French Canada to Ireland and the Scottish Highlands. In all three places, relatively small groups of poorly armed men could inflict great damage to the powerful, well-populated British Empire. Consequently, all three

Figure 12. In 1759 British bombardment severely damaged Quebec. This print shows the city as it appeared in 1760. (John Verelst. Library and Archives Canada, C-092414.)

places had to be under British control.[131] Soldiers would be needed, and Britain would have to encourage a wave of immigration, to "fill Canada with double the number of English than it now has of French inhabitants." Franklin thought that this could be done in ten years. He predicted that a large number of the French colonists would flee to Europe, and those who remained, "from the crowds of English settling round and among them," would eventually be "blended and incorporated with our people both in language and manners."[132] Franklin's pamphlet circulated widely in Britain and America and changed some minds, even among the soldiers in the British garrison of Quebec.[133]

The debates that Cumberland and his officers had engaged in never ended. Controversy continued over the role of British army in Britain's governmental structure, particularly in the colonies after 1763. Britain's military leaders would still repeatedly face quandaries over military codes of conduct and criminal procedure. As before, these problems seemed most daunting in the context of Britain's overseas domains. Everywhere in the empire, but particularly in North America, the absorption of new populations through conquest and immigration would revive, over and again, the debate over cultural mixing and almost continuously renew the question Defoe had raised in 1700, over what it means to be "True-born" among the English. In the middle years of the eighteenth century Cumberland and his subordinate officers had joined these discussions, but they had not achieved resolution. On such questions, in truth, they had resolved nothing.

Nonetheless, Cumberland's army made an impact, and of all the legacies of its service in North America, one of the most dramatic and unmistakable was the effect it had on the Scottish Highlands and the reputation of the Highlanders as servants of the empire. The Forty-second Regiment, the famous "Black Watch," had never served in the colonies before 1756. Loudon brought the unit with him when he crossed the ocean to serve as commander in chief. One year later, two more battalions came to America from Highland Scotland, and Highlanders would continue to fight for the British on the American continent and in the Caribbean, for the duration of the war and beyond. Gaelic-speaking Highlanders constituted a significant part of the forces Britain sent across the Appalachian Mountains in 1763 to confront Pontiac and suppress yet another Native American "insurrection."[134]

The idea of sending Highland troops to America had been circulating for years. Some ministers and military officers believed that service overseas could function as a substitute for exile and prevent young Gaelic-speaking men from causing trouble in Britain.[135] Others, more generously, suggested that enlistment in the army would reform the character of the soldiers and tie them economically and emotionally to the ruling regime.[136] Even after the Highland units arrived in America, these ideas remained controversial, however. Hardwicke, for example, argued in 1756 that the Highlanders were a "dangerous resource" militarily because their loyalty could not be trusted. Others had long maintained, more generally, that the Gaelic-speakers' purported militaristic impulses should be suppressed, and that "savages addicted to arms and rapine must be civilized by the arts of peace and not war."[137]

As it happened, complex political negotiations led to the deployment of the Highlanders across the ocean. Cumberland and Newcastle had long supported the idea, but William Pitt was more reluctant and became convinced only in 1756.[138] For all these men, one of the difficult aspects of the decision was that it brought them into a pragmatic alliance with several prominent and powerful landlords in the Highlands, and it seemed, temporarily at least, that the recruitment process would strengthen the militaristic traditions of the clans. Soldiers were enlisted into the army through the operation of well-established, family-based patronage networks.[139] Though the ministry ordered its recruiters not to exploit clanship, the process seemed to follow predictable lines.[140] Expressing the trend more openly than most ministers did, a report in the *London Magazine* in 1757 indicated that two new battalions destined for service in America would be recruited from "the Campbells, the Mackenzies, the Frasers, the Macdonalds, and the Grants."[141]

Argyll and a few other prominent and powerful Highland landlords saw military recruitment and provisioning as a way to increase their own patronage power in Scotland, their political leverage in London, and their fortunes generally. The Highlands were suffering economically in the mid-1750s, and many landlords worked in cooperation with the army's press gangs to evict surplus laborers and potentially troublesome young men. On the Atholl estates, for example, orders were issued to seize "all able-bodied, idle, and disorderly persons" and enlist them for service across the ocean.[142] One officer serving in the Highland regiments in America reported that his company was "mostly composed of impressed men."[143] Many of those forcibly recruited began to plead for release before they left Scotland. One recruiter complained, "I am plagued to death with them. Every one of them wants to be at home."[144] One of Humphrey Bland's last duties as commander in chief in Scotland, before his retirement in 1756, was to arrange for the transportation of the new recruits.[145] This was in many ways fitting, because military recruitment served several of the goals he had long sought to achieve in his reform proposals. It put young men to work, exposed them to the wider world, and had the effect of diversifying the regional economy and increasing the circulation of cash. Many of the recruits left impoverished parents, wives, and children behind.[146] To support them they sent money home.[147]

One of the landlords who saw military recruitment as a great opportunity was Aeneas MacKintosh, the husband of the famous "Lady Anne," and Loudon's old friend. MacKintosh felt certain that economic necessity would convince many of his tenants to enlist and cross the Atlantic. He told Loudon in 1757, "If there is another year as this you'll have us all in America."[148] From the start, MacKintosh also believed that vigorous support for the war effort would restore the political reputation of his home region and dispel its lingering association with Jacobitism. In early May 1756 he assembled the freeholders of Inverness and had them endorse a petition to George II which was published in the *London Gazette*. The petition declared that the British colonists in North America were facing the same adversary that the government's forces had faced in Scotland in 1745, a coalition of the French and traitorous British subjects, vaguely identified as "the Common Enemy of our Peace." The petition went on to praise Cumberland's 1746 military campaign, the subsequent trials and punishment of the Jacobite prisoners, and the investments the government had made since that time for "training up even the lowest order of the inhabitants [of the Highlands] to industry."

In conclusion the petitioners vowed that a sense of gratitude, and an eagerness to demonstrate their fidelity to the reigning royal family, had motivated them to raise soldiers for the defense of British North America.[149]

Aeneas and Anne MacKintosh actively encouraged enlistment over the next few years. They opened their house to the commanders of the Highland battalions, who stayed with them in Inverness for several days recruiting.[150] With their diverse family connections and political histories, they sought reconciliation between former adversaries, including Jacobites and old allies of Cumberland and Loudon. In particular, Aeneas MacKintosh vouched for the character of Simon Fraser (the son of Lord Lovat), whom Loudon had met in 1746. "The longer you know Col. Fraser," he promised, "you'll love him the better."[151] For the most part, however, the Highlanders who came to fight in America after 1756 were not former Jacobites.[152] Most of them were too young to have participated in the 1745 rising.[153] Fraser was exceptional, and his appointment as commander of a battalion had caused controversy on the floor of the House of Commons.[154] Some of Loudon's supporters suspected that Fraser had been chosen to embarrass him.[155]

After they arrived in the colonies, the Highland soldiers were seldom perceived as a political threat, however. The 1745 rising had been frightening as it was occurring, but it had changed little in North America permanently, and among the colonists memories were fading. Moreover, because there were few concentrated Gaelic-speaking communities in North America outside North Carolina, the leaders of the Highland units could maintain a clear boundary between military and civilian life, which led some colonists to prefer Highlanders to other British troops. The soldiers spoke Gaelic and therefore did not engage in recruiting, which allowed them to avoid an array of controversies.[156] Furthermore, desertion rates from the units were low, because it was difficult for the men to slip unnoticed into the colonial population.[157] More generally, the Highland soldiers gained a reputation for orderliness and circumspection, in all probability because they had difficulty communicating with the colonists and found little entertainment in the colonial towns. After a body of Highlanders spent the winter in Connecticut, several townspeople declared that the men had been "thrifty, consequently sober and less liable to get into squabbles" than other soldiers.[158] Listening to the advice they received from Connecticut, the authorities in Boston asked for Highlanders in the event that Massachusetts had to quarter any troops.[159]

The Highlanders, in general, pleased the colonists, not only because they were easy guests but also because they quickly gained a reputation as effective soldiers. Even Wolfe, who hated Highlanders in Scotland, praised the Highland units in his American command.[160] By the time of the fall of Quebec, a legend was developing that the men of the Scottish Highlands were peculiarly suited for service in America. As one writer put it, "The Highlanders seem particularly calculated for this country. Their patience, temperance, and hardiness, their bravery, their agility, nay, their very dress contributes to adapt them to the climate, and render them formidable to the enemy."[161]

When they arrived in North America, the Highlanders had carried with them (at least in some quarters) a reputation for savagery comparable to the one attached to native North Americans. Loudon went so far as to claim that the Iroquois thought of the Highlander as a "kind of Indian."[162] The soldiers' manner of close combat, their loose-fitting clothing, and their practice of yelling as they ran toward their enemies linked them, it seemed, to America's native warriors.[163] Early reports reaching Britain indicated that the Highlanders readily adopted Native American customs, including the taking of scalps.[164] Even as these stories were told, however, most of the English-language commentary on the Highlanders during the war emphasized their alleged superiority over the native warriors. The Highlanders, it was widely claimed, operated with discipline in coherent units, and though they fought with occasional brutality, their resort to scalping and other similar practices was motivated primarily by righteous anger.[165] At its most extreme, this way of interpreting the Highlanders' experience in the Seven Years' War celebrated acts of massive retaliatory violence. In one published war memoir, for example, the Highlander Robert Kirk claimed to have participated in an attack on a Catholic mission among the Abenaki in which he and his fellow soldiers were ordered to set fire to every house and "kill every one without mercy."[166] Kirk almost certainly exaggerated the effectiveness of the action, but he insisted that "in less than a quarter of an hour the whole town was in a blaze, and the carnage terrible . . . Thus the inhumanity of these savages was rewarded with calamity." It had been "dreadful indeed," he admitted, "but justly deserved."[167]

Others among the Highland troops had a slightly more constructive response to the native communities they encountered. Their response depended to a great extent on where they were posted and whether their first exposure to native people was in battle. In Iroquois country, in particular, Highlanders lived near native villages in conditions sometimes approaching peace. They were more likely than other British soldiers to be stationed in frontier outposts.[168] This was so not only because they were thought to be hardy and well suited to wilderness conditions but also because they were assumed to be poorly trained and unprepared for conventional garrison duty.[169] When they were posted near native villages, many of the soldiers, lonely and far from home, established friendly relations with their new neighbors, and they occasionally found love, though often only temporarily. Some of the officers of the Highland companies discouraged this.[170] Other commanders, however, including Simon Fraser, sought out temporary loves of their own. These were not equal relationships. Fraser never shed his aristocratic bearing or his assumption of cultural superiority over the people near his camp. Almost without pausing for thought, he could turn from boasting of his sexual conquests among the Iroquois to recounting daydreams in which he reformed them by placing them under the benevolent guidance of a Scottish philosopher-king. Specifically, Fraser fantasized about making Henry Home, Lord Kames, governor of the Iroquois. "This is the country for a philosopher," he wrote. "What a find for his favorite investigation, the human mind! . . . What is most wanted here is persons to think for the people and to put them in motion."[171]

Almost invariably, the Highlanders took their supremacy for granted and saw themselves as part of a civilized, conquering group. This was equally true whether they boasted of killing "Indians" or of having sex with them. It was even more the case with respect to Fraser and others like him who imagined providing the tribes good government. Nonetheless, the most permanently intrusive assertion of supremacy the Highlanders made, over the native peoples and over the French, was their claim on North American lands. Robert Grant, a merchant from Aberdeen, wrote to his family from Halifax, Nova Scotia, in May 1756, describing the opportunities offered ordinary settlers by the removal of the Acadians. "We have got rid entirely of the French . . . I don't hear of anybody coming in their rooms. There are many hundred of as fine farms and orchards as any in Britain laying waste, the cattle perishing for want of anybody to look after them."[172] Ongoing combat delayed the onset of immigration, but as early as the spring of 1757, families in the Scottish Highlands who had contributed soldiers to the American war effort were declaring their intention to cross the ocean as soon as the fighting was over and the "disturbers" were gone. They vowed to "improve what is reckoned here a fine country."[173]

*   *   *

The Seven Years' War altered the landscape of both North America and Scotland. Canada was slowly rebuilt, and beginning almost from the moment of Wolfe's death, new accommodations were reached between the British and the colony's French-speaking, Catholic inhabitants.[174] From 1763 onward, the French colonists owed formal allegiance to Great Britain, and they had to accommodate themselves, whether they liked it or not, to the arrival of thousands of newcomers in the valley of the St. Lawrence and elsewhere on the continent.[175] Responding to offers of land, more than 150 noncommissioned officers and soldiers from Simon Fraser's battalion stayed in North America after the fighting ended. They were offered free land, and many of them chose to live in the heart of formerly French Canada.[176] Hundreds of other soldiers established new homes along the St. Lawrence and on Ile St.-Jean, in New York, and in North Carolina. Over the next twelve years, thousands more from the Highlands—including women, children, and men who had not served in the army—crossed the ocean and settled in the colonies.[177] Emigration, not just to America but also to Britain's other, expanding possessions, accelerated after 1763 and transformed the Scottish Highlands' economy. From that time forward, Highland soldiers were deployed nearly everywhere the British Empire spread, and settlers often followed. Eventually on nearly every continent, and on islands around the world, Highlanders became, often proudly, consummate representatives of Britain's imperial project.

Cumberland's Death and the End of the Officers' Careers

The 1745 Jacobite rising allowed Cumberland, and the soldiers he led, to present themselves as the ultimate defenders of Protestantism and constitutional order. Once Charles Edward was defeated, many believed that Cumberland's regiments had warded off chaos, despotism, and Catholic rule in Britain. The army had also, according to some observers, defended the nation's sovereignty. The crisis had heightened fears of Catholic influence in Britain's domestic affairs, fears that centered on the alleged secret intentions of the French as well as the Church in Rome. This way of thinking had special significance in the British colonies, particularly in North America, where Cumberland's victory at Culloden was celebrated as a defense of Britain's colonial territories, thwarting (at least for the time being) the imperial ambitions of France.

The events of 1745 and 1746 gained support for the army throughout the British Empire and strengthened Cumberland's position as he struggled to secure political backing for the maintenance of large land forces after the cessation of hostilities in Europe in 1748. The deployment of soldiers in peacetime carried deep ideological significance, both for Cumberland and for his opponents in Britain. He and the officers under him associated the army with security, enlightenment, and social progress, while many of his political adversaries argued that maintaining regiments, except in a time of war, threatened individual liberty and constitutional order, especially if the soldiers were placed under the overall command of a member of the royal family.

The Scottish Highlands were an arena at the center of this debate. It was the Highlands, after all, that had received the concentrated attention of Cumberland's forces in the immediate aftermath of the insurrection, and for years thereafter the Highlanders suffered more than others in Britain from the continuous presence of garrisons. Cumberland's opponents in Lowland Scotland and England cited the Highlanders' experience as a premonition of what all Britons could face if the army were allowed to expand its powers unchecked. Cumberland and his officers responded to these charges by insisting that the policies they adopted in Scotland were transitional measures, justified by the primitive social customs prevailing in the Highlands and the prominent role of the clans in the 1745 rising. Cumberland did not intend to extend military government over all of Britain. On the contrary, the aim of his actions in the Highlands was to establish a new peaceful order there. In cooperation with the civilian authorities, he hoped to secure the uncontested sovereignty of the king in Parliament, introduce new legal institutions, reform the backward and violent customs of the inhabitants, build a new economic infrastructure, and gradually incorporate the Highlands more fully into the cosmopolitan orbit of Britain as a whole.

The dispute over the meaning of the army's actions in the Highlands paralleled other, ongoing controversies over the governance of Britain's colonies. Cumberland's officers, after they were stationed in colonial posts, differed from their predecessors in their zeal for advancing British civilization. In a variety of contexts, in the Mediterranean as well as in North America, they sought to promote the use of the English language, serve the cause of Protestantism, and encourage commercial exchange. They also generally hoped to establish English-style law courts, though their interest in legal reform was subordinated to an overriding concern to assert the supremacy of the British government under George II.

The years between 1745 and 1759 were pivotal for both Britain and its empire. The reforms the government implemented in the Highlands after 1746 hardly achieved all its purposes, but the end of wardholding and the abolition of heritable jurisdictions diminished the local prerogatives of the Highlanders. Jacobitism lost its power as a military threat, and partly as a consequence, new political alliances were formed, facilitating cooperation between the leaders of the Highlands and the authorities in Westminster. The ongoing presence of garrisons in the Highlands, and the mobilization of Highlanders in the Seven Years' War, promoted the circulation of money in the region and enlisted more of the region's inhabitants into Britain's imperial enterprise. Strengthened politically by their operations in Scotland, the leaders of the army could devote greater resources to the defense and expansion of the empire. They sought to consolidate control over marginal territories overseas by promoting immigration, Protestantism, commerce, legal reform, and the use of the English language. After the resumption of warfare in 1754, they turned their attention to the French in North America, and laid much of the groundwork for the conquest of New France.

Since we live in a world shaped by the legacies of British and Anglo-American imperialism, it can be difficult to recover the sense of contingency that surrounded the spread of British influence in the middle decades of the eighteenth century. Yet it is necessary to understand the fears of the imperialists, and the perceived uncertainties of the time, in order to comprehend the empire's political dynamics. In Cumberland's lifetime no one was certain about the future of British power—the ability of the government in Westminster to maintain political stability at home, and to protect and expand its territories and influence abroad. Moreover, there were uncertainties surrounding the aims of British imperial policy, the value of governing foreign territories and peoples, and the rights of the inhabitants of colonized lands. It is necessary to recognize the quandaries and controversies surrounding these issues, not only to understand events in the eighteenth century, but to comprehend developments in later eras as well, because the questions that troubled Cumberland and his contemporaries were never coherently or permanently resolved. What were the rights of the inhabitants of the scattered sections of Britain's domains? How should the authorities respond when culturally distinct communities resisted incorporation into the empire? In the middle years of the eighteenth century, Britain's political leaders debated the loyalty, and legal rights, of Scottish Highlanders, Catholics, and the native peoples of North America, among others. Long before the status of those groups was resolved, still more communities would be examined and debated in similar terms, and indeed the discussions continued as long as the empire continued to expand.

When Cumberland resigned from command of the army in 1757, the legal and administrative structures of the empire remained thoroughly confused.[1] In the early 1760s, the government's ministers argued over the status of the inhabitants of its newly conquered territories. In North America, uncertainties surrounded the rights of the native peoples of the Great Lakes region and the French-speaking Catholic colonists in the old territories of New France. Long before those issues were resolved, new questions arose over the constitutional status of Britain's colonial governments and the rights of the colonists. In time these controversies would become particularly perplexing in the string of colonies running from Georgia to New England.

Cumberland continued to participate in politics between 1757 and 1765. He was still widely admired as a military hero, and he retained a popular following. Nonetheless, his resignation from the army had destroyed most of his patronage power. Especially after the death of his father and the accession of George III in 1760, Cumberland's influence on policy was limited.[2] In 1763, under the terms of the Peace of Paris, the British claimed sovereignty over Canada and regained Minorca. Cumberland had shown an interest in both territories earlier in his career, but he did not play a major role in the debates over their administration under George III.[3] Though the king was his nephew, Cumberland stayed outside the inner circles of government until the spring of 1765, when a spate of riots in London, coming after weeks of political wrangling in Parliament, convinced George III that his ministers had to be dismissed.[4] Cumberland had a rare conversation with the king and agreed to help him form a new government. By late summer he had assumed a prominent position in the ministry.

Almost immediately thereafter, reports began to arrive from America indicating that protesters representing a wide cross-section of the colonial population intended to prevent the recently enacted Stamp Act from taking effect. The colonists insisted that the proposed stamp duties would violate their constitutional rights, because Parliament could not tax them in that way without granting them representation in the House of Commons.[5] Cumberland summoned the cabinet to his apartment on October 31, 1765 to formulate a response to the protests. The meeting was cancelled, however, because an hour before the appointed time, Cumberland was struck by a sharp pain in his chest and died.[6] In the weeks after his death, many of his contemporaries, remembering his career as captain general and recent statements he had made about the need to assert British authority in the colonies, assumed that he would have steered the government more assertively than his successors in the ministry did. In the spring of 1766 the government arranged for the repeal of the Stamp Act, which had the effect of postponing Parliament's confrontation with America. Some believed that if Cumberland had lived he would have taken charge of the debate, kept the law in place, and made every effort to enforce the Stamp Act, with soldiers if necessary.[7]

In the 1740s and 1750s, in the Scottish Highlands as well as in the Mediterranean and in North America, Cumberland's officers and soldiers had never shown much respect for the peculiar legal institutions and customary prerogatives of local communities. On the contrary, they had insisted on the undiluted authority of the king and Parliament, and they had adopted a punitive stance toward those who resisted them. Cumberland and his officers expressed a preference for arresting purported rebels and punishing them only after formal criminal trials, but in situations where the law courts were unequal to that task, they were ready to deploy military force and pursue retribution against whole communities collectively. Along with Cumberland, Blakeney, Bland, Cornwallis, Loudon, and Wolfe had all believed that a period of military rule might be necessary to reform the political institutions of rebellious provinces—at least outside England in the less anglicized margins of Britain's domains. It is impossible to know for certain how they would have responded to the challenge of imposing order in the predominantly English-speaking and Protestant colonies of North America. Nonetheless, there is reason to suspect that several of Cumberland's officers might have considered it a righteous enterprise to use troops to collect taxes from the American colonists. Indeed Loudon's supporters had hoped that he might perform exactly that kind of service after he was appointed military commander in North America in 1756.[8]

The five officers were not, however, at the height of their powers at the time of the Stamp Act crisis. Bland had retired in 1756, after receiving a sinecure appointment as governor of Edinburgh Castle. Shortly thereafter he left Scotland. By then he was already an ailing man, and he died in London at the age of seventy-seven in 1763.[9] Blakeney, for his part, retired from active service in 1757. He died four years later, at the age of eighty-nine, and was entombed in Westminster Abbey.[10] Wolfe, of course, was also gone. His death at the gates of Quebec had made him a legend.[11] Only Cornwallis and Loudon remained.

Cornwallis had never fully recovered, emotionally or professionally, from the events of 1756. As a member of Byng's council of war, he had barely escaped prosecution alongside the admiral. One year later he had faced another similar scandal, after he participated in a shipboard council of war that resolved not to proceed with an attack on the French port of Rochefort, on the Bay of Biscay.[12] Again a court martial was convened, and though Cornwallis was not formally charged with a crime, the inquiry jeopardized his reputation and career.[13] Wolfe had also been involved in the council of war before Rochefort, but unlike Cornwallis he had argued in favor of aggressive action and therefore could not be blamed for the cancellation of the expedition.[14] After the controversy began, Wolfe worried for Cornwallis. "There is a storm gathering over the head of my unfortunate friend," he had written, "such a one as must necessarily crush him."[15] Wolfe's worst fears were not realized, but after these incidents Cornwallis was passed over for promotion repeatedly, on occasion in spite of his seniority.[16] Nonetheless, by 1762 Cornwallis had obtained the governorship of Gibraltar.[17] His performance at that post, especially compared to his earlier career in Nova Scotia, exhibited disillusionment, a loss of energy, and a decline in his enthusiasm for the imperial cause.

On his arrival in the Mediterranean, Cornwallis was told that the "Moors in Barbary were growing troublesome," and for the next three years he was engaged in intermittent negotiations similar to those conducted by Bland more than a decade before.[18] Cornwallis was less personally engaged in the diplomatic process than Bland had been, however. The British political elite was barely paying attention to his activities, and Cornwallis himself questioned the value of his efforts. Within a year he had despaired of maintaining peace. That would be impossible, he asserted, because the "inveterate enmity subsisting between the Spaniards and the Moors," combined with the polyglot nature of the merchant community on Gibraltar, guaranteed that disputes would always arise over the rights and liabilities of particular traders. He maintained that commercial life at the outpost would be fraught with violent controversy until "native British subjects" came to Gibraltar in greater numbers, but Cornwallis expressed no hope of encouraging immigration.[19]

While he believed that the peoples of the North African coast were violent and untrustworthy, Cornwallis did not draw out the contrast between Europe and Africa as sharply as Bland had done. Britain was at war with the Spanish Empire in 1762, and Cornwallis had nothing good to say about Spain. To make matters worse, the British-ruled enclave itself depressed him. While some of Bland's reforms had taken effect—a civilian law court was established in 1753—overall, Cornwallis believed, Gibraltar remained a center of corruption.[20] Bland's scheme to tax liquor had been repealed, and instead of collecting license fees, fines, and duties, Gibraltar's military officials routinely supported themselves and subsidized their operations by demanding bribes.[21] Cornwallis admitted that, as a consequence, his governorship had become one of the most "lucrative" positions in the British army.[22] Nonetheless, though he enriched himself, he considered the outpost a place of exile, and he lamented his situation.

Cornwallis had started his career with enormous advantages—he had lived among members of the royal household since childhood—but now it seemed he had no powerful friends in the government. He wrote to Loudon in the winter of 1762 to complain about his alienation from the ministry. Since his arrival at Gibraltar, he declared, he had been left "totally ignorant of all public affairs."[23]

Cornwallis's sense of isolation was compounded by his separation from his wife. He had married while still in active military service, in 1753.[24] His wife Mary, however, had not joined him in Gibraltar, and by 1765 she was helping her husband plead for permission to return to England.[25] Cornwallis, by that time, was frantic. He complained that he had felt a "decline in vigor of body and mind" since his posting in Gibraltar.[26] Specifically, he wrote that he suffered from a "disorder in my head," that stupefied him, affected his strength, and rendered him "incapable of doing any business."[27] In the summer of 1765 Cornwallis received permission to return to England for one year.[28] He was not, however, formally relieved of his post and remained governor of Gibraltar. He returned twice and left for the last time in 1773. He died three years later.[29]

Like Cornwallis, Loudon never fully recovered from the controversy that had surrounded him in the early, unsuccessful period of the Seven

Years' War. After he was dismissed from his command in North America he returned to Britain in 1758 and began preparing for a possible court martial or public inquiry into his actions as commander.[30] According to his accusers, Loudon had violated his duty by postponing the attack on Louisbourg in 1757. Some, however, raised wider objections to his behavior, suggesting that he was corrupt and a tyrant, that he had trammeled the rights of the American colonists, refused to inform the ministry of his plans, and intentionally prolonged the fighting in order to enrich himself and his supporters.[31] Loudon's removal from command not only hurt him; it undercut the position of those who had depended on his patronage for the advancement of their careers.[32] His friends were anxious to salvage his public standing and influence. In one publication, somewhat desperately, they compared him to Blakeney, a hero who had been unjustly slandered in a moment of political crisis.[33] No one succeeded in presenting Loudon as a hero, however. His reputation, it seemed, had been effectively destroyed. In the months following his dismissal from military command, some doubt lingered over his status as governor of Virginia, but in the autumn of 1759 that post was taken from him too.[34]

Years later, Loudon still complained stridently about what had happened to him. In the winter of 1762 he wrote to Cumberland's old ally in the ministry, Henry Fox, to argue that his downfall had come solely as a result of petty factional politics. Loudon complained that he had had "suffered every persecution" at the hands of those in the government who opposed Cumberland and Fox: "Removed from my command, a government taken from me, my character traduced, my enemies abetted and protected, the lowest, basest and most improbable calumnies against me encouraged, and their authors screened from justice and sometimes rewarded."[35] Loudon presented himself as a victim, and almost, perhaps, as a martyr, though he retained a hope that Cumberland's friends in the ministry might return to power.

Loudon's military career was not quite over. In 1762 he commanded troops in Portugal, but the posting made him miserable.[36] After peace was restored with Spain in 1763, he returned to his home in Scotland, and after Bland's death in that year he succeeded him as governor of Edinburgh Castle.[37] It was a comfortable post, though not a powerful one. In 1778 Loudon was called out of his effective retirement from military service for a high-profile assignment, to preside over an inquiry into General John Burgoyne's failed expedition into revolutionary New York. Loudon and his fellow officers did not proceed with their planned investigations, however, because they feared that conducting the inquiry might be interpreted as a violation of sworn agreements Burgoyne had entered into when he surrendered to the American patriots.[38] In 1746

Cumberland had refused to respect the terms of similar promises his subordinate officers and soldiers had made when they surrendered to Charles Edward's men. Nonetheless, by 1778 America's revolutionary movement was much stronger, and more viable, than the Jacobites in Britain had ever been. Furthermore, surrendering to the patriots in North America never seemed as subversive as giving in to the Jacobites. Since America's revolutionaries did not seek sovereignty over the entire kingdom and empire, their demands were always more negotiable, from the British perspective. Still, in 1778 respecting the terms of Burgoyne's surrender represented a significant concession. Loudon and his fellow officers, in effect, acknowledged the enduring power of the Continental Congress, its army, and the patriots generally in the United States.

Almost until his death in 1782, Loudon remained involved in imperial politics and the affairs of the army, but for the last nineteen years of his life most of his energies were consumed in the management of his Scottish estates. Loudon had inherited his title and land in Ayrshire in 1731, four years after his enlistment in the army. His time had been divided ever since, and when military service called him away from home, he continued to receive letters from family members, tenants, and neighbors seeking direction, assistance, and advice. In the 1740s and 1750s Loudon's mother, Margaret Campbell, the Countess of Loudon, oversaw many of the routine operations of the estate. While she gloried in her son's military successes, she had pleaded with him repeatedly to spend more time at home, both for his own good and for that of the community. In 1746 she had disapproved of his spending the summer in the Highlands sleeping without a tent.[39] In 1755 she had argued more vehemently that he should not go to North America and enlisted friends and neighbors into the effort to dissuade him. There was no glory to be won fighting "a few French troops assisted by some Indian savages," they insisted. On the other hand Loudon might die "hideously," they warned, and he would be slandered if his campaigns did not succeed.[40] After Loudon returned to Scotland in 1758, he may have remembered those warnings and recognized the wisdom of his mother's advice: he could live comfortably, distinguish himself, and serve the empire without going overseas to fight or occupying colonial posts. From 1763 forward he devoted most of his time to Ayrshire, his tenants, and his land.

Since the early 1730s Loudon had expressed an interest in improving his estates by taking advantage of new technologies and new trends in industry. Working in consultation with his mother and James Arnot, his principal factor, Loudon experimented with lead mining, and established a coal mine and a stone quarry.[41] He and Arnot viewed these projects as an expression of their benevolence rather than simply as money-making ventures. In 1757, when crops were failing across Scotland,

Arnot told Loudon that his coal mine was a "great relief to this country" because everyone needed money to eat. Few were able to grow their own food.[42]

Like many of his aristocratic compatriots across Scotland, Loudon believed that the improvements he introduced onto his estates reflected his general interest in human progress. Throughout his career he had worked to educate himself, and he stayed familiar with the currents of contemporary thought.[43] Even in America his education continued. One of the first men to meet him after his arrival in New York was Benjamin Franklin. His conversations with Franklin ranged widely and covered issues that may have been relevant to the war effort but also carried a general utility. They discussed road construction, for example, and the mechanics of delivering the mail.[44] Loudon's military experience and his contact with the outer reaches of the empire informed and facilitated some of the innovations he brought onto his estates. With the assistance of the army, he carried aspects of colonial life back to southern Scotland. His most visible imports were new varieties of livestock and crops.

Taking advantage of his far-flung connections, Loudon collected seeds from cedars in Lebanon, coconuts from India, silk grass from the Mosquito coast, and sunflowers from eastern North America.[45] An orchard at Loudon's estate in Scotland had more than sixty varieties of fruit trees.[46] Elsewhere on the grounds he grew dozens of different cedars, spruces, and pines. Along with his interest in trees, Loudon examined the properties of food crops, including potatoes, kidney beans, and watermelons.[47] He collected ornamental and fragrant flowers and medicinal herbs.[48] With his aristocratic colleagues, he also experimented with exotic livestock and fowl, including swine from India and turkeys and quail from the American woods.[49]

In the middle years of the eighteenth century, seeds, roots, cuttings, and whole plants were common gifts between aristocrats, courtiers, ministers, and military officials. Loudon distributed botanical specimens to other aristocrats in Scotland including Argyll, Stair, Milton, and Bute.[50] He also received grafts of fruit trees from other collectors and experimenters.[51] As well as seeds and specimens, Loudon and his associates exchanged advice on the transportation and planting of crops, watering, and soil conditions. For many of them, this was a labor of love with deep ideological significance, for it tied Scotland to the margins of the empire and served the people of Britain by expanding knowledge and potentially introducing new products and industries to promote the British economy. Despite the public service these men believed they were performing, none of them openly considered gardening to be work. They were ministers and leaders of the empire, and in their own estimation, at least, their concerns and interests rose far above those of "Farmer Grover," the archetypical, ordinary agriculturalist.[52]

In a race to find varieties of plants that had never reached Britain before, Loudon's seed collectors ventured into war-torn provinces. For more than a year his friends in Nova Scotia tried to hire men to venture into the woods surrounding Halifax, but none was willing to risk entering the area, which was under the effective control of the Mi'kmaq.[53] His correspondent in Asia was similarly unable to enter the countryside surrounding Europe's trading posts in China, the Malay Peninsula, and India.[54] Loudon's botanical collections, like those of his British contemporaries, directly depended on British (or at least European) political influence and military power. Nothing could be gathered from uncolonized regions where indigenous peoples resisted the plant collectors. To console Loudon for his lack of access to Nova Scotia's woods, one friend sent him souvenirs that could be gathered more easily, including a shipment of dried fish.[55] Loudon received seeds from trees in Nova Scotia only in 1757, after the removal of the Acadians and the conclusion of peace treaties between the British and the local Mi'kmaq bands. Even then, he was unable to acquire a coveted specimen of larch.[56] In 1760 the fall of Montreal afforded an opportunity to gather mayapple seeds, though Loudon's friends in the field protested that they were too busy to gather as many seeds as he might have wished.[57]

Loudon's gardens, orchards, and cultivated forests reflected a British cultural trend, an enthusiasm that was spreading through the ranks of the wealthy, the powerful, and the privileged not only in Scotland but in England as well. Before 1765, one of the most prominent plant collectors had been Cumberland himself. Beginning in 1746 Cumberland oversaw the Great Park in Windsor, and in his enthusiasm to gather plants for this and other royal properties, he took advantage of his position of authority in the army.[58] He, like Loudon, sent subordinate officers and soldiers into areas of intermittent combat, on the coasts of North Africa and in North America, to collect seeds and exotic birds for his increasingly complex parks.[59] Cumberland's brother Frederick had similar ambitions, and while Cumberland was remaking Windsor, Frederick was creating his own enormous "garden of exotics" on the grounds of the royal family's "White House" at Kew.[60]

These gardens were a direct reflection of the British Empire.[61] They grew physically and became more elaborate as the imperial authorities consolidated their control over their scattered territories and, through economic leverage, diplomatic influence, and military power, expanded Britain's geographical reach. For those who came to Loudon's estate in Ayrshire, the Great Park at Windsor, or Kew, the exotically cultivated landscape seemed to demonstrate what Britain could achieve by expanding its overseas domain. The grand parks of eighteenth-century Britain were not simply retreats from the concerns of the world. They were places of study, education, and industrious labor as well as rest. Loudon and his fellow collectors believed that by importing the products of divergent climates they could expand human knowledge and initiate technological innovations that would improve the material circumstances of the people of Britain, and perhaps benefit everyone on the globe. There was an assumption of global hierarchy underlying the way they went about this mission. The owners and custodians of the gardens assumed that progress could be achieved only if exotic plants and animals were removed from their original countries and taken to Britain, so that British gardeners and scholars could study and manipulate them without facing the expense, danger, disorientation, and discomfort of venturing into hostile lands.

Cumberland and Loudon, and Britain's aristocrats and political leaders generally, achieved something within the confines of their parks that they could never accomplish on a national or imperial scale. They made their project seem peaceful. To be sure, military men were sent to gather seeds, cuttings, and small plants along with new specimens of livestock and fowl. Nonetheless, for those who visited the gardens there was seldom any occasion to consider the implicit threat of violence that made soldiers effective collectors. Even in the years of warfare in the eighteenth century, it was comforting to forget that the peace, stability, and prosperity of the empire required the deployment of military force.

Notes

In citing archives, abbreviations have been used, as follows.

Aberdeen University, Special Collections and Archives (AU)
British Library (BL)
Huntington Library (HL)
  Abercromby Papers (AB)
  Loudon Papers, North America (LO (NA))
  Loudon Papers, Scotland (LO (SC))
The National Archives (TNA)
  Colonial Office correspondence (CO)
  Records of the Privy Council (PC)
  State Papers (SP)
  Treasury Papers (T)
National Archives of Scotland (NAS)
National Library of Scotland (NLS)
Nova Scotia Archives and Records Management (NSARM)
Royal Archives, Windsor Castle (RAWC)
  Cumberland Papers (CP)

Introduction

1. For the military history of the 1745 rising, see Jeremy Black, *Culloden and the '45* (New York: St. Martin's Press, 1990), and W. A. Speck, *The Butcher: The Duke of Cumberland and the Suppression of the '45* (London: Blackwell, 1981). For more detail, see Christopher Duffy, *The '45: Bonnie Prince Charlie and the Untold Story of the Jacobite Rising* (London: Cassell, 2003), and John Prebble, *Culloden* (London: Penguin, 1996).

2. Biographical works on Cumberland include Rex Whitworth, *William Augustus, Duke of Cumberland, A Life* (London: Lee Cooper, 1992); Evan Edward Charteris, *William Augustus, Duke of Cumberland, His Early Life and Times* (London: E. Arnold, 1913); and Evan Edward Charteris, *William Augustus, Duke of Cumberland and the Seven Years' War* (London: Hutchinson, 1925). See also W. A. Speck, "William Augustus, Prince, duke of Cumberland (1721–1765)," in H. C. G. Matthew and Brian Harrison, eds., *Oxford Dictionary of National Biography*, 60 vols. (Oxford: Oxford University Press, 2004), 59:105–13.

3. For the life of Charles Edward Stuart, see Frank McLynn, *Charles Edward Stuart: A Tragedy in Many Acts* (New York: Routledge, 1988).

4. For an introduction to Jacobitism, see Bruce P. Lenman, *The Jacobite Risings*

in Britain, 1689–1746 (Aberdeen: Scottish Cultural Press, 1995). See also Murray
G. H. Pittock, *The Myth of the Jacobite Clans* (Edinburgh: Edinburgh University
Press, 1995); Paul Kléber Monad, *Jacobitism and the English People, 1688–1788*
(Cambridge: Cambridge University Press, 1989); Daniel Szechi, *The Jacobites,
Britain, and Europe, 1688–1788* (Manchester: Manchester University Press, 1994);
Eveline Cruickshanks, *Political Untouchables: The Tories and the '45* (New York:
Holmes and Meier, 1979); Peter David Garner Thomas, *Politics in Eighteenth-
Century Wales* (Cardiff: University of Wales Press, 1998), 133–49.

5. William Harper, *The Advice of a Friend to the Army and People of Scotland*
(1745), 2–3.

6. *The Rise of the Present Unnatural Rebellion Discover'd* (London, 1745), 4.

7. Andrew Henderson, *The History of the Rebellion, 1745 and 1746* (Edinburgh,
1748), 186.

8. For an overview of outsiders' stereotypes of the Highlanders, see Robert
Clyde, *From Rebel to Hero: The Image of the Highlander, 1745–1830* (East Linton,
Scotland: Tuckwell, 1995), and Peter Womack, *Improvement and Romance: Con-
structing the Myth of the Highlands* (London: Macmillan, 1989).

9. See generally Annette M. Smith, *Jacobite Estates of the Forty-Five* (Edinburgh:
John Donald, 1982); Byron Frank Jewell, "The Legislation Relating to Scotland
after the Forty-Five" (Ph.D. diss., University of North Carolina at Chapel Hill,
1975); A. J. Youngson, *After the Forty-Five: The Economic Impact on the Scottish Highlands* (Edinburgh: Edinburgh University Press, 1973).

10. See Howard Mumford Jones, "Origins of the Colonial Idea in England,"
Proceedings of the American Philosophical Society 85 (1942): 448–65; D. B. Quinn,
"Ireland and Sixteenth-Century European Expansion," *Historical Studies* 1
(1958): 20–32; Nicholas P. Canny, "The Ideology of English Colonization: From
Ireland to America," *William and Mary Quarterly*, 3d ser. 30 (1973): 575–98;
David Armitage, *The Ideological Origins of the British Empire* (Cambridge: Cam-
bridge University Press, 2000), 24–60; Jane H. Ohlmeyer, " 'Civilizinge those
Rude Partes': Colonization within Britain and Ireland, 1580s–1640s," in Nicho-
las Canny, ed., *The Oxford History of the British Empire*, vol. 1: *The Origins of Empire*
(Oxford: Oxford University Press, 1998), 124–47. For a recent effort to survey
British imperial history in a comprehensive fashion incorporating developments
in Britain, Ireland, and the colonies simultaneously, see Bruce P. Lenman,
England's Colonial Wars, 1550–1688: Conflicts, Empire, and National Identity (London: Longman, 2001), and its sequel, Bruce P. Lenman, *Britain's Colonial Wars,
1688–1783* (London: Longman, 2001).

11. Linda Colley, *Britons: Forging the Nation, 1707–1837* (New Haven, Conn.:
Yale University Press, 1992). The "British Problem" has engaged the attention
of a wide range of scholars and increased the level of dialogue between Irish,
Scottish, Welsh, and English historians. See, for example, Alexander Grant and
Keith J. Stringer, eds., *Uniting the Kingdom: The Making of British History* (New
York: Routledge, 1995), and Steven G. Ellis and Sarah Barber, eds., *Conquest and
Union: Fashioning a British State, 1485–1725* (New York: Longman, 1995). Histori-
ans of Britain's North American colonies have also been involved in these discus-
sions. See Ned C. Landsman, *From Colonials to Provincials: American Thought and
Culture, 1680–1760* (New York: Twayne, 1997), and Ned C. Landsman, ed.,
Nation and Province in the First British Empire: Scotland and the Americas, 1600–1800
(Lewisburg, Pa.: Bucknell University Press, 2001). The implications of the "New
British History" for historians of the Atlantic world is discussed by several promi-
nent scholars in "AHR Forum: The New British History in Atlantic Perspective,"
American Historical Review 104 (1999): 426–500.

12. Aaron Garrett, "Anthropology: The 'Original' of Human Nature," in Alexander Brodie, ed., *The Cambridge Companion to the Scottish Enlightenment* (Cambridge: Cambridge University Press, 2003), 79–93. See also more generally J. G. A. Pocock, *Barbarism and Religion*, vol. 2: *Narratives of Civil Government* (Cambridge: Cambridge University Press, 1999).

13. Anthony Pagden, *The Fall of Natural Man: The American Indian and the Origins of Comparative Ethnology* (Cambridge: Cambridge University Press, 1982), 80–81; T. M. Devine, *Clanship to Crofter's War: The Social Transformation of the Scottish Highlands* (Manchester: Manchester University Press, 1994), 1–2.

14. See A. M. Archibald, *Scotland: The Making of the Kingdom* (New York: Barnes and Noble, 1975), 449–51.

15. Peter Hume Brown, ed., *Scotland before 1700 from Contemporary Documents* (Edinburgh: D. Douglas, 1893), 12, quoting John of Fordun, circa 1380.

16. *Westminster Journal*, July 26, 1746. For a discussion of the gendered meanings of eighteenth-century stage-theories of human development, see Rosemarie Zagarri, "Morals, Manners, and the Republican Mother," *American Quarterly* 44 (1992): 192–215.

17. For an introduction to clanship, see Allan I. Macinnes, *Clanship, Commerce, and the House of Stewart, 1603–1788* (East Linton, Scotland: Tuckwell, 1996), 1–29.

18. On Highlanders in Glasgow, see Memorial of the Glasgow Highland Society, January 8, 1760, Huntington Library, San Marino, Cal. (hereafter HL) LO (SC) 8937.

19. See Margaret Campbell, Countess of Loudon, to John Campbell, Earl of Loudon, May 14, 1746, HL LO (SC) 11259; John Forbes to Loudon, May 28, 1745, HL LO (SC) 11519; John Dalrymple, Earl of Stair, to Loudon, June 28, 1746, HL LO (SC) 11348.

20. William, Earl of Home, to Loudon, September 11, 1747, HL LO (SC) 7111.

21. See especially Donald Cameron of Lochiel and Alexander MacDonald, *Copy of a Letter &c, Glenivis, March 20, 1746* (1746), reprinted in John Marchant, *The History of the Present Rebellion* (London, 1746), 367–69, and *The Life of Dr. Archibald Cameron* (London, 1753), 17–19. See also HL LO (SC) 10902 and The National Archives, Kew, England (hereafter TNA) SP 54/30, 76.

22. Alexander Boswell, Lord Auchinleck, to Loudon, March 12, 1757, HL LO (NA) 3029. See also William Cunningham, Earl of Glencairn, to Loudon, May 5, 1745, HL LO (SC) 7364; John Campbell, Earl of Breadalbane, to Loudon, August 24, 1745, HL LO (SC) 7566. For a capsule biography of Loudon, see Stephen Brumwell, "Campbell, John, fourth earl of Loudon (1705–1782)," in Matthew and Harrison, eds., *Oxford Dictionary of National Biography*, 9:820–21.

23. Margaret Sankey and Daniel Szechi, "Elite Culture and the Decline of Scottish Jacobitism, 1716–1745," *Past and Present* 173 (2001): 90–128, 98–9.

24. Daniel Defoe, *A Tour Thro' the Whole Island of Great Britain*, 2 vols. (London: Peter Davies, 1927), 2:813.

25. See Allan I. Macinnes, "Scottish Gaeldom: The First Phase of Clearance," in T. M. Devine and Rosalind Mitchell, eds., *People and Society in Scotland*, vol. 1 (Edinburgh: John Donald, 1988), 70–90.

26. T. C. Smout, "The Landowner and the Planned Village in Scotland, 1730–1830," in N. T. Phillipson and Rosalind Mitchison, eds., *Scotland in the Age of Improvement* (Edinburgh: Edinburgh University Press, 1996), 73–102, 74.

27. Macinnes, *Clanship, Commerce, and the House of Stewart*, 144–6; A.J. Young-

son, *After the Forty-five*, 20; R. H. Campbell, "The Scottish Improvers and the Course of Agrarian Change in the Eighteenth Century," in L. M. Cullen and T. C. Smout, eds., *Comparative Aspects of Scottish and Irish Economic and Social History, 1600–1800* (Edinburgh: John Donald, 1977), 204–15, 208.

28. Defoe, *Tour Thro' the Whole Island of Great Britain*, 2:821.

29. Edward Burt, *Letters from a Gentleman in the North of Scotland*, 2 vols. (London, 1754), 1:6.

30. SSPCK committee minutes, November 10, 1714, National Archives of Scotland, Edinburgh (hereafter NAS) GD 95/2/2, 40.

31. Address of the General Assembly of the Scottish Kirk, April 19, 1709, NAS GD 95/2/1, 13.

32. Letters patent dated July 14, 1709, NAS GD 95/2/1, 1.

33. Victor Edward Durkacz, *The Decline of the Celtic Languages: A Study of Linguistic and Cultural Conflict in Scotland, Wales, and Ireland from the Reformation to the Twentieth Century* (Edinburgh: John Donald, 1983), 26–30, 47–72. See also Leah Leneman, *Living in Atholl, 1685–1785* (Edinburgh: Edinburgh University Press, 1986), 116–27.

34. See SSPCK minutes, November 1, 1739, NAS GD 95/1/4, 117.

35. Address of the General Assembly of the Scottish Kirk, April 19, 1709, NAS GD 95/2/1, 13. See generally David Spadafora, *The Idea of Progress in Eighteenth-Century Britain* (New Haven, Conn.: Yale University Press, 1990), 267.

36. SSPCK minutes, March 19, 1719, May 3 and June 2, 1720, NAS GD 95/1/2, 36, 92 and 104.

37. SSPCK minutes, November 3, 1737, NAS GD 95/1/4, 57.

38. SSPCK committee minutes, July 26, 1733, NAS GD 95/2/5, 103.

39. See SSPCK minutes, June 2 and November 3, 1737, NAS GD 95/1/4, 52 and 57.

40. SSPCK minutes, November 3, 1737, and March 2, 1738, NAS GD 95/1/4, 57 and 66. See also SSPCK minutes, January 4, 1739 and January 3, 1740, NAS GD 95/1/4, 96 and 124.

41. For an indication of the impact of the SSPCK missions in North America, see Jonathan Edwards, *An Account of the Life of the Late Reverend Mr. David Brainerd* (Boston, 1749); Joseph Conforti, "Jonathan Edwards' Most Popular Work: The Life of David Brainerd and Nineteenth-Century Evangelical Culture," *Church History* 54 (1985): 188–201; Joseph Conforti, "David Brainerd and the Nineteenth-Century Missionary Movement," *Journal of the Early Republic* 5 (1985): 309–29.

42. See, for example, SSPCK minutes, March 15, 1723, NAS GD 95/1/2, 234.

43. Canny, "Ideology of English Colonization."

44. See Nicholas P. Canny, *Making Ireland British, 1580–1650* (Oxford: Oxford University Press, 2001), for the fullest statement of his views.

45. For a discussion of efforts to establish colonies on the west coast of Scotland at the start of the seventeenth century, see Macinnes, *Clanship, Commerce, and the House of Stewart*, 60–63.

46. See Daniel Defoe, *A True-Born English-Man* (London, 1708), 10, 11.

47. For an exception, an account of the Highlanders that emphasizes their diverse cultural inheritances, see Henderson, *History of the Rebellion*, 57–61.

48. Burt, *Letters from a Gentleman in the North of Scotland*, 2:70.

49. See Macinnes, *Clanship, Commerce, and the House of Stewart*, 109, 120 n.45; Abbott Emerson Smith, *Colonists in Bondage: White Servitude and Convict Labor in America, 1607–1776* (Chapel Hill: University of North Carolina Press, 1947), 157–58.

50. F. D. Dow, *Cromwellian Scotland, 1651–1660* (Edinburgh: John Donald, 1979), 124–26.

51. Defoe, *Tour Thro' the Whole Island of Great Britain*, 2:818.

52. See, for example, *To the People of England*, British Library (hereafter BL) Add. 35,889, 4; *Declaration and Admonitory Letter*, BL Add. 35,889, 2, TNA SP 54/26, 192, reprinted in *A Full and True Collection of all the Orders, Proclamations, and Papers &c. Published by Authority of Charles Prince of Wales, Part II* (Glasgow, 1746), 22–24.

53. The quotation is from *Declaration and Admonitory Letter*, BL Add. 35,889, 2, SP 54/26, 192, 2; reprinted in *Full and True Collection, Part II*, 22–24.

54. See Lenman, *Jacobite Risings in Britain*, 30–31.

55. See J. M. Sosin, *English America and the Revolution of 1688* (Lincoln: University of Nebraska Press, 1982); David S. Lovejoy, *The Glorious Revolution in America* (New York: Harper and Row, 1972); Richard R. Johnson, *Adjustment to Empire: The New England Colonies, 1675–1715* (New Brunswick, N.J.: Rutgers University Press, 1981). Stephen Saunders Webb, *Lord Churchill's Coup: The Anglo-American Empire and the Glorious Revolution Reconsidered* (New York: Knopf, 1995), analyzes the revolution on a wide imperial scale.

56. On James VII's view of the Celts, see Lenman, *Jacobite Risings in Britain*, 49.

57. See, for example, William Blakeney to Robert D'Arcy, Earl of Holdernesse, October 21, 1752, Royal Archives, Windsor Castle (hereafter RAWC) CP Box 44/282. For a capsule biography of Blakeney, see H. M. Stephens, "Blakeney, William, Baron Blakeney (1671/2–1761)," rev. Richard Harding, in Matthew and Harrison, eds., *Oxford Dictionary of National Biography* 6:133–34.

58. John Childs, "The Williamite War, 1689–1691," in Thomas Bartlett and Keith Jeffery, eds., *A Military History of Ireland* (Cambridge: Cambridge University Press, 1996), 188–210.

59. Lenman, *Jacobite Risings in Britain*, 88–89.

60. Ibid.

61. See Black, *Culloden and the '45*, 22.

62. See Lenman, *Jacobite Risings in Britain*, 127–44.

63. See, for example, Defoe, *Tour Thro' the Whole Island of Great Britain*, 2:799–800.

64. For a typical comment, see "Some hints anent disarming the Highlands and suppressing the Jacobite Meeting Houses," n.d., 1746, RAWC CP Box 10/289. For a mixed assessment of the value of the government's disarmament program after 1715, see the marginal notes of James Ogilvy, Earl of Findlater and Earl of Seaforth, on "Abbreviate of the proposals transmitted by General Bland and Lord Justice Clerk," March 1748, TNA SP 54/38, 347.

65. Smith, *Colonists in Bondage*, 197–200. See also letters of Colonel Rapin, April 8, 20, 29, May 4, 6 15, 1716, in *State Papers Domestic, George I* (London: List and Index Society, 1977), 41–43; Bruce Gordon Seton and Jean Gordon Arnot, *The Prisoners of the '45*, 3 vols. (Edinburgh: Scottish History Society, 1928–29), 1:24; See also Lenman, *Jacobite Risings in Britain*, 158–59; George Home to his sister, July 7, 1716, in Edgar Erskine Hume, "A Colonial Scottish Jacobite Family: Establishment in Virginia of a Branch of the Humes of Wedderburn," *Virginia Magazine of History and Biography* 38 (1930): 1–37, 10–11; John Granville, Earl of Carteret, to Alexander Spotswood, February 26, 1722, in *Calendar of State Papers, Colonial Series: America and West Indies* (London: Public Record Office, 1860-) 34:22–23. See also Sankey and Szechi, "Elite Culture and the Decline of Scottish Jacobitism," 114–22.

66. Smith, *Colonists in Bondage*, 198.

67. Lenman, *Jacobite Risings in Britain*, 161–79; Sankey and Szechi, "Elite Culture and the Decline of Scottish Jacobitism."

68. See instructions for George Wade, July 3, 1724, RAWC CP Box 61/B/2.

69. See George Wade, instructions to the Officers Commanding the Highland Companies, September 22, 1725, RAWC CP Box 61/B/4/2.

70. Andrew Mackillop, *"More Fruitful than the Soil": Army, Empire, and the Scottish Highlands, 1715–1815* (East Linton, Scotland: Tuckwell, 2000), closely examines the impact of military service on the economy and society of the Highlands through the eighteenth century.

71. "A Remonstrance of the Gentlemen of the Highland Clans to General Wade 1725," RAWC CP Box 61/B/3.

72. See George Wade, "Report &c Relating to the Highlands," 1724, in James Allardyce, ed., *Historical Papers Relating to the Jacobite Period, 1699–1750*, 2 vols. (Aberdeen: New Spaulding Club, 1895), 1:131–49; George Wade, "Report &c Relating to the Highlands," 1727, in Allardyce, ed., *Historical Papers Relating to the Jacobite Period*, 1:150–65.

73. See James Smollet to Robert Craigie, September 1, 1745, TNA SP 54/26, 5; statement of John Chisholm, September 2, 1745, TNA SP 54/26, 7.

74. See Lenman, *Jacobite Risings in Britain*, 222.

75. Burt, *Letters from a Gentleman in the North of Scotland*, 2:351. For a discussion of road building in Minorca, see Bruce Laurie, *The Life of Richard Kane, Britain's First Lieutenant-Governor of Minorca* (Rutherford, N.J.: Farleigh-Dickinson University Press, 1994), 137–39. See also Janet Sloss, *Richard Kane, Governor of Minorca* (Bagpath, England: Bonaventure Press, 1995).

76. Richard Beresford to the Board of Trade, June 23, 1716, in *Calendar of State Papers, Colonial Series: America and West Indies*, 30:130–31.

77. For an introduction to the "rules of war," see Richard Tuck, *The Rights of War and Peace: Political Thought and the International Order from Grotius to Kant* (Oxford: Oxford University Press, 1999), and Michael Howard, George J. Andreopoulos, and Mark R. Shulman, eds., *The Laws of War: Constraints on Warfare in the Western World* (New Haven, Conn.: Yale University Press, 1994). Among Europeans the rules of war served an important ideological function in the middle years of the eighteenth century, as one of several markers that helped delineate the distinctions they drew between civilization and savagery, or, according to another formulation, between Europe and the rest of the world. See Eliga H. Gould, "Zones of Law, Zones of Violence: The Legal Geography of the British Atlantic, circa 1772," *William and Mary Quarterly*, 3d ser. 60 (2003): 471–510. In practice, however, the rules were not applied in detail according to any simple geographical pattern. In North America, British colonists and combatants treated war captives according to a variety of codes of behavior and altered their conduct if they classified their enemy as savage. See Ian K. Steele, "Surrendering Rites: Prisoners on Colonial North American Frontiers," in Stephen Taylor, Richard Connors, and Clyve Jones, eds., *Hanoverian Britain and Empire: Essays in Memory of Philip Lawson* (Woodbridge, Suffolk: Boydell Press, 1998), 137–57; Gould, "Zones of Law, Zones of Violence," 483. Through a close analysis of one episode, Ian K. Steele, *Betrayals: Fort William Henry and the "Massacre"* (Oxford: Oxford University Press, 1990), examines the consequences of the confusion surrounding codes of conduct in eighteenth-century colonial American warfare.

78. See David Cole, *Enemy Aliens: Double Standards and Constitutional Freedoms in the War on Terrorism* (New York: New Press, 2003); Steven R. Swanson, "Enemy

Combatants and the Writ of Habeas Corpus," *Arizona State Law Journal* 35 (2003): 939–1006; *Yaser Esam Hamdi v. Donald H. Rumsfeld*, 124 S.Ct. 2633 (2004).

79. See Robert M. Cover, "Violence and the Word," *Yale Law Journal* 95 (1986): 1601–29.

80. William Augustus, Duke of Cumberland, to Thomas Hollis-Pelham, Duke of Newcastle, March 15, 1746, TNA SP 54/29, 114.

81. This episode is discussed in more detail in Chapter 2, below.

82. For a discussion of the ongoing political controversies surrounding the mid-eighteenth-century army, see Eliga H. Gould, "To Strengthen the King's Hands: Dynastic Legitimacy, Militia Reform, and Ideas of National Unity in England, 1745–1760," *Historical Journal* 34 (1991): 329–48. See also more generally John Brewer, *The Sinews of Power: War, Money, and the English State, 1688–1783* (Cambridge. Mass.: Harvard University Press, 1990), 29–63.

83. On Cumberland's efforts to reform the army, see J. A. Houlding, *Fit for Service: The Training of the British Army, 1715–1795* (Oxford: Clarendon, 1981), passim.

84. Cumberland's relations with various members of the ministry in the mid-to-late 1740s are analyzed in detail in Jewell, "Legislation Relating to Scotland after the Forty-Five." There is an extensive scholarly literature on high politics in Britain in the 1740s and 1750s. See, for example, Philip Lawson, *George Grenville: A Political Life* (Oxford: Clarendon, 1984); J. C. D. Clark, *The Dynamics of Change: The Crisis of the 1750s and English Party Systems* (Cambridge: Cambridge University Press, 1982); Marie Peters, *Pitt and Popularity: The Patriot Minister and London Opinion during the Seven Years' War* (Oxford: Clarendon, 1980); Reed Browning, *The Duke of Newcastle* (New Haven, Conn.: Yale University Press, 1975); John W. Wilkes, *A Whig in Power: The Political Career of Henry Pelham* (Evanston, Ill.: Northwestern University Press, 1964); Lewis M. Wiggin, *The Faction of Cousins: A Political Account of the Grenvilles, 1733–1763* (New Haven, Conn.: Yale University Press, 1958). For the debates within successive ministries on imperial issues, see Fred Anderson, *Crucible of War: The Seven Years' War and the Fate of Empire in British North America, 1754–1766* (New York: Knopf, 2000); Richard Middleton, *The Bells of Victory: The Pitt-Newcastle Ministry and the Conduct of the Seven Years' War, 1757–1762* (Cambridge: Cambridge University Press, 1985); James Henretta, *"Salutary Neglect": Colonial Administration under the Duke of Newcastle* (Princeton, N.J.: Princeton University Press, 1972); and, generally, Lawrence Henry Gipson, *The British Empire before the American Revolution*, 15 vols. (New York: Knopf, 1936–70).

85. See Linda Colley, *Captives: The Story of Britain's Pursuit of Empire and How Its Soldiers and Civilians Were Held Captive by the Dream of Global Supremacy* (New York: Pantheon, 2003); Bob Harris, *Politics and the Nation: Britain in the Mid-Eighteenth Century* (Oxford: Oxford University Press, 2002); Nicholas Rogers, *Crowds, Culture and Politics in Georgian Britain* (Oxford: Clarendon, 1998); Kathleen Wilson, *The Sense of the People: Politics, Culture, and Imperialism in England, 1715–1785* (Cambridge: Cambridge University Press, 1995).

86. See, for example, Kathleen Wilson, "Empire, Trade, and Popular Politics in Mid-Hanoverian Britain: The Case of Admiral Vernon," *Past and Present* 121 (1988): 74–109; Gerald Jordan and Nicholas Rogers, "Admirals as Heroes: Patriotism and Liberty in Hanoverian England," *Journal of British Studies* 28 (1989): 210–24.

87. Of all the recent studies of the political controversies surrounding imperi-

alism in the middle years of the eighteenth century, Eliga H. Gould's *The Persistence of Empire: British Political Culture in the Age of the American Revolution* (Chapel Hill: University of North Carolina Press, 2000) maintains the sharpest focus on the distinctive positions taken by the supporters of the army. Not coincidentally, Gould also pays more attention to members of the royal family.

88. Stephen Saunders Webb's work concentrates on the interplay between colonial events and the politics of Britain, by focusing on the role of the army in imperial expansion and governance. See especially Webb, *Lord Churchill's Coup.* There are no similarly ambitious works examining the navy's impact on the eighteenth-century empire. John Brewer's *The Sinews of Power* emphasizes the navy's influence in Britain. Jerry Bannister's *The Rule of the Admirals: Law, Custom, and Naval Government in Newfoundland, 1699–1832* (Toronto: University of Toronto Press, 2003) examines the navy as a governing institution in one colony.

89. Devine, *Clanship to Crofter's War,* provides a useful introduction to the history of the Highlands. See also MacInnes, *Clanship, Commerce, and the House of Stuart,* and Bruce P. Lenman, *The Jacobite Clans of the Great Glen, 1650–1784* (Aberdeen: Scottish Cultural Press, 1995). For an overview of the British administration of Minorca, see Desmond Gregory, *Minorca, the Illusory Prize: A History of the British Occupations of Minorca between 1708 and 1802* (Rutherford, N.J.: Farleigh Dickinson University Press, 1990). There is no comparable academic work on Gibraltar. For British conceptions of North Africa, see Colley, *Captives,* 23–134, and Ann Thomson, *Barbary and Enlightenment: European Attitudes toward the Maghreb in the Eighteenth Century* (Leiden: Brill, 1987). British policy toward French colonists in North America is analyzed in Geoffrey Plank, *An Unsettled Conquest: The British Campaign against the Peoples of Acadia* (Philadelphia: University of Pennsylvania Press, 2001), and Philip Lawson, *The Imperial Challenge: Quebec and Britain in the Age of the American Revolution* (Montreal: McGill-Queen's University Press, 1990). For an analysis of the contested status of Native Americans as subjects of the British Empire, see Gregory Evans Dowd, *War under Heaven: Pontiac, the Indian Nations, and the British Empire* (Baltimore: Johns Hopkins University Press, 2002).

90. See Anderson, *Crucible of War,* Fred Anderson, *A People's Army: Massachusetts Soldiers and Society in the Seven Years' War* (New York: Norton, 1984); Alan Rogers, *Empire and Liberty: American Resistance to British Authority, 1755–1763* (Berkeley: University of California Press, 1974); Stanley McCrory Pargellis, *Lord Loudon in North America* (New Haven, Conn.: Yale University Press, 1933).

91. For an overview of emigration patterns in the eighteenth century see Alex Murdoch, "Emigration from the Scottish Highlands to America in the Eighteenth Century," *British Journal for Eighteenth-Century Studies* 21 (1998): 161–74.

92. For the role of military service in redefining the Highlanders' reputation and role in the empire, see Andrew Mackillop, "For King, Country, and Regiment?: Motive and Identity within Highland Soldiering, 1746–1815," in Steve Murdoch and A. Mackillop, eds., *Fighting for Identity: Scottish Military Experience c. 1550–1900* (Leiden: Brill, 2002), 185–211. See also Clyde, *From Rebel to Hero,* 150–80, and Stephen Brumwell, *Redcoats: The British Soldier and War in the Americas, 1755–1763* (Cambridge: Cambridge University Press, 2002), 264–89.

Chapter 1. Rebellion

1. Newcastle to Cumberland, August 2, 1745, RAWC CP Box 4/43; *Edinburgh Evening Courant,* August 12, 1745.

2. See proclamation of August 22, 1745, in *Full and True Collection, Part II*, 48; McLynn, *Charles Edward Stuart*, 144.

3. See, for example, warrant for the arrest of James Rollo, August 21, 1745, TNA T 1/348, 59; Craigie to Gabriel Napier, August 21, 1745, TNA T 1/348, 58.

4. Charles Edward Stuart, warrant for the arrest of Duncan Forbes, October 17, 1745, RAWC CP Box 6/229.

5. See instructions for Cumberland, November 25, 1745, RAWC CP Box 7/117.

6. See Seton and Arnot, *Prisoners of the '45*, 1:39–40, 154–55.

7. Black, *Culloden and the '45*, and Speck, *The Butcher*, contain strong narrative accounts of the military action. For more detail, see Duffy, *The '45*.

8. See Hugo Grotius, *The Illustrious Hugo Grotius of the Law of Warre and Peace* (London, 1654), 538–42, 589–97; Montesquieu, *The Spirit of the Laws*, trans. Anne M. Cohler, Basia Carolyn Miller, and Harold Samuel Stone (Cambridge: Cambridge University Press, 1989), 247 n. 2; Emmerich de Vattel, *The Law of Nations*, 2 vols. (London, 1760), 2:49, 2:53, 2:110. See also Emmerich de Vattel, *Le Droit des gens* (London, 1758), 107, 149–50, 245. For indications of the dissemination of these ideas, see *Truth, but no Treason, or Oppression often the Cause of Rebellion* (London, 1748), 45 n.; James Foster, *An Account of the Behaviour of the Late Earl of Kilmarnock* (London, 1746), 18; *Maryland Gazette*, March 24, 1747; Robert Forbes, *The Lyon in Mourning*, ed. Henry Patton, 3 vols. (Edinburgh: Scottish Academy Press, 1975), 1:29.

9. Minutes of the Privy Council, February 3, 1746, TNA SP 36/81, 28; Newcastle to James Sinclair, February 26, 1746, RAWC CP Box 11/124; memorial for Captain James St. Clair, TNA SP 54/37, 100; Cumberland to Newcastle, November 1747, TNA SP 54/37, 102; "Names of the French Officers lately taken by Commodore Knowles, who have leave to go to Canterbury on their parole," March 3, 1746, RAWC CP Box 11/222; "A list of prisoners on board his Majesty's ship the Sheerness," April 7, 1746, RAWC CP Box 13/218; see also *The Trial of Aeneas MacDonald* (London, 1747).

10. See John Gordon to George Forbes of Skellater, September 7, 1745, RAWC CP, Box 5/256–7; Assynt parish inhabitants of Sutherlandshire to William, Earl of Sutherland, November 14, 1745, HL LO (SC) 10023; Alexander Brodie to Loudon, February 19, 1746, HL LO (SC) 10880; letter from Lewis Gordon, December 6, 1745, HL LO (SC) 8944. See also Hugh Horn to Loudon, November 16, 1745, HL LO (SC) 10441; John Grant to Lodovick Grant, January 7, 1746, HL LO (SC) 11698; letter from Findlater and Seaforth, January 9, 1746, HL LO (SC) 12514; Andrew Logie to Loudon, January 20, 1746, HL LO (SC) 10755.

11. See Leneman, *Living in Atholl*, 226.

12. Charles Edward Stuart to Lachlan MacLachlan, September 24, 1745, RAWC CP Box 5/302. See also James Murray to Alexander Robertson of Struan, August 28, 1745, RAWC CP Box 4/332; Charles Edward Stuart to John Gordon of Glenbucket, August 30, 1745, RAWC CP Box 4/338.

13. Assynt parish inhabitants of Sutherlandshire to William, Earl of Sutherland, November 14, 1745, HL LO (SC) 10023; depositions of John McGilespuk and John Fraser, January 16, 1747, HL LO (SC) 9344, 14–15.

14. *A Brief Account of the Life and Family of Miss Jenny Cameron* (London, 1746), 60.

15. Maggie Craig, *Damn' Rebel Bitches: The Women of the '45* (Edinburgh: Mainstream Publishing, 1997), 42–50.

16. Macinnes, *Clanship, Commerce, and the House of Stewart*, 168. See Anne Mackintosh to William, Marquis of Tullibardine, the Jacobite Duke of Atholl, October 16, 1745, in *Jacobite Correspondence of the Atholl Family* (Edinburgh, 1840), 95–96.

17. See Lachlan Cuthbert to George Cuthbert, January 26, 1746, HL LO (SC) 11038.

18. Macinnes, *Clanship, Commerce, and the House of Stuart*, 167; Mackillop, "For King, Country, and Regiment?," 192; Lewis Gordon to Glenarrock's factor, December 6, 1745, HL LO (SC) 8944; Cosmo George, Duke of Gordon, advertisement, November 16, 1745, HL LO (SC) 7164. See also John Gordon to Forbes of Skellater, September 7, 1745, RAWC CP, Box 5/257.

19. Alexander Mackenzie to Loudon, 1746, HL LO (SC) 9145; Cosmo George, Duke of Gordon, to Loudon, HL LO (SC) 7166; letter from Lachlan Shaw, January 1, 1746, HL LO (SC) 12613.

20. James Drummond, Jacobite Duke of Perth, to John Drummond and William Dow, October 16, 1745, RAWC CP Box 6/222.

21. See, for example, Michael Foster, *A Report of Some Proceedings on the Commission of Oyer and Terminer and Goal Delivery* (Oxford, 1762), 13; "Information against Glengarry," July 16, 1746, in Charles Sanford Terry, ed., *The Albemarle Papers*, 2 vols. (Aberdeen: New Spalding Club, 1902), 2:407–8.

22. See Horn to Loudon, November 16, 1745, HL LO (SC) 10441.

23. Foster, *Account of the Late Earl of Kilmarnock*, 10–11. See also John Campbell to Campbell of Carwin, May 2, 1746, HL LO (SC) 11234.

24. Loudon to Robert Napier, June 27, 1746, RAWC CP Box 16/321; *The Life of Nicholas Mooney* (Dublin, 1752), 11.

25. See *Caledonian Mercury*, October 9, 1745.

26. See Pittock, *Myth of the Jacobite Clans*, 54–79.

27. Allan L. Carswell, " 'The Most Despicable Enemy That Are'—The Jacobite Army of the '45," in Robert C. Woosnam-Savage, ed., *1745: Charles Edward Stuart and the Jacobites* (Edinburgh: Glasgow Museums, 1995), 29–40.

28. Charles Edward Stuart, order of October 22, 1745, in *Full and True Collection, Part II*, 50; see also *Caledonian Mercury*, October 23, 1745; orders of Charles Edward Stuart, November 30, 1745, RAWC CP Box 7/444.

29. Cumberland to Newcastle, September 20, 1745, in William Coxe, *Memoirs of the Administration of the Right Honourable Henry Pelham*, 2 vols. (London, 1829), 1:245.

30. Peregrine Lascelles to Loudon, January 16, 1746, HL LO (SC) 10595; *The Counterpoise: Being Thoughts on a Militia and a Standing Army* (London, 1753), 37; Henderson, *History of the Rebellion*, 20.

31. Letter from Loudon, HL LO (SC) 11785.

32. *Caledonian Mercury*, September 27, 1745. See also *A True and Full Account of the Late Bloody and Desperate Battle fought at Gladsmuir* (1745), 5.

33. *London Evening Post*, February 1–4, 1746.

34. Henderson, *History of the Rebellion*, 186.

35. *True and Full Account of Gladsmuir*, 5.

36. Ibid., 7; *Declaration and Admonitory Letter of the Nobility, Gentry, and Free-born Subjects* (1745), BL Add. 35,889, 2, TNA SP 54/26, 192, 2; reprinted in *Full and True Collection, Part II*, 22–24, 22.

37. Duncan Forbes to Tweeddale, August 8, 1745, in H. R. Duff, ed., *Culloden Papers* (London, 1815), 205; Andrew Fletcher, Lord Milton, to John Hay, Marquis of Tweeddale, September 6, 7, 12, and 16, 1745, in John Home, *The*

History of the Rebellion in the Year 1745 (London, 1802), 294, 296, 298, and 301–5; Tweeddale to Milton, September 21, 1745, in Home, *History of the Rebellion*, 309. See also John Campbell, Lord Glenorchy, to Philip Yorke, Earl of Hardwicke, August 27, 1745, BL Add. 35,450, 40; Stair to Loudon, August 31 and September 5, 1745, HL LO (SC) 7642 and 7604; Rosalind Mitchison, "The Government and the Highlands, 1707–1745," in N. T. Phillipson and Rosalind Mitchison, eds., *Scotland in the Age of Improvement* (Edinburgh: Edinburgh University Press, 1996), 24–46, 39–42; Harris, *Politics and the Nation*, 151.

38. "Some few of the cases of loyal and zealous subjects," 1752, BL Egerton 3433, 10. See also Milton to Tweeddale, September 6, 1745, TNA SP 54/26, 17; abstract of Craigie to Gabriel Napier, September 6, 1745, TNA T 1/348, 77; affidavit of James Grassan, February 22, 1746, TNA T 1/348, 63; memorial of Gabriel Napier, April 1, 1749, RAWC CP Box 43/172.

39. Newcastle to Cumberland, August 17 and 20, 1745, RAWC CP Box 4/172 and 204.

40. William Stanhope, Earl of Harrington, to Cumberland, July 15, 1745, RAWC CP Box 3/270; Cumberland to Newcastle, August 1, N.S., 1745, RAWC CP Box 3/315; Newcastle to Cumberland, July 26, 1745, RAWC CP Box 3/241.

41. Horatio Walpole to Everard Fawkener, September 6, 1745, RAWC CP Box 5/51. See Gould, *Persistence of Empire*, 1–34.

42. Cumberland to Newcastle, August 1, N.S. (new style), and September 6, N.S., 1745, RAWC CP Box 3/315, and BL Add. 32,705, 106; see also Harrington to Cumberland, August 17, 1745, RAWC CP Box 4/176.

43. Cumberland to Harrington, September 6, N.S., 1745, RAWC CP Box 4/246.

44. Cumberland to Newcastle, Steptember 20, 1745, in Coxe, *Memoirs*, 1:244–5; Wilkes, *A Whig in Power*, 152.

45. Cumberland to Newcastle, September 20, 1745, in Coxe, *Memoirs*, 1:245.

46. Harrington to Cumberland, October 8 1745, RAWC CP Box 6/61.

47. See Newcastle to Cumberland, August 20, 1745, RAWC CP Box 4/204, also BL Add. 32,705,92; Cumberland to Harrington, September 13 and 20, N.S., 1745, RAWC CP Box 5/13 and 68; Harrington to Cumberland, September 4 and 25, October 1, 1745, RAWC CP Box 5/29, 5/179 and 6/5.

48. See, for example, orders of February 8, 9, and 10, March 6, and April 24 and June 14, 1746, in order book beginning January 28, 1746, NAS GD1/322/1, 19, 21, 23, 51, and 123–24.

49. For a discussion of the complexity of financing military operations in this period, see Wilkes, *A Whig in Power*, 111.

50. Newcastle to Cumberland, November 30, 1745, RAWC CP Box 7/195; Cumberland to George Wade, December 12, 1745, RAWC CP Box 8/23; Newcastle to Wade, December 25, 1745, RAWC CP Box 8/116; Cumberland to John, Earl of Crawford, March 9, 1746, RAWC CP Box 12/27.

51. Amos Aschbach Ettinger, *James Edward Oglethorpe, Imperial Idealist* (Oxford: Clarendon, 1936), 259–60; Margaret Yorke, Countess of Hardwicke, to Hardwicke, September 28, 1745, in Philip C. Yorke, *The Life and Correspondence of Philip Yorke, Earl of Hardwicke*, 3 vols. (Cambridge: Cambridge University Press, 1913), 1:461; letter from Baron Idle, September 25, 1745, BL Add. 35,446, 79; Thomas Herring to Hardwicke, September 27, 1745, in R. Garnett, ed., "Correspondence of Archbishop Herring and Lord Hardwicke during the Rebellion of 1745," *English Historical Review* 19 (1904): 528–50, 543–45.

52. Edward J. Cashin, "Oglethorpe's Acount of the 1745 Escape of the Scots

at Shad," in John C. Inscoe, ed., *James Edward Oglethorpe: New Perspectives on his Life and Legacy* (Savannah: Georgia Historical Society, 1997), 92–104. See also Joseph Yorke to Hardwicke, December 19, 1745, in Yorke, *Life and Correspondence of Hardwicke*, 1:484–87; Ettinger, *James Edward Oglethorpe*, 266–68; *Caledonian Mercury*, August 21, 1746; *Both Sides of the Question; or, a Candid Enquiry into a Certain Doubtful Character, in a Letter to a General Officer Remarkably Acquitted by a C——T M——L* (2d ed., London, 1749).

53. See generally order book beginning January 28, 1746, NAS GD1/322/1.

54. General and staff officers serving in Flanders, December 24, 1744, RAWC CP Box 1/282. For a capsule biography of Bland, see J. A. Houlding, "Bland, Humphrey (1685/6–1763)," in Matthew and Harrison, eds., *Oxford Dictionary of National Biography*, 6:158–59.

55. Houlding, *Fit for Service*, 171, 182–84; Humphrey Bland, *A Treatise of Military Discipline* (Dublin, 1743).

56. *The French Flail, or A Letter to His Excellency, the Commander in chief of his Majesty's New Raised Regiment of Ladies* (London, 1746), 8. See Craig, *Damn Rebel Bitches*, 53–54.

57. *French Flail*, 5.

58. Ibid., 6.

59. Warrant, March 8, 1745, RAWC CP Box 44/23.

60. See James Wolfe to Charles Lennox, Duke of Richmond, March 17, 1756, in R. H. Whitworth, ed., "Some Unpublished Wolfe Letters, 1755–1758," *Journal of the Society for Army Historical Research* 53 (1975): 65–86, 71. For a critical comment on this pattern, see Richard Bentley, *An Attempt Towards an Apology for His R——H—— the D——* (London, 1751), 16–17.

61. J. Murray Beck, "Cornwallis, Edward," *Dictionary of Canadian Biography*, vol. 4 (Toronto: University of Toronto Press, 1979), 168–70, 168. For more on Cornwallis, see John Oliphant, "Cornwallis, Edward (1713–1776)," in Matthew and Harrison, eds., *Oxford Dictionary of National Biography*, 13:482–83.

62. For a capsule biography of Wolfe, see Stuart Reid, "Wolfe, James (1727–1759)," in Matthew and Harrison, eds., *Oxford Dictionary of National Biography*, 59:960–67.

63. L. B. Namier, *The Structure of Politics at the Accession of George III* (London: Macmillan, 1957), 25–26; John Brooke, *King George III* (New York: McGraw-Hill, 1970), 32; Brewer, *Sinews of Power*, 45.

64. William Anne Keppel, 2d Earl of Albemarle, to Fawkener, October 8, 1746, RAWC CP Box 18/294; Colonel J. Lee to Fawkener, RAWC CP Box 18/368.

65. Henry Fox to Fawkener, June 9, 1747, RAWC CP Box 23/157.

66. See Col. J. Munro to Fawkener, June 10, 1747, RAWC CP Box 23/214; Fox to Fawkener, June 12, 1747, RAWC CP Box 23/236; James Abercromby to Fawkener, June 16 and 19, 1747, RAWC CP Box 23/354 and 396; Philip Dormer Stanhope, Earl of Chesterfield, to Cumberland, June 23, 1747, RAWC CP Box 23/430; Loudon to Fawkener, July 5, 1747, RAWC CP Box 24/184; Felton Hervey to Cumberland, July 6, 1747, RAWC CP Box 24/210; Newcastle to Fawkener, July 7, 1747, RAWC CP Box 24/229; Lord Ancrum to Cumberland, July 8, 1747, RAWC CP Box 24/247.

67. Fox to Loudon, July 7, 1747, HL LO (SC) 11524.

68. Fox to Fawkener, July 7, 1747, RAWC CP Box 24/231. According to the *OED*, the word "campaign" did not acquire its current political meaning until the nineteenth century. See *Oxford English Dictionary*, 2d ed. (Oxford: Oxford University Press, 1989), 2:811.

69. See Stanley Pargellis, *Military Affairs in North America, 1748–1765* (New York: American Historical Association, 1936), ix–xii.

70. Wolfe to his father, September 1, 1743, in Bickles Willson, ed., *The Life and Letters of James Wolfe* (London: William Heinemann, 1909), 40–41, 41, and Robert Wright, ed., *The Life of Major-General James Wolfe* (London, 1864), 50–51, 51.

71. Order of April 24, 1746, in order book beginning January 28, 1746, NAS GD1/322/1, 122.

72. Orders for June 10, 1746, in order book beginning January 28, 1746, NAS GD1/322/1, 199.

73. See Alexander Dallas, "Return of the people inhabiting the huts around the garrison," Fort Augustus, August 13, 1746, HL LO (SC) 11319.

74. For a description of Cumberland's efforts to display himself, see Henderson, *History of the Rebellion*, 168.

75. See Cumberland to Newcastle, September 3, 1745, and February 16, 1746, BL Add. 32,705, 106 and 32,706, 157.

76. Cumberland to Newcastle, December 11, 1746, RAWC CP LR (letter register) 1/92.

77. See, for example, Craigie to Tweeddale, September 10, 1745, BL Add. 35,446, 73; Findlater and Seaforth to Hardwicke, October 15, 1745, BL Add. 35,446, 85.

78. George Wade, printed proclamation of October 30, 1745; see also *Edinburgh Evening Courant*, November 8, 1745.

79. Duncan Forbes to Loudon, November 16, 1745, HL LO (SC) 11469.

80. Stair to Loudon, October 2, 1745, HL LO (SC) 7676.

81. Frank McLynn, *The Jacobite Army in England, 1745* (Edinburgh: John Donald, 1983), 34–59; Katherine Tomasson, *The Jacobite General* (London: Blackwood, 1958), 74–75; *London Magazine*, 1745, 565–66.

82. Joseph Yorke to Hardwicke, December 24 and 30, 1745, in Yorke, *Life and Correspondence of Hardwicke*, 1:487–88, 492–93; See Black, *Culloden and the '45*, 131–32; James Johnstone, *Memoir of the Rebellion in 1745 and 1746* (London, 1821), 373–74.

83. Cumberland to Newcastle, December 30, 1745, RAWC CP LR 1/111; *London Magazine*, 1745, 626.

84. Black, *Culloden and the '45*, 132. See James Miller, "Diary," J. H. Leslie, ed., in *Journal of Army Historical Research* 3 (1923): 208–26.

85. Cumberland to Newcastle, December 30, 1745, RAWC CP LR 1/111; Fawkener to John Colleton, January 1, 1746, RAWC CP Box 65/vi.23.14. See also Chancellor of Carlisle to Newcastle, n.d., RAWC CP Box 7/62; James Durand to Lt. General Folliet, n.d., RAWC CP Box 7/130.

86. See letter from Hardwicke, March 28, 1746, BL Add. 32,706, 349. See also Chancellor of Carlisle to Newcastle, n.d., RAWC CP Box 7/62; Durand to Folliet, n.d., RAWC CP Box 7/130.

87. Henderson, *History of the Rebellion*, 24. See also David Hume, *A True Account of the Behavior and Conduct of Archibald Stewart, Late Provost of Edinburgh* (London, 1748), 32.

88. Milton to Newcastle, October 31, 1747, in Terry, ed., *Albemarle Papers*, 2:466–67; Speck, *Butcher*, 48.

89. Humphrey Bland to Hardwicke, December 25, 1753, BL Add. 35,448, 51.

90. Inquiry into the surrender of the castle at Inverness, March 15, 1746, TNA SP 54/29, 78; "Copy of the sentence of the court martial upon Major

Grant," TNA SP 54/31, 116; Brodie to Loudon, April 29, 1746, HL LO (SC) 10882; orders for June 7, 1746, in order book beginning January 28, 1746, NAS GD1/322/1; *Caledonian Mercury*, September 16, 18, and 22, 1746.

91. Cumberland to Newcastle, April 30, 1746, RAWC CP Box 14/234 and LR 2/79; also TNA SP 54/30, 234.

92. "Narrative of the transactions at the siege of Fort Augustus . . . with other papers relating thereto, given in by Lieutenant General Bland," RAWC CP Box 69/xi.37.65.

93. Ettinger, *James Edward Oglethorpe*, 266–68; *The Report of the Proceedings and Opinion of the Board of General Officers* (London, 1747).

94. Letter from Henry Hawley, January 20, 1746, TNA SP 54/27, 137.

95. Milton to Newcastle, January 20, 1746, TNA SP 54/27, 137; *A Compleat and Authentick History of the Rise, Progress and Extinction of the Late Rebellion* (Dublin, 1747), 26; Henderson, *History of the Rebellion*, 149.

96. *London Chronicle*, September 19–22, 1761, 286.

97. See Grotius, *Illustrious Hugo Grotius*, 294.

98. For examples of conditional threats, see Cumberland to Newcastle, February 5 and March 26, 1746, TNA SP 54/28, 31; TNA SP 54/29, 185 and RAWC CP LR 2/52.

99. *Caledonian Mercury*, October 2, 1745. See also *Caledonian Mercury*, September 25, 1745; Robert Wightman to Duncan Forbes, September 26, 1745, in Duff, ed., *Culloden Papers*, 225; *London Magazine*, 1745, 465, 539; Henderson, *History of the Rebellion*, 45–46; *A True and Full Account of Gladsmuir*, 5.

100. *Caledonian Mercury*, September 30, 1745. See also statement of Robert Bowey, October 4, 1745, TNA SP 54/26, 150.

101. *Caledonian Mercury*, September 30, 1745; Henderson, *History of the Rebellion*, 45–46; Dr. Colvill to James Scott, October 1, 1745, in *Jacobite Correspondence of the Atholl Family*, 39–40; Jacobite Duke of Atholl to the Earl of Airly, October 1, 1745, in *Jacobite Correspondence of the Atholl Family*, 41; Robertson of Kilichangy to Mr. Mercer of Aldie, October 3, 1745, in *Jacobite Correspondence of the Atholl Family*, 55–56; instructions of the Jacobite Duke of Atholl, October 1, 1745, in *Jacobite Correspondence of the Atholl Family*, 42.

102. *Caledonian Mercury*, October 4, 1745.

103. These terms had been offered to officers. See "Copy of the obligation signed by the officers on parole dated Hollyrood house September 28, 1745," TNA SP 54/27, 142.

104. *Caledonian Mercury*, October 21, 1745 and March 19, 1746; letter from Shaw, January 1, 1746, HL LO (SC) 12613; passport dated April 11, 1746, RAWC CP Box 13/389.

105. Johnstone, *Memoir of the Rebellion*, 166. See also 340–41.

106. Cumberland to Newcastle, January 30, 1746, TNA SP 54/27, 211.

107. William, Earl of Sutherland, to Loudon, December 1 and 2, 1745, HL LO (SC) 12720, 12721, and 12706.

108. Sutherland to Loudon, December 1, 1745, HL LO (SC) 12720.

109. Alexander Mackay to Loudon, December 12 and 15, 1745, HL LO (SC) 11927 and 11928.

110. See *Caledonian Mercury*, January 20 and February 4, 1746; "The report of the examination of Ensign Erwin of General Guise's," February 7, 1746, RAWC CP Box 10/98. See also Johnstone, *Memoir of the Rebellion*, 166–67.

111. Printed broadside dated February 10, 1746, TNA SP 54/28, 203.

112. *Edinburgh Evening Courant*, January 6, 1746; *Caledonian Mercury*, January

24, 1746; orders for April 19, 20, 26, and 27, 1746, in order book beginning January 28, 1746, NAS GD1/322/1, 108, 113, 125, 128, and 131; *London Evening Post,* June 24–26, 1746.

113. Orders for February 16, 1746, in order book beginning January 28, 1746, NAS GD1/322/1, 33.

114. See, for example, John McKeek and William McVicar, examination, April 16, 1746, HL LO (SC) 12022; Henderson, *History of the Rebellion,* 149.

115. Lochiel and Alexander MacDonald, *Copy of a Letter &c, Glenivis, March 20, 1746* (1746), reprinted in Marchant, *History of the Present Rebellion,* 367–69, and *Life of Dr. Archibald Cameron,* 17–19. See also HL LO (SC) 10902, and TNA SP 54/30, 76.

116. Harry Innes to Duncan Forbes, February 16, 1746, HL LO (SC) 10557.

117. See "Some of the Few Cases of Loyal and Zealous Subjects," 1752, BL Egerton 3433, 5, and RAWC CP Box 44/230.

118. Joseph Yorke to Hardwicke, December 19, 1745, in Yorke, *Life and Correspondence of Hardwicke,* 1:484–87, 486.

119. See Marchant, *History of the Present Rebellion,* 220.

120. "Copy of the orders given by Colonel John Campbell to Captain Campbell of Knockbowie of the Argyllshire Milita, and which was taken from the original order found amongst Knockbowie's papers and baggage which was seized when the greatest part of his men were made prisoners at Bannoch by Lord George Murray" (purported orders dated February 20, 1746), RAWC CP Box 11/9.

121. Brodie to Loudon, April 29, 1746, HL LO (SC) 10882.

122. Account of the Battle of Culloden, HL LO (SC) 8848.

123. For Jacobite, or otherwise dissenting, accounts of the battle, see Forbes, *Lyon in Mourning,* 1:32–33, 48–50, 90; *Caledonian Mercury,* September 4, 1746; "An Account of the Signal Escape of John Fraser," appendix to George Murray, *A Particular Account of the Battle of Culloden* (London, 1749), 1.

124. Orders for April 17, 1746, in order book beginning January 28, 1746, NAS GD1/322/1, 103.

125. See Foster, *An Account of the Earl of Kilmarnock,* 18; Forbes, *Lyon in Mourning,* 1:251–52.

126. Wolfe to Henry Delabene, April 17, 1746, in Willson, *Life and Letters of Wolfe,* 62–64, 63. See also Wolfe to William Sotheron, April 17, 1746, in Willson, *Life and Letters of Wolfe,* 65–66, 65; and Wright, *Life of Wolfe,* 84–85, 84.

127. Henderson, *History of the Rebellion,* 185–86.

128. Cumberland to Newcastle, April 18, 1746, RAWC CP Box 14/58 and LR 2/71; also TNA SP 54/30, 183.

129. Bland to Napier, May 22, 1746, RAWC CP Box 15/129.

130. *Oxford English Dictionary,* 2d ed., 5:158.

131. Milton to Wade, December 22, 1745, RAWC CP Box 8/97.

132. *Caledonian Mercury,* January 17, 1746. See also orders for February 3, 1746, in order book beginning January 28, 1746, NAS GD1/322/1, 11; Charles Howard to Cumberland, January 13, 1746, RAWC CP Box 9/73.

133. Henderson, *History of the Rebellion,* 153.

134. See minutes of the Privy Council, February 3, 1746, TNA SP 36/81, 28; Newcastle to Cumberland, June 5, 1746, RAWC CP Box 15/372, and TNA SP 54/32, 3.

135. Seton and Arnot, *Prisoners of the '45,* 1:6–7. See also Forbes, *Lyon in Mourning,* 1:178–82.

136. See Terry, ed., *Albemarle Papers*, 2:xxxv.

137. Certificate of Bland, December 10, 1746, TNA T 1/348, 74, and RAWC CP Box 19/162A; Bland to Albemarle, August 3, 1746, in Terry, ed., *Albemarle Papers*, 1:33–35, 35; Milton to Newcastle, August 11, 1746, in Terry, ed., *The Albemarle Papers*, 2:410–11.

138. Newcastle to Milton, July 11, 1746, in Terry, ed., *Albemarle Papers*, 1:7–8, 8. See also instructions for David Bruce, July 1746, RAWC CP Box 17/1.

139. Bland to Fawkener, July 28, 1746, RAWC CP Box 17/424.

140. Bland to Fawkener, August 4, 1746, RAWC CP Box 18/20.

141. Bland to Fawkener, August 4, 1746, RAWC CP Box 18/20.

142. See Milton to Newcastle, March 15, 1746, TNA SP 54/29, 118; Newcastle to Milton, March 21, 1746, TNA SP 54/29, 166; Joseph Yorke to Bruce, May 25, 1746, BL Add. 35,889, 119; Cranfield Spencer Powell to Loudon, September 1, 1746, HL LO (SC) 12439.

143. *Act to Attaint Alexander Earl of Kellie . . .* (London, 1746); Jewell, "Legislation Relating to Scotland," 96.

144. See Milton to Newcastle, March 10 and 15, 1746, TNA SP 54/29, 43 and 118.

145. Foster, *Report of Some Proceedings*, 14 n. The rules of criminal procedure were very much in flux in the middle years of the eighteenth century. Not all trials were conducted so carefully. See Stephan Landsman, "The Rise of the Contentious Spirit: Adversary Procedure in Eighteenth-Century England," *Cornell Law Review* 75 (1990): 497–609; John H. Langbein, "Shaping the Eighteenth-Century Criminal Trial: A View from the Ryder Sources," *University of Chicago Law Review* 50 (1983): 1–136.

146. Foster, *Report of Some Proceedings*, 7, 63 n.

147. Ibid., 8; *A Genuine Account of the Lives, Behavior, Confession and Dying Words of the Five Rebels . . .* (London, 1746), 7–9; "Third List of Rebel Prisoners Tried or Who Have Pleaded Guilty," September 22, 1746, RAWC CP Box 18/212.

148. *Caledonian Mercury*, September 11 and 16, October 7, 1746. See Milton to Newcastle, July 26, 1746, in Terry, ed., *Albemarle Papers*, 2: 398–99, 399.

149. *Caledonian Mercury*, September 23, 1746.

150. Jewell, "Legislation Relating to Scotland," 89–90; Foster, *Report of Some Proceedings*, 1.

151. Newcastle to Cumberland, May 12 and 23, 1746, RAWC CP Boxes 14/392 and 15/137, and TNA SP 54/31, 70.

152. Bland to Hardwicke, December 25, 1753, BL Add. 35,448, 51.

153. Cumberland to Newcastle, February 2, 1746, TNA SP 54/28, 9.

154. Newcastle to Milton, August 1, 1746, BL Egerton 3433, 32. See also Milton to Newcastle, August 7, 1746, in Terry, ed., *Albemarle Papers*, 2:401–404, 401.

155. See, generally, depositions at Jacobite trials, 1746, in Allardyce, ed., *Historical Papers Relating to the Jacobite Period*, 2:372–486. See also Forbes, *Lyon in Mourning*, 1:24, 29, 47, 50; *Genuine Account of the Five Rebels*, 9; *To Mr. S . . . M . . . On His Turning Evidence* (London, 1747).

156. *Caledonian Mercury*, September 18, 1746.

157. Ibid., September 25, 1746.

158. Ibid., October 6, 1746. See also Philip Carteret Webb to Fawkener, September 27, 1746, RAWC CP Box 18/251.

159. Execution speech of David Morgan, tried in London and executed on July 30, 1746, in Forbes, *Lyon in Mourning*, 1:47.

160. *A Genuine Account of the Behaviour, Confession, and Dying Words of Francis Townley . . .* (Dublin, 1746), 18.

161. Seton and Arnot, *Prisoners of the '45*, 1:96.

162. Foster, *Report of Some Proceedings*, 8. On the distinction between "quarter" and "mercy," see Barbara Donagan, "Atrocity, War Crime, and Treason in the English Civil War," *American Historical Review* 99 (1994): 1137–66, 1150.

163. Foster, *Report of Some Proceedings*, 14.

164. See especially *Rise of the Present Unnatural Rebellion*, 13.

165. As it happened, coercion defenses succeeded in only a handful of cases. See *Caledonian Mercury*, September 18 and 23, 1746; "Second List of Rebel Prisoners Tried or who had Pleaded guilty at York," October 6, 1746, RAWC CP Box 18/288.

166. *Caledonian Mercury*, September 30, October 28, and November 11, 1746 *Genuine Account of Francis Townley*, 31.

167. George II to Newcastle, July 27, 1746, BL Add. 32,707, 492. See also Newcastle to Stair, November 11, 1746, TNA SP 54/34, 82.

168. See *Caledonian Mercury*, November 17 and 18, 1746.

169. "Abstract of Mr. Sharpe's letters," n.d., TNA SP 54/26, 599.

170. On plea bargaining, see John H. Langbein, "Understanding the Short History of Plea-Bargaining," *Law and Society Review* 13 (1979): 261–72.

171. See Newcastle to Albemarle, October 7, 1746, TNA SP 54/34, 5.

172. *Caledonian Mercury*, December 22, 1746.

173. Ibid., July 29, 1746.

174. *Scots Magazine* 9 (1747): 243.

175. Smith, *Colonists in Bondage*, 201; see also generally Seton and Arnot, *The Prisoners of the '45*.

176. See, for example, Macinnes, *Clanship, Commerce, and the House of Stuart*, 212.

177. See, for example, Alan J. Guy, "King George's Army, 1714–1750," in Robert C. Woosnam-Savage, ed., *1745: Charles Edward Stuart and the Jacobites* (Edinburgh: Glasgow Museums, 1995), 41–56, 51.

178. This may have changed later in the century. On the shifting meaning of being a British subject in the eighteenth century, see Dowd, *War under Heaven*, 177–85.

Chapter 2. Savagery

1. See Cumberland to Newcastle, September 3, 1745, N.S., BL Add. 32,705, 106; Newcastle to Chesterfield, September 6, 1745, BL Add. 32,705, 143, and TNA SP 63/408, 72; Thomas, *Politics in Eighteenth-Century Wales*, 143–49; *The Parliamentary History of England*, 36 vols. (London: 1806–20), 13:1363–82.

2. See Chesterfield to Newcastle, November 2, 1745, BL Add. 32,705, 300.

3. *Parliamentary History of England*, 13:1363–82. See Gould, "To Strengthen the King's Hands," 335–36.

4. See, for example, Stair to Loudon, August 31, September 10, and October 5, 1745, HL LO (SC) 7642, 7639, and 7636.

5. Memorial of Stair, September 5, 1745, HL LO (SC) 7641.

6. See Stair to Loudon, October 5, 1745, HL LO (SC) 7636; Loudon to Simon Fraser, Baron Lovat, November 11 and November 24, 1745, *Transactions of the Gaelic Society of Inverness* 14 (1887–88): 10–11, 14–16; Loudon to John Campbell of Ensay, April 7, 1746, HL LO (SC) 11829; Richard Howe to Loudon,

April 10, 1746, HL LO (SC) 7336; Cumberland to Loudon, April 25, 1746, HL LO (SC) 9505.

7. *London Evening Post,* January 16–18, 1746; *South Carolina Gazette,* May 19, 1746.

8. Loudon to Lovat, November 11, 1745, *Transactions of the Gaelic Society of Inverness* 14 (1887–88): 10–11; Wolfe to William Rickson, March 7, 1755, in Willson, *Life and Letters of Wolfe,* 252–54, 253; also in Wright, *The Life of Wolfe,* 307–11, 308–9.

9. For a poignant illustration, see Forbes, *Lyon in Mourning,* 1:178.

10. See, for example, Bland, *Treatise of Military Discipline,* 173.

11. General and staff offices serving in Flanders, December 24, 1744, RAWC CP Box 1/282; Bland to Fawkener, June 22, N.S., 1745, RAWC CP Box 3/83; Bland to Robert Napier, August 14, N.S., 1745, RAWC CP Box 4/70; John Napier to Bland, July 1745, RAWC CP Box 4/71; certificate of Bland, October 8, 1745, RAWC CP Box 6/81.

12. Bland to Richmond, November 27, 1745, RAWC CP Box 7/149.

13. See letter from Shaw, January 1, 1746, HL LO (SC) 12613; Innes to Duncan Forbes, February 16, 1746, HL LO (SC) 10557; Charles Edward Stuart to the Magistrates of Haddington, November 2, 1745, RAWC CP Box 7/380.

14. See C. McLaurin to Rev. Mr. Hill, November 21, 1745, BL Add. 35,889, 46.

15. Philalethes, "A Letter to the Archbishop of York," in *Full and True Collection, Part II,* 25–35, 26.

16. See, for example, Lochiel and Alexander MacDonald, *Copy of a Letter &c, Glenivis, March 20, 1746* (1746), reprinted in Marchant, *The History of the Present Rebellion,* 367–69, and *Life of Dr. Archibald Cameron,* 17–19. See also HL LO (SC) 10902, and TNA SP 54/30, 76.

17. This argument was advanced explicitly in *Traduccion de la reponse du roi Jacques à la lettre du regent d'ecosse* (Paris, 1745), 2.

18. See orders of September 30, 1745, *A Full Collection of all the Proclamations and Orders Published by Authority of Charles Prince of Wales* (Glasgow, 1745), 20–21; orders of October 15 and 28, 1745, in *Full and True Collection, Part II,* 48–49, 52–53; Gregor MacGregor of Glengyle to Gabriel Napier, 1745, TNA T 1/348, 79, and BL Egerton 3433, 254.

19. Collector of Customs at Ayr to the Secretaries of State, September 30, 1745, TNA SP 54/26, 127.

20. See "Some Few of the Instances where Jacobites or Nonjurors have been Provided for," 1752, BL Egerton 3433, 5, and RAWC CP Box 44/331.

21. See, for example, order of September 23, 1745, in *Full Collection of all the Proclamations,* 16–17.

22. *London Magazine,* 1745, 565.

23. Order of James, Duke of Perth, November 17, 1745, TNA SP 54/26, 528.

24. See McLaurin to Hill, November 21, 1745, BL Add. 35,889, 46.

25. Milton to Newcastle, September 25, 1745, TNA SP 54.26, 104.

26. *Caledonian Mercury,* October 16 and 18, 1745.

27. Order of October 22, 1745, in *A Full and True Collection, Part II,* 50; *Caledonian Mercury,* October 23, 1745. See also *Caledonian Mercury,* October 30, 1745.

28. Craigie to Gabriel Napier, September 4, 1745, TNA T 1/348, 61; Craigie to Tweeddale, September 5 and 10, 1745, TNA SP 54/26, 11 and 42; Affidavit of James Paterson, February 10, 1746, TNA T 1/348, 64; memorial of Gabriel Napier, April 1, 1749, RAWC CP Box 43/172.

29. Affidavit of Paterson, February 10, 1746, TNA T 1/348, 64.

30. Craigie to Tweeddale, September 10, 1745, TNA SP 54/26, 42; Affidavit of Paterson, February 10, 1746, TNA T 1/348, 64; Statement of David Duncan, February 1746, TNA T 1/348, 65.

31. For indications of the financial disruption, see Findlater and Seaforth to Loudon, January 1, 1746, HL LO (SC) 12412; Logie to Loudon, January 20, 1746, HL LO (SC) 10755; Archibald Dunbar to Brodie, January 21, 1746, HL LO (SC) 11397; David Campbell to Loudon, April 3, 1746, HL LO (SC) 11089.

32. Cumberland to the lord lieutenant of the County of Lancaster, December 12, 1745, RAWC CP LR 1/96; John Beynon to the postmaster at Coventry, November 26, 1745, RAWC CP Box 7/138; William Douglass to Richmond, November 27, 1745, RAWC CP Box 7/148; Newcastle to Cumberland, November 30, 1745, RAWC CP Box 7/195.

33. Orders for February 1, 1746, in order book beginning January 28, 1746, NAS GD1/322/1, 8.

34. Bland to Fawkener, March 19, 1746, RAWC CP Box 12/181 and 12/182.

35. Blakeney to Henry Pelham, November 22, 1745, TNA SP 54/26, 227; Blakeney to Milton, March 17, 1746, TNA T 1/348, 62.

36. Affidavit of James Wallace and Robert Banks, February 22, 1746, TNA T 1/348, 67; affidavit of Andrew Malcome, February 22, 1746, TNA T 1/348, 69; affidavit of Andrew Turnbell, February 15, 1746, TNA T 1/348, 71.

37. Blakeney to Milton, March 17, 1746, TNA T 1/348, 62; affidavit of Wallace and Banks, February 22, 1746, TNA T 1/348, 67; affidavit of Malcome, February 22, 1746, TNA T 1/348, 69; affidavit of Turnbell, February 15, 1746, TNA T 1/348, 71; Blakeney to Gabriel Napier, October 27, 1746, TNA T 1/348, 74; abstract of Craigie to Gabriel Napier, September 8, 1745, TNA T 1/348, 77; affidavit of James Grassan, February 22, 1746, TNA T 1/348, 63; affidavit of Duncan Drummond, February 22, 1746, TNA T 1/348, 65; affidavit of Thomas Blackader, February 22, 1746, TNA T 1/348; certificate of Bland, December 10, 1746, TNA T 1/348, 74; memorial of Gabriel Napier, 1752, TNA T 1/348, 54.

38. MacGregor of Glengyle to Gabriel Napier, 1745, TNA T 1/348, 79, and BL Egerton 3433, 254; memorial of Gabriel Napier, April 1, 1749, RAWC CP Box 43/172.

39. Memorial of Gabriel Napier, April 1, 1749, RAWC CP Box 43/172; memorial of Gabriel Napier, 1752, TNA T 1/348, 54. See also Gabriel Napier to James West, March 10, 1752, TNA T 1/348, 53; "Some Few of the Cases of the Loyal and Zealous Subjects," 1752, BL Egerton 3433, 10, and RAWC CP Box 44/230.

40. Affidavit of Malcome, February 22, 1746, TNA T 1/348, 69.

41. Charles Edward Stuart, commission for Lewis Gordon, October 16, 1745, RAWC CP Box 6/221. See also Horn to Loudon, November 16, 1745, HL LO (SC) 10441; James More to Lewis Gordon, November 21 and 22, 1745, RAWC CP Box 7/419 and 7/420; William More to the magistrates of Aberdeen, December 27, 1745, RAWC CP Box 8/207.

42. William Moir to Lewis Gordon, November 27, 1745, RAWC CP Box 7/439.

43. James Morison to Loudon, December 14, 1745, HL LO (SC) 12306; see also Roderick Merchant to Normand MacLeod, January 4, 1746, HL LO (SC) 9189.

44. Cumberland to Newcastle, March 9, 1746, TNA SP 54/29, 38; Milton to the sheriff of Aberdeen, March 8, 1746, TNA SP 54/29, 45.

45. Loudon to Tweeddale, October 11, 1745, TNA SP 54/26, 162; See cabinet minutes, November 27, 1745, RAWC CP Box 7/207.

46. Loudon to Lovat, November 11, 1745, *Transactions of the Gaelic Society of Inverness* 14 (1887–88): 14–16, 15.

47. Anonymous letter to Lovat, *Transactions of the Gaelic Society of Inverness* 14 (1887–88): 30–31.

48. See Lenman, *The Jacobite Clans of the Great Glen,* 101–48; instructions for Wade, July 24, 1724, RAWC CP Box 61/B/2. See also Lovat, "Memorial Concerning the Highlands of Scotland," RAWC CP Box 61/B/3.2.

49. See Lenman, *Jacobite Clans of the Great Glen,* 167–68; Duncan Forbes to Tweeddale, December 22, 1745, TNA SP 54/26, 284; Forbes, *Lyon in Mourning,* 2:284–85; McLynn, *Charles Edwards Stuart,* 202.

50. McLynn, *Charles Edward Stuart,* 223.

51. See Speck, *The Butcher,* 117–20.

52. Instructions for Cumberland, November 25, 1745, RAWC CP Box 7/117.

53. "List of persons chiefly on suspicion of treason," January 3, 1746, RAWC CP Box 9/27; "Abstract of Mr. Sharpe's letters," n.d., TNA SP 54/26, 599.

54. Cumberland to the keeper of the prison in Applebee, December 20, 1745, RAWC CP Box 65/vi.23.14, 54; Charles Howard to Cumberland, January 13, 1746, RAWC CP Box 9/73; Fawkener to the commissioners for sick and wounded seamen, etc., January 16, 1746, RAWC CP Box 9/92; S. Machel, "List of Prisoners in Westmorland," January 23, 1746, RAWC CP Box 9/137; list of prisoners at Carlisle, January 25, 1746, CP Box 10/3.

55. Charles Howard to Cumberland, January 13, 1746, RAWC CP Box 9/73.

56. Newcastle to Milton, July 11, 1746, in Terry, ed., *Albemarle Papers,* 1:7–8, 8.

57. *The Sinfulness of Compliance with the Rebels Detected* (1745), preface.

58. Cumberland to Newcastle, February 2 and 28, 1746, TNA SP 54/28, 9 and 196.

59. Loudon to Lovat, November 24, 1745, *Transactions of the Gaelic Society of Inverness* 14 (1887–88): 14–16, 15.

60. Cumberland to Duke of Newcastle, February 2 and 28, 1746, TNA SP 54/28, 9 and 196.

61. Milton to Fawkener, February 10, 1746, RAWC CP Box 10/165.

62. Cumberland to Newcastle, March 5, 1746, RAWC CP LR 2/32, and TNA SP 54/29, 14.

63. Proclamation of Cumberland, February 24, 1746, RAWC CP Box 11/65; Seton and Arnot, *Prisoners of the '45,* 1:1.

64. Milton to Fawkener, February 10, 1746, RAWC CP Box 10/165; draft of proclamation dated February 24, 1746, RAWC CP Box 11/64. See also proclamation of Cumberland, March 8, 1746, RAWC CP Box 12/14.

65. Proclamation of Cumberland, February 24, 1746, RAWC CP Box 11/65, and TNA SP 54/29, 21.

66. Milton to Fawkener, March 12, 1746, RAWC CP Box 12/75; Speck, *The Butcher,* 125–27.

67. Cumberland to Newcastle, March 15, 1746, TNA SP 54/29, 114.

68. Newcastle to Cumberland, March 21, 1746, TNA SP 54/29, 164.

69. Newcastle to Cumberland, March 21, 1746, BL Add. 32,706, 325.

70. See John Garden to David Blair, March 14, 1746, RAWC CP Box 12/101.

71. *London Evening Post,* June 17–19, 1746.

72. Letter from Alexander Campbell, February 17, 1746, TNA SP 54/28, 158; Archibald Campbell to John Campbell, future 5th Duke of Argyll, February 20, 1746, TNA SP 54/28, 152.

73. Cumberland to Newcastle, March 26, 1746, RAWC CP LR 2/52, and TNA

SP 54/29, 185. See also Cumberland to Newcastle, March 31, 1746, RAWC CP Box 13/88, and TNA SP 54/29, 243.

74. Wolfe to Rickson, March 7, 1755, in Bickles Willson, *Life and Letters of Wolfe*, 252–54, 253; and in Wright, *Life of Wolfe*, 307–11, 308–9.

75. See Alexander Cameron to Loudon, August 18, 1746, HL LO (SC) 7354; see also Isabel Cameron to Loudon, September 1746, HL LO (SC) 7352; Joseph Yorke to Hardwicke, March 31, 1746, in Yorke, *Life and Correspondence of Hardwicke*, 1:514–16, 515.

76. Chesterfield to Newcastle, September 29, 1745 and March 11, 1746, BL Add. 32,705, 225 and 32,706, 286.

77. Chesterfield to Newcastle, March 11, 1746, BL Add. 32,706, 286.

78. Chesterfield to Newcastle, March 23, 1746, BL Add. 32,706, 330.

79. Milton to Bruce, March 31, 1746, RAWC CP Box 13/75.

80. Newcastle to Cumberland, April 17, 1746, BL Add. 32,707, 67; Jewell, "Legislation Relating to Scotland," 91, 126.

81. Orders for February 10 and April 20, 21 and 27, 1746, in order book beginning January 28, 1746, NAS GD1/322/1, 23–24, 115, 116, and 130.

82. Bland, *Treatise of Military Discipline*, 134–38. See also Bland to Napier, May 19, 1746, RAWC CP Box 15/90.

83. Orders for June 3, 1746, in order book beginning January 28, 1746, NAS GD1/322/1, 192–93.

84. Orders for June 15, July 2 and 4, 1746, in order book beginning January 28, 1746, NAS GD1/322/1, 204, 220, and 222.

85. Wolfe to Captain Hamilton, June 11 and July 1746, in Willson, *Life and Letters of Wolfe*, 68 and 69.

86. Forbes, *Lyon in Mourning*, 3:174–75.

87. Cumberland to Newcastle, April 30, 1746, RAWC CP LR 2/79; Loudon to John Campbell, future 5th Duke of Argyll, May 3, 1746, HL LO (SC) 11793; George Munro of Culcairn to Loudon, July 28, 1746, HL LO (SC) 12337; Loudon to George Munro, August 2, 1746, HL LO (SC) 11796; petition of Patrick and William Grant, n.d., HL LO (SC) 7321.

88. George Munro of Culcairn to Loudon, June 4, 1746, HL LO (SC) 12328; Allan MacLeod, et al., depositions, June 4, 1746, HL LO (SC) 12096; letter from Loudon, March 13, 1747, HL LO (SC) 11806.

89. See Kenneth Bethune, list of persons who have not surrendered arms with the parish of Laggan, June 1, 1746, HL LO (SC) 10839. There are dozens of such lists in the Cumberland Papers, RAWC CP Boxes 15 and 16.

90. *Caledonian Mercury*, October 6, 1746.

91. Joseph Yorke to Hardwicke, June 3, 1746, in Yorke, *Life and Correspondence of Hardwicke*, 1:542–43, 543.

92. Orders for April 16, 1746, in order book beginning January 28, 1746, NAS GD1/322/1, 103.

93. Joseph Yorke to Hardwicke, April 18, 1746, in Yorke, *Life and Correspondence of Hardwicke*, 1: 521–25, 524.

94. Cumberland to Loudon, April 25, 1746, HL LO (SC) 9505.

95. Loudon to Cumberland, April 23, 1746, HL LO (SC) 11792; John Campbell, future 5th Duke of Argyll, to Loudon, July 2, 1746, HL LO (SC) 11199; order of George Munro, August 4, 1746, in Terry, ed., *Albemarle Papers*, 1:53–54, and HL LO (SC) 12346; *Caledonian Mercury*, May 27, June 12, 16, and 19, 1746; *London Evening Post*, June 24–26, July 8–10, 1746.

96. See Terry, ed., *Albemarle Papers*, 2:xxxiii.

97. *Caledonian Mercury*, June 19, 1746.

98. Lochiel and Alexander MacDonald, *Copy of a Letter &c, Glenivis, March 20, 1746* (1746), reprinted in Marchant, *The History of the Present Rebellion*, 367–69, and *Life of Dr. Archibald Cameron*, 17–19. See also HL LO (SC) 10902, and TNA SP 54/30, 76.

99. Bland to Napier, May 22, 1746, RAWC CP Box 15/129.

100. George Howard to Bland, May 24, 1746, RAWC CP Box 15/178; "List of prisoners taken by the detachment under th command of Lieutenant Howard," May 26, 1746, RAWC CP Box 15/212. According to one of the men taken prisoner, there had been 380 Jacobite men under arms in the vicinity of Lochiel's house at start of this episode. See Loudon to Humphrey Bland, May 25, 1746, RAWC CP Box 15/191. For another account of this encounter, see Cumberland to Newcastle, RAWC CP Box 15/221. See John Sibbold Gibson, *Lochiel of the '45: The Jacobite Chief and the Prince* (Edinburgh: Edinburgh University Press, 1994), 129–30.

101. Loudon to Cumberland, May 25, 1746, RAWC CP Box 15/183; George Howard to Napier, May 25, 1746, RAWC CP Box 15/188.

102. Submission of the Camerons, May 25, 1746, RAWC CP Box 15/190.

103. Cumberland to Newcastle. May 27, 1746, RAWC CP Box 15/221, and TNA SP 54/31, 141.

104. Newcastle to Cumberland, June 5, 1746, RAWC CP Box 15/372, and TNA SP 54/32, 3.

105. Albemarle to Loudon, July 24 and 25, 1746, HL LO (SC) 7142 and 7143; Prebble, *Culloden*, 205.

106. Cumberland to James Campbell, RAWC CP Box 15/271.

107. Cumberland to Newcastle, June 5, 1746, RAWC CP Box 15/396 and LR 2/95, and TNA SP 54/32, 20.

108. Forbes, *Lyon in Mourning*, 1:92–93. See also "Journal of the Young Pretender . . . taken from the manuscript found among the papers of Mrs. Cameron, wife of Doctor Cameron, when she was taken up at Breda, in her way to Paris, January 1748," RAWC CP Box 69/xi.41.18.

109. See, for example, Mungo Grame to the Duke of Montrose, June 12, 1746, TNA SP 54/32, 59.

110. See Allan MacDonald, information, June 11, 1746, HL LO (SC) 10772.

111. Joseph Yorke to Hardwicke, February 8, 1746, in Yorke, *Life and Correspondence of Hardwicke*, 1:496–98, 497–98.

112. Adam Gordon, memorandum, March 17, 1746, HL LO (SC) 11635; Alexander MacKay to Loudon, June 30, 1746, HL LO (SC) 11933.

113. *London Evening Post*, March 25–27, 1746. See also *Caledonian Mercury*, April 18, 1746.

114. Defoe, *A Tour Thro' the Whole Island of Great Britain*, 2:772–73. For an example of the typical humor surrounding these accounts, see the *London Evening Post*, April 29, 1746.

115. See "Declaration of Miss MacDonald," July 1, 1746, TNA SP 54/32, 216; "Journal of the Young Pretender . . . taken from the manuscript found among the papers of Mrs. Cameron, wife of Doctor Cameron, when she was taken up at Breda, in her way to Paris, January 1748," RAWC CP Box 69/xi.41.18; McLynn, *Charles Edward Stuart*, 284–85. For Margaret MacDonald's version of these events, see Margaret MacDonald to John MacKenzie, July 24, 1746, National Library of Scotland (hereafter NLS) 1309/29.

116. Vattel, *Law of Nations* (London, 1760), 51. See also Vattel, *Droit des gens*, 113; Grotius, *The Illustrious Hugo Grotius*, 551–52.

117. Lochiel and Alexander MacDonald, *Copy of a Letter &c, Glenivis, March 20, 1746* (1746), reprinted in Marchant, *The History of the Present Rebellion*, 367–69, and *Life of Dr. Archibald Cameron*, 17–19. See also HL LO (SC) 10902, and TNA SP 54/30, 76.

118. Vattel, *Law of Nations*, 52; Vattel, *Droit des gens*, 113.

119. Normand MacLeod to Duncan Forbes, February 12 and March 16, 1746, HL LO (SC) 12145 and 12147; Innes to Duncan Forbes, February 16, 1746, HL LO (SC) 10557; orders for May 3, 1746, in order book beginning January 28, 1746, NAS GD1/322/1, 142.

120. *Copy of a Letter from a Young Lady in the Country to a Lady in Edinburgh* (1745); *A Journey Through Part of England and Scotland along with the Army under the Command of His Highness the Duke of Cumberland* (London, 1746), 51.

121. Marchant, *History of the Present Rebellion*, 216. See also Craig, *Damn' Rebel Bitches*, 42–50.

122. *Brief Account of Jenny Cameron*, 17.

123. Ibid., 24.

124. See also Archibald Arburthnot, *Memoirs of the Remarkable Life and Surprizing Adventures of Miss Jenny Cameron* (London, 1746, rep. New York: Garland, 1974); *Harlequin Incendiary* (London, 1746).

125. *A Letter to the Author of the National Journal* (1746).

126. See *The History of the Present Rebellion in Scotland* (London, 1745), 15; *London Evening Post*, November 15–18, 1746; Henderson, *History of the Rebellion*, 84; McLynn, *Jacobite Army in England*, 49.

127. *Caledonian Mercury*, November 4, 1745.

128. Abel Darley to Loudon, November 30, 1745, HL LO (SC) 11365.

129. See letter from D. Baily, November 22, 1745, RAWC CP Box 7/83a.

130. Alexander Cameron to Loudon, August 18, 1746, HL LO (SC) 7354; see also Isabel Cameron to Loudon, September 1746, HL LO (SC) 7352; Forbes, *Lyon in Mourning*, 1:91; "Journal of the Young Pretender . . . taken from the manuscript found among the papers of Mrs. Cameron, wife of Doctor Cameron, when she was taken up at Breda, in her way to Paris, January 1748," RAWC CP Box 69/xi.41.18; Johnstone, *Memoir of the Rebellion*, 153–54.

131. *A Letter to the Author of the National Journal.*

132. See proclamation dated October 26, 1745, TNA SP 63/409, 169; Chesterfield to Newcastle, March 11, 1746, BL Add. 32,706, 286. See also Chesterfield to Newcastle, March 20 and 23, 1746, BL Add. 32,706, 323 and 330.

133. Chesterfield to Newcastle, March 11, 1746, BL Add. 32,706, 286. See also Chesterfield to Newcastle, March 23, 1746, BL Add. 32,706, 330.

134. For an indication of the Privy Council's response, see Newcastle to Chesterfield, April 6, 1746, BL Add. 32,707, 21, but see also Newcastle to Chesterfield, TNA SP 63/409, 120.

135. *A Letter to the Author of the National Journal; Truth, but no Treason*, 50.

136. Loudon to Stair, March 2, 1746, TNA SP 54/29, 53. See also Loudon to Cumberland, March 10, 1746, RAWC CP Box 12/31.

137. Bland to Fawkener, March 20, 1746, RAWC CP Box 12/209.

138. See Cumberland to Newcastle, February 10, 1746, TNA SP 54/28, 58.

139. Chesterfield to Newcastle, December 6, 1745, BL Add. 32,705, 415.

140. Bland to Fawkener, March 17, 1746, TNA SP 54/29, 128; *Edinburgh Evening Courant*, March 31, 1746.

141. See Glenorchy to Hardwicke, April 27, 1746, BL Add. 35,450, 105. See also *London Evening Post*, May 10–13, 1746.

142. Henderson, *History of the Rebellion*, 14–15.

143. See John Campbell, future 5th Duke of Argyll, to Loudon, June 4, 1746, HL LO (SC) 11197.

144. Fawkener to James Campbell, May 17, 1746, RAWC CP Box 15/64; *Caledonian Mercury*, August 26, 1746; Albemarle to Loudon, August 27, 1746, HL LO (SC) 7138; "Dates of which the Independent Companies were disbanded," September 1746, HL LO (SC) 10142.

145. Craigie to Tweeddale, September 10, 1745, TNA SP 54/26, 42; William Mackenzie to Loudon, May 29, 1746, HL LO (SC) 12056; Norman MacLeod to John MacLeod, July 24, 1746, February 24, 1747, HL LO (SC) 12132 and 12137.

146. Bland to Fawkener, March 19, 1746, RAWC CP Box 12/182; Orders of Archibald Campbell, March 27, 1746, RAWC CP Box 13/14. On the apprehension of allegedly "nonjuring" Episcopalians, and the destruction of their places of worship, see also Craigie to Tweeddale, September 10, 1745, TNA SP 54/26, 42; Mungo Grame to the Duke of Montrose, June 12, 1746, TNA SP 54/32, 59.

147. William Mackenzie to Loudon, May 29, 1746, HL LO (SC) 12056. See also Norman MacLeod to John MacLeod, July 24, 1746, February 24, 1747, HL LO (SC) 12132 and 12137.

148. *London Evening Post*, November 27–29, 1746; SSPCK minutes, June 4, 1747, NAS GD 95/1/4, 392.

149. See Harris, *Politics and the Nation*, 155–56.

150. Joseph Yorke to Hardwicke, February 13, 1746, in Yorke, *Life and Correspondence of Hardwicke*, 1:500.

151. Printed proclamation, May 1, 1746, TNA SP 54/31, 135.

152. Charles Falconer to Loudon, August 25, 1746, HL LO (SC) 7347; William Gordon, declaration concerning Thomas MacPherson, February 4, 1747, HL LO (SC) 7325; William Blair, memorial Anent Thomas MacPherson, February 5, 1747, HL LO (SC) 7362.

153. Bland to Fawkener, March 19, 1746, RAWC CP Box 12/182. See Speck, *The Butcher*, 128.

154. John Stuart to Loudon, October 12, 1746, HL LO (SC) 12672. See also John Campbell of Archalader to Loudon, May 29, 1746, HL LO (SC) 11219; Archibald Campbell to Loudon, December 5, 1746, HL LO (SC) 11073.

155. Loudon to Adam Gordon, September 20, 1746, HL LO (SC) 11799.

156. See Patrick Grant to James MacDonald, June 6, 1746, HL LO (SC) 11725; Archibald McCorkell to Albemarle, August 9, 1746, HL LO (SC) 10728; Adam Gordon to Loudon, September 17 and October 3, 1746, HL LO (SC) 11629 and 11632; Loudon to Adam Gordon, September 20, 1746, HL LO (SC) 11799.

157. Alexander Gun, advertisement, November 21, 1746, HL LO (SC) 11777. See also Gun to Loudon, November 24, 1746, HL LO (SC) 11767.

158. See Cumberland to Newcastle, April 19, 1746, RAWC CP Box 14/58 and LR 2/71.

159. Arbthnot, *Memoirs of Jenny Cameron* (London ed.), 251.

160. Brodie to Loudon, April 29, 1746, HL LO (SC) 10882.

161. Albemarle to Newcastle, October 27, 1746, TNA SP 54/34, 61.

162. See John Stuart to Loudon, July 17, 1745, HL LO (SC) 12665.

163. John Farquharson to Loudon, August 4, 1746, HL LO (SC) 11444. See also John Farquharson to Loudon, August 25 and 26, 1746, HL LO (SC) 11445 and 11446.

164. Cumberland to Newcastle, March 14, 1746, RAWC CP Box 12/108, and TNA SP 54/29, 73.

165. See M. Murray to Anne MacKintosh, n.d., February 1746, RAWC CP Box 11/280.

166. The subordinate officer had the rank of major, and may have been the notorious "Major Lockhart." See Prebble, *Culloden*, 205; Albemarle to Loudon, July 24 and 25, 1746, HL LO (SC) 7142 and 7143. Alternatively he might have been one Major Caulfield, who in January 1747 sent Albemarle and Cumberland a collection of documents regarding the rising in and around Inverness. See RAWC CP Box 19/71–79.

167. Home to Loudon, August 10, 1747, HL LO (SC) 7112.

168. John Sutherland to Loudon, November 1 and 3, 1746, HL LO (SC) 12697 and 12698. See also Margaret MacDonald to Loudon, November 13, 1746, HL LO (SC) 11892.

169. John Farquharson to Duncan Forbes, August 18, 1747, in Duff, ed., *Culloden Papers*, 478–79.

170. John Stuart to Loudon, October 31, 1746, HL LO (SC) 12677.

171. See Hew Dalrymple, Lord Drummore, to Loudon, November 8, 1746, HL LO (SC) 11342; Home to Loudon, August 10, 1747, HL LO (SC) 7112.

172. Loudon to Albemarle, August 18, 1746, in Terry, ed., *Albemarle Papers*, 1:125–26. See also Simon Fraser to Loudon, August 10, 1746, in Terry, ed., *Albemarle Papers*, 1:89–90; Loudon to Albemarle, August 14, 1746, in Terry, ed., *Albemarle Papers*, 1:110

173. Declaration of nine Presbyterian ministers, *Transactions of the Gaelic Society of Inverness* 14 (1887–88): 37.

174. Milton to Newcastle, August 29, 1747, in Terry, ed., *Albemarle Papers*, 2:453–54, 453; obligation by the Master of Lovat, August 12, 1747, in Terry, ed., *Albemarle Papers*, 2:454–55, 454.

175. See Sankey and Szechi, "Elite Culture and the Decline of Scottish Jacobitism."

176. *A Candid and Impartial Account of the Behaviour of Simon Lord Lovat* (London, 1747), 18.

177. See *An Answer to a Dangerous Pamphlet Entitled a Candid and Impartial Account of the Behaviour of Simon, Lord Lovat* (London, 1747).

Chapter 3. The 1745 Crisis in the Empire

1. Statement of W. Brett, June 5, 1746, TNA SP 54/32, 42; statement of John McBride, June 4, 1746, TNA SP 54/32, 45; statement of Philip McGuire, June 4, 1746, TNA SP 54/32, 47; statement of Patrick McGuire, June 4, 1746, TNA SP 54/32, 48; Milton to W. Brett, June 7, 1746, TNA SP 54/32, 49.

2. Statement of Philip McGuire, June 4, 1746, TNA SP 54/32, 47.

3. Loudon to Robert Napier, June 27, 1746, RAWC CP Box 16/321; *The Life of Nicholas Mooney* (Dublin, 1752), 11.

4. Statement of Patrick McGuire, June 4, 1746, TNA SP 54/32, 48.

5. Statement of John McBride, June 4, 1746, TNA SP 54/32, 45.

6. Statement of W. Brett, June 5, 1746, TNA SP 54/32, 42.

7. See generally Cruickshanks, *Political Untouchables*; Monad, *Jacobitism and the English People*, 330–41; Thomas, *Politics in Eighteenth-Century Wales*, 133–49.

8. Jeremy Black, *A System of Ambition? British Foreign Policy, 1660–1793* (New York: Longman, 1991), 173.

9. For an extreme statement of this view, see the *Gentleman's Magazine,* December 13, 1745, quoted in Devine, *Clanship to Crofter's War,* 21–22.

10. *Journey Through Part of England and Scotland,* 31.

11. Murray G. H. Pittock, *Celtic Identity and the British Image* (Manchester: Manchester University Press, 1999), 26–28.

12. *Rise of the Present Unnatural Rebellion,* 7–8.

13. Chesterfield to Newcastle, September 29, 1745 and February 8, 1746, BL Add. 32,705, 225 and TNA SP 63/409, 58; Andrew Mitchell to Duncan Forbes, November 19, 1745, in Duff, ed., *Culloden Papers,* 253.

14. Chesterfield to Newcastle, September 29, 1745, BL Add. 32,705, 225.

15. See, for example, Newcastle to Cumberland, September 4 and 11, 1745, BL Add. 32,705, 135 and RAWC CP Box 5/77.

16. See proclamation of Charles Edward Stuart, October 10, 1745, RAWC CP Box 6/206.

17. Pittock, *Myth of the Jacobite Clans,* 54–87.

18. See David Allan, "Protestantism, Presbyterianism, and National Identity in Eighteenth-Century Scottish History," in Tony Claydon and Ian McBride, eds., *Protestantism and National Identity* (Cambridge: Cambridge University Press, 1998), 182–205, 192–93.

19. See Harris, *Politics and the Nation,* 155–56.

20. *Caledonian Mercury,* September 30, October 2, 7, 14, 1745.

21. Cumberland to Newcastle, February 28, 1746, in Duncan Warrand, ed., *More Culloden Papers* 5 vols. (Inverness: Robert Carruthers and Sons, 1923–30), 5:36.

22. David Jennings, *Success from God Alone, and the Vanity of Human Endeavours without His Blessing* (London, 1745), 3; *Sinfulness of Compliance with the Rebels Detected,* 3.

23. See Françoise Deconinck-Brossard, "The Churches and the '45," *Studies in Church History* 20 (1983): 253–62; Ebenezer Pemberton, *A Sermon Delivered at the Presbyterian Church in New York, July 31, 1746* (New York, 1746), 16; Charles Chauncy, *A Sermon Occasion'd by the Present Rebellion in Favour of the Pretender* (Boston, 1746), 40; Jonathan Edwards, letter to a correspondent in Scotland, November 20, 1745, in *The Works of Jonathan Edwards* (New Haven, Conn.: Yale University Press, 1957-), 3:444–60, 459–60.

24. See Robert Blackey, "A War of Words: The Significance of the Propaganda Conflict between English Catholics and Protestants, 1715–1745," *Catholic Historical Review* 58 (1972–73): 534–55, 536. See also generally Colin Haydon, *Anti-Catholicism in Eighteenth-Century England* (Manchester: Manchester University Press, 1993); SSPCK minutes, March 15, 1723, NAS GD 95/1/2, 236; *Maryland Gazette,* February 25, March 23, and July 1, 1746, February 10 and March 3, 1747.

25. Manifesto, May 16, 1745, in *Full Collection of all the Proclamations,* 9–13; proclamation of Charles Edward Stuart, October 10, 1745, RAWC CP Box 6/206. See also *Declaration and Admonitory Letter* (1745), BL Add. 35,889, 2, TNA SP 54/26, 192, reprinted in *Full and True Collection, Part II,* 22–24; *To the People of England* (1745), BL Add. 35,889, 4.

26. *Caledonian Mercury,* October 11, 1745.

27. Devine, *Clanship to Crofter's War,* 86, quoting from W. Donaldson, *The Jacobite Song* (Aberdeen, 1988), 46.

28. See Speck, *The Butcher,* 38–41; Haydon, *Anti-Catholicism in Eighteenth-Century England,* 131–33; Wilkes, *A Whig in Power,* 150; *History of the Present Rebellion in Scotland,* 24; *London Evening Post,* January 16–18, 1746.

29. Wilkes, *A Whig in Power*, 150.
30. Newcastle to John Williamson, September 12, 1745, BL Add. 32,705, 171.
31. Newcastle to Chesterfield, September 6, 1745, BL Add. 32,705, 143,; also TNA SP 63/408, 72.
32. Cumberland to Harrington, September 27, 1745, RAWC CP Box 5/127.
33. See, for example, letter from D. Baily, November 22, 1745, RAWC CP Box 7/83a; Newcastle to Cumberland, November 30, 1745, postscript dated December 1, 1745, RAWC CP Box 7/195.
34. Cumberland to the Lord Lieutenant of the County of Lancaster, December 12, 1745, RAWC CP LR 1/96.
35. Cumberland to Newcastle, December 11, 1746, RAWC CP LR 1/92.
36. Milton to Archibald Campbell, Duke of Argyll, November 21, 1745, in Home, *History of the Rebellion*, 336; Marchant, *History of the Present Rebellion*, 251.
37. Marchant, *History of the Present Rebellion*, 251.
38. Gould, *Persistence of Empire*, 24–29.
39. J. R. Western, *The English Militia in the Eighteenth Century: The Story of a Political Issue* (London: Routledge, 1965), 117–18.
40. Haydon, *Anti-Catholicism in Eighteenth-Century England*, 155.
41. *London Evening Post*, January 2–4, 1746.
42. Ibid., January 23–30 and July 24–26, 1746. See also Haydon, *Anti-Catholicism in Eighteenth-Century England*, 155–56; Speck, *The Butcher*, 69, 111.
43. *London Evening Post*, January 30-February 1, 1746.
44. Ibid., July 24–26, 1746.
45. See Haydon, *Anti-Catholicism in Eighteenth-Century England*, 130–31, 163; Speck, *The Butcher*, 41; McLynn, *Jacobite Army in England*, 6–7.
46. Henderson, *History of the Rebellion, 1745 and 1746*, 70.
47. Cumberland to Newcastle, September 3, N.S., 1745, BL Add. 32,705, 106.
48. For an overview of Protestant Ireland in the eighteenth century, see S. J. Connolly, *Religion, Law, and Power: The Making of Protestant Ireland, 1660–1760* (Oxford: Clarendon, 1992).
49. Chesterfield to Newcastle, August 31, 1745, BL Add. 32,705, 129; letter from R. Liddell, August 31, 1745, TNA SP 63/408, 66.
50. Thomas Gordon, *The Free Briton's Answer to the Pretender's Declaration* (Dublin, 1745), 4.
51. Henry Brooke, *The Farmer's Letter to the Protestants of Ireland, Number 1* (Dublin, 1745), 3.
52. Ibid., 7.
53. Chesterfield to Newcastle, September 2, 1745, BL Add. 32,705, 133.
54. Chesterfield to Newcastle, November 2, 1745, BL Add. 32,705, 300; Newcastle to Chesterfield, November 19, 1745, TNA SP 63/408, 221; proclamation dated October 10, 1745, TNA SP 63/408, 171.
55. See *Honest Advice to the People of Ireland Occasioned by the Present Attempt in Favour of the Pretender* (Dublin, 1745), 18–19.
56. Chesterfield to Newcastle, September 9, 1745, BL Add. 32,705, 153.
57. Chesterfield to Newcastle, September 29, 1745, BL Add. 32,705, 225.
58. Chesterfield to Newcastle, October 5, 1745, BL Add. 32,705, 241.
59. Chesterfield to Newcastle, September 29, 1745, BL Add. 32,705, 225. See also Chesterfield to Newcastle, October 4, 1745, BL Add. 32,705, 237.
60. Chesterfield to Newcastle, October 5, 1745, BL Add. 32,705, 241.
61. Ibid.
62. Chesterfield to Newcastle, September 10, 1745, BL Add. 32,705, 162.

63. Howe to Loudon, April 10, 1746, HL LO (SC) 7336.

64. Chesterfield to Fawkener, March 25, 1746, RAWC CP Box 12/341.

65. George Thomas to the Pennsylvania Assembly, January 8, 1746, in George Edward Reed, ed., *Pennsylvania Archives*, ser. *4, vol. 1: Papers of the Governors, 1681–1747* (Harrisburg: State of Pennsylvania, 1900), 879–83, 882. For the first arrival of the news in Pennsylvania, see Jonathan Hawkins, "Imperial '45: The Jacobite Rebellion in Transatlantic Context," *Journal of Imperial and Commonwealth History* 24 (1996): 24–47, 26.

66. Daniel Wadsworth, *Diary of Rev. Daniel Wadsworth* (Hartford, Conn., 1894), 127.

67. Ibid., 129.

68. See *Maryland Gazette*, March 4 and 11, 1746.

69. Wadsworth, *Diary*, 132.

70. See generally Hawkins, "Imperial '45."

71. See Chauncy, *A Sermon Occasion'd by the Present Rebellion*, 24 n.

72. *South Carolina Gazette*, March 10, 1746.

73. See Lovejoy, *Glorious Revolution in America*; Johnson, *Adjustment to Empire*.

74. Chauncy, *A Sermon Occasion'd by the Present Rebellion*, 28.

75. Ibid., 28, 29.

76. Ibid., 43.

77. Benjamin Franklin, "Poor Richard's Almanac," 1748, in *The Papers of Benjamin Franklin* (New Haven, Conn.: Yale University Press, 1959–), 3:255.

78. See generally John Mack Faragher, *A Great and Noble Scheme: The Tragic Story of the Expulsion of the French Acadians from their American Homeland* (New York: Norton, 2005); John G. Reid, et al., *The "Conquest" of Acadia, 1710: Imperial, Colonial, and Aboriginal Constructions* (Toronto: University of Toronto Press, 2004).

79. George A. Rawlyk, *Yankees at Louisbourg* (Orono: University of Maine Press, 1967).

80. *Boston Evening Post*, July 15 and August 5, 1745, July 22 and September 9, 1745; *Boston Postboy*, July 22, 1745. See also Louis Effingham De Forest, ed., *Louisbourg Journals* (New York: Society of Colonial Wars, 1932), 92, 94, 98; Julian Gwyn and Christopher Moore, eds., *La chute de Louisbourg: Le journal du 1er siège de Louisbourg du 25 mars au 17 juillet 1745 par Gilles Lacroix-Girard* (Ottawa: Éditions de l'Université d'Ottawa, 1978), 101.

81. *Full and True Collection, Part II*, 51. See also Harper, *Advice of a Friend to the Army*, 3.

82. *To the People of England* (1745), BL Add. 35,889, 4. This question was asked in the context of an overall critique of alleged German influence in George II's government, which was inextricably linked to issues of foreign policy and imperialism. The Jacobites opposed the government's concern for the interests of Hanover as well as its general anti-French stance.

83. Thomas Prince, *A Sermon Delivered at the South Church in Boston, N.E., August 14, 1746* (Boston, 1746), 18.

84. See, for example, *Pennsylvania Gazette*, April 24, 1746; *Boston Evening Post*, August 11, 1746.

85. Edwards, *Account of the Life of . . . David Brainerd*, 173, quoting Brainerd's diary entry for February 2, 1746.

86. Ibid., 173–74, quoting Brainerd's diary entry for February 3, 1746.

87. See Tim Hanson, "Gabriel Johnston and the Portability of Patronage in the Eighteenth-Century North Atlantic World," in A. Mackillop and Steve Murdoch, eds., *Military Governors and Imperial Frontiers, c. 1600–1800* (Leiden: Brill, 2003), 119–40, 129–32.

88. George Montagu Dunk, Earl of Halifax, et al. to John Russell, Duke of Bedford, February 20, 1749, in William L. Saunders, ed., *The Colonial Records of North Carolina*, 10 vols. (Raleigh: State of North Carolina, 1886), 4:933. See also 4:938, 4:940–41.

89. Hugh Talmage Lefler and William S. Powell, *Colonial North Carolina: A History* (New York: Scribners, 1973), 92; Duane Gilbert Meyer, *The Highland Scots of North Carolina, 1732–1776* (Chapel Hill: University of North Carolina Press, 1961), 27–28, 81.

90. On Georgia, see Anthony W. Parker, *Scottish Highlanders in Colonial Georgia: Recruitment, Emigration, and Settlement at Darien, 1735–1748* (Athens: University of Georgia Press, 1997); SSPCK minutes, January 7, 1742, NAS GD 95/1/4, 272. For the New York project, see memorial of Donald Campbell to the Board of Trade, in E. B. O'Callaghan, ed., *Documents Relative to the Colonial History of the State of New York* 15 vols. (Albany, N.Y.: Weed, Parsons, 1850–83), 7:629–31. See also George Clarke to Board of Trade, June 15, 1739, in O'Callaghan, ed., *Documents Relative to the Colonial History of the State of New York*, 6:145.

91. For an account of the early North Carolina settlement, see SSPCK minutes, April 3, 1740, NAS GD 95/2/5, 477. See also Lefler and Powell, *Colonial North Carolina*, 93; minutes of the Presbytery of Inverary, November 3, 1741, quoted in Meyer, *Highland Scots of North Carolina*, 113. Georgia's Highlanders were dispersed by the Spanish in 1741, and the New York emigrants never received title to land.

92. Gabriel Johnston to Board of Trade, May 10, 1749, in Saunders, ed., *Colonial Records of North Carolina*, 4:935–36.

93. John Lax and William Pencak, "The Knowles Riot and the Crisis of the 1740's in Massachusetts," *Perspectives in American History* 10 (1976): 163–214.

94. William Shirley to Board of Trade, December 13, 1747, in Charles Henry Lincoln, ed., *The Correspondence of William Shirley*, 2 vols. (New York: Macmillan, 1912), 1:412.

95. See, for example, ibid., 415.

96. William Douglass, *A Summary, Historical and Political, of the First Planting, Progressive Improvements, and Present State of the British Settlements in North America*, 2 vols. (Boston, 1749–53), 1:254 n.

97. *Independent Advertiser*, August 28, 1749; John Noble, *The Libel Suit of Knowles v. Douglass*, 1748 and 1749 (Cambridge, Mass., 1897).

98. For an account of Douglass's life, see Charles J. Bullock, "The Life and Writings of William Douglass," *Economic Studies* 2 (1897): 265–90. See also John M. Bumsted, "Doctor Douglass's *Summary*: Polemic for Reform," *New England Quarterly* 37 (1964): 242–50; Margot Minardi, "The Boston Inoculation Controversy of 1721–1722: An Incident in the History of Race," *William and Mary Quarterly* 3d ser. 61 (2004): 47–76.

99. Beatriz Betancourt Hardy, "Papists in a Protestant Age: The Catholic Gentry and Community in Colonial Maryland, 1689–1776" (Ph.D. diss., University of Maryland, 1993), 179.

100. See *Maryland Gazette*, June 17, 1746; Council minutes, December 3, 1746, in *Archives of Maryland* (Baltimore: Maryland Historical Society, 1883–), 28:370–76.

101. Hardy, "Papists in a Protestant Age," 246.

102. Summons, March 21, 1746, in *Archives of Maryland*, 28:356.

103. Council minutes, March 21, 1746, in *Archives of Maryland*, 28:356–57.

104. Proclamation of Thomas Bladen, July 13, 1746, in *Archives of Maryland*, 28:363–64.

105. John Mynard to Newcastle, October 25, 1745, TNA CO 174/2, 24.

106. Emanuel Sifantos and Nicholas Alexano Malvasia to Blakeney, September 16, 1749, TNA CO 174/2, 162. See Gregory, *Minorca, The Illusory Prize*, 133–34.

107. William Matthew to Board of Trade, November 6, 1746, TNA CO 152/25, 234. See also Matthew to the Board of Trade, September 19, 1746, TNA CO 152/25, 221; R. Plumer to Matthew, June 16, 1747, TNA CO 153/16, 160; representation of the Lords Justices, August 25, 1748, TNA CO 153/17, 36; minutes of the Privy Council, November 28, 1748, TNA CO 152/26, 92.

108. *Virginia Gazette*, July 3–11, 1746.

109. Newcastle to Shirley, May 30, 1747, in Lincoln, ed., *Correspondence of William Shirley*, 1:386; Shirley to George Clinton, August 15, 1747, in Lincoln, ed., *Correspondence of William Shirley*, 1:393; *Boston Evening Post*, June 9, 1746; *Maryland Gazette*, October 21 and November 25, 1746; Lawson, *George Grenville*, 46.

110. Pemberton, *Sermon Delivered at the Presbyterian Church*; George Whitefield, *Britain's Mercies, and Britain's Duty* (London, 1746).

111. Address of the governor and council, September 4, 1746, in *Archives of Maryland*, 28:364; New Jersey Council minutes, November 1, 1746, in *Archives of the State of New Jersey, First Series*, 33 vols. (Trenton: New Jersey Historical Society, 1883–1928), ser. 1, 15:474; *Pennsylvania Gazette*, January 13 and June 4, 1747.

112. *Maryland Gazette*, September 2, 1746; *Virginia Gazette*, July 24–31, 1746.

113. Whitefield, *Britain's Mercies*, 18.

114. Benjamin Franklin, "Poor Richard's Almanac," 1748, in *Papers of Benjamin Franklin*, 3:255.

115. Jedediah Morse, *The American Universal Geography* (Boston, 1802), 151, 157, 174, 580, 602–3, 819.

116. Ava Harriet Chadbourne, *Maine Place Names, and the Peopling of its Towns* (Portland, Me.: Bond Wheelwright, 1955), 3; Erik Achorn, "Geographical and Place Names taken from 'A Map of the Most Inhabited Part of New England . . . Nov. 29, 1774'," *Essex Institute Historical Collections* 89 (1953): 275–87, 284; see also Morse, *American Universal Geography*, 491, 639, 815; New Jersey council minutes, January 19, 1748, in *Archives of New Jersey*, ser. 1, 15:608. See also *Archives of New Jersey*, ser. 1, 15:550, 552, 582, 603, 607; Martha W. Hiden, *How Justice Grew: Virginia Counties: An Abstract of their Formation* (Williamsburg: Virginia 350th Anniversary Celebration Corporation, 1957), 27; George R. Stewart, *Names on the Land: A Historical Account of Place-Naming in the United States* (Boston: Houghton Mifflin, 1958), 142; Meyer, *Highland Scots of North Carolina*, 81; A. Howry Espenshade, *Pennsylvania Place Names* (State College: Pennsylvania State College, 1925), 44. Several counties in Pennsylvania are named for counties in England, and some inhabitants of the state have insisted that their "Cumberland County" was named with only the northern English county in mind. Nonetheless, given when the county was named (1750), its location on the frontier, and the pattern of naming at the time elsewhere in colonial America, it is likely that Pennsylvania's county, like the others, was named to honor the Duke of Cumberland.

117. Douglass, *Summary*, 1:400, 2:90, 92; Morse, *American Universal Geography*, 664, map of Massachusetts following page 364, and map of Rhode Island and Connecticut following 414; *Archives of Maryland*, 46:223, 225, 294; Stewart, *Names on the Land*, 146.

118. See Frederick Jackson Turner, "The Significance of the Frontier in American History," in Frederick Jackson Turner, ed., *The Frontier in American History* (New York: Holt, 1920), 1–38, 12.

119. See Newcastle to Albemarle, October 7, 1746, TNA SP 54/34, 5.

120. See Petition of the prisoners from the *Elizabeth and Anne,* 1716, in *Calendar of Virginia State Papers and Other Manuscripts,* 11 vols. (Richmond: Virginia State Library, 1875–93), 1:187–88; see also minutes of the council of Virginia, October 24, 1716, in Henry Reed McIlwaine, ed., *Executive Journals of the Council of Colonial Virginia,* 6 vols. (Richmond: Virginia State Library, 1925–28), 3:430–32; Carteret to Spotswood, February 26, 1722, in *Calendar of State Papers, Colonial Series: America and West Indies,* 34:22–23.

121. "A List of One Hundred and Twenty-Eight Rebels," August 3, 1747, TNA CO 28/49, 22.

122. Edward Tyrawley to Newcastle, October 29, 1747, TNA CO 137/58, 40; "A list of the rebel prisoners," October 1747, TNA CO 137/58, 42.

123. See contract of indenture, NAS GD103/2/382–38.

124. Edward Tyrawley to Bedford, April 15, 1749, TNA CO 137/58, 136; affidavit of Daniel Coal, April 14, 1749, TNA CO 137/58, 138.

125. *Maryland Gazette,* July 21 and 28, August 4, 1747; Smith, *Colonists in Bondage,* 202.

126. See Burt, *Letters from a Gentleman in the North of Scotland,* 1:250–56; Donald MacPherson to his father, June 2, 1717, in *Maryland Historical Magazine* 1 (1906): 345–48. *Maryland Gazette,* May 20, September 30, October 7, 14, and 21, 1746. A runaway-servant advertisement involving a Highlander living in present-day Delaware appeared in the *Pennsylvania Gazette* for March 8, 1739.

127. See proclamation of Samuel Ogle, September 16, 1747, in *Archives of Maryland,* 28:394.

128. "Two Jacobite Prisoners," *Maryland Historical Magazine* 1 (1906): 346–52, 350.

129. *Maryland Gazette,* September 8, 1747.

130. Minutes of the council of Maryland, December 18, 1747, in *Archives of Maryland,* 28:402; Hardy, "Papists in a Protestant Age," 246.

131. Robert Wightman, *A Letter from a Scots Gentleman at Berwick* (Newcastle upon Tyne, 1745), 6.

132. Cumberland to Newcastle, May 8, 1746, RAWC CP Box 14/349, and TNA SP 54/31, 28. See also Duncan Forbes, "Memorandum for His Highness the Duke," May 20, 1746, RAWC CP Box 15/101.

133. Loudon to Cumberland, April 22, 1746, RAWC CP Box 14/80; Loudon to Cumberland, April 26, 1746, HL LO (SC) 11792, and RAWC CP Box 14/131; Alexander MacDonald to "The Officers Commanding the two Island Sky Companies," May 3, 1746, HL LO (SC) 11868; Alexander MacKenzie, Memorial to Loudon, 1746, HL LO (SC) 9145; Joseph Yorke to Hardwicke, June 5, 1746, in Yorke, *Life and Correspondence of Hardwicke,* 1:543–45, 544.

134. See Captain O'Brien to Fawkener, April 5, 1746, TNA SP 54/30, 99.

135. John Dalrymple, future 5th Earl of Stair, to Loudon, May 17, 1746, HL LO (SC) 11351.

136. Devine, *Clanship to Crofter's War,* 16; Meyer, *The Highland Scots of North Carolina,* 42; W. C. MacKenzie, *The Western Isles: Their History, Traditions, and Place-Names* (Paisley: Alexander Gardner, 1932), 45–49. For MacDonald's version of the 1739 episode, see Margaret MacDonald to Milton, January 1, 1740, in Duff, ed., *Culloden Papers,* 154–55; Alexander MacDonald of Sleat to James Douglas, Earl of Morton, December 29, 1739, NLS 3142/21; John MacKenzie to MacDonald of Sleat, January 12, 1740, NLS 1136/108.

137. Cumberland to Newcastle, June 5, 1746, RAWC CP Box 15/396 and LR 2/95, and TNA SP 54/32, 20.

138. Cumberland to Newcastle, May 8, 1746, RAWC CP Box 14/349, and TNA SP 54/31, 28.

139. Cumberland to Newcastle, May 27, 1746, RAWC CP Box 15/221 and LR 2/92, and TNA SP 54/31, 141.

140. Newcastle to Cumberland, May 23, 1746, RAWC CP Box 15/137; *Letter to the Author of the National Journal* (1746); *Gentleman's Magazine* 16 (1746): 261; "Notes concerning regulations in the Highlands," March 3, 1748, TNA SP 54/38, 147.

141. See *Westminster Journal,* July 26, 1746.

142. Bedford to Cumberland, October 11, 1748, in Pargellis, ed., *Military Affairs in North America,* 6–7; Cumberland to Bedford, October 15, 1748, in John Russell, ed., *Correspondence of John, fourth Duke of Bedford,* 3 vols. (London, 1842–46), 1:563–64, 564. Cumberland was cautious in his support, however. See Cumberland to Bedford, November 12, 1748, RAWC CP Box 41/117.

143. Bedford to Cumberland, October 28, 1748, RAWC CP Box 41/73.

144. Return of men "that have not been sick since landed in Holland," October 16, 1748, HL LO (SC) 10529; Henry Fox to Loudon, December 21, 22, 24, 29, 30, and 31, 1748, HL LO (SC) 11525, 11535, 11526, 11527, 11530, 8620, and 11531; passes issued by Loudon, January 4, 1749, HL LO (SC) 11848.

145. Wolfe to Rickson, June 9, 1751, in Willson, *Life and Letters of Wolfe,* 139–45, 141, and Wright, *Life of Wolfe,* 165–73, 168–69.

146. *Pennsylvania Gazette,* April 24, 1746; *South Carolina Gazette,* May 19, 1746; *Maryland Gazette,* July 1, 1746.

147. See, for example, James Macpherson, *The History of the Present Rebellion in Scotland* (Boston, 1746); John Marchant, *The History of the Late Rebellion* (New York, 1747); P. Doddridge, *Some Remarkable Passages in the Life of the Honourable Col. James Gardner* (Boston, 1748).

148. Archibald Arburthnot, *Memoirs of the Remarkable Life and Surprising Adventures of Miss Jenny Cameron* (Boston, 1750).

149. See Meyer, *Highland Scots of North Carolina,* 79; James Oglethorpe to the Georgia Trustees, June 1736, in Mills Lane, ed., *General Oglethorpe's Georgia: Colonial Letters, 1733–1743,* 2 vols. (Savannah, Ga.: Beehive Press, 1990), 1:268–78, 274–75. On the broad imperial effort to bring "foreign Protestants" to the British colonies, see Warren R. Hofstra, "'The Extension of His Majesties Dominions': The Virginia Backcountry and the Reconfiguration of Imperial Frontiers," *Journal of American History* 84 (1998): 1281–312. See also Beresford to the Board of Trade, June 23, 1716, in *Calendar of State Papers, Colonial Series: America and West Indies,* 30:130–31.

150. McLachlan to ?, May 9, 1735, in *The Colonial Records of the State of Georgia,* 39 vols. (Atlanta, 1904-), 20:338–40, 339.

151. Shirley to Newcastle, November 21, 1746, Nova Scotia Archives and Records Management (hereafter NSARM) RG1 13, 33.

152. Petition of Philip Feneyer, et al., to King George II, in Saunders, ed., *Colonial Records of North Carolina,* 4:954–56, 956; Meyer, *Highland Scots of North Carolina,* 24.

Chapter 4. Cumberland's Army in Scotland

1. For an overview of public perceptions of the Highlanders after 1745, see Womack, *Improvement and Romance.*

2. See Youngson, *After the Forty-Five;* Smith, *Jacobite Estates of the Forty-Five.*

3. Jewell, "Legislation Relating to Scotland," 109–11.

4. Orders dated March 7, August 17, and October 4, 1749, and May 30, 1750, in James Wolfe, *General Wolfe's Instructions to Young Officers* (London, 1780), 8–9, 15, 16, 22.

5. See Francis Grant, dates of the present commissions of the 42d Regiment, October 23, 1756, HL LO (NA) 3008.

6. Adam Fergusson, *A Sermon in the Ersh Language to His Majesty's First Highland Regiment of Foot, Commanded by Lord John Murray, at their Cantonment at Camberwell, on the 18ᵗʰ day* of December, 1745 (London, 1746), 7–9.

7. See Pocock, *Barbarism and Religion*, 2:330–45; Zagarri, "Morals, Manners, and the Republican Mother."

8. See generally Richard B. Sher, *Church and University in the Scottish Enlightenment* (Princeton, N.J.: Princeton University Press, 1985), 37–64.

9. See particularly David Hume, "Of the Protestant Succession," in *Political Essays*, ed. Knud Haakonssen (Cambridge: Cambridge University Press, 1994), 213–20, and Hume, *True Account of Archibald Stewart*.

10. See Youngson, *After the Forty-Five*, 25–46.

11. Newcastle to Cumberland, February 22, 1746, TNA SP 54/28, 130; Cumberland to Newcastle, February 28, 1746, TNA SP 54/28, 196.

12. Cumberland to Newcastle, June 28, 1746, RAWC CP LR 2/99, and TNA SP 54/32, 83; "Sketch of Regulations to be made in Scotland, 1746," TNA SP 54/32, 90.

13. Cumberland to Newcastle, April 4 and 23, 1746, in Coxe, *Memoirs of Henry Pelham*, 1:300, 302. See also Cumberland to Newcastle, April 30, 1746, BL Add. 32,707, 128; Newcastle to Cumberland, May 10, 1746, BL Add. 32,707, 184. Findlater's correspondence with Hardwicke could fill a small volume. Much of it can be found in the Hardwicke Papers, BL Add. 35,446–47.

14. Cumberland to Newcastle, April 30, 1746, BL Add. 32,707, 128.

15. Jewell, "The Legislation Relating to Scotland," provides an excellent overview of the legislative process.

16. Youngson, *After the Forty-Five*, 25–26.

17. Devine, *Clanship to Crofter's War*, 86. See "Memorandums relating to the present state of Scotland," NAS GD248/654/2; letter dated October 15, 1746, NAS GD248/654/2.

18. Smith, *Jacobite Estates of the Forty-Five*, 2.

19. Lenman, *Jacobite Risings in Britain*, 278. See generally Philip Yorke, Earl of Hardwicke, *Two Speeches in the House of Lords: I, On the Bill for Abolishing the Heritable Jurisdictions in Scotland: II, On the Militia Bill* (London, 1770), 1–23.

20. *Parliamentary History of England*, 14:1–57.

21. See Bland and Milton, "Proposals for Civilizing the Highlands," December 1747, in Terry, ed., *Albemarle Papers*, 2:480–92, 484; David Bruce, Report, 1750, BL Add. 35,447, 89, and RAWC CP Box 59/8; Bland to Hardwicke, December 25, 1753, BL Add. 35,448, 51; Coxe, *Memoirs of Henry Pelham*, 2:218–19. The phrase "royal district" appears in "Abbreviate of the proposals transmitted by General Bland and Lord Justice Clerk for civilizing and reforming the Highlands," n.d., TNA SP 54/38, 347.

22. See Hume, *True Account of Archibald Stewart*, 8–9; "On the subject of civilizing the Highlands," 1748, NAS GD248/654/1; "The Real Highlands," NAS GD248/654/2.

23. "Memorial in Relation to Service Duties According to the Present Practice in Scotland," BL Add. 35,446, 137.

24. Hume, *True Account of Archibald Stewart*, 8–9.

25. *London Evening Post*, March 24–26, 1747; Smith, *Jacobite Estates*, 21.

26. Smith, *Jacobite Estates*, 143–44; Youngson, *After the Forty-five*, 35. See "Causes of the Present Disorderly State of the Highlands of Scotland," NAS GD248/654/1; "Observations on the Present State of the Highlands and the Means of Improving Them," NAS GD248/954/4.

27. *Parliamentary History of England*, 14:1252.

28. See Duncan Forbes, "Some Thoughts Concerning the State of the Highlands in Scotland," n.d., NAS GD248/654/2, and TNA SP 54/34, 24. See also "Causes of the Present Disorderly State of the Highlands of Scotland," NS GD248/654/1; Andrew Lang, ed., *The Highlands of Scotland in 1750* (Edinburgh, 1898), 144.

29. See Duncan Forbes, "Some Thoughts Concerning the State of the Highlands in Scotland," n.d., NAS GD248/654/2, and TNA SP 54/34, 24.

30. Bland and Milton, "Proposals for Civilizing the Highlands," December 1747, in Terry, ed., *Albemarle Papers*, 2:480–92, 490.

31. Cumberland to Newcastle, April 30, 1746, BL Add. 32,707, 128.

32. Duncan Forbes, "Some Thoughts Concerning the State of the Highlands in Scotland," n.d., NAS GD248/654/2, and TNA SP 54/34, 24. See also Lang, ed., *Highlands of Scotland in 1750*, 144.

33. Bland and Milton, "Proposals for Civilizing the Highlands," December 1747, in Terry, ed., *Albemarle Papers*, 2:480–92; Milton to Newcastle, December 4, 1747, in Terry, ed., *Albemarle Papers*, 2:479.

34. See Alex Murdoch, *The People Above: Politics and Administration in Eighteenth-Century Scotland* (Edinburgh: John Donald, 1980), 38–39, 80; John Stuart Shaw, *The Management of Scottish Society, 1707–1764* (Edinburgh: John Donald, 1983), 175–76; Smith, *Jacobite Estates*, 21–23; Coxe, *Memoirs of Henry Pelham*, 2:215–16. For an early expression of this view, see *London Evening Post*, June 24–25, 1746.

35. Instructions for David Bruce, August 1749, RAWC CP Box 43/292; Robert Napier to Stone, August 21, 1749, RAWC CP Box 43/301; David Bruce, Report, 1750, BL Add. 35,447, 89, and CP Box 59/8.

36. Jewell, "Legislation Relating to Scotland," 240–43.

37. Smith, *Jacobite Estates*, 4; Youngson, *After the Forty-Five*, 27.

38. Smith, *Jacobite Estates*, 38–39.

39. Hardwicke to Cumberland, April 16, 1747, RAWC CP Box 21/261.

40. Bland and Milton, "Proposals for Civilizing the Highlands," December 1747, in Terry, ed., *Albemarle Papers*, 2:480–92, 483.

41. "The Real Highlands," NAS GD248/654/2. See also "Suggestions for Civilizing the Highlands," 1750, RAWC CP Box 44/148. For a succinct discussion of Georgia's character as a governmentally subsidized social experiment see J. E. Crowley, *This Sheba Self: The Conceptualization of Economic Life in Eighteenth-Century America* (Baltimore: Johns Hopkins University Press, 1974), 16–34.

42. See *An Abstract of the Proceedings of the Incorporated Society in Dublin for Promoting English Protestant Schools in Ireland* (London, 1737).

43. *A Brief Review of the Rise and Progress of the Incorporated Society in Dublin for Promoting English Protestant Schools in Ireland* (Dublin, 1744), 13.

44. See, for example, Laurel Thatcher Ulrich, *The Age of Homespun: Objects and Stories in the Creation of an American Myth* (New York: Vintage, 2001), 159–61. For more on the empire-wide influence of Ireland's charter schools see Geoffrey Plank, "Childhood and the Expansion of the Eighteenth-Century British Empire," in Peter Benes, ed., *The Worlds of Children, 1620–1920* (Boston: Boston University, 2004), 93–111.

45. See, for example, *London Evening Post,* July 19–22, 1746. See also *Westminster Journal,* July 26, 1746.

46. See especially *An Abstract of the Proceedings of the Society in Dublin,* 14. See also Thomas Sherlock, *A Sermon Preached before the Society Corresponding with the Incorporated Society in Dublin* (London, 1738), 4–5.

47. *A Brief Review of the Rise and Progress of the Society in Dublin,* 4.

48. *An Abstract of the Proceedings of the Society in Dublin,* 14.

49. Findlater and Seaforth to Hardwicke, December 29, 1749, NAS GD248/572/8, 21(2).

50. On Findlater's influence on policy in the Highlands, see Cumberland to Newcastle, April 4 and 23, 1746, in Coxe, *Memoirs of Henry Pelham,* 1:300, 302; Smith, *Jacobite Estates,* 39.

51. Adam Fergusson to Findlater and Seaforth, May 25, 1753, NAS GD248/954.5, 43.

52. SSPCK minutes, December 11, 1729, NAS GD 95/2/4, 241. See also Patrick Lindsay, *The Interest of Scotland Considered* (Edinburgh, 1733), 31–32.

53. "Memorandums relating to the present state of Scotland," NAS GD248/654/2. See also John McCaulay to Bruce, February 2, 1750, BL Add. 35,447, 151.

54. "Memorandums relating to the present state of Scotland," NAS GD248/654/2. See also "The Real Highlands," NAS GD248/654/2; Findlater and Seafield to Hardwicke, December 29, 1749, NAS GD248/572/8, 21(2).

55. SSPCK minutes, December 15, 1747, NAS GD 95/2/6, 461.

56. SSPCK minutes, December 28, 1750 and May 2 and 23, 1751, NAS GD 95/2/7, 22, 35 and 37.

57. Deposition of John Grant, January 17, 1753, BL Add. 35,447, 379.

58. See Milton to Newcastle, November 3 and 21, December 15 and 29, 1747, in Terry, ed., *Albemarle Papers,* 2:468–69, 473–75, 473–74, 492–94, 493, 516.

59. See Bland to Hardwicke, December 25, 1753, BL Add. 35,448, 51.

60. For typical comments see Bland to Fawkener, February 2, 1748, RAWC CP Box 32/3.

61. Bland to Fawkener, February 2, 1748, RAWC CP Box 32/3.

62. Bland, *Treatise of Military Discipline,* 147.

63. Milton to Newcastle, February 29, 1748, TNA SP 54/38, 111; Jewell, "Legislation Relating to Scotland," 217.

64. Terry, ed., *Albemarle Papers,* 2:xxxi–xxxii, xxxvii; H. Manners Chichester, "Bland, Humphrey," in Leslie Stephen, ed., *Dictionary of National Biography,* 66 vols. (London: Smith, Elder, 1886), 5:196–97, 197.

65. Smith, *Jacobite Estates,* 39, 239.

66. Blakeney to Fawkener, June 9, 1746, RAWC CP Box 16/18. See also "Proposals offered to Major General Blakeney," n.d., 1747, RAWC CP Box 29/174; "Proposals from Lieut. General Blakeney," n.d., 1747, RAWC CP Box 29/175; "Copy of Lieut. General Blakeney's orders of the 28th October 1747," RAWC CP Box 29/176.

67. Advertisement published at Tarland, July 4, 1747, RAWC CP Box 29/173. See also "Proposals from Lieut. General Blakeney," n.d., 1747, RAWC CP Box 29/175.

68. Loudon to Fossfern, November 13, 1746, HL LO (SC) 11801; see also John Cameron to Loudon, November 17, 1746, HL LO (SC) 10909.

69. Stair to Loudon, June 28, 1746, HL LO (SC) 11348.

70. Wolfe to his father, July 15, 1750, in Willson, *Life and Letters of Wolfe,* 126–27, 127.

71. Wolfe to his mother, April and December 15, 1749, and May 13, 1753, in Willson, *Life and Letters of Wolfe*, 96–98, 110–11, 211–12, and Wright, *Life of Wolfe*, 127–28, 140, 264–66; Wolfe to Rickson, April 2, 1749, in Willson, *Life and Letters of Wolfe*, 92–94, 94, and Wright, *Life of Wolfe*, 122–24, 123.

72. Wolfe to his father, October 3, 1751, in Willson, *Life and Letters of Wolfe*, 155–56, 155, and Wright, *Life of Wolfe*, 177.

73. Wolfe to his father, September 17, 1753, in Willson, *Life and Letters of Wolfe*, 220–21, 221, and Wright, *Life of Wolfe*, 275–76, 276.

74. Albemarle to Newcastle, February 19, 1747, TNA SP 54/35, 175; Fawkener to Bland, January 25, 1748, RAWC CP LR 12/85; Bland to the Magistrates of Stirling, January 31, 1747, TNA SP 54/35, 179; memorial of the Magistrates of Stirling, February 1747, TNA SP 54/34, 177; Bland to Fawkener, February 2, 1748, RAWC CP Box 32/3; Bland to Newcastle, February 2, 1748, RAWC CP Box 32/4; Newcastle to Bland, February 18, 1748, TNA SP 54/38, 69.

75. Bland to Pelham, November 17, 1747, Aberdeen University, Special Collections and Archives (hereafter AU), Ms 954.

76. Bland to Newcastle, June 2, 1748, TNA SP 54/39, 136.

77. Wolfe to his father, April 28, 1749, in Willson, *Life and Letters of Wolfe*, 98–99, 99, and Wright, *Life of Wolfe*, 129–30, 130; Wolfe to his mother, June 25, 1753, in Willson, *Life and Letters of Wolfe*, 214–15, 214, and Wright, *Life of Wolfe*, 268.

78. Orders dated May 25, 1749, in Wolfe, *Instructions*, 11.

79. Letter from Findlater and Seaforth, August 8, 1747, BL, Add. 35,446, 203; see also Clyde, *From Rebel to Hero*, 50.

80. Harris, *Politics and the Nation*, 169; Bland to Newcastle, December 12, 1747, TNA SP 54/37, 175; Bland to Captain Ferguson, January 18, 1754, TNA T 1/360, 1; Bland to Henry Fox, January 21, 1755, TNA T 1/360, 15.

81. Bland to Stone, March 31, 1748, TNA SP 54/38, 288; Bland to Fox, January 21, 1755, TNA T 1/360, 15.

82. Bland, "Circular Letter to the Four Regiments in the North," December 15, 1747, TNA SP 54/37, 198. Bland's letter employs the term "nonjurors," a word commonly used to refer to the Scottish Episcopalians and Anglicans who had refused, since 1688, to swear allegiance to the king. In the context of this letter, however, it appears that Bland included within the "nonjuring" category all Scottish Episcopalians who failed to comply with the requirements of the recent legislation.

83. Ibid.

84. Orders dated December 22, 1748, in Wolfe, *Instructions*, 4.

85. Jewell, "Legislation Relating to Scotland," 114–21; Shaw, *Management of Scottish Society*, 169. See also Milton to Newcastle, April 26, 1746, TNA SP 54/30, 224; "Memorial and Queries," in Terry, ed., *Albemarle Papers*, 2:531–35.

86. See "Process and Sentence against the Rev. George Semple," in Terry, ed., *Albemarle Papers*, 2:507–14; Bland to Newcastle, January 16, 1748, TNA SP 54/38, 23.

87. See Bland to John Potter, November 17, 1748, TNA SP 54/39, 278; Charles Areskine to Newcastle, December 20, 1748, TNA SP 54/39, 300; Bland, "Circular letter to the several commanding officers in the Highlands," December 22, 1748, TNA SP 54/39, 304.

88. Orders dated December 22, 1748, in Wolfe, *Instructions*, 4. See Robert Scott to George Churchill, August 10, 1749, BL Egerton 3433, 109.

89. See Wolfe to Churchill, October 24, 1751, BL Egerton 3433, 113.

90. Robert Richard Maitland to Churchill, March 17, 1749, BL Egerton 3433,

109. See also William Rufane to Bland, December 29, 1748, TNA SP 54/40, 9; Charles Forbes to David Dalrymple, December 29, 1748, TNA SP 54/40, 9; Bland to Newcastle, January 3, 1749, TNA SP 54/40, 7.

91. Powell to Churchill, June 29, 1749, BL Egerton 3433, 109.

92. Robert Scott to Churchill, August 10, 1749, BL Egerton 3433, 109.

93. Shaw, *Management of Scottish Society*, 170; see also "Substance of Capt. Mollesworth's Memorial about the Highlands," 1750, NAS GD248/654/1.

94. John Reydon Hughes to Churchill, September 1, 1749, BL Egerton 3433, 110; James Erskine to Captain Collier, October 3, 1749, BL Egerton 3433, 137.

95. Harris, *Politics and the Nation*, 180.

96. Bland to Potter, July 16, 1748, TNA SP 54/39, 172.

97. Bland to Hardwicke, February 22, 1754, BL Add. 35,448, 57.

98. Blakeney to Newcastle, April 8, 1747, TNA SP 54/36, 5; Bob Harris, *Politics and the Nation*, 165. See also Albemarle to Newcastle, September 1, 1746, TNA SP 54/33, 70.

99. Bland, "Circular Letter to the Four Regiments in the North," December 15, 1747, TNA SP 54/37, 198; Bland to Newcastle, December 15, 1747, TNA SP 54/37, 194.

100. Orders dated December 22, 1748, in Wolfe, *Instructions*, 4.

101. Bland to Pelham, December 19, 1747, AU Ms 954; Wolfe to Churchill, October 24, 1751, BL Egerton 3433, 113.

102. Robert Scott to Churchill, August 10, 1749, BL Egerton 3433, 109.

103. Harris, *Politics and the Nation*, 175 (spelling modernized). See also Bland to Newcastle, February 23, 1748, TNA SP 54/38, 86; Harris, *Politics and the Nation*, 160; Lenman, *Jacobite Risings in Britain*, 269.

104. Inverness Magistrates and Council, disposition regarding General Guise's Regiment of Foot, April 19, 1750, HL LO 10463.

105. William Alston to Areskine, November 2, 1752, BL Egerton 3433, 90.

106. Orders dated October 4, 1750, in Wolfe, *Instructions*, 25.

107. See information against Patrick Wallace and Richard Ferres, February 25, 1747, TNA SP 54/35, 227; trial record of Patrick Wallace and Richard Ferres, March 1747, TNA SP 54/35, 236; letter from William Grant, April 3, 1747, TNA SP 54/36, 1; Wolfe, *Instructions*, 28.

108. Erskine to Captain Collier, October 3, 1749, BL Egerton 3433, 137; information against Patrick Wallace and Richard Ferres, February 25, 1747, TNA SP 54/35, 227; trial record of Patrick Wallace and Richard Ferres, March 1747, TNA SP 54/35, 236; letter from William Grant, April 3, 1747, TNA SP 54/36, 1.

109. See Wolfe, *Instructions*, 28.

110. Inverness Magistrates and Council, disposition regarding General Guise's Regiment of Foot, April 19, 1750, HL LO 10463.

111. Mungo Grame to the Duke of Montrose, June 12, 1746, TNA SP 54/32, 59.

112. Jewell, "Legislation Relating to Scotland," 91, 126.

113. See Milton to Newcastle, August 7, 1746, in Terry, ed., *Albemarle Papers*, 2:401–4, 403; Bland to Stone, February 18, 1748, TNA SP 54/38, 67; "Abuses, or Neglects, in the General Management in Scotland since the Rebellion," 1752, BL Egerton 3433, 1, and RAWC CP Box 44/229; Alston to Areskine, November 2, 1752, BL Egerton 3433, 90.

114. Fawkener to Bland, December 15, 1747, RAWC CP LR 12/37.

115. Alston to Areskine, November 2, 1752, BL Egerton 3433, 90.

116. William Grant to Bedford, August 4, 1748, RAWC CP Box 38/160; Bedford to Cumberland, August 12, 1748, RAWC CP Box 38/159.

117. Alston to Areskine, November 2, 1752, BL Egerton 3433, 90.
118. Bland to Stone, February 18, 1748, TNA SP 54/38, 67.
119. See "Abuses, or Neglects, in the General Management in Scotland since the Rebellion," 1752, BL Egerton 3433, 1, and RAWC CP Box 44/229.
120. Wilkes, *A Whig in Power*, 167–68; Clark, *Dynamics of Change*, 37; Newcastle to Hardwicke, March 21, 1752, in Coxe, *Memoirs of Henry Pelham*, 2:412–13; Pelham to Newcastle, May 8 and July 3, 1752, in Coxe, *Memoirs of Henry Pelham*, 2:416–17, 440; Newcastle to Pelham, May 15, 1752, in Coxe, *Memoirs*, 2:420; "Names of Rebels omitted in the first bill of attainder," 1752, BL Egerton 3433, 18, and RAWC CP Box 44/234; "Names of some of the attainted and excepted rebels," BL Egerton 3433, 21, and RAWC CP Box 44/235; Hardwicke to Findlater and Seaforth, June 29, 1752, BL Add. 35,447, 233.
121. Wilson, *Sense of the People*, 174–76. See John Martin to Loudon, January 1747, HL LO (SC) 12228. For an example of effusive praise of Cumberland, see *London Evening Post*, November 13–15, 1746. See also *Harlequin Incendiary*, 23–24.
122. Jewell, "Legislation Relating to Scotland," 47–48.
123. Western, *English Militia*, 120.
124. Pelham to Newcastle, October 11, 1748, in Coxe, *Memoirs of Henry Pelham*, 2:327–8. See also Pelham to Newcastle, October 4, 1748, BL Add. 32,717, 23; Pelham to Newcastle, October 14, 1748, in Coxe, *Memoirs of Henry Pelham*, 2:300.
125. Wilkes, *A Whig in Power*, 129. See Pelham to Newcastle, October 25, 1748, in Coxe, *Memoirs of Henry Pelham*, 2:331.
126. "Estimates of the Forces in the Plantations, Minorca and Gibraltar," 1748, RAWC CP Box 39/145; "H.R.'s Scheme and Mr. Pelham's Compared," 1748, RAWC CP Box 39/154; Houlding, *Fit for Service*, 19–20. See also Alan J. Guy, *Oeconomy and Discipline: Officership and Administration in the British Army, 1714–63* (Manchester: Manchester University Press, 1985), 118.
127. Pelham to Newcastle, June 1, 1750, in Coxe, *Memoirs of Henry Pelham*, 2:343.
128. Speck, "William Augustus, Prince, duke of Cumberland (1721–1765)," in Matthew and Harrison, eds., *Oxford Dictionary of National Biography*, 59:111; Coxe, *Memoirs of Henry Pelham*, 2:140–41; Wilkes, *A Whig in Power*, 188;. For a similar statement, more circumspectly expressed, see *Seasonable and Affecting Observations on the Mutiny-Bill* (London, 1750), 60.
129. Browning, *The Duke of Newcastle*, 172–73; Wiggin, *Faction of Cousins*, 142–43; Clark, *Dynamics of Change*, 35–36; Brooke, *King George III*, 27–28, 32, 46.
130. Mackillop, *"More Fruitful than the Soil"*, 79–80.
131. "Measures Taken by the Military Since the Rebellion and the Effects Thereof," 1752, BL Egerton 3433, 15, and RAWC CP Box 44/233.
132. Bland to Potter, November 5, 1748, BL Add. 35,446, 318.
133. Wolfe to his father, December 13, 1751, in Willson, *Life and Letters of Wolfe*, 163, and Wright, *Life of Wolfe*, 187–88.
134. Wolfe to his mother, October 2, 1749, in Willson, *Life and Letters of Wolfe*, 108–9, 109, and Wright, *Life of Wolfe*, 137.
135. Wolfe to his mother, November 10, 1748, in Willson, *Life and Letters of Wolfe*, 85–6, 86, and Wright, *Life of Wolfe*, 110–11, 111.
136. Bland's experiences in Gibraltar are discussed in Chapter Five, below.
137. James Pritchard, *Anatomy of a Naval Disaster: The 1746 Naval Expedition to North America* (Montreal: McGill-Queen's University Press, 1995), 33–34, 213.
138. Johnstone, *Memoir of the Rebellion*, 332.

139. Bedford to Cumberland, October 28, 1748, RAWC CP Box 41/73.

140. Pehlham to Newcastle, July 2, 1750, in Coxe, *Memoirs of Henry Pelham*, 2:351.

141. Edward Cornwallis to Board of Trade, July 10, 1750, in Thomas B. Akins, ed., *Selections from the Public Documents of the Province of Nova Scotia* (Halifax: Charles Annand, 1869), 617.

142. Wolfe to his mother, March 25, 1749, in Willson, *Life and Letters of Wolfe*, 89–91, 90, and Wright, *Life of Wolfe*, 121.

143. Wolfe to Rickson, April 2, 1749, in Willson, *Life and Letters of Wolfe*, 92–94, 94, and Wright, *Life of Wolfe*, 122–24, 124.

144. Wolfe to Rickson, 1750, in Willson, *Life and Letters of Wolfe*, 133–35, and Wright, *Life of Wolfe*, 157–59.

145. Montesquieu, *Spirit of the Laws*, 140.

146. Ibid., 149–50.

147. See "On the subject of civilizing the Highlands," 1748, NAS GD248/654/1; "The Real Highlands," NAS GD248/654/2; "Suggestions for Civilizing the Highlands," 1750, RAWC CP Box 44/148.

148. Wolfe to Rickson, 1750, in Willson, *Life and Letters of Wolfe*, 133–35, 134, and Wright, *Life of Wolfe*, 157–59, 158.

149. Wolfe to Rickson, June 9, 1751, in Willson, *Life and Letters of Wolfe*, 139–45, 141, and Wright, *Life of Wolfe*, 165–73, 168.

150. Wolfe to his mother, November 25, 1752, in Willson, *Life and Letters of Wolfe*, 190–92, 192; Wolfe to Rickson, March 7, 1755, in Willson, *Life and Letters of Wolfe*, 252–55, 252, and Wright, *Life of Wolfe*, 307–11, 308.

151. See Clyde, *From Rebel to Hero*, 150–80; Brumwell, *Redcoats*, 264–89.

152. See, for example, Robert Kirk, *The Memoirs and Adventures of Robert Kirk* (Limerick, 1770), 43–44.

153. See generally McLynn, *Charles Edward Stuart*, 308–77.

154. Frank McLynn, *1759: The Year Britain Became Master of the World* (London: Jonathan Cape, 2004), 79–83.

155. *London Evening Post*, November 27–29, 1746. See SSPCK committee minutes, November 14 and 18, 1746, NAS GD 95/2/6, 366 and 370; SSPCK minutes, January 1 and June 4, 1747, NAS GD 95/1/4, 378 and 392.

156. Bland to Newcastle, December 23, 1748, TNA SP 54/39, 302; Wolfe to his father, July 15, 1750, in Willson, *Life and Letters of Wolfe*, 126–27, 127, and Wright, *Life of Wolfe*, 150.

157. See generally Womack, *Improvement and Romance*.

158. See "Declaration of Miss MacDonald," July 1, 1746, TNA SP 54/32, 216; Margaret MacDonald to John MacKenzie, July 24, 1746, NLS 1309/29; "Journal of the Young Pretender . . . taken from the manuscript found among the papers of Mrs. Cameron, wife of Doctor Cameron, when she was taken up at Breda, in her way to Paris, January 1748," RAWC CP Box 69/xi.41.18; McLynn, *Charles Edward Stuart*, 284–85.

159. Margaret MacDonald to Loudon, November 13, 1746, HL LO (SC) 11892; Margaret MacDonald to Fawkener, December 29, 1746, RAWC CP Box 19/242.

160. Margaret MacDonald to Fawkener, December 29, 1746, RAWC CP Box 19/242; abstract of Sir James MacDonald's affairs, 1754, BL Add. 35,448, 172.

161. Normand MacLeod to Cumberland, May 19, 1747, RAWC CP Box 22/217. See also Albemarle to Newcastle, December 6, 1746, TNA SP 54/34, 159.

162. Bland to Hardwicke, July 6, 1754, BL Add. 35,448, 110.

163. Bland to Hardwicke, July 6, 1754, BL Add. 35,448, 110. See also Morton to Hardwicke, July 2, 1754, BL Add. 35,448, 106; Bland to Hardwicke, July 27, August 24, and October 17, 1754, BL Add. 35,448, 120, 140, and 178.

164. Bland to Hardwicke, August 13, 1754, BL Add. 35,448, 142; Morton to Hardwicke, October 11 and 25, 1754, BL Add. 35,448, 170 and 180.

165. A. MacDonald and A. MacDonald, *The Clan Donald*, 3 vols. (Inverness: Northern Counties Publishing, 1904), 3:92–97.

166. Douglass, *Summary*, 1:22.

167. Ibid., 1:193–94 n.

168. Ibid., 1:239, 2:111, 2:117 n.

169. Ibid., 2:123.

170. Ibid., 2:137 n.

171. Ibid., 1:208–9.

172. Ibid., 1:209–10, 235.

173. Ibid., 1:209–10. See Defoe, *A True-Born English-Man*.

174. Douglass, *Summary*, 1:209–10.

175. On Douglass's role in the debates over the Acadians, see Plank, *Unsettled Conquest*, 118–20. On Douglass, Franklin and Canada, see generally Benjamin Franklin, "The Interest of Great Britain Considered, with Regard to her Colonies, and the Acquisitions of Canada and Guadeloupe," 1760, in *Papers of Benjamin Franklin*, 9:47–100.

Chapter 5. Cumberland's Army in the Mediterranean

1. Bland to Bedford, March 22, 1750, TNA CO 91/11, 8. See also Cumberland to Bland, November 24, 1748, N.S., RAWC CP Box 41/237; Bland to Colonel Napier, n.d., RAWC CP Box 61/B/14.

2. Bland to Captain Richardson, April 6, 1750, TNA CO 91/11, 16.

3. See, for example, testimony of Philip Anstruther, January 28, 1742, BL Add. 35,876, 187. See also Houlding, *Fit for Service*, 12.

4. See Bland to Colonel Napier, n.d., RAWC CP Box 61/B/14.

5. *Parliamentary History of England*, 12:379–98.

6. Bland, "An Account of Lieut. General Bland's Conduct During the Time he was Governor of Gibraltar," 1751, BL Landsdowne 1234, 94.

7. See, for example, Blakeney to Holdernesse, October 21, 1752, RAWC CP Box 44/282.

8. For a fleeting indication of Bland's views on the relationship between Highlanders and Africans, see Bland to Bedford, March 14, 1751, TNA CO 91/11, 183.

9. James Lind, *Three Letters Relating to the Navy, Gibraltar, and Port Mahon, Wrote in the Years 1747 and 1748* (London, 1757), 136; John Armstrong, *The History of the Island of Minorca* (London, 1752), 221–22.

10. Armstrong's *History of Minorca* was hastily reprinted in London during the French siege of Port Mahon.

11. See Minutes of the Privy Council, TNA PC 1/6/41, 1.

12. Joseph Bennet, "Some Remarks Concerning Gibraltar," November 22, 1712, BL Add. 10034, 136.

13. Petition of Francis Bolhousia, n.d., TNA CO 91/1, 3; report of the Commission of the Public Accounts of Gibraltar, March 14, 1713, TNA CO 91/1, 17.

14. Richard Kane to Townsend, August 18, 1725, TNA CO 91/4, 122.

15. Civilian census of Gibraltar, August 20, 1725, TNA CO 91/4, 146; letter from Joseph Sabine, June 15, 1730, TNA CO 91/9, 73–81.

16. The case of Peter Romero, John de la Rosa and their families, July 8, 1752, TNA CO 91/11, 282.

17. See Gregory, *Minorca, the Illusory Prize*, 15–34; Laurie, *Life of Richard Kane*, 67–86.

18. See letter from Jonathan Fermor, November 17, 1712, TNA CO 174/15, 3; memorial of Lorenzo Beltrano, n.d., TNA CO 174/15, 107; petition of Juan Sauro, 1753, TNA CO 174/16, 169.

19. See John Campbell, 2d Duke of Argyll, to William Legge, Baron Dartmouth, November 13, 1712, TNA CO 174/15, 43.

20. Census of Minorca, 1750, TNA CO 174/2, 218.

21. Petition dated January 16, 1743, TNA CO 174/2, 154; petition dated July 5, 1744, TNA CO 174/2, 1; Miguel Morera to Blakeney, September 26, 1749, TNA CO 174/2, 160; Blakeney to Bedford, January 14, 1751, TNA CO 142/2, 212.

22. See the records of a court martial of George Wright, Thomas Richardson, and Robert Hutchinson, July 15, 1719, TNA CO 174/15, 211.

23. Gregory, *Minorca, the Illusory Prize*, 133–34; Sifantos and Malvasia to Blakeney, September 16, 1749, TNA CO 174/2, 162.

24. John Campbell, 2d Duke of Argyll, to Dartmouth, November 13, 1712, TNA CO 174/15, 43. For an outline of Minorca's complex legal institutions, see "Abstract of the Constitution of Minorca," March 6, 1755, TNA CO 174/16, 253. See also Laurie, *Life of Richard Kane*, 103; Roman Piña Homs, *Las Instituciones de Menorca en el sigle XVIII* (Palma, Spain: La Nostra, 1986); petition of the jurats of Minorca to John Campbell, 2d Duke of Argyll, December 5, 1712, TNA CO 174/1, 1, and CO 174/16, 241.

25. Bland to Bedford, June 19 and 29, 1749, TNA CO 91/11, 58 and 61.

26. Bland, "An Account of Lieut. General Bland's Conduct During the Time he was Governor of Gibraltar," 1751, BL Landsdowne 1234, 99.

27. Bland to Bedford, May 14, 1750, PRO CO 91/11, 42.

28. See Bland to Hardwicke, May 2, 1749, BL Add. 35,590, 283; Bland to Colonel Napier, n.d., RAWC CP Box 61/B/14.

29. Proposals from Bland, March 1748/9, BL Add. 35590, 284, and RAWC CP Box 43/171.

30. See Bland to Hardwicke, May 2, 1749, BL Add. 35,590, 283.

31. Bland, "An Account of Lieut. General Bland's Conduct During the Time he was Governor of Gibraltar," 1751, BL Landsdowne 1234, 102.

32. Ibid., 103–4.

33. Ibid., 125–27.

34. Ibid., 131.

35. Bland to Bedford, December 1, 1750, TNA CO 91/11, 148.

36. Bland to Bedford, November 11, 1749, TNA CO 91/11, 127.

37. Bland to Bedford, January 5, 1750, TNA CO 91/11, 6.

38. Bland, "Rules for the Governance of Gibraltar," February 29, 1752, BL Add. 38,331, 185.

39. Summons of Bland, April 16, 1750, TNA CO 91/11, 26; see also Bland to Bedford, April 21, 1750, TNA CO 91/11, 24; report of the governor of Gibraltar, 1755, TNA T 1/348, 30.

40. Bland to Bedford, April 21, 1750, TNA CO 91/11, 24.

41. Report on property rights in Gibraltar, July 1756, BL Add. 10034, 143;

Bland, "Rule Humbly Proposed for the Better Government of His Majesty's Town of Gibraltar," March 1749, BL Add. 35,590, 284.

42. Bland, "An Account of Lieut. General Bland's Conduct During the Time he was Governor of Gibraltar," 1751, BL Landsdowne 1234, 94. See also report on property rights in Gibraltar, July 1756, BL Add. 10034, 143; Bland to Fawkener, September 3, 1750, RAWC CP Box 44/105.

43. Bland to Fawkener, September 3, 1750, RAWC CP Box 44/105.

44. Ibid.; Bland, "An Account of Lieut. General Bland's Conduct During the Time he was Governor of Gibraltar," 1751, BL Landsdowne 1234, 94.

45. Bland to John Colebrooke, March 29, 1751, TNA CO 91/11, 209.

46. Bland, "An Account of Lieut. General Bland's Conduct During the Time he was Governor of Gibraltar," 1751, BL Landsdowne 1234, 120.

47. Bland to Bedford, May 6, 1750, TNA CO 91/11, 38.

48. Bland to Bedford, November 11, 1749, TNA CO 91/11, 127. See also Bland to Colonel Napier, n.d., RAWC CP Box 61/B/14; Bland to Captain Richardson, December 13, 1750, TNA CO 91/11, 166.

49. Bland to Bedford, December 1, 1750, TNA CO 91/11, 148.

50. Bland, "An Account of Lieut. General Bland's Conduct During the Time he was Governor of Gibraltar," 1751, BL Landsdowne 1234, 97.

51. Bland to Bedford, April 6, 1750, TNA CO 91/11, 10; W. Herbert to Holdernesse, January 1, 1753, TNA CO 91/11, 296; resolution of the justices, January 1, 1753, TNA CO 91/11, 298; Bland to West, April 4, 1753, TNA T 1/353, 10.

52. See George Forbes to Jurats, before November 20, 1717, TNA CO 174/15, 137. See also Jurats of Minorca to George Forbes, November 22, 1717, TNA CO 174/15, 135.

53. Lind, *Three Letters*, 126.

54. Ibid., 130.

55. Ibid., 136.

56. Ibid., 137.

57. Blakeney to Raphael di Lugagnano, March 17, 1749, TNA CO 174/2, 146. See also John Wynard to Blakeney, June 6, 1748, TNA CO 174/2, 144.

58. See Blakeney to Bedford, January 13 and 31, TNA CO 174/2, 76 and 96; Morera to Blakeney, December 14, 1748, TNA CO 174/2, 78; Blakeney to Morera et al., January 21, 1749, TNA CO 174/2, 103; report of Henry Malcolm et al., February 6, 1749, TNA CO 174/2, 104.

59. Blakeney to Morera, January 27, 1749, TNA CO 174/2, 100. Blakeney asked Morera to "publish" this letter "to the people, and the clergy." See Blakeney to Bedford, January 31, 1749, TNA CO 174/2, 96.

60. Bland to Bedford, February 14, 1751, TNA CO 91/11, 174; Bland, "Rules for the Governance of Gibraltar," February 29, 1752, BL Add. 38,331, 185; Bland to the Lords Commissioners of the Treasury, n.d., BL Add. 38,331, 187.

61. *Memoirs of the Life and Actions of General W. Blakeney* (London, 1756), 13–14.

62. Blakeney to di Lugagnano, March 17, 1749, TNA CO 174/2, 146.

63. Ibid.

64. James O'Hara, Baron Tyrawley, to Fox, May 23, 1753, BL Add. 23,638, 95.

65. See Blakeney to Holdernesse, August 27, 1753, TNA CO 174/16, 159; memorial of Blakeney, September 16, 1749, TNA CO 174/2, 156.

66. Remonstrance of the merchants of Mahon, 1750, TNA CO 174/2, 172.

67. Blakeney to Holdernesse, August 27, 1753, TNA CO 174/16, 159.

68. Blakeney to Holdernesse, November 6, 1752, RAWC CP Box 44/284; abstract of Blakeney to Holdernesse, November 6, 1752, BL 35,885, 174.

69. Abstract of Blakeney to Holdernesse, February 10, 1753, BL Add. 35,885, 183.

70. Blakeney to Bedford, January 14, 1751, TNA CO 174/2, 212.

71. Blakeney to Bedford, August 2, 1748 and January 14, 1751, TNA CO 174/2, 60 and 212.

72. See Memorial of the merchants of Mahon, 1750, TNA CO 174/2, 188; Blakeney to Newcastle, August 23, 1750, TNA CO 174/2, 196; John Henry Desguliers to Bedford, October 21, 1750 [1749?] and January 29, 1750, TNA CO 174/2, 72 and 73. See also Baron Tyrawley to Fox, May 23, 1753, BL Add. 23,638, 95.

73. Blakeney to Bedford, January 13, May 23, July 5, and September 16, 1749, TNA CO 174/2, 76, 117, 138, and 150.

74. Minutes of the Privy Council, TNA PC 1/6/41, 1.

75. Abstract of a letter from Blakeney, November 9, 1755, TNA CO 174/16, 274.

76. See minutes of the Privy Council, TNA PC 1/6/41, 1.

77. Blakeney to Thomas Robinson, October 15, 1755, TNA PC 1/6/41, 4. See also Jurats of Mahon to Robinson, October 1755, TNA PC 1/6/41, 7.

78. Fox to Baron Tyrawley, May 20, 1753, BL Add. 23,638, 93; Baron Tyrawley to Fox, May 23, 1753, BL Add. 23,638, 95; Bland to Blakeney, May 29, 1753, TNA CO 174/16, 74; Gregory, *Minorca, the Illusory Prize*, 51.

79. Gregory, *Minorca, the Illusory Prize*, 51. See Baron Tyrawley to Fox, May 23, 1753, BL Add. 23,638, 95; Baron Tyrawley, "Considerations upon the Heads of Instructions to the Governor of Minorca, submitted to the Privy Council," 1753, TNA CO 174/16, 94, and BL Add. 23,638, 104.

80. Baron Tyrawley to Fox, May 23, 1753, BL Add. 23,638, 99; representation of James O'Hara, Baron Tyrawley, to the Privy Council, May 23, 1753, BL Add. 23,638, 104, and TNA CO 174/16, 94.

81. See Baron Tyrawley to Fox, May 23, 1753, BL Add. 23,638, 95. See also Baron Tyrawley, "Considerations upon the Heads of Instructions to the Governor of Minorca, submitted to the Privy Council," 1753, TNA CO 174/16, 94, and BL Add. 23,638, 104.

82. See N. A. M. Rodger, "Sea Power and Empire, 1688–1793," in P. J. Marshall, ed., *The Oxford History of the British Empire: The Eighteenth Century* (Oxford: Oxford University Press, 1998), 169–83.

83. See, for example, Cumberland to Fox, September 23, 1757, BL Add. 51,375, 132.

84. See Baron Tyrawley to Fox, May 23, 1753, BL Add. 23,638, 99; Blakeney to Bedford, January 14, 1751, TNA CO 174/2, 212.

85. Bland to the Alcaide of Tetuan, November 16, 1750, TNA CO 91/11, 138.

86. Bland to the Alcaide of Tetuan, April 23, May 13, and November 16, 1750, TNA CO 91/11, 30, 36, and 138.

87. Bland to Bedford, November 16, 1750, TNA CO 91/11, 138.

88. See, for example, copy of a letter from Mahon, October 24, 1748, TNA CO 174/2, 66; Blakeney to Bedford, November 8, 1748, March 24, 1749 and November 24, 1750, TNA CO 174/2, 68, 108, and 208.

89. See Bland to Bedford, April 20, 1750, TNA CO 91/11, 22.

90. Copy of a letter from Mahon, October 24, 1748, TNA CO 174/2, 66; Blakeney to Bedford, November 8, 1748, March 24, 1749, and November 24, 1750, TNA CO 174/2, 68, 108, and 208.

91. See Blakeney to Bedford, June 2, 1750, TNA CO 174/2, 168, report of the merchants of Mahon, 1750, TNA CO 174/2, 170.

92. Bland to Bedford, July 17, 1750, TNA CO 91/11, 71.

93. Bland to Bedford, July 1, 1750, TNA CO 91/11, 64. See also Bland to Bedford, May 6, 1750, TNA CO 91/11, 34; Bland, "An Account of Lieut. General Bland's Conduct During the Time he was Governor of Gibraltar," 1751, BL Landsdowne 1234, 114.

94. William Hargrove to Newcastle, June 24, 1743, TNA CO 91/10, 839; Bland to Bedford, May 6, 1750, TNA CO 91/11, 34.

95. Bland to Captain Richardson, April 6, 1750, TNA CO 91/11, 16; Bland to Bedford, May 14, 1750, TNA CO 91/11, 42.

96. See statement of Hadgi Manoeli Zinfantos, May 10, 1749, TNA CO 174/2, 115; Blakeney to Bedford, September 19, 1749, TNA CO 174/2, 150; Blakeney to Holdernesse, November 1 and December 30, 1751, September 20, 1752, TNA CO 174/2, 222, 224 and 250; Blakeney to Newcastle, July 5, 1752, TNA CO 174/2, 236.

97. Richard Whatley to Robinson, February 26, 1755, TNA CO 174/16, 247.

98. Blakeney to Bedford, September 18, 1748, TNA CO 174/2, 62. See also Whatley to Robinson, February 26, 1755, TNA CO 174/16, 247.

99. See Bland to Alcaide of Tetuan, April 23, 1750, TNA CO 91/11, 30.

100. Thomas Troughton, *Barbarian Cruelty, or an Accurate and Impartial Narrative of the Unparallel'd Sufferings and Almost Incredible Hardships of the British Captives* (London, 1751), 190–93.

101. Bland to Bedford, April 14, 1751, TNA CO 91/11, 213.

102. See generally Colley, *Captives*, 23–134. Edward Said's *Orientalism* (New York: Vintage, 1978) provides an overview of Western perceptions of North Africa and the Middle East but does not concentrate on the first half of the eighteenth century. Thomson's *Barbary and Enlightenment* contains more relevant detail on European ideas in Bland's lifetime, though most of her evidence comes from the 1760s or later in the century.

103. Bland to Bedford, February 22, 1750, TNA CO 91/11, 203. See also Bland, "Revolutions of Fez and Morocco since the Death of the Emperor Muly Ismael," TNA CO 91/11, 194; Bland, "An Account of Lieut. General Bland's Conduct During the Time he was Governor of Gibraltar," 1751, BL Landsdowne 1234, 112.

104. Bland to Bedford, April 21 and 23, May 6, July 1, 1750, TNA CO 91/11, 24, 28, 34, 38, and 64; Bland to Alcaide of Tetuan, April 23, 1750, TNA CO 91/11, 30.

105. Bland to Bedford, April 23, August 7 and 20, 1750, TNA CO 91/11, 28, 81, and 85. The quotation is from Bland to Bedford, November 16, 1750, TNA CO 91/11, 138.

106. Bland to Bedford, July 1, 1750, TNA CO 91/11, 64.

107. Bland to the Alcaide of Tetuan, April 23, 1750, TNA CO 91/11, 30.

108. Bland, "An Account of Lieut. General Bland's Conduct During the Time he was Governor of Gibraltar," 1751, BL Landsdowne 1234, 113.

109. Bland to Alcaide of Tetuan, April 23, 1750, TNA CO 91/11, 30. See also Bland to Bedford, August 7 and 20, 1750, February 14, 1751, TNA CO 91/11, 81, 85, and 174.

110. Bland, "An Account of Lieut. General Bland's Conduct During the Time he was Governor of Gibraltar," 1751, BL Landsdowne 1234, 104.

111. Bland to Bedford, February 22 and July 17, 1750, TNA CO 91/11, 203 and 71.

112. Bland to Bedford, October 20, 1750, TNA CO 91/11, 117.

113. Bland, "An Account of Lieut. General Bland's Conduct During the Time he was Governor of Gibraltar," 1751, BL Landsdowne 1234, 109.

114. Ibid.

115. Ibid., 125.

116. Bland to Bedford, April 6, 1750, TNA CO 91/11, 10. See also Bland to Bedford, October 9, 1750, TNA CO 91/11, 105.

117. Bland, "An Account of Lieut. General Bland's Conduct During the Time he was Governor of Gibraltar," 1751, BL Landsdowne 1234, 112.

118. Bland to the Alcaide of Tetuan, April 23, 1750, TNA CO 91/11, 30; Bland to Mahomet Lucas, November 26, 1750, TNA CO 91/11, 146.

119. Bland, "An Account of Lieut. General Bland's Conduct During the Time he was Governor of Gibraltar," 1751, BL Landsdowne 1234, 122.

120. Ibid., 120.

121. Bland to Captain Richardson, April 6, 1750, TNA CO 91/11, 16.

122. Bland to Bedford, March 14, 1751, TNA CO 91/11, 183.

123. Blakeney to Fox, February 10, 1756, RAWC CP Box 47/13.

124. Israel Mauduit, *A Letter to the Right Honourable the Lord B——y* (London, 1757), 34–35; *A Full Answer to an Infamous Libel, Intituled A Letter to the Right Honourable Lord B——y* (London, 1757), 28–29.

125. Blakeney to Fox, n.d., 1756, RAWC CP Box 47/13. See generally Gregory, *Minorca, the Illusory Prize*, 173–78.

126. Blakeney to Fox, April 20, 1756, TNA CO 174/16, 284, and RAWC CP Box 47/13.

127. Blakeney to Fox, July 29, 1756, CO 91/2.

128. Blakeney to Bedford, May 23, 1749, TNA CO 174/2, 117; Blakeney to di Lugagnano, March 17, 1749, TNA CO 174/2, 146.

129. Blakeney to Holdernesse, winter 1753–54, TNA CO 174/16, 206.

130. Mauduit, *Letter to Lord B——y*, 26–34.

131. Armstrong, *History of Minorca*, 214.

132. Ibid., 221–22.

133. *London Evening Post*, May 29 to June 1, 1756.

134. *The Importance of the Island of Minorca and Harbour of Port-Mahon* (London, 1756), 34.

135. Ibid., 58.

136. Ibid., 59.

137. Articles of capitulation, RAWC CP Box 47/212.

138. Julian S. Corbett, *England in the Seven Years' War* (New York: Longmans, Green, 1907), 107.

139. Minutes of a council of war, May 24, 1756, RAWC CP Box 47/89; John Byng to J. Cleveland, May 25, 1756, RAWC CP Box 47/88.

140. John Rutherford to Loudon, August 12, 1756, HL LO (NA) 1473.

141. Henry Collins to Stephen Greenleaf, August 20, 1756, HL LO (NA) 1535.

142. Ibid.

143. John Young to Loudon, September 2, 1756, HL LO (NA) 1681.

144. Jeremy Black, *Pitt the Elder* (Cambridge: Cambridge University Press, 1992), 119; *Public Advertiser*, June 24, 1756.

145. Rogers, *Crowds, Culture, and Politics*, 58–64. See also Wilson, *Sense of the People*, 180–85.

146. W. A. Speck, *Stability and Strife: England, 1714–1760* (Cambridge, Mass.: Harvard University Press, 1977), 263–64; Wilson, *Sense of the People*, 183.

147. See *A Serious Call to the Corporation of London* (London, 1756); *Considerations on the Addresses lately Presented to His Majesty* (London, 1756).

148. Speck, *Stability and Strife*, 263–64.

149. Minutes of a council of war, May 4, 1756, RAWC CP Box 47/59; see also Thomas Fawke to William Wildman, Lord Barrington, May 6, 1756, RAWC CP Box 47/58.

150. Minutes of a council of war, May 24, 1756, RAWC CP Box 47/89; Byng to Cleveland, May 25, 1756, RAWC CP Box 47/88.

151. Wolfe to his father, November 27, 1756, in Willson, *Life and Letters of Wolfe*, 309, and Wright, *Life of Wolfe*, 355.

152. *The Report of the General Officers Appointed to Enquire into the Conduct of Major General Stuart, and Colonel Cornwallis and Earl of Effingham* (London, 1757), 22.

153. *A Full Account of the Siege of Minorca by the French in 1756* (London, 1757), 5; *Memoirs of General W. Blakeney*, 11–12.

154. *Memoirs of General W. Blakeney*, 12.

155. Ibid., 19.

156. Henry Dell, *Minorca, A Tragedy in Three Acts* (London, 1756), 21. See also *A Poem for the Better Success of His Majesty's Arms Against the French this Spring* (London, 1757).

157. John Railton, *Introduction to an Extract, entitled, Zealous Remonstrances, &c.* (London, 1758), 7–8.

158. Mauduit, *Letter to Lord B——y*, 8–9; *Westminster Journal*, October 16, 1756.

159. *A Letter to Lord Robert Bertie, Relating to his Conduct in the Mediterranean and his Defence of Admiral Byng* (London, 1757), 27. See also Rogers, *Crowds, Culture, and Politics*, 62.

160. See, for example, *More Birds for the Tower, or Who'll Confess First* (London, 1756).

161. *A Letter to the Right Honourable William Pitt, Esq.* (London, 1756), 3.

162. See George Germain, Viscount Sackville, to Loudon, February 4, 1757, HL LO (NA) 2778.

163. Black, *Pitt the Elder*, 136–38. See John Calcraft to Loudon, February 5, 1757, HL LO (NA) 2785.

164. See George Burges to the Lords Commissioners of the Treasury, January 9, 1752, TNA T 1/348, 2.

165. Minutes of a meeting at St. James's, June 3, 1756, RAWC CP Box 47/106.

166. See Abercromby to Loudon, August 3, 1756, HL LO (NA) 1410; Halifax to Loudon, August 13, 1756, HL LO (NA) 1478.

167. Alexander McMillan to Loudon, August 29, 1756, HL LO (NA) 1565.

168. Milton to Loudon, April 26, 1757, HL LO (NA) 3475.

169. Calcraft to Loudon, September 8, 1757, HL LO (NA) 4422.

170. James Abercromby, declaration relative to Lord Charles Hay, August 7, 1757, HL LO (NA) 3873, and RAWC CP Box 56/9. See also Loudon to Cumberland, August 6, 1757, RAWC CP Box 55/42; Loudon to Holdernesse, September 1, 1757, RAWC CP Box 56/4; Peregrine Thomas Hopson to Loudon, October 23, 1757, HL LO (NA) 4693.

Chapter 6. Cumberland's Army in North America

1. Stephen E. Patterson, "1744–1763: Colonial Wars and Aboriginal Peoples," in Phillip A. Buckner and John G. Reid, eds., *The Atlantic Region to Confederation: A History* (Toronto: University of Toronto Press, 1994), 125–55, 127.

2. Cornwallis to Bedford, July 23, 1749, in Akins, ed., *Selections from the Public Documents of Nova Scotia*, 561–64.

3. Cornwallis to Board of Trade, August 20, 1749, in Akins, ed., *Selections from the Public Documents of Nova Scotia*, 574–76, 575.

4. Cornwallis to Bedford, October 17, 1749, in Akins, ed., *Selections from the Public Documents of Nova Scotia*, 593–95.

5. Cornwallis to Board of Trade, April 30, 1750, in Akins, ed., *Selections from the Public Documents of Nova Scotia*, 608.

6. Minutes of the Governor's Council, July 17, 1749 and May 27, 1751, in Akins, ed., *Selections from the Public Documents of Nova Scotia*, 570 and 640; proclamation dated November 19, 1750, in Akins, ed., *Selections from the Public Documents of Nova Scotia*, 629.

7. Cornwallis to Bedford, September 11, 1749, in Akins, ed., *Selections from the Public Documents of Nova Scotia*, 585–87.

8. Minutes of the Governor's Council, November 6, 1749, in Akins, ed., *Selections from the Public Documents of Nova Scotia*, 595.

9. Minutes of the Governor's Council, January 14, 1751, in Akins, ed., *Selections from the Public Documents of Nova Scotia*, 639.

10. Cornwallis to Bedford, September 11, 1749, in Akins, ed., *Selections from the Public Documents of Nova Scotia*, 585–87; indictment of Peter Cartel, August 31, 1749, NSARM RG1 vol. 342, 1; minutes of the governor's council, August 31, 1749, TNA CO 217/9, 97; Ronald Rompkey, ed., *Expeditions of Honour: The Journal of John Salusbury in Halifax, Nova Scotia, 1749–1753* (Newark: University of Delaware Press, 1982), 62–63.

11. Cornwallis to Board of Trade, July 24, 1749, TNA CO 217/9, 70.

12. See Thomas Hill to Cornwallis, May 29, 1750, in Akins, ed., *Selections from the Public Documents of Nova Scotia*, 610. See generally Winthrop Pickard Bell, *The "Foreign Protestants" and the Settlement of Nova Scotia: The History of a Piece of Arrested British Colonial Policy in the Eighteenth Century* (Toronto: University of Toronto Press, 1961).

13. Cornwallis to Board of Trade, July 24, 1749, TNA CO 217/9, 70.

14. Cornwallis to Board of Trade, March 19, 1750, in Akins, ed., *Selections from the Public Documents of Nova Scotia*, 605.

15. Cornwallis to Bedford, January 16, 1750/51, TNA CO 217/33, 110.

16. Minutes of the Governor's Council, October 1, 1749, in Akins, ed., *Selections from the Public Documents of Nova Scotia*, 581.

17. George Fothrington to Loudon, March 13 and July 28, 1751, HL LO (NA) 207 and 305.

18. Wolfe to Rickson, June 9, 1751, in Willson, *Life and Letters of Wolfe*, 139–45, 141, and Wright, *Life of Wolfe*, 165–73, 168.

19. See Wolfe to Rickson, 1750, in Willson, *Life and Letters of Wolfe*, 133–35, 134, and Wright, *Life of Wolfe*, 157–59, 158.

20. Browning, *The Duke of Newcastle*, 210; Anderson, *Crucible of War*, 66–71; Clark, *Dynamics of Change*, 102–4.

21. John Inglis to Loudon, October 14, 1753, HL LO (NA) 453; Charles Schaw, Baron Cathcart, to Loudon, August 30 and September 13, 1755, HL LO (SC) 7088 and 7087; Eleanor Wallace to Loudon, September 7, 1755, HL LO (SC) 9470; Pargellis, *Lord Loudon in North America*, 42.

22. Fox to Loudon, October 31, 1754, HL LO (SC) 8622.

23. See Anderson, *Crucible of War*, 94–108.

24. See, for example, *Public Advertiser*, August 27, 1755, and *Whitehall Evening*

Post, August 30 to September 2, 1755, reprinted in N. Darnell Davis, ed., "British Newspaper Accounts of Braddock's Defeat," *Pennsylvania Magazine of History and Biography* 23 (1899): 310–28, 314–15.

25. Wolfe to Richmond, October 25, 1755, in Whitworth, ed., "Some Unpublished Wolfe Letters," 68.

26. See "Heads of Lord Temple's Speech," November 3, 1755, BL Add. 32,996, 281.

27. Cathcart to Loudon, August 26, 28, and 30, September 13, 16, and 30, October 11, 1755, HL LO (SC) 7089, 7090, 7088, 7087, 7086, 7084, and 7083; letter from Fox, September 28, 1755, BL Add. 32,859, 255.

28. Cathcart to Loudon, August 30, 1755, HL LO (SC) 7088.

29. Cathcart to Loudon, September 13, 1755, HL LO (SC) 7087. See also James Lindsay, Earl of Balcarres, to Loudon, February 16, 1756, HL LO (NA) 825.

30. "Lord Halifax's Paper," January 7, 1756, BL Add. 32,996, 3.

31. Ibid.; "Hints from Lord Halifax relating to a tax in North America," October 31, 1755, BL Add. 32,996, 265.

32. Minutes of the Privy Council, January 20, 1756, BL Add. 32,996, 352.

33. See generally Pargellis, *Lord Loudon in North America*; Rogers, *Empire and Liberty*.

34. Rogers, *Empire and Liberty*, 78–87.

35. See Anderson, *Crucible of War*, 209–10; Anderson, *A People's Army*, 123, 135–41.

36. See Shirley to William Johnson, May 16, 1756, HL LO (NA) 1153.

37. On the origins of scalping, see James Axtell and William C. Sturtevant, "The Unkindest Cut, or Who Invented Scalping," *William and Mary Quarterly* 3d ser. 37 (1980): 551–72.

38. *Pennsylvania Gazette,* April 15, 1756. See Francis Jennings, *Empire of Fortune: Crowns, Colonies, and Tribes in the Seven Years' War in America* (New York: Norton, 1988), 268. See also *Pennsylvania Gazette,* June 26 and November 17, 1755.

39. Terms of enlistment, n.d., in Randolph Boehm, ed., *Records of the British Colonial Office, Class 5* (microfilm) (Frederick, Md.: University Publications of America, 1983–84), part 3, 47:754.

40. For an indication of Franklin's views, see Benjamin Franklin to Thomas Pownall, August 19, 1756, in *Papers of Benjamin Franklin,* 6:486–87.

41. Provincial commissioners to Robert Hunter Morris, June 13, 1756, in *Papers of Benjamin Franklin,* 6:455–6.

42. Jonathan Belcher to Abercromby, July 19, 1756, HL LO (NA) 1318; Loudon to Fox, August 19, 1756, in Boehm, ed., *Records of the British Colonial Office,* part 3, 47:699–715, 704–5; and HL LO (NA) 1522.

43. Loudon to Fox, August 19, 1756, in Boehm, ed., *Records of the British Colonial Office,* part 3, 47:699–715, 704–5; and HL LO (NA) 1522. See also Loudon to Belcher, July 25, 1756, HL LO (NA) 1355; Belcher to Loudon, July 30, 1756, HL LO (NA) 1375.

44. See William Sparke to Loudon, August 25, 1756, HL LO (NA) 1584; Phineas Lyman to Loudon, September 9, 1756, HL LO (NA) 1753; Loudon to Johnson, September 10, 1756, HL LO (NA) 1760; Peter Wraxall, "Information of a party of Indians who brought in two French scalps," September 1756, HL LO (NA) 1938.

45. Loudon to Cumberland, November 22, 1756, in Pargellis, ed., *Military Affairs in North America,* 263–80, 269.

46. Proclamation from Cornwallis, October 2, 1749, TNA CO 217/9, 118, and CO 217/40, 148.

47. Order for June 26, 1755, in "Halkett's Orderly Book," in Charles Hamilton, ed., *Braddock's Defeat* (Norman: University of Oklahoma Press, 1959), 113.

48. Charles Lawrence, orders for attacking Louisbourg, May 1758, HL AB 303. See also Jeffery Amherst, Address to the Officers and Men of the Army before Attacking Louisbourg, June 3, 1758, HL LO (NA) 5847.

49. Vattel, *Law of Nations*, 2:49; see Vattel, *Droit des gens*, 107.

50. Minutes of the Governor's Council, October 1, 1749, in Akins, ed., *Selections from the Public Documents of Nova Scotia*, 581.

51. Cornwallis to Board of Trade, September 11, 1749, in Placide Gaudet, ed., "Acadian Genealogy and Notes," in *Report Concerning Canadian Archives for the Year 1905* (Ottawa: National Archives of Canada, 1906), 53–55.

52. See Treaty of August 15, 1749, NSARM RG1, vol. 163, 10.

53. *Maryland Gazette*, March 24, 1747.

54. *Maryland Gazette*, November 25, 1746. See also *Maryland Gazette*, March 24, 1747; Douglass, *Summary*, 1:99 n.

55. For a discussion of the dangers posed by dispersed French colonists, see Benjamin Hallowell to Loudon, February 17, 1759, HL LO (NA) 6042.

56. Middleton, *Bells of Victory*, 22.

57. Loudon to Cumberland, October 2, 1756, RAWC CP Box 48/97; Cumberland to Loudon, December 2, 1756, in Pargellis, ed., *Military Affairs in North America*, 253–56, 255.

58. William March, "Observations on the Attacking of Canada," November 20, 1747, HL LO (NA) 4168.

59. For an early expression of this aspiration, see Lawrence to Halifax, August 23, 1754, RAWC CP Box 45/72. See also Shirley to Fox, August 12 and September 28, 1755, HL LO (NA) 624 and 657; John Forbes, "Plan of operations on the Mississippi, Ohio, etc.," February 1, 1758, HL LO (NA) 5515; Dowd, *War under Heaven*, 61.

60. See articles of capitulation for Fort Niagara in Boehm, ed., *Records of the British Colonial Office*, part 3, 56:524–27, 524; Johnson to Amherst, August 9, 1759, in Boehm, ed., *Records of the British Colonial Office*, part 3, 56:744.

61. See Bland to Bedford, August 1, 1750, TNA CO 91/11, 73; Blakeney to Bedford, January 13, 1749, TNA CO 174/2, 76.

62. See Richard White, *The Middle Ground: Indians, Empires, and Republics in the Great Lakes Region, 1650–1815* (Cambridge: Cambridge University Press, 1991).

63. See opinion of Jonathan Belcher, Jr., July 28, 1755, in Gaudet, ed., "Acadian Genealogy and Notes," 63–65.

64. For a discussion of one of the most provocative of these episodes, see Geoffrey Plank, "The Changing Country of Anthony Casteel: Language, Religion, Geography, Political Loyalty, and Nationality in Mid-Eighteenth Century Nova Scotia," *Studies in Eighteenth-Century Culture* 27 (1998): 55–76.

65. See generally Faragher, *Great and Noble Scheme*, 335–92; Plank, *Unsettled Conquest*, 140–57.

66. Newcastle to Hardwicke, October 12, 1754, BL Add. 32,737, 107. See also Newcastle to Hardwicke, October 2, 1754, BL Add. 32,737, 24; Hardwicke to Newcastle, October 13, 1754, BL Add. 32,737, 147; Newcastle to Horace Walpole, October 26, 1754, BL Add. 32,737, 207.

67. See especially Robinson to Lawrence, August 13, 1755, BL Add. 19,073, 42.

68. Newcastle, "Points of business for the meeting at the Duke's," BL Add. 32,996, 389.

69. James Campbell to Loudon, December 13, 1755, HL LO (NA) 698.

70. Gipson, *British Empire before the American Revolution*, 6:314.

71. Loudon to William Pitt, April 25, 1757, in Boehm, ed., *Records of the British Colonial Office*, part 3, 48:292–323, 306–9; and HL LO (NA) 3467.

72. See, especially, instructions for Cornwallis, April 29, 1749, in Gaudet, ed., "Acadian Genealogy and Notes," 49–52, 51. See also Shirley to Newcastle, November 21, 1746 and July 8, 1747, NSARM RG1, vol. 13, 33, vol. 13A, 27; Charles Knowles and Shirley to Newcastle, April 28, 1747, NSARM RG1, vol. 13A, 25; Act of the Maryland Assembly, May 22, 1756, in *Archives of Maryland*, 52:542; Horatio Sharpe to the Lower House of Assembly, April 19, 1756, in *Archives of Maryland*, 52:373; Goldsbrow Banyar to Johnson, April 30, 1756, in James Sullivan, ed., *The Papers of William Johnson*, 14 vols. (Albany: State of New York, 1922), 2:458–62; New York Provincial Council Minutes, April 30, 1756, quoted in Sullivan, ed., *Papers of William Johnson*, 2:459–60 n.

73. Bell, *"Foreign Protestants,"* 500–501; Loudon to Pitt, April 25, 1757, in Boehm, ed., *Records of the British Colonial Office*, part 3, 48:292–323, 307–9; and HL LO (NA) 3467. See also William Cotterell to Antoine Benezet, May 16, 1757, HL LO (NA) 3632.

74. Loudon to Pitt, April 25, 1757, in Boehm, ed., *Records of the British Colonial Office*, part 3, 48:292–323, 306–9; and HL LO (NA) 3467.

75. Shirley to Fox, September 4, 1756, in Boehm, ed., *Records of the British Colonial Office*, part 3, 46:466–73, 471–72.

76. Hopson, "Minutes in regard to a descent proposed to be made upon the island," July 11, 1757, in Pargellis, ed., *Military Affairs in North America*, 302–10, 305–6.

77. See Calcraft to Loudon, December 28, 1757, HL LO (NA) 5125. See also Loudon to Pitt, March 1757, HL LO (NA) 6938; Loudon to Abercromby, March 10, 1758, HL LO (NA) 5744.

78. Cumberland to Fox, September 23, 1757, BL Add. 51,375, 132.

79. Gipson entitled volume 6 of his multivolume work *The British Empire before the American Revolution, The Great War for the Empire: The Years of Defeat, 1754–1757.*

80. Calcraft to Loudon, November 12, 1757, HL LO (NA) 4814.

81. Anderson, *Crucible of War*, 212. For Cumberland's interpretation of the politics of this period, see Cumberland to Fox, May 2 and 23, September 23, 1757, BL Add. 51,375, 101, 109, and 132.

82. Cumberland to Loudon, November 26, 1757, RAWC CP Box 57/88, and HL LO (NA) 4907.

83. Cumberland to Fox, September 23, 1757, BL Add. 51,375, 132.

84. Gipson, *British Empire before the American Revolution*, 6:316.

85. See Gould, "To Strengthen the King's Hands," 338–48.

86. See Stanley Ayling, *The Elder Pitt, Earl of Chatham* (London: Collins, 1976), 197.

87. Anderson, *Crucible of War*, 234–35. On the question of timing, see Calcraft to Loudon, December 25, 1757, HL LO (NA) 5092; Loudon to Abercromby, March 10, 1758, HL LO (NA) 5744.

88. Middleton, *Bells of Victory*, 53.

89. See Wolfe to Richmond, March 17, 1756, in Whitworth, ed., "Some Unpublished Wolfe Letters," 71.

90. Wolfe to Richmond, July 28, 1758, in Whitworth, ed., "Some Unpublished Wolfe Letters," 83.

91. Loudon to Hopson, December 28, 1757, HL LO (NA) 5134. On the truth behind these rumors, see Peter Way, "The Cutting Edge of Culture: British Soldiers Encounter Native Americans in the French and Indian War," in Martin Daunton and Rick Halpern, eds., *Empire and Others: British Encounters with Indigenous Peoples, 1600–1850* (Philadelphia: University of Pennsylvania Press, 1999), 123–48, 133; Earle Lockerby, "The Deportation of the Acadians from Ile St.-Jean, 1758," *Acadiensis* 27 (1998): 45–94, 72–73.

92. Journal of the proceedings of the fleet and army, May 28–June 15, 1758, HL AB 291.

93. Lawrence, orders for attacking Louisbourg, May 1758, HL AB 303.

94. Journal of the proceedings of the fleet and army, May 28–June 15, 1758, HL AB 291; Nelson, journal of the siege of Louisbourg, June 3–July 2, 1758, HL LO (NA) 5844; Thomas Bill to Calcraft, 1758, HL LO (NA) 6975; Wolfe to Sackville, July 30, 1758, in Willson, *Life and Letters of Wolfe*, 387–88, 388. See also Robert J. Allison, ed., *The Interesting Narrative of the Life of Olaudah Equiano, Written by Himself* (Boston: Bedford Books, 1995), 69; Way, "Cutting Edge of Culture," 128.

95. James Wolfe to Walter Wolfe, July 27, 1758, in Willson, *Life and Letters of Wolfe*, 384–85, 385, and Wright, *Life of Wolfe*, 448.

96. Wolfe to Richmond, July 28, 1758, in Whitworth, ed., "Some Unpublished Wolfe Letters," 83.

97. Anderson, *Crucible of War*, 253–54.

98. Amherst to Abercromby, August 10, 1758, in Boehm, ed., *Records of the British Colonial Office*, part 3, 50:92–93, 92; Edward Boscowen to Pitt, September 13, 1758, in Boehm, ed., *Records of the British Colonial Office*, part 3, 53:539–41, 541.

99. See generally Lockerby, "Deportation from Ile St.-Jean."

100. John Clarence, Webster, ed., *The Journal of Jeffery Amherst* (Toronto: Ryerson Press, 1931), 74; A. J. B. Johnston, *Control and Order in French Colonial Louisbourg, 1713–1758* (East Lansing: Michigan State University Press, 2001), 90–91.

101. Wolfe to his mother, July 27, 1758, in Willson, *Life and Letters of Wolfe*, 382–83, and Wright, *Life of Wolfe*, 446.

102. Wolfe to Richmond, July 28, 1758, in Whitworth, ed., "Some Unpublished Wolfe Letters," 83.

103. Resolution of Boscowen and Amherst, August 8, 1758, in Boehm, ed., *Records of the British Colonial Office*, part 3, 53:532–33, 532; Amherst to Wolfe, August 15, 1758, in Boehm, ed., *Records of the British Colonial Office*, part 3, 53:637–40, 637. A parallel operation, under the command of Colonel Robert Monckton, destroyed French Catholic settlements along the banks of the St. John River. See Geoffrey Plank, "New England Soldiers in the St. John River Valley, 1758–1760," in Stephen Hornsby and John G. Reid, eds., *New England and the Maritime Provinces: Connections and Comparisons* (Montreal: McGill-Queens University Press, 2005), 59–73.

104. Wolfe to his father, August 21, 1758, in Willson, *Life and Letters of Wolfe*, 396; and Wright, *Life of Wolfe*, 455.

105. Amherst to Wolfe, August 15, 1758, in Boehm, ed., *Records of the British Colonial Office*, part 3, 53:637–40, 637–38.

106. James Murray to Wolfe, September 24, 1758, in Boehm, ed., *Records of the British Colonial Office*, part 3, 53:670–74, 671; and HL AB 682.

107. Letter from Wolfe, November 1, 1758, in Boehm, ed., *Records of the British Colonial Office*, part 3, 53:665–69. See also Wolfe to Abercromby, September 30, 1758, HL AB 705.

108. John Knox, *An Historical Journal of the Campaigns in North America, for the Years 1757, 1758, 1759 and 1760*, ed. Arthur G. Doughty, 3 vols. (Toronto: Champlain Society, 1914), 1:274–75, 274.

109. Letter from Wolfe, November 1, 1758, in Boehm, ed., *Records of the British Colonial Office*, part 3, 53:665–69. See also Wolfe to Abercromby, September 30, 1758, HL AB 705.

110. Knox, *Historical Journal of the Campaigns*, 1:274–75, 275.

111. M. Joannes, "Mémoire sur le campagne de 1759," in A. Doughty and G. W. Parmelee, eds., *The Siege of Quebec and the Battle of the Plains of Abraham*, 6 vols. (Quebec: Dusaault and Proulx, 1901), 4:219–29, 211; Knox, *Historical Journal of the Campaigns*, 1:378.

112. James Wolfe's proclamation on the Island of Orleans, June 28, 1759, in Willson, *Life and Letters of Wolfe*, 439–40, 439; and Wright, *Life of Wolfe*, 517–18, 517. See also "An Accurate and Authentic Journal of the Siege of Quebec," in Doughty and Parmelee, eds., *Siege of Quebec*, 4:279–94, 285.

113. "An Accurate and Authentic Journal of the Siege of Quebec," in Doughty and Parmelee, eds., *Siege of Quebec*, 4:279–94, 290.

114. Wolfe to Holderness, September 9, 1759, in Willson, *Life and Letters of Wolfe*, 472–75, 473; and Wright, *Life of Wolfe*, 564.

115. 1759 orders issued onboard the *Richmond* frigate, in Wolfe, *Instructions*, 73.

116. Wolfe's orders of July 5, 1759, in Willson, *Life and Letters of Wolfe*, 446–47, 446; and Wright, *Life of Wolfe*, 527–28, 528. See also Wolfe, *Instructions*, 79.

117. For a list of seized items, see "A Journal of the Expedition up the River St. Lawrence," in Doughty and Parmelee, eds., *Siege of Quebec*, 5:1–11, 4.

118. Brumwell, *Redcoats*, 184; orders of August 10, 1759, in Wolfe, *Instructions*, 95. See also letter dated September 2, 1759, in "Genuine Letters from a Volunteer," in Doughty and Parmelee, eds., *Siege of Quebec*, 5:13–31, 17; John Montrésor, "Journal of the Siege of Quebec," in Doughty and Parmelee, eds., *Siege of Quebec*, 4:301–34, 309.

119. Knox, *Historical Journal of the Campaigns*, 1:389–90; "Journal abrégé de la campagne de 1759," in Doughty and Parmelee, eds., *Siege of Quebec*, 5:282–301, 293; "An Accurate and Authentic Journal of the Siege of Quebec," in Doughty and Parmelee, eds., *Siege of Quebec*, 4:279–94, 288–89. See also "A Journal of the Expedition up the River St. Lawrence," in Doughty and Parmelee, eds., *Siege of Quebec*, 5:1–11, 6–7; "Journal of Major Moncrief," in Doughty and Parmelee, eds., *Siege of Quebec*, 5:23–58, 45–46; John Montrésor, "Journal of the Siege of Quebec," in Doughty and Parmelee, eds., *Siege of Quebec*, 4:301–34, 329.

120. Order given at Montmorenci, July 9, 1759, in Wolfe, *Instructions*, 89.

121. "An Accurate and Authentic Journal of the Siege of Quebec," in Doughty and Parmelee, eds., *Siege of Quebec*, 4:279–94, 282.

122. Ibid., 285; "Journal of a Voyage to America and Campaign against Quebec," in Doughty and Parmelee, eds., *Siege of Quebec*, 5:225–70, 251. For the official French response, see "Journal de Foligné," in Doughty and Parmelee, eds., *Siege of Quebec*, 4:163–217, 187–88.

123. "Journal de Foligné," in Doughty and Parmelee, eds., *Siege of Quebec*, 4:163–217, 193, 202. See also "Journal of a French officer," in Doughty and Parmelee, eds., *Siege of Quebec*, 4:231–58, 244; "An Accurate and Authentic Journal of the Siege of Quebec," in Doughty and Parmelee, eds., *Siege of Quebec*, 4:279–94, 287, 289; John Montrésor, "Journal of the Siege of Quebec," in Doughty and Parmelee, eds., *Siege of Quebec*, 4:301–34, 315, 322, 329; "A Journal of the Expedi-

tion up the River St. Lawrence," in Doughty and Parmelee, eds., *Siege of Quebec*, 5:1–11, 2; John Johnson, "Memoirs of the Siege of Quebec," in Doughty and Parmelee, eds., *Siege of Quebec*, 5:71–166, 81–82, 89–90; "Journal of the Particular Transactions during the Siege of Quebec," in Doughty and Parmelee, eds., *Siege of Quebec*, 5:167–89, 168, 171; "Journal of a Voyage to America and Campaign against Quebec," in Doughty and Parmelee, eds., *Siege of Quebec*, 5:225–70, 248.

124. George Townshend to Lady Ferers, September 6, 1759, in Doughty and Parmelee, eds., *Siege of Quebec*, 5:194–95, 195.

125. "An Accurate and Authentic Journal of the Siege of Quebec," in Doughty and Parmelee, eds., *Siege of Quebec*, 4:279–94, 285; see also James Gibson to Charles Lawrence, August 1, 1759, in Doughty and Parmelee, eds., *Siege of Quebec*, 5:61–69, 65; "Journal of the Particular Transactions during the Siege of Quebec," in Doughty and Parmelee, eds., *Siege of Quebec*, 5:167–89, 173; "Relation du siège de Quebec," in Doughty and Parmelee, eds., *Siege of Quebec*, 5:303–26, 315.

126. Letter dated September 2, 1759, in "Genuine Letters from a Volunteer," in Doughty and Parmelee, eds., *Siege of Quebec*, 5:13–31, 20.

127. "A Journal of the Expedition up the River St. Lawrence," in Doughty and Parmelee, eds., *Siege of Quebec*, 5:1–11, 3, 7.

128. Wolfe to Holderness, September 9, 1759, in Willson, *Life and Letters of Wolfe*, 472–75, 473; and Wright, *Life of Wolfe*, 563.

129. "A Journal of an Expedition up the River St. Lawrence," in Doughty and Parmelee, eds., *Siege of Quebec*, 5:1–11, 11.

130. James Murray's journal beginning September 18, 1759, in Boehm, ed., *Records of the British Colonial Office*, part 3, 64:27–104, 52.

131. Franklin, "The Interest of Great Britain Considered, with Regard to her Colonies, and the Acquisitions of Canada and Guadeloupe," 1760, in *Papers of Benjamin Franklin*, 9:47–100, 74.

132. Ibid., 95.

133. John Brown to Loudon, May 8, 1761, HL LO (NA) 6310.

134. See generally Dowd, *War under Heaven*. For an example of the use of the word "insurrection," see Ibid., 111.

135. See Mackillop, *"More Fruitful than the Soil,"* 57.

136. See, for example, Stair to Loudon, June 28, 1746, HL LO (SC) 11348; William Pepperell to Newcastle, June 24, 1746, TNA CO 5/45, 41.

137. Letter dated October 15, 1746, NAS GD248/654/2. See also "Hints Towards a Settlement of the Forfeited Estates in the Highlands of Scotland," NAS GD248/654/2.

138. Ayling, *Elder Pitt*, 192; Middleton, *The Bells of Victory*, 10; Shaw, *Management of Scottish Society*, 179. See also Yorke, *The Life and Correspondence of Hardwicke*, 2:379.

139. See, for example, "Scotch Officers Proposed for Command of Two Highland Battalions, Approved by H.M., January 3, 1757," RAWC CP Box 49/5.

140. See Mackillop, *"More Fruitful than the Soil,"* 84–88.

141. *London Magazine* 26 (1757) 42.

142. Leneman, *Living in Atholl*, 134–35.

143. Kirk, *Memoirs and Adventures*, 2.

144. James Grant to Robert Grant, March 2, 1757, BL Add. 25,411, 240.

145. Bland to Barrington, March 11, 1756, RAWC CP Box 46/183; Bland to Loudon, March 16 and 20, April 1, 1756, HL LO (NA) 941, 942, 952, 5301, 999.

146. See Penuel Grant to Robert Grant, February 17, 1757, BL Add. 25,441, 230.

147. See generally Mackillop, *"More Fruitful than the Soil"*.

148. Aeneas Mackintosh to Loudon, March 18, 1757, HL LO (NA) 3089.

149. *London Gazette*, May 25–29, 1756.

150. Aeneas Mackintosh to Loudon, March 18, 1757, HL LO (NA) 3089; William Mackintosh to Loudon, April 16, 1757, HL LO (NA) 3369; Charles Farquharson to Loudon, October 24, 1757, HL LO (NA) 4698.

151. Aeneas McIntosh to Loudon, April 12, 1757, LO (NA) 3348.

152. For specific references to a few former Jacobites among the Highland soldiers in America, see Allan Whiteford to Loudon, May 7, 1757, LO (NA) 3577.

153. See Calcraft, officers in his Majesty's first battalion of Highlanders, February 5, 1757, HL LO (NA) 5257.

154. Horace Walpole, *Memoirs of King George II*, ed. John Brooke, 3 vols. (New Haven, Conn.: Yale University Press, 1985), 3:207; Calcraft to Loudon, February 5, 1757, HL LO (NA) 2785.

155. James St. Clair to Loudon, March 15, 1757, HL LO (NA) 3053.

156. See Rogers, *Empire and Liberty*, 37–58; Pargellis, *Lord Loudon in North America*, 104–31.

157. For an account of one incident, see Abercromby to Loudon, December 20, 1756, HL LO (NA) 2373.

158. Lawrence to Abercromby, April 2, 1758, HL AB 99.

159. Ibid.; see also Simon Fraser to Abercromby, April 23, 1758, HL AB 188. The townspeople of Albany also reportedly liked the Highlanders. See Abercromby to Loudon, June 30, 1756, HL LO (NA) 1263; Abercromby to Loudon, December 20, 1756, HL LO, (NA) 2373.

160. Wolfe to Sackville, May 12 and July 30, 1758, in Willson, *Life and Letters of Wolfe*, 363–64, 387–88.

161. Letter of Captain Calcraft, September 20, 1759, in Doughty and Parmelee, eds., *Siege of Quebec*, 6:142–46, 146.

162. Loudon to Cumberland, November 22, 1756, in Pargellis, ed., *Military Affairs in North America*, 263–80, 264.

163. On the yell, see Brumwell, *Redcoats*, 225. On the clothing, see Knox, *Historical Journal of the Campaigns*, 1:73–75.

164. *Scots Magazine* 18 (1756): 559. See Loudon to Fox, October 3, 1756, HL LO (NA) 1961.

165. See, for example, *Scots Magazine* 20 (1758): 439.

166. Kirk, *Memoirs and Adventures*, 44.

167. Ibid., 45. See Jennings, *Empire of Fortune*, 200; Amherst to Pitt, October 22, 1759, in Boehm, ed., *Records of the British Colonial Office*, part 3, 56:578–608, 594. See also Webster, ed., *Journal of Jeffery Amherst*, 168.

168. See Loudon to Johnson, August 31, 1756, HL LO (NA) 1651.

169. Loudon to Cumberland, November 22, 1756, in Pargellis, ed., *Military Affairs in North America*, 263–80, 264; Hopson to Loudon, October 16 and 23, 1757, HL LO (NA) 4646 and 4693.

170. Brumwell, *Redcoats*, 167.

171. Simon Fraser to William Johnstone, February 23, 1759, HL PU 1790.

172. Robert Grant to William Grant, May 1, 1756, BL Add. 25,411, 152.

173. David Baillie to Loudon, April 12, 1757, HL LO (NA) 3345.

174. James Murray's journal beginning September 18, in Boehm, ed., *Records of the British Colonial Office*, part 3, 64:27–104, 27; oath proffered to the Canadians, 1759, in Boehm, ed., *Records of the British Colonial Office*, part 3, 57:189.

175. See generally Lawson, *Imperial Challenge.*

176. Brumwell, *Redcoats,* 297–98.

177. For an overview of the Highland emigration to America, see Murdoch, "Emigration from the Scottish Highlands." See also Bernard Bailyn, *Voyagers to the West: A Passage in the Peopling of America on the Eve of the Revolution* (New York: Knopf, 1986), 57–66; Eric Richards, "Leaving the Highlands: Colonial Destinations in Canada and Australia," in Marjory Harper and Michael E. Vance, eds., *Myth, Migration and the Making of Memory: Scotia and Nova Scotia c. 1700–1990* (Halifax, N.S.: Fernwood, 1999), 105–26; John M. Bumsted, *The People's Clearance: Highland Emigration to North America, 1770–1815* (Edinburgh: Edinburgh University Press, 1982).

Epilogue

1. See Gould, "Zones of Law, Zones of Violence."

2. See Peter David Garner Thomas, *British Politics and the Stamp Act Crisis: The First Phase of the American Revolution, 1763–1767* (Oxford: Clarendon, 1975), 117.

3. See Lawson, *Imperial Challenge;* Gregory, *Minorca, the Illusory Prize,* 73–97.

4. Paul Langford, *The First Rockingham Administration, 1765–1766* (Oxford: Oxford University Press, 1973), 4–39, 70–108; Peter David Garner Thomas, *George III: King and Politicians, 1760–1770* (Manchester: Manchester University Press, 2002), 116–19, 126–29; Brooke, *King George III,* 113–18, 121–22; Lawson, *George Grenville,* 215–19.

5. See generally Edmund S. Morgan and Helen M. Morgan, *The Stamp Act Crisis: Prologue to Revolution* (Chapel Hill: University of North Carolina Press, 1953).

6. See Thomas, *British Politics and the Stamp Act Crisis,* 139–40.

7. See Langford, *The First Rockingham Administration,* 83; Michael G. Kammen, *A Rope of Sand: The Colonial Agents, British Politics, and the American Revolution* (Ithaca, N.Y.: Cornell University Press, 1968), 123.

8. Cathcart to Loudon, September 13, 1755, HL LO (SC) 7087. See also Balcarres to Loudon, February 16, 1756, HL LO (NA) 825; "Lord Halifax's Paper," January 7, 1756, BL Add. 32,996, 3; "Hints from Lord Halifax relating to a tax in North America," October 31, 1755, BL Add. 32,996, 265.

9. See Houlding, "Bland, Humphrey (1685/6–1763)," in Matthew and Harrison, eds., *Oxford Dictionary of National Biography,* 6:159.

10. Stephens, "Blakeney, William Baron Blakeney (1671/2–1761)," in Matthew and Harrison, eds., *Oxford Dictionary of National Biography,* 6:134.

11. For an evocative discussion of the celebration of Wolfe, see Simon Schama, *Dead Certainties (Unwarranted Speculations)* (New York: Knopf, 1991).

12. Minutes of a council of war, September 28, 1757, RAWC CP Box 57/78.

13. Middleton, *Bells of Victory,* 26, 43; Wolfe to his father, October 21, 1757, in Willson, *Life and Letters of Wolfe,* 337, and Wright, *Life of Wolfe,* 394.

14. Middleton, *Bells of Victory,* 26, 43.

15. Wolfe to his father, October 21, 1757, in Willson, *Life and Letters of Wolfe,* 337; and Wright, *Life of Wolfe,* 394.

16. See Pownall to Loudon, February 4, 1757, HL LO (NA) 2768; Calcraft to Loudon, February 7, 1757, and January 14, 1758, HL LO (NA) 2793 and 5271.

17. Cornwallis to Charles Wyndham, Earl of Egremont, June 25, 1762, TNA CO 91/14.

18. See Cornwallis to Egremont, June 25, 1762, February 10, and September

11, 1763, TNA CO 91/14; Valentine Cannon to Joseph Popham, December 25, 1762, TNA CO 91/14; Halifax to Cornwallis, May 25, 1764, and January 1, 1765, TNA CO 91/14; Cornwallis to Halifax, July 2 and October 15, 1764, February 4, 1765, TNA CO 91/14.

19. Cornwallis to Egremont, September 11, 1763, TNA CO 91/14.

20. On Bland and the civilian courts, see Herbert to Holdernesse, January 1, 1753, TNA CO 91/11; resolution of the justices, January 1, 1753, TNA CO 91/11; Bland to West, April 4, 1753, TNA T 1/353, 10.

21. See Burges to the Lords Commissioners of the Treasury, January 9, 1752, TNA T 1/348, 2; letter from Bland, January 2, 1755, TNA T 1/360, 5.

22. Cornwallis to Halifax, March 4, 1765, TNA CO 91/14.

23. Cornwallis to Loudon, October 13, 1762, HL LO (SC) 10093.

24. Oliphant, "Cornwallis, Edward (1713–1776)," in Matthew and Harrison, eds., *Oxford Dictionary of National Biography*, 13:482. The only other officer prominently featured in this narrative to take a wife was Bland, who married a twenty-three-year-old woman in 1755, when Bland was sixty-nine. Bland's wife outlived him by fifty-three years. See Houlding, "Bland, Humphrey (1685/6–1763)," in Mathew and Harrison, eds., *Oxford Dictionary of National Biography*, 159;" Chichester, "Bland, Humphrey," in Stephen, ed., *Dictionary of National Biography*, 5:197.

25. Cornwallis to Halifax, May 17, 1765, TNA CO 91/14.

26. Cornwallis to Halifax, March 4, 1765, TNA CO 91/14; Halifax to Cornwallis, June 14, 1765, TNA CO 91/14.

27. Cornwallis to Halifax, May 17, 1765, TNA CO 91/14.

28. Halifax to Cornwallis, June 14, 1765, TNA CO 91/14.

29. Oliphant, "Cornwallis, Edward (1713–1776)," in Matthrew and Harrison, eds., *Oxford Dictionary of National Biography*, 13:482–83.

30. See Calcraft to Loudon, December 28, 1757, HL LO (NA) 5125. See also Loudon to Pitt, March 1757, HL LO (NA) 6938; Loudon to Abercromby, March 10, 1758, HL LO (NA) 5744.

31. Calcraft to Loudon, December 25 and 29, 1757, HL LO (NA) 5092 and 5140; *London Magazine*, June 1758, 267.

32. See David Cunningham to Loudon, June 19, 1758, HL LO (SC) 8643.

33. *The Conduct of a Noble Commander in America, Impartially Reviewed* (London, 1758), 5–6.

34. See Calcraft to Loudon, January 8, 1758, HL LO (NA) 5361; Halifax to Loudon, September 11, 1759, HL LO (NA) 6141.

35. Loudon to Fox, December 11, 1762, HL LO (SC) 10685.

36. Loudon to John Stuart, Earl of Bute, July 25, September 12 and October 11, 1762, HL LO (SC) 10711, 10644, and 10645.

37. Brumwell, "Campbell, John, fourth earl of Loudon (1705–1782)," in Matthew and Harrison, eds., *Oxford Dictionary of National Biography*, 821.

38. Loudon, report of the general officers, May 23, 1778, HL LO (NA) 6577.

39. Margaret Campbell, Countess of Loudon, to Loudon, May 14, 1746, HL LO (SC) 11259.

40. Eleanor Wallace to Loudon, September 7, 1755, HL LO (SC) 9470.

41. Margaret Campbell, Countess of Loudon, to Loudon, March 7, May 18, 1737, LO (SC) 7437 and 7451; James Arnot to Loudon, April 27, 1757, HL LO (NA) 6719.

42. Arnot to Loudon, April 27, 1757, HL LO (NA) 6719.

43. See, for example, bill from Kincaid and Donaldson, 1754, HL LO (SC) 9629; receipt from Samuel Johnson, January 30, 1759, HL LO (NA) 9626.

44. Franklin to Fawkener, July 27, 1756, in *Papers of Benjamin Franklin*, 6:472. See also *Papers of Benjamin Franklin*, 7:174.

45. Alexander Drummond to Loudon, March 4, 1745, HL LO (SC) 11389; Thomas Brown to Loudon, June 20, 1756, HL LO (NA) 1229; Robert Johnston to Loudon, July 25, 1757, HL LO (NA) 3989; John Lawrie to Loudon, January 8, 1759, HL LO (NA) 6011.

46. Robert Johnston, list of fruit trees grafted in the new orchard, July 25, 1757, HL LO (NA) 4652.

47. Arnot to Loudon, April 27, 1757, HL LO (NA) 6719; Robert Johnston to Loudon, July 25, 1757, HL LO (NA) 3989.

48. See James Alexander to Loudon, January 8, 1758, HL LO (NA) 5357.

49. Home to Loudon, December 13, 1752, HL LO (SC) 10437; Arnot to Loudon, April 27, 1757, HL LO (NA) 6719.

50. Alexander Drummond to Loudon, March 4, 1745, HL LO (SC) 11389; Milton to Loudon, February 5, 1757, HL LO (NA) 2790; Loudon to Alexander, June 6, 1759, and June 5, 1760, HL LO (NA) 6106 and 6248.

51. John Leslie, Earl of Rothes, to Loudon, September 29, 1752, and January 23, 1753, LO (SC) 10602 and 7469.

52. See William Fordyne to Loudon, February 7, 1757, HL LO (NA) 2797.

53. Fothringham to Loudon, September 15, 1750, and July 28, 1751, HL LO (NA) 224 and 305.

54. Brown to Loudon, June 20, 1756, HL LO (NA) 1229.

55. Fothringham to Loudon, July 28, 1751, HL LO (NA) 305.

56. Alexander Murray to Loudon, November 6, 1757, HL LO (NA) 4770.

57. Abercromby to Loudon, October 17, 1760, HL LO (NA) 6270.

58. See Whitworth, *William Augustus, Duke of Cumberland, A Life*, 133–34, 140–42, 157–58, 222.

59. James Lockhart to Fawkener, September 1, 1749, RAWC CP Box 43/308; Fothringham to Loudon, September 15, 1750, HL LO (NA) 224; Whitworth, *William Augustus, Duke of Cumberland, A Life*, 140–41.

60. Richard Drayton, *Nature's Government: Science, Imperial Britain, and the "Improvement" of the World* (New Haven, Conn.: Yale University Press, 2000), 40–41.

61. See generally ibid.

Index

Abenaki, 178
Abercromby, James, 161
Aberdeen, 59, 71, 81, 179
Acadia and the Acadians, 88, 123, 129, 156–57, 163–67, 169–70, 179, 190, 232 n.175
Africa and the Africans, 9, 12, 131, 133, 138, 141–46, 163, 185–86, 190, 200 n.89, 232 n.8, 236 n.102
African Americans, 78–79, 91, 95–96
Albany, 246 n.159
Algiers and the Algerians, 139, 142
American Revolution, 25–26, 187–88
Amherst, Jeffery, 168–69
Anglo-Normans, 8, 15
Anglo-Saxons, 8–9, 15
Annexing Act, 111
Antigua, 18, 92, 149
Appalachian Mountains, 88, 90, 93, 175
Argyll, Archibald Campbell, Duke of, 35, 72, 121, 176, 189
Armstrong, John, 147–48, 232 n.10
Arnot, James, 188–89
Atholl, 43, 72
Atlas Mountains, 146
Austria and the Austrians, 4
Ayr, 56

Barbados, 18, 95
Bedford, John Russell, Duke of, 98, 123, 146
Belcher, Jonathan, Jr., 163
Bermuda, 128
Bladen, Thomas, 91
Blakeney, William, 5, 7, 16, 34, 40–41, 57–60, 114–15, 117, 122, 130–33, 136–43, 146–47, 149–53, 163, 184–85, 187, 197 n.57, 234 n.59
Bland, Humphrey, 5, 7, 36–38, 40, 44–48, 55, 64–66, 71–73, 110–11, 113–18, 120,

122, 126–27, 130–38, 140–46, 153, 163, 176, 184–87, 204 n.54, 232 n.8, 248 n.24
Boston, Massachusetts, 87–88, 90, 92, 155, 177
bound labor, 3, 15, 18, 51, 77, 79, 95–97, 99, 128, 134, 143–44, 165, 223 n.126
Braddock, Edward, 150, 158, 160–61
Brainerd, David, 89–90, 92
British Army, 1–3, 5–8, 10–11, 15, 18–25, 29–31, 34–48, 51, 54–55, 57–76, 79–80, 86, 88–89, 98–100, 103–6, 108–11, 113–27, 129–82, 184–91, 193 n.1, 199 nn.82–83, 199–200 n.87, 200 n.88, 203 n.49
Burgoyne, John, 187–88
Burt, Edward, 12, 15, 147
Bute, John Stuart, Earl of, 189
Byng, John, 132, 149–52, 154, 166, 185

Cameron, Donald, of Lochiel, 44, 65, 69, 214 n.100
Cameron, Jenny, 32, 49, 69, 98
Campbell, Margaret, Countess of Loudon, 188
Canada and the Canadians, 25–26, 93, 129, 162, 169–74, 179–80, 183, 232 n.175
Canny, Nicholas, 14
Cape Breton Island, 88, 90, 122, 155, 166, 168
Caribbean Sea, 4, 15, 24, 51, 79–80, 87–89, 92, 95–97, 175
Carlisle, 40, 42, 48–51, 56
Catalan, 130, 133, 138–39, 141, 143
Catholics and Catholicism, 4–8, 13–16, 19–21, 32, 53, 72, 76, 78–79, 81–89, 91–92, 96, 100, 111–12, 116, 123–25, 129–31, 133, 135–41, 145–48, 156–57, 163, 165, 167, 170–71, 179, 181–83, 243 n.103
Caulfield, Major, 217 n.166
Chalmers, George, 151
Charles Edward Stuart, 1–4, 23, 25–26, 29–34, 36, 39–41, 44, 46, 49–50, 53–61, 65–

Charles Edward Stuart (*continued*)
  70, 74, 77–78, 80–86, 88–89, 93–94,
  96–99, 111–12, 118, 122, 125–26, 151,
  181, 188, 193 n.3
Chauncy, Charles, 87–88
Chester, 50–51
Chesterfield, Philip Dormer Stanhope, Earl
  of, 53, 63, 70–71, 80, 85–86, 91
children, 1, 5, 9, 13, 54, 60, 63, 65–70, 96,
  105–6, 108–13, 126–28, 131, 135, 137,
  160–61, 164–65, 167–68, 170–72, 176,
  180, 226 n.44
China and the Chinese, 80, 190
civilization, 4–15, 19–25, 73, 98, 100, 103–
  17, 121, 123–31, 136–41, 147–49, 153,
  155–58, 164–66, 174, 176, 179, 181–82,
  188–91, 226 n.44
clanship, 9–10, 15, 25, 31–32, 35, 39–40,
  49–50, 53–54, 59–60, 65, 71, 79, 96–97,
  106–10, 114–18, 121, 125–27, 175–76,
  182, 195 n.17
Colley, Linda, 8
commerce, 5–7, 9, 12, 19, 24–25, 39, 57, 92,
  97, 103, 106–15, 121, 127–28, 131, 134–
  45, 148, 155–58, 176, 182, 186, 188–91
Connecticut, 86, 89, 149, 177
Continental Congress, 188
Cope, John, 41
Cornwall, 8
Cornwallis, Edward, 5, 7, 38, 41, 65–66, 70,
  123, 150–51, 153, 155–57, 161–62, 164–
  65, 173, 184–86, 204 n.61
Cornwallis, Mary, 186
courts martial, 40–41, 43–44, 57, 64, 104,
  119, 132, 134, 150–53, 166, 185, 187–88
criminal procedure, 1–3, 6, 16–18, 22–23,
  29–32, 40, 46–52, 58–65, 72–77, 83, 85,
  95, 97–98, 103–4, 106, 114, 116–19,
  124–25, 136, 155–58, 162–64, 176, 184,
  208 n.145, 209 n.165
Cromwell, Oliver, 15, 72, 111, 121
Culloden, Battle of, 1, 6, 45, 48, 60, 65–66,
  71, 73–74, 76, 79, 86, 88, 93, 100, 103,
  106, 118, 120, 152, 181, 207 n.123
Cumberland, Rhode Island, 94
Cumberland, William Augustus, Duke of, 1,
  5–8, 21–26, 29, 33–43, 45–49, 51, 55,
  57–66, 70–74, 79–81, 83–84, 89, 93–94,
  97–100, 103, 106, 110–11, 113–16, 119–
  27, 129, 131–32, 134, 136–37, 140–41,
  152–53, 157–59, 161–64, 166–67, 173–

77, 181–85, 187–88, 190–91, 193 n.2,
  199 n.84, 205 n.74, 224 n.142, 230 n.121,
  242 n.81
Cumberland River, 93–94

Defoe, Daniel, 10, 12, 15, 128–29, 175
Delaware, 223 n.126
Derby, 1
Detroit, 163
disarmament, 1, 6, 18–19, 61–66, 72, 82–
  83, 91, 106–7, 126, 139, 197 n.64
Douglass, William, 90, 92, 127–29, 221
  n.98, 232 n.175
Dublin, 77, 85

East Indies, 12
Edinburgh, 1, 33–35, 40–42, 46, 57, 63, 69,
  71, 80–82, 113, 116–17, 122, 153
Edinburgh Castle, 1, 43, 46, 48, 57, 75, 80,
  185, 187
education, 5, 10–13, 69, 105–13, 126–28,
  131, 137–38, 147–49, 165, 226 n.44
Elizabeth, New Jersey, 89
Elizabeth I, 14
England, 1, 4–5, 8–10, 12, 14–17, 19, 24,
  31, 33–36, 39–41, 46, 48–51, 53–58, 60,
  70, 76, 78–88, 91, 95, 104–5, 111, 114–
  16, 120–21, 126, 132, 135, 149–50, 155,
  164–68, 181, 184–86, 190, 194 n.11
English, 5, 6, 10, 13, 15, 25, 48, 104, 108–
  10, 112–13, 128, 136, 148, 162, 164–65,
  174, 178, 182, 184
Episcopalians and Episcopalianism, 32, 72,
  81, 106, 116–17, 128, 137, 216 n.146,
  228 n.82
Ethiopia and the Ethiopians, 147
ethnography, 7–15, 19–22, 31, 52–54, 80–
  81, 84, 96–99, 103–6, 114–17, 123–24,
  127–29, 134, 144–47, 179
Eton, 126

Falkirk, 58
Falkirk, Battle of, 36
Fergusson, Adam, 105–6, 108, 112
Findlater, James Ogilvy, Earl of (and Earl of
  Seaforth), 71, 106, 112, 225 n.13
Flanders and the Flemish, 33, 34–36, 55, 83
Forbes, Duncan, 29, 71, 75, 97, 106, 108–10
forfeited Jacobite estates, 6, 18, 103, 107–
  11, 113–14, 134
Fort Augustus, 65–66, 75

Forth, River, 115
Fort William Henry, 166
Fox, Henry, 140, 147, 158, 164, 167, 187
France and the French, 1, 4–5, 7, 8, 17–18,
  21, 24–25, 30–31, 34–35, 45, 55, 67, 78–
  79, 82–83, 87–89, 92–93, 97, 99, 116,
  121–25, 129, 131–32, 138–39, 143, 146–
  47, 149–52, 154, 156–57, 162–74, 176,
  179, 181–82, 188, 200 n.89, 220 n.82,
  241 n.55, 243 n.103
Franklin, Benjamin, 87, 93, 129, 160, 173,
  189, 232 n.175, 240 n.40
Fraser, Simon, "The Master of Lovat," 59–
  60, 75–76, 177, 179–80
Frederick, Prince of Wales, 120–21, 190

Gaelic, 1, 3, 8–16, 31, 48, 53–54, 71, 78–80,
  89–90, 98–99, 103, 105–6, 108–10, 114,
  118, 125, 146, 175, 177
gender issues, 1, 7, 9–10, 15, 21, 32, 36–39,
  49, 54, 60, 63–70, 73–77, 80, 85, 96, 98,
  110, 112–13, 117–19, 128, 136–37, 160–
  61, 163–65, 168–72, 176, 179–80, 195
  n.16, 214 n.114, 248 n.24
George I, 17–18, 39, 59
George II, 1, 6, 22–24, 29–30, 32–34, 38,
  50–51, 53, 60, 63, 67, 71–72, 76, 81–84,
  88, 93, 97, 105–6, 116, 132, 150, 152,
  161, 164–66, 169, 176, 182, 220 n.82
George III, 121, 183–84
Georgia, 36, 41, 90, 98, 111, 183, 221 n.90,
  226 n.41
Germany and the Germans, 90, 99, 142,
  156, 220 n.82
Gibraltar, 5, 88, 100, 120, 122, 130–37,
  141–46, 149–50, 153, 185–86, 200 n.89
Gipson, Lawrence Henry, 166, 242 n.79
Glasgow, 10, 76, 90, 195 n.18
Gordon, Lewis, 59
Grant, Robert, 179
Great Lakes region, 183
Greece and the Greeks, 130, 133, 139–40,
  142

Halifax, George Montagu Dunk, Earl of,
  159
Halifax, Nova Scotia, 123, 155–57, 161,
  168, 172–73, 179, 190
Hanover and the Hanoverians, 17, 34–35,
  142–43, 159, 166, 220 n.82

Hardwicke, Philip Yorke, Earl of, 106, 108,
  111–12, 175, 225 n.13
Hargrove, William, 134
Hartford, Connecticut, 86
Hawley, Henry, 63–64
Henderson, Andrew, 84
Hercules, 93
Hesse and the Hessians, 36
Highland regiments, 10–11, 18–19, 26, 34–
  35, 43, 55, 59, 70–72, 75, 97–98, 105–6,
  116, 127, 158, 175–80, 198 n.70, 200
  n.92, 246 nn. 152, 159, 163
Hume, David, 126

Ile St.-Jean (Prince Edward Island), 168–
  69, 180
immigration, 5, 7, 10–12, 14–15, 19–21,
  108, 114, 123, 126–28, 130–31, 133,
  135–37, 139–41, 155–57, 164, 174, 179–
  80, 182, 186
India and the Indians, 190
intermarriage, 7, 15, 124, 133, 136–37, 165
Inverlochy, 63
Inverness, 1, 10, 15, 35, 44, 59–61, 97, 114,
  118–19, 176
Ireland and the Irish, 3, 5, 8, 14, 16, 30, 35–
  36, 53, 77–80, 82, 84–86, 91, 95, 104,
  111–13, 116, 120, 128, 133, 135–37, 146,
  148, 158, 173–74, 194 n.11, 219 n.48,
  226 n.44
Iroquois, 178–79
Italy and the Italians, 1, 82, 127, 130, 133–
  34, 135, 138

Jacobite army, 1–4, 29–36, 39–46, 51–66,
  70–71, 75, 77–83, 86, 95, 97–99, 151–52,
  181, 188, 193 n.1
Jacobite Rising of 1715, 17–18, 21, 36, 50,
  59, 76, 95
Jacobites, 1–4, 16–18, 25–26, 29–88, 91,
  94–99, 103, 111, 115, 120, 122, 125,
  151–52, 161, 176–77, 181, 188, 193 n.4,
  220 n.82, 246 n.152
Jamaica, 18, 51, 88, 95, 158
James I and VI, 14
James II and VII, 1, 4, 16, 84–85, 87
James Francis Edward Stuart, 1, 4, 17
Japan and the Japanese, 147
Jews and Judaism, 130, 133–35, 142, 144,
  146
Johnston, William, 89–90, 92

Kames, Henry Home, Lord, 179
Kew, 190
kilts, 3, 10–11, 33, 80, 106–7, 116–18, 178
Kirk, Robert, 178

Lancaster, 50–51
legal reform, 5, 6, 7, 19, 53, 55, 71–73,
    103–7, 110–11, 113–20, 124, 131, 133–
    36, 138–41, 146–48, 153, 155–57, 159,
    182, 184, 186
Lenape (the Delaware), 160
Lewis, Isle of, 77
Limerick, Treaty of, 16
Lincoln, 50–51
Liverpool, 51, 84
livestock, 1, 9, 39, 54, 57–58, 62–63, 65–66,
    69, 73, 114, 117, 134, 155, 170, 179, 189,
    191
Lochaber, 146
Locke, John, 112
Lockhart, Major, 216 n.166
London, 33, 41, 48–50, 80, 82, 85, 87, 105,
    121, 150, 176, 184
Loudon, John Campbell, Earl of, 5, 7, 10–
    11, 33–35, 38, 40, 43, 46, 54–56, 59–61,
    65–66, 70–76, 98, 114, 126, 153–54,
    157–68, 173, 175–77, 184–91, 195 n.22
Louisbourg, 88, 122–23, 154, 168–69, 187
Lovat, Simon Fraser, Lord, 59, 75–76, 113,
    177

MacDonald, Alexander of Sleat, 67, 71, 97,
    106, 126, 223 n.136
MacDonald, Flora, 67, 70, 74
MacDonald, James, 126–27
MacDonald, Margaret, 67, 70, 97, 126–27,
    223 n.136
MacKintosh, Aeneas, 32, 75–76, 176–77
MacKintosh, Anne, 32, 60, 73–76, 176–77
Madeira, 150
Maine, 13, 93
Malay Peninsula, 190
Malta, 138
Manchester, 35, 70
Marseilles, 143
Maryland, 18, 78–79, 91–94, 96, 162
Massachusetts, 87–88, 90, 92–94, 99, 127–
    28, 149, 155, 160, 177
Mediterranean Sea, 5–7, 22, 24, 31, 129–
    53, 163, 182, 184–85

Mi'kmaq, 123, 155–56, 161–64, 168–69,
    190
military execution, 32, 58–59, 61–73, 75,
    170–72
militia, 16, 34–35, 55, 70–72, 83–84, 97,
    160–61, 163, 167–68, 170–71
Milton, Andrew Fletcher, Lord, 47, 59, 61–
    62, 110–11, 114, 117, 153, 189
Minorca, 5, 19, 24, 88, 92, 100, 120, 122,
    125, 130–33, 136–43, 146–53, 183, 200
    n.89, 233 n.24
Mississippi River, 25
Moidart, 1, 4
Molyneux, Richard, 91
Monacy River, 91
Monckton, Robert, 243 n.103
Montesquieu, 123–24
Montreal, 163, 190
Montserrat, 88, 92
Morera, Miguel, 234 n.59
Morocco, 142–45
Munro, Harry, 72
Murray, James, 172
Muslims and Islam, 133, 135, 142–45

Napier, Gabriel, 47, 58
Native Americans, 9, 13, 52, 78–79, 88–89,
    92–93, 123, 125, 127–28, 143, 154–58,
    160–63, 165, 168–72, 175, 178, 183, 188,
    200 n.89, 240 nn. 37, 40, 243 n.91
Netherlands and the Dutch, 12, 34–36,
    114, 129, 139, 163
Newcastle, 84
Newcastle, Thomas Hollis-Pelham, Duke of,
    23, 47–48, 61–62, 83, 106, 110, 120–21,
    150–51, 158, 175
New England, 13, 87–88, 90, 92, 122, 128,
    183
Newfoundland, 88
New Jersey, 89, 93, 160–61
Newport, Rhode Island, 149
New York, 90, 129, 150, 158, 180, 187, 189,
    221 n.90
Niagara, 163
North America, 4–9, 12–13, 15, 16, 18, 21–
    22, 25–26, 31, 51, 54, 76–80, 82, 86–99,
    105, 122–24, 127–29, 132, 143, 146, 150,
    153–82, 184–85, 187–90, 200 n.89
North Carolina, 89–90, 93, 98–99, 177,
    180, 221 n.91
Nova Scotia, 5, 88, 93–94, 98–100, 122–24,

129–30, 141, 153, 155–57, 161–64, 168, 179, 185, 190

Oglethorpe, James, 36, 41
Ohio River, 100, 158, 163
Olivar y Pardo, Gabriel, 139–41
Oxford, 126

Paris, 126
Paris, Peace of, 183
Parliament, 6, 17, 18, 23–24, 38–39, 48, 53, 55, 64, 103, 106–8, 111, 115, 118–21, 123, 143, 156, 159, 177, 182, 184
Pelham, Henry, 38, 120–21, 123
Pennsylvania, 86, 88, 93, 149, 158, 160, 165, 220 n.65, 222 n.116
Pequot, 128
Perth, James Drummond, Jacobite Duke of, 32, 57
Philadelphia, 93, 149, 165
Pitt, William, 167, 175
Pittock, Murray, 80–81
Pontiac, 175
Port Mahon, 139, 149, 151, 153
Portsmouth, England, 150
Portugal and the Portuguese, 135, 187
Presbyterians and Presbyterianism, 6, 12–13, 43, 55, 60–62, 64, 72, 75, 81–82, 104–6, 108, 113, 115, 122, 137
Preston, Battle of, 18
Prestonpans, Battle of, 33–35, 41–43, 54, 56, 158
Protestantism, 4–7, 39, 81–82, 84–86, 91–92, 96, 98, 108, 112–13, 126, 130–31, 135–37, 139, 147, 153, 156–57, 165, 181–82, 184, 224 n.149

quartering of soldiers, 55–57, 59, 61, 159
Quebec, 6, 26, 124, 162–63, 166, 170–74, 178, 185

race, 10, 21, 71, 91, 138, 144
rape, 54, 66–70, 85, 104, 118–19, 170–73
rebellion, 3, 8, 15–18, 22–23, 29–31, 40–52, 58–59, 63–65, 73–74, 77–85, 88–92, 98–99, 106–11, 116, 119, 121, 124–26, 135, 137–40, 142, 146–49, 153, 156–57, 160–66, 169, 175–76, 181, 184–85, 187–88, 245 n.134
Revolution of 1688, 1, 15–16, 23, 84–85, 87, 197 n.55
Rhode Island, 93, 149

Richard III, 121
roads and transportation infrastructure, 5, 7, 19–21, 57–58, 104, 108–10, 115–16, 121, 134–35, 155, 182, 189, 198 n.75
Rochefort, 185
Rodohan, Alexandre de, 165
Romans, 15
Royal Navy, 24, 46, 74, 77, 90, 92–93, 132, 136, 138–41, 146, 149–52, 168, 200 n.88
rules of war, 3, 16–17, 22–23, 30–33, 39–46, 49, 51, 55–57, 61–63, 67–69, 124–25, 156–58, 160–62, 168–73, 178, 184, 187–88, 198 n.77, 206 n.98, 209 n.162, 240 nn. 37, 40, 243 n.91

St. John River, 163, 166
St. Kitts, 18
St. Lawrence River, 93, 162–63, 170, 180
savagery, 3–4, 7–14, 19–22, 30, 33–34, 52–54, 69–72, 80, 82, 84–85, 96–99, 103–11, 114–15, 117–18, 124–25, 127–29, 131, 141–45, 157–66, 168–72, 175, 178–79, 182, 185–86, 188, 209 n.178, 218 n.9, 236 n.102, 241 n.64, 246 n.163
Scotland, 1–84, 86–131, 134–35, 137, 141, 146–48, 151, 153, 157–58, 161–62, 172–85, 187–88, 194 n.11
Scottish Highlands, 1–26, 31–35, 43–45, 50–57, 59–82, 84, 87–90, 94–131, 134, 137, 141, 146–48, 151, 157–58, 161–62, 172–84, 188, 194 n.8, 195 n.18, 196 nn. 45, 47, 198 n.70, 200 nn. 89, 92, 218 n.9, 224 n.1, 232 n.8
Scottish Lowlands, 3, 8–9, 12, 16–17, 33, 48, 53, 57–59, 78–82, 89–91, 110, 113, 115, 122, 137, 181, 187–90
Scottish Society for Propagating Christian Knowledge, 12–14, 72, 89, 112–13, 125, 128, 196 n.41
Seven Years' War, 7, 24–25, 55, 76, 99–100, 105, 124, 146, 157, 162, 164, 166, 178–79, 182, 186–87
Shirley, William, 90, 99, 160, 166
Skye, Isle of, 67, 77, 126
Smith, Adam, 126
South America, 14
South Carolina, 18, 21, 51, 87
Spain and the Spanish, 4, 14, 24, 80, 86–88, 92–93, 132, 135, 138–39, 145–46, 149, 186–87

Stair, John Dalrymple, Earl of, 54, 56, 114, 189
Stamp Act, 25, 159, 184–85
Stewart, Archibald, 40
Stirling, 41, 58–59, 115, 119, 151
Stirling Castle, 34, 40–41, 47, 57–58, 138, 152
Stokesley, 84
Stornoway, 77
Susquehanna, 89
Switzerland and the Swiss, 156

Tetuan, 142, 145
Ticonderoga, 166
Tories, 24, 167
Tower of London, 50, 76
Townshend, George, 172–73
transportation to the colonies, 3, 7, 15, 18, 21, 26, 29, 50–51, 77, 79, 95–99, 110, 113, 123, 127, 176, 200 n.91, 224 n.142, 247 n.177
Trembleau, 172
Turkey and the Turks, 80
Tyrawley, James O'Hara, Baron, 140

Union, Treaty of, 17, 81
United States of America, 25, 188
Utrecht, Treaty of, 88, 169

Vattel, Emerich de, 67–69, 161
Vermont, 93
Vesting Act, 111
Virginia, 15, 18, 77–78, 93, 150, 159, 187

Wade, George, 18–20, 39–40, 59, 104, 115
Wadsworth, Daniel, 86
Wales and the Welsh, 8, 15, 24, 35, 53, 78–80, 83, 148, 194 n.11
Walker, Thomas, 93
Walpole, Robert, 18, 24
War of Jenkins' Ear, 4, 24, 80, 87
War of the Austrian Succession, 4, 87–88, 122, 130
War of the Spanish Succession, 36, 132, 145
Washington, George, 158
West Indies, 12
Westminster Abbey, 185
Whigs, 24, 38–39, 89, 113, 122
Whitefield, George, 93
Windsor, 190
Wolfe, James, 5, 7, 38, 44–45, 54, 63–65, 98, 115–17, 119, 122–24, 150, 157, 167–73, 178–79, 184–85, 204 n.62, 247 n.11
Wuastukwiuk, 169

York, 50–51

Acknowledgments

This book is dedicated to my parents, Eleanor and John Plank, who encouraged me even as a boy to think about the world and justice.

There is no way for me to thank everyone who has helped me on this project with advice, hospitality, and gifts, or with formal grants and privileges. There are too many to mention, too many, indeed (to be honest), to remember, and behind each benefactor there are others I do not know who made possible the assistance I have received. When I think about acknowledgments in the abstract, they tend to multiply exponentially.

Nonetheless, moving to specifics, I want to thank John Murrin. As my professor at Princeton, he tolerated—indeed encouraged—an eclectic approach to research and allowed me to work in an open-ended, expansive way. I am not at all sure I would have ever started on this project if I had I been more restrictively supervised at the beginning of my career. I am thankful to John Murrin for allowing me to range. I also benefited greatly from a pilot project launched by the Andrew W. Mellon Foundation, which subsidized a brief exploratory research trip to the archives then known as the Public Record Office in Kew, England. It was there, in January 1992, that I started reading the Colonial Office documents on Minorca.

The Mellon Foundation supported me again in 2003, with a fellowship that subsidized two months of research at the Huntington Library. The Loudon Papers at the Huntington were indispensable for my research. I had been at the Huntington once before, in 1993 when the library granted me a Robert Middlekauff Fellowship. During that earlier stay I met Allan Macinnes, who encouraged me to look into the connections between policy making in the Scottish Highlands and Nova Scotia. Several years later he introduced me to his colleague at the University of Aberdeen, Andrew Mackillop, whose advice and encouragement have been very helpful to me. I am particularly grateful to Mackillop for directing me to Simon Fraser's correspondence from Iroquois country.

The University of Cincinnati's University Research Council and the Charles Phelps Taft Foundation provided support for my research in Britain in the summer of 1998. The Taft Foundation also awarded me a fellowship in the 2001–2 academic year. I spent much of that year work-ing happily and productively at the Newberry Library in Chicago. The URC supported me on another trip to Britain, in the summer of 2003, and the Taft Foundation gave me yet more support by purchasing the Cumberland Papers on microfilm from the Royal Archives at Windsor Castle. Sally Moffitt, the tireless history librarian at the University of Cin-cinnati's Langsam Library, helped me in my application for that pur-chase, as did Professor Jill Rubenstein in our English department. The Cumberland Papers have been invaluable. I have used them with the permission of Her Majesty Queen Elizabeth II, and I am grateful.

Colin Calloway, Catherine Desbarats, and Ian Steele provided useful comments at conferences where I presented papers based on my research. The questions from the audience at the 2000 meeting of the Omohundro Institute of Early American History and Culture, in Toronto, were particularly helpful in clarifying my thoughts. I must also thank Maurice Basque and Stephen White, of the Centre d'études aca-diennes at the University of Moncton, for helping me identify Alexandre de Rodohan.

Barbara Ramusack, as the head of Cincinnati's history department, arranged my teaching assignments in the 2003–4 academic year in a way that gave me time and space for writing. I am indebted to her and to my colleagues in general for their patience with that (unusual) arrange-ment. My colleague Willard Sunderland read an early draft of my manu-script and gave me helpful advice.

This is the second book I have published with the University of Penn-sylvania Press. Everyone associated with the press has been good to work with. I am particularly grateful for the help and guidance I have received from Bob Lockhart, the history editor, who for more than five years has been providing me intelligent, direct, and constructive advice. When I applied for my second contract from the press, Michael Zuckerman reviewed my proposal and took the time to send me detailed comments. Daniel Richter did me a similar service after I submitted the first draft of this book. My outside readers, Ned Landsman and Eliga Gould, gave me their views both early and late in the writing process, with helpful specificity. I learned a great deal from them as I worked. I am especially happy to have met Eliga Gould, who has become a new friend. I would also like to thank Erica Ginsburg and Ellie Goldberg at the Press, who helped me in the final stages of preparing the manuscript for publica-tion, and the copyeditor, Lynn Walterick.

I received a series of additional favors in the last stage of preparing for the publication of this book. The Taft Foundation awarded me a grant to pay for the reproduction of the cover art. Stephen Brumwell and Con-rad Graham, a curator at the McCord Museum in Montreal, shared with me their thoughts concerning the attribution of the caricature on page 173, Figure 11. Finally, Daniel P. Glenn, Douglas Link, and Justin Pope helped me review the page proofs. My thanks to them all.

Ina Zweiniger-Bargielowska read several drafts of the manuscript. She is unlike the other scholars I have mentioned because we shared our lives together as I considered her suggestions, reworked my ideas, and pondered the comments of everyone else. I am grateful to her for many things. After we married, Ina gave up her adopted home country, and she has risen to the challenge of living in the United States. We have moved a few times, and we travel extensively. Over the past five years I have been commuting nearly three hundred miles to work. Home, for me, is not one place but wherever our family can be together. For now that is usually Oak Park, Illinois. With the help of Sonja Bargielowska, our two cats Milo and Silk, and two dogs—Usher and Jive—we have found a way to enjoy daily chaos. I love them all deeply. There is more to life than books.